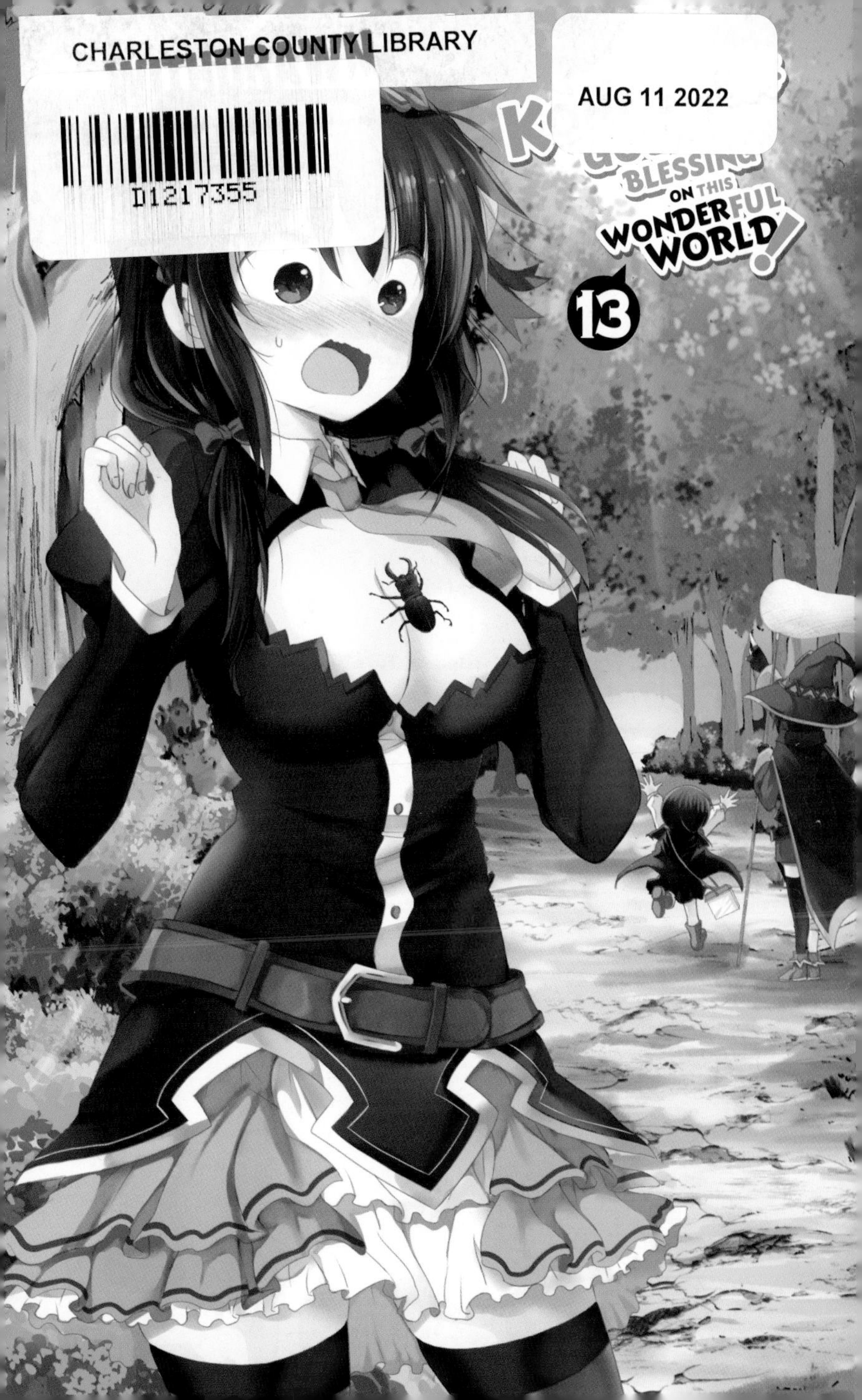
BLESSING
ON THIS
WONDERFUL
WORLD!
13

13

GOD'S
BLESSING
ON THIS
WONDERFUL
WORLD!
CONTENTS

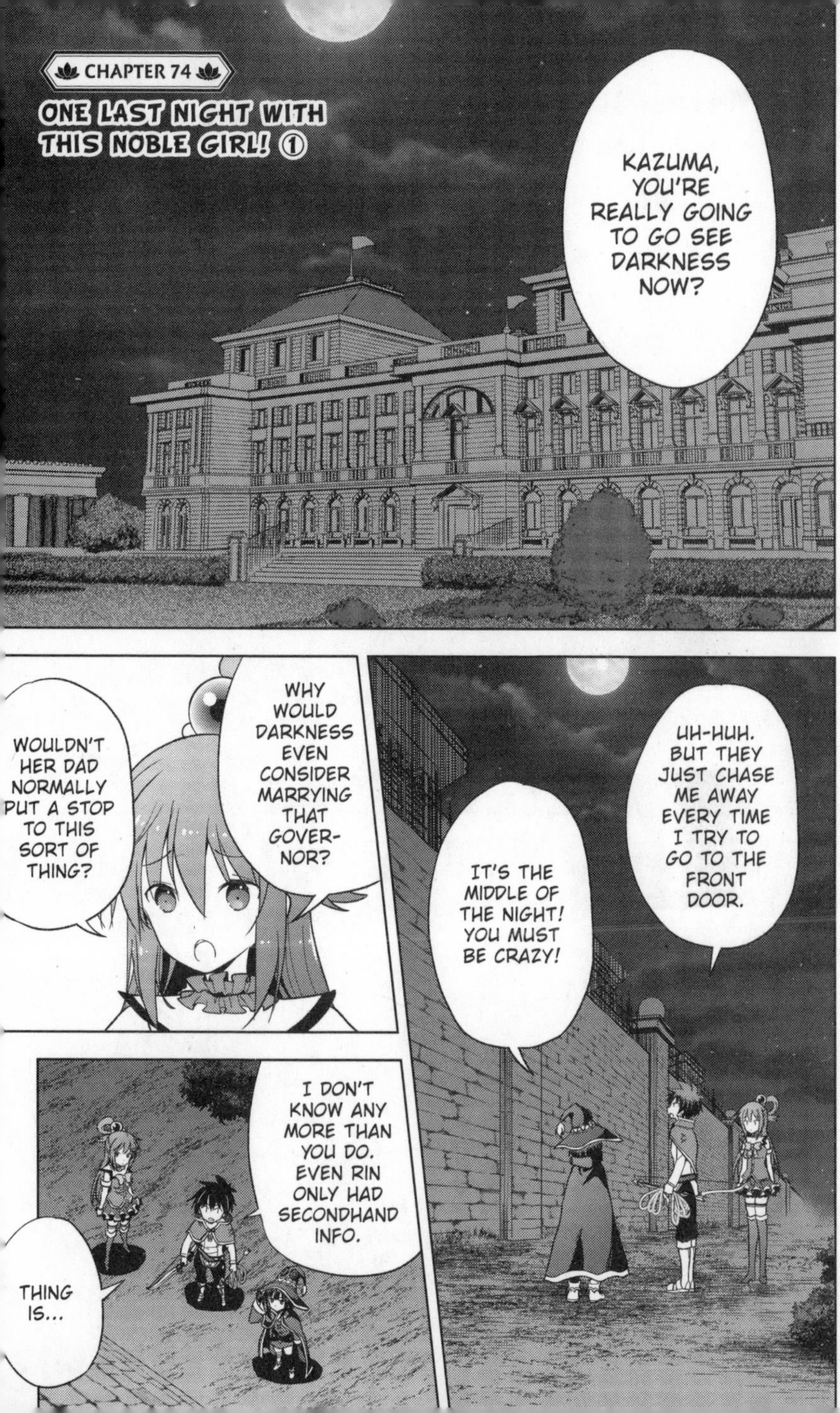
CHAPTER 74
ONE LAST NIGHT WITH THIS NOBLE GIRL! ①
KAZUMA, YOU'RE REALLY GOING TO GO SEE DARKNESS NOW?
UH-HUH. BUT THEY JUST CHASE ME AWAY EVERY TIME I TRY TO GO TO THE FRONT DOOR.
IT'S THE MIDDLE OF THE NIGHT! YOU MUST BE CRAZY!
WHY WOULD DARKNESS EVEN CONSIDER MARRYING THAT GOVERNOR?
WOULDN'T HER DAD NORMALLY PUT A STOP TO THIS SORT OF THING?
I DON'T KNOW ANY MORE THAN YOU DO. EVEN RIN ONLY HAD SECONDHAND INFO.
THING IS...

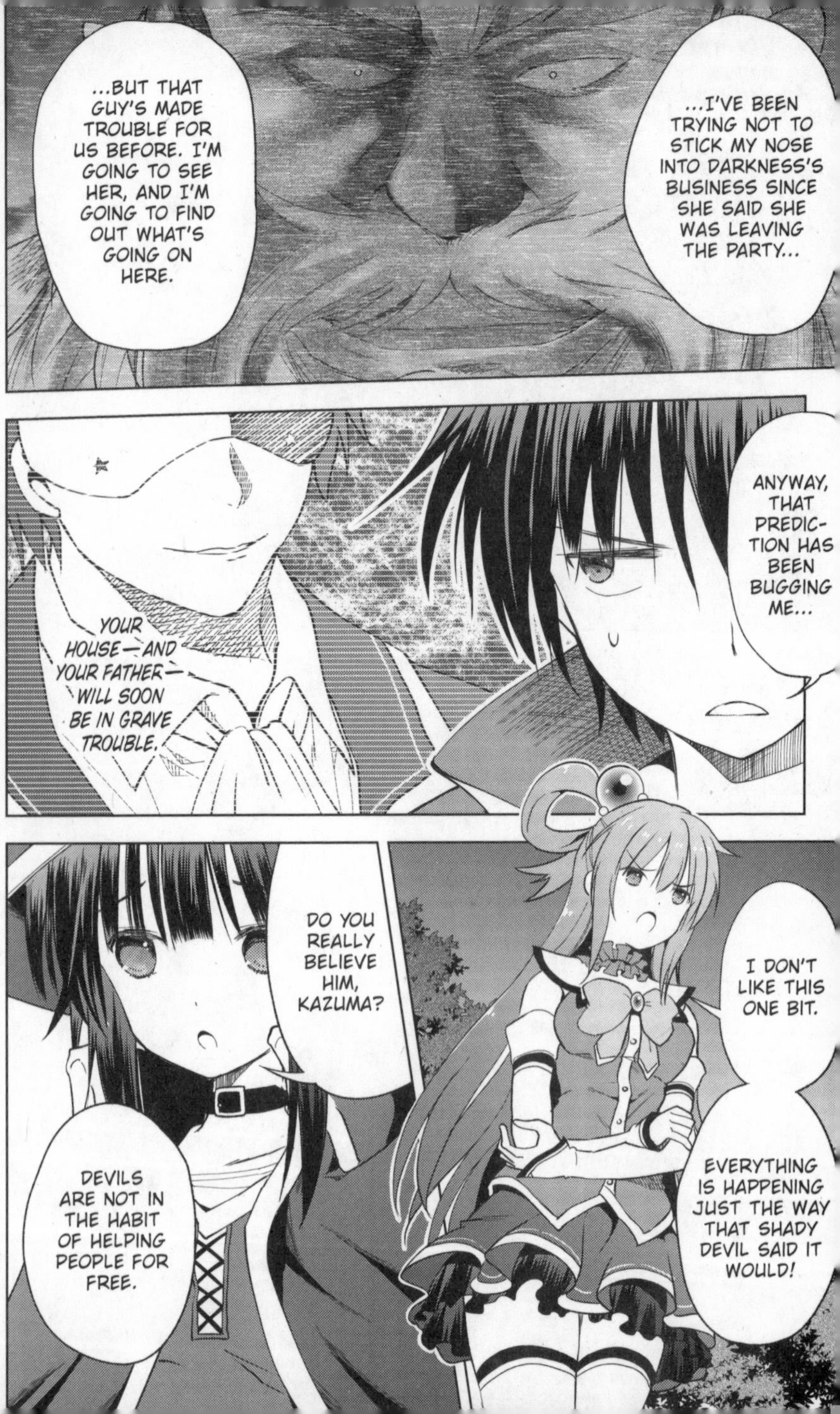
...I'VE BEEN TRYING NOT TO STICK MY NOSE INTO DARKNESS'S BUSINESS SINCE SHE SAID SHE WAS LEAVING THE PARTY...
...BUT THAT GUY'S MADE TROUBLE FOR US BEFORE. I'M GOING TO SEE HER, AND I'M GOING TO FIND OUT WHAT'S GOING ON HERE.
ANYWAY, THAT PREDICTION HAS BEEN BUGGING ME...
YOUR HOUSE—AND YOUR FATHER—WILL SOON BE IN GRAVE TROUBLE.
I DON'T LIKE THIS ONE BIT.
DO YOU REALLY BELIEVE HIM, KAZUMA?
EVERYTHING IS HAPPENING JUST THE WAY THAT SHADY DEVIL SAID IT WOULD!
DEVILS ARE NOT IN THE HABIT OF HELPING PEOPLE FOR FREE.

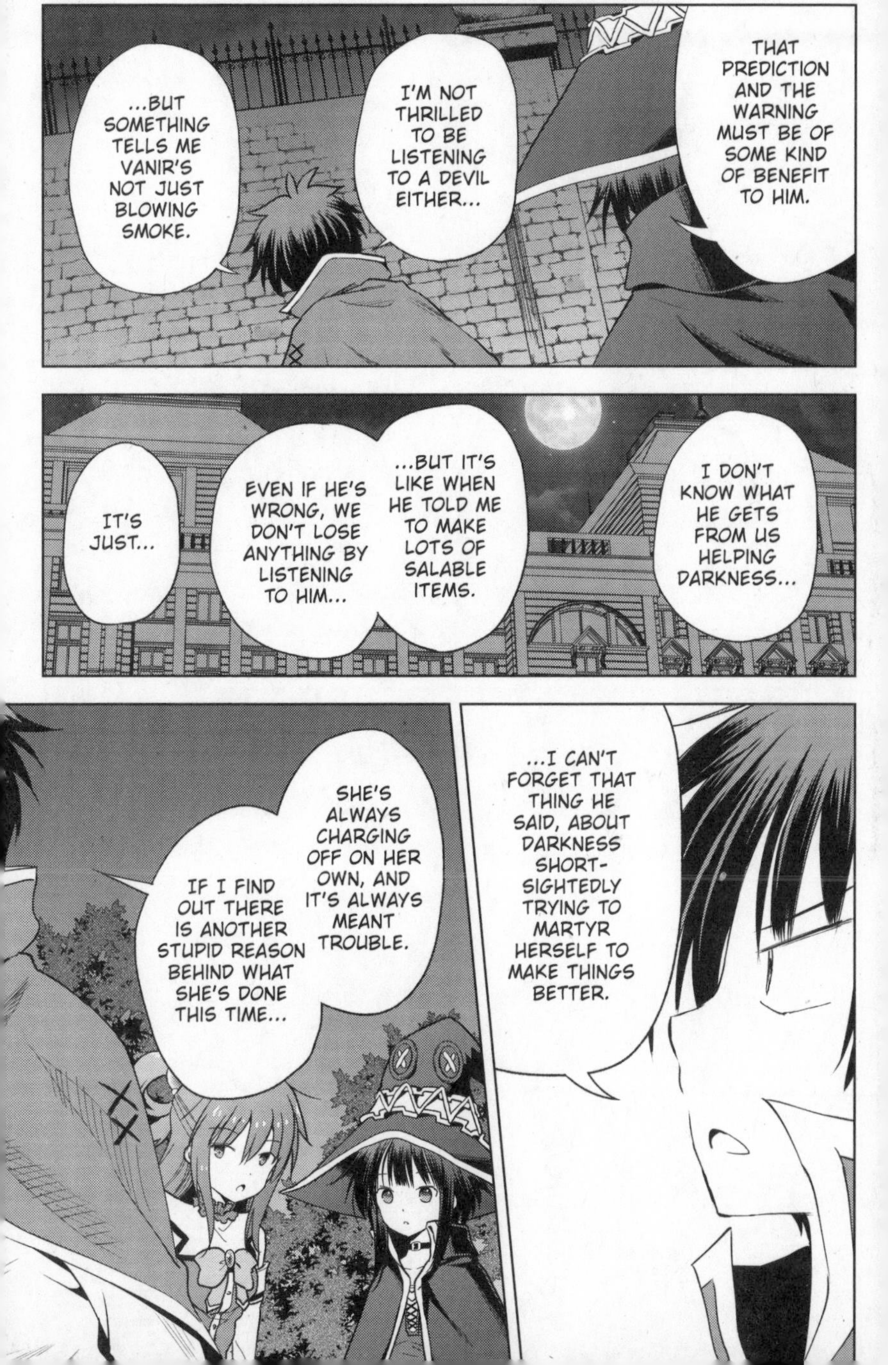
THAT PREDICTION AND THE WARNING MUST BE OF SOME KIND OF BENEFIT TO HIM.
I'M NOT THRILLED TO BE LISTENING TO A DEVIL EITHER...
...BUT SOMETHING TELLS ME VANIR'S NOT JUST BLOWING SMOKE.
I DON'T KNOW WHAT HE GETS FROM US HELPING DARKNESS...
...BUT IT'S LIKE WHEN HE TOLD ME TO MAKE LOTS OF SALABLE ITEMS.
EVEN IF HE'S WRONG, WE DON'T LOSE ANYTHING BY LISTENING TO HIM...
IT'S JUST...
...I CAN'T FORGET THAT THING HE SAID, ABOUT DARKNESS SHORT-SIGHTEDLY TRYING TO MARTYR HERSELF TO MAKE THINGS BETTER.
SHE'S ALWAYS CHARGING OFF ON HER OWN, AND IT'S ALWAYS MEANT TROUBLE.
IF I FIND OUT THERE IS ANOTHER STUPID REASON BEHIND WHAT SHE'S DONE THIS TIME...

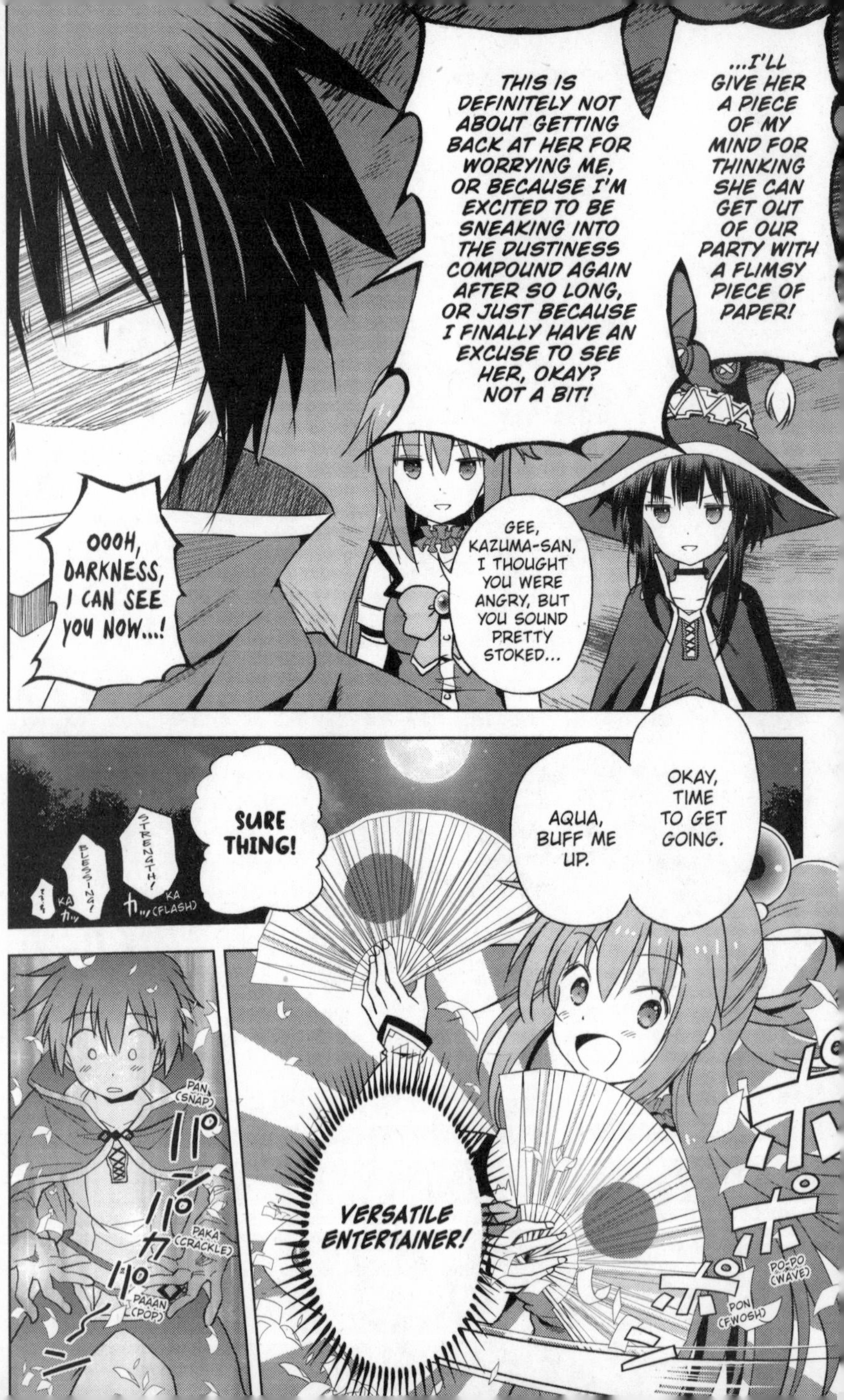
...I'LL GIVE HER A PIECE OF MY MIND FOR THINKING SHE CAN GET OUT OF OUR PARTY WITH A FLIMSY PIECE OF PAPER!
THIS IS DEFINITELY NOT ABOUT GETTING BACK AT HER FOR WORRYING ME, OR BECAUSE I'M EXCITED TO BE SNEAKING INTO THE DUSTINESS COMPOUND AGAIN AFTER SO LONG, OR JUST BECAUSE I FINALLY HAVE AN EXCUSE TO SEE HER, OKAY? NOT A BIT!
GEE, KAZUMA-SAN, I THOUGHT YOU WERE ANGRY, BUT YOU SOUND PRETTY STOKED...
OOOH, DARKNESS, I CAN SEE YOU NOW...!
OKAY, TIME TO GET GOING.
AQUA, BUFF ME UP.
SURE THING!
STRENGTH!
BLESSING!
KA (FLASH)
VERSATILE ENTERTAINER!
PO-PO (WAVE)
PON (FWOSH)
PAN (SNAP)
PAKA (CRACKLE)
PAAAN (POP)

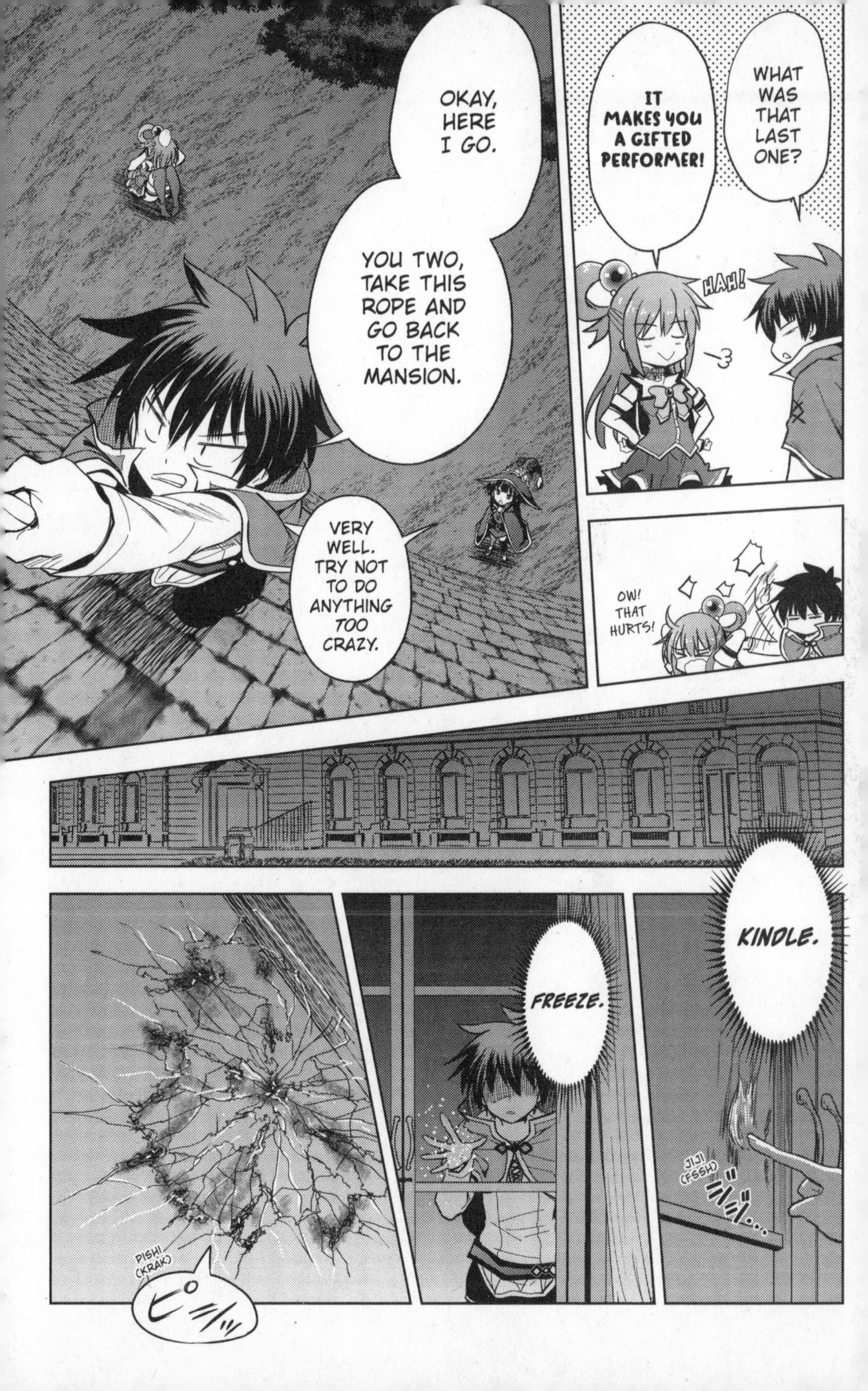

WHAT WAS THAT LAST ONE?
IT MAKES YOU A GIFTED PERFORMER!
HAH!
OW! THAT HURTS!
OKAY, HERE I GO.
YOU TWO, TAKE THIS ROPE AND GO BACK TO THE MANSION.
VERY WELL. TRY NOT TO DO ANYTHING *TOO* CRAZY.
KINDLE.
JIJI (FSSH)
FREEZE.
PISHI (KRAK)

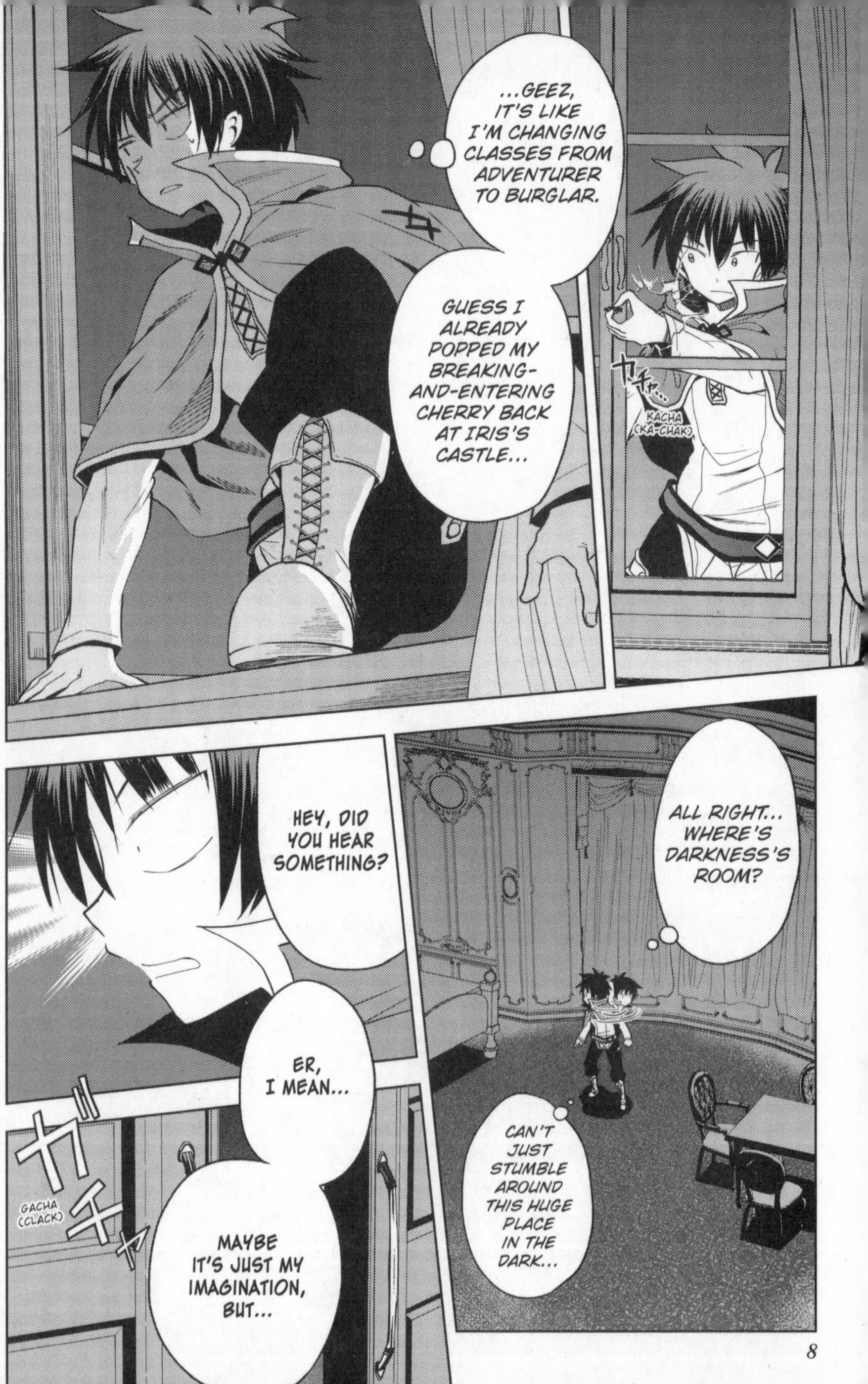
KACHA (KA-CHAK)
...GEEZ, IT'S LIKE I'M CHANGING CLASSES FROM ADVENTURER TO BURGLAR.
GUESS I ALREADY POPPED MY BREAKING-AND-ENTERING CHERRY BACK AT IRIS'S CASTLE...
ALL RIGHT... WHERE'S DARKNESS'S ROOM?
CAN'T JUST STUMBLE AROUND THIS HUGE PLACE IN THE DARK...
HEY, DID YOU HEAR SOMETHING?
ER, I MEAN...
MAYBE IT'S JUST MY IMAGINATION, BUT...
GACHA (CLACK)

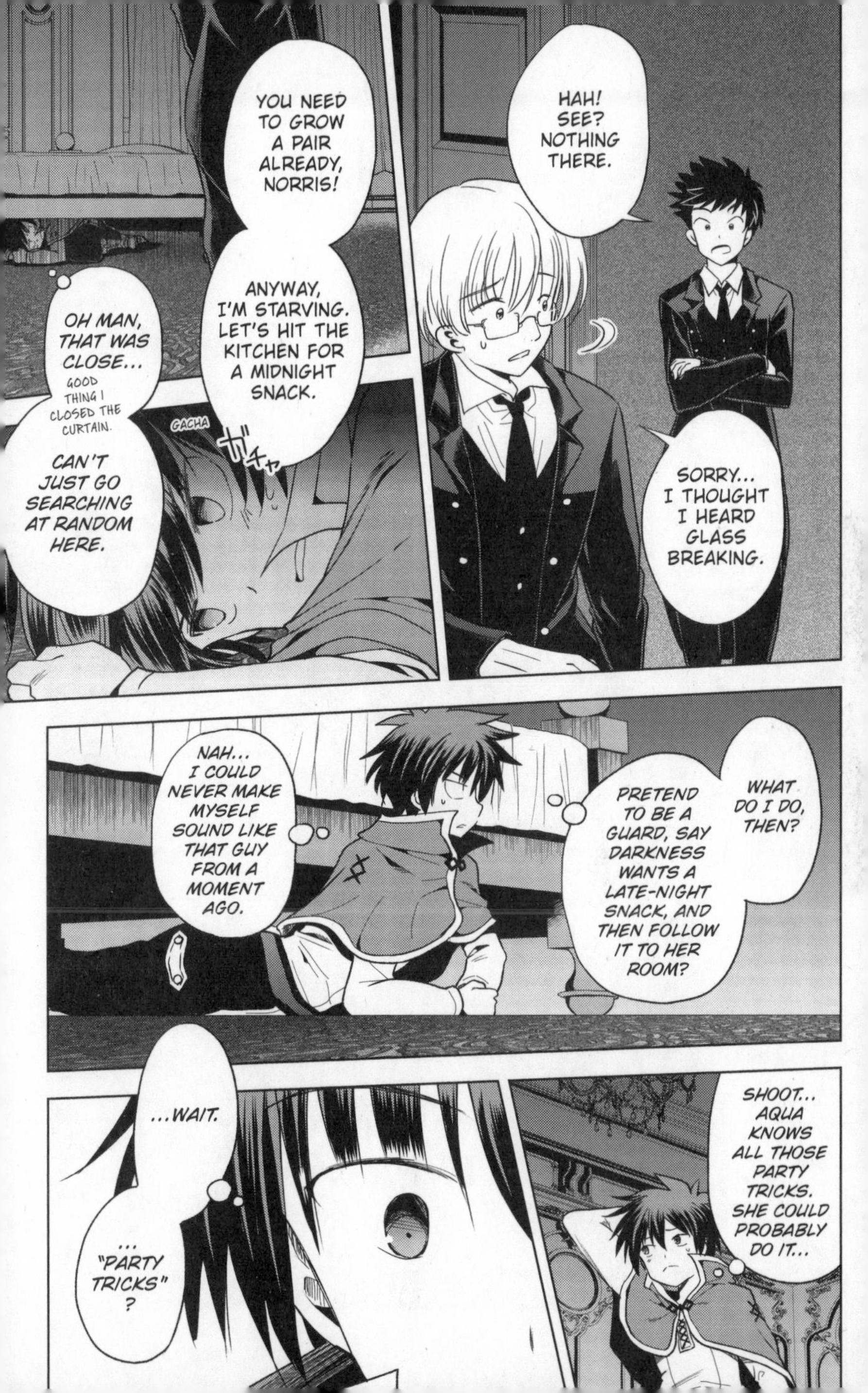
HAH! SEE? NOTHING THERE.
SORRY... I THOUGHT I HEARD GLASS BREAKING.
YOU NEED TO GROW A PAIR ALREADY, NORRIS!
ANYWAY, I'M STARVING. LET'S HIT THE KITCHEN FOR A MIDNIGHT SNACK.
GACHA
ガチャ
OH MAN, THAT WAS CLOSE...
GOOD THING I CLOSED THE CURTAIN.
CAN'T JUST GO SEARCHING AT RANDOM HERE.
WHAT DO I DO, THEN?
PRETEND TO BE A GUARD, SAY DARKNESS WANTS A LATE-NIGHT SNACK, AND THEN FOLLOW IT TO HER ROOM?
NAH... I COULD NEVER MAKE MYSELF SOUND LIKE THAT GUY FROM A MOMENT AGO.
SHOOT... AQUA KNOWS ALL THOSE PARTY TRICKS. SHE COULD PROBABLY DO IT...
...WAIT.
... "PARTY TRICKS" ?

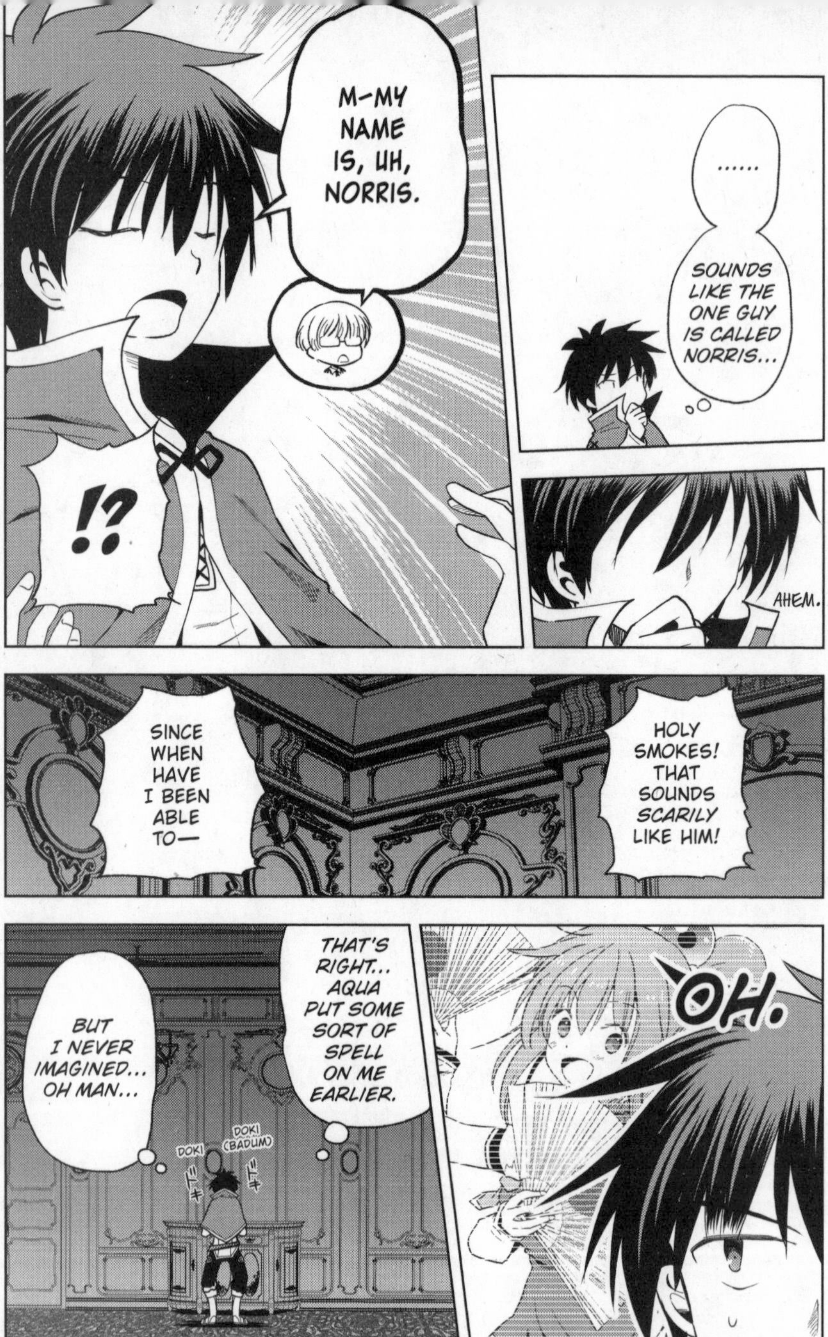
......
SOUNDS LIKE THE ONE GUY IS CALLED NORRIS...
AHEM.
M-MY NAME IS, UH, NORRIS.
!?
HOLY SMOKES! THAT SOUNDS SCARILY LIKE HIM!
SINCE WHEN HAVE I BEEN ABLE TO—
OH.
THAT'S RIGHT... AQUA PUT SOME SORT OF SPELL ON ME EARLIER.
BUT I NEVER IMAGINED... OH MAN...
DOKI DOKI (BADUM)

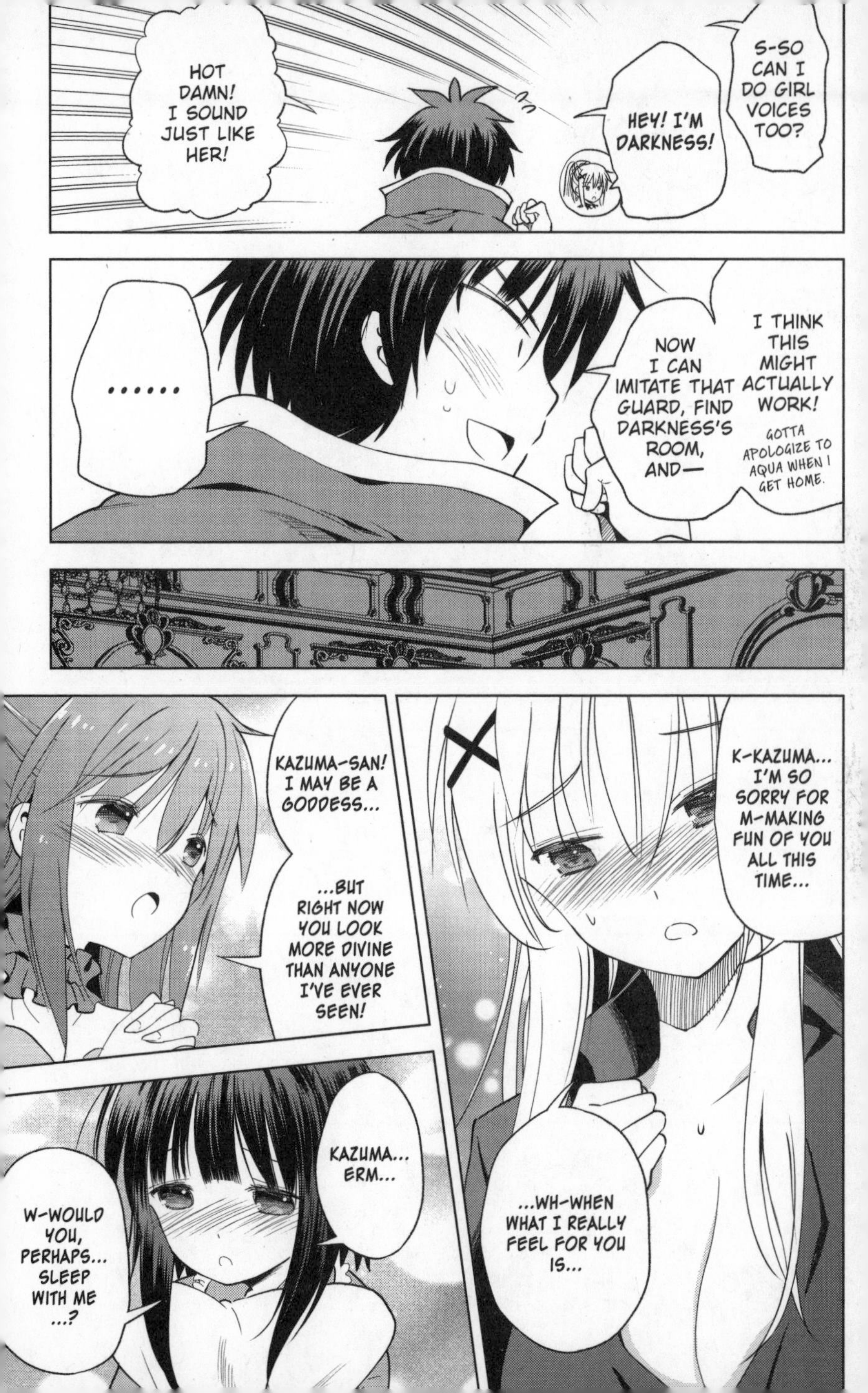
S-SO CAN I DO GIRL VOICES TOO?
HEY! I'M DARKNESS!
HOT DAMN! I SOUND JUST LIKE HER!
I THINK THIS MIGHT ACTUALLY WORK!
GOTTA APOLOGIZE TO AQUA WHEN I GET HOME.
NOW I CAN IMITATE THAT GUARD, FIND DARKNESS'S ROOM, AND—
......
K-KAZUMA... I'M SO SORRY FOR M-MAKING FUN OF YOU ALL THIS TIME...
...WH-WHEN WHAT I REALLY FEEL FOR YOU IS...
KAZUMA-SAN! I MAY BE A GODDESS...
...BUT RIGHT NOW YOU LOOK MORE DIVINE THAN ANYONE I'VE EVER SEEN!
KAZUMA... ERM...
W-WOULD YOU, PERHAPS... SLEEP WITH ME ...?

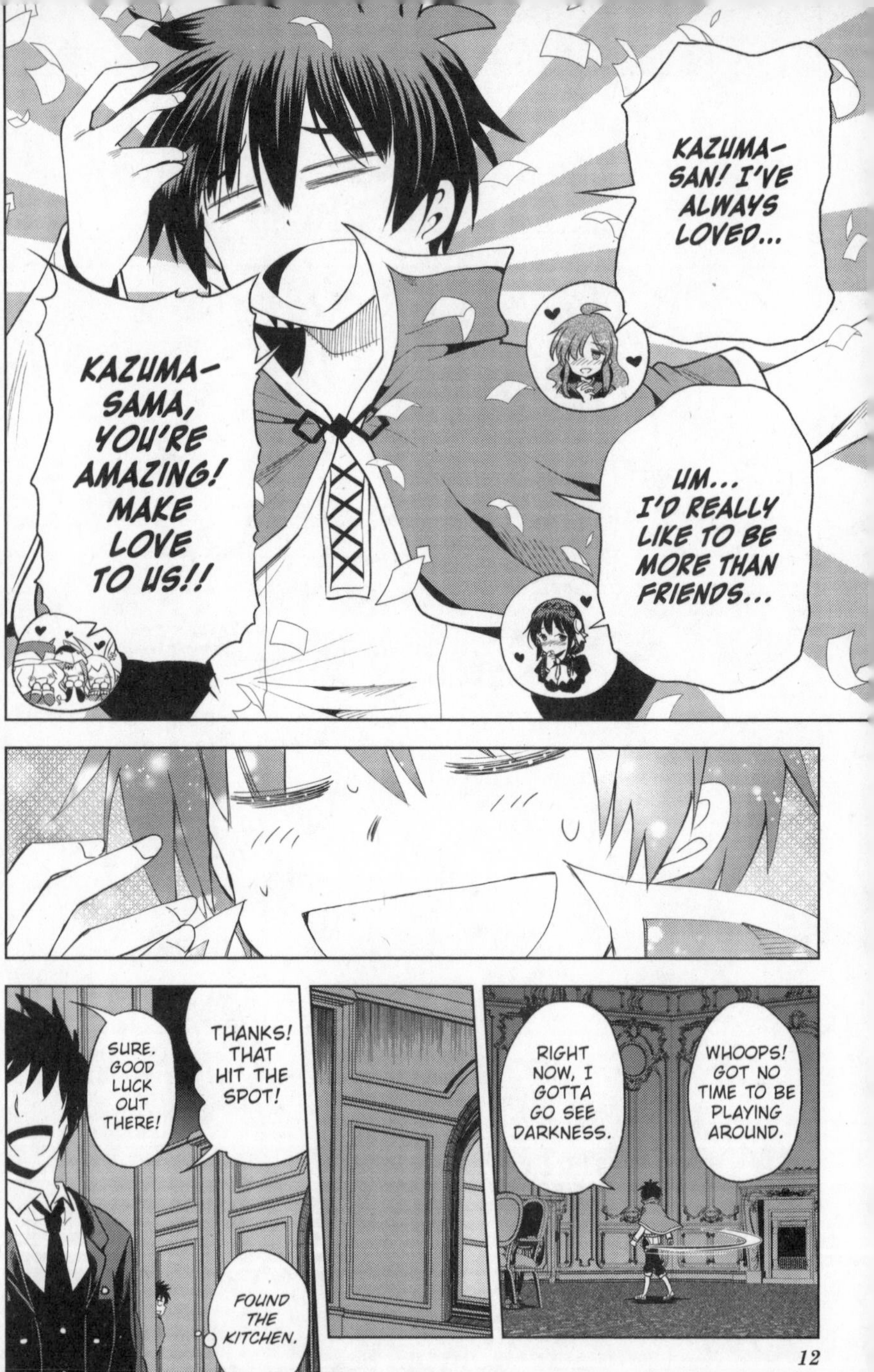
KAZUMA-SAN! I'VE ALWAYS LOVED...
UM... I'D REALLY LIKE TO BE MORE THAN FRIENDS...
KAZUMA-SAMA, YOU'RE AMAZING! MAKE LOVE TO US!!
WHOOPS! GOT NO TIME TO BE PLAYING AROUND.
RIGHT NOW, I GOTTA GO SEE DARKNESS.
THANKS! THAT HIT THE SPOT!
SURE. GOOD LUCK OUT THERE!
FOUND THE KITCHEN.

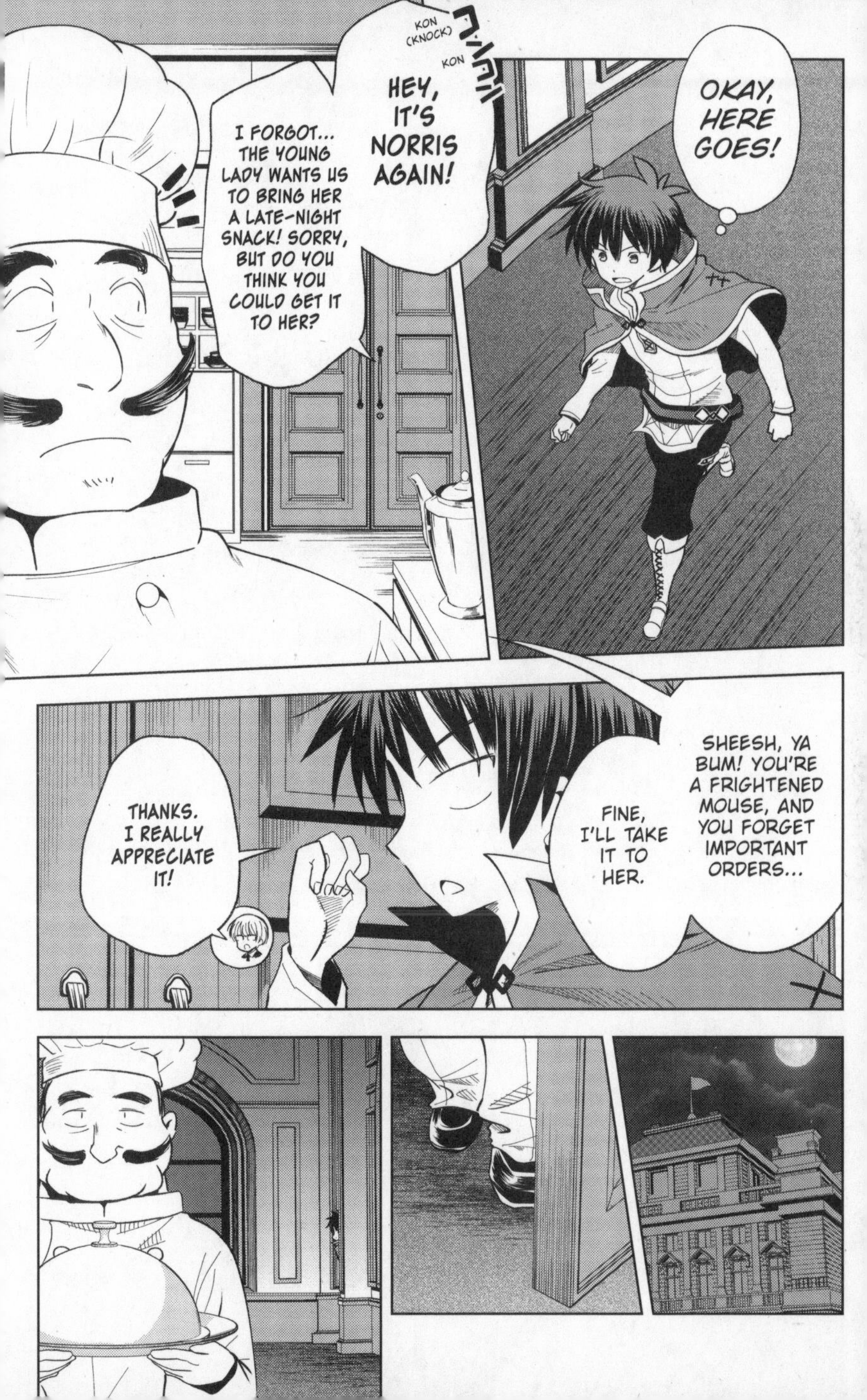
OKAY, HERE GOES!
KON (KNOCK) KON
HEY, IT'S NORRIS AGAIN!
I FORGOT... THE YOUNG LADY WANTS US TO BRING HER A LATE-NIGHT SNACK! SORRY, BUT DO YOU THINK YOU COULD GET IT TO HER?
SHEESH, YA BUM! YOU'RE A FRIGHTENED MOUSE, AND YOU FORGET IMPORTANT ORDERS...
FINE, I'LL TAKE IT TO HER.
THANKS. I REALLY APPRECIATE IT!

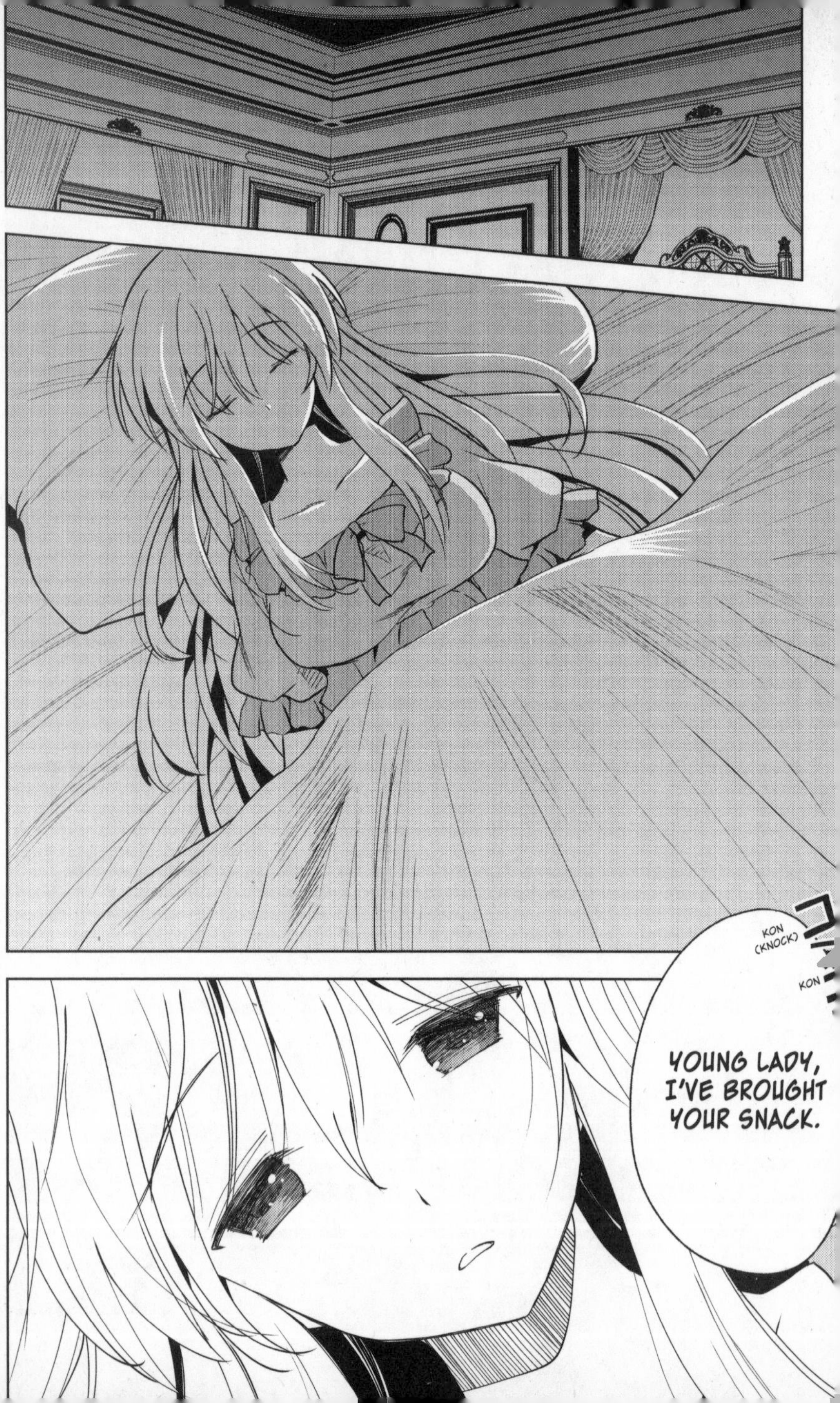
KON (KNOCK)
KON
YOUNG LADY, I'VE BROUGHT YOUR SNACK.

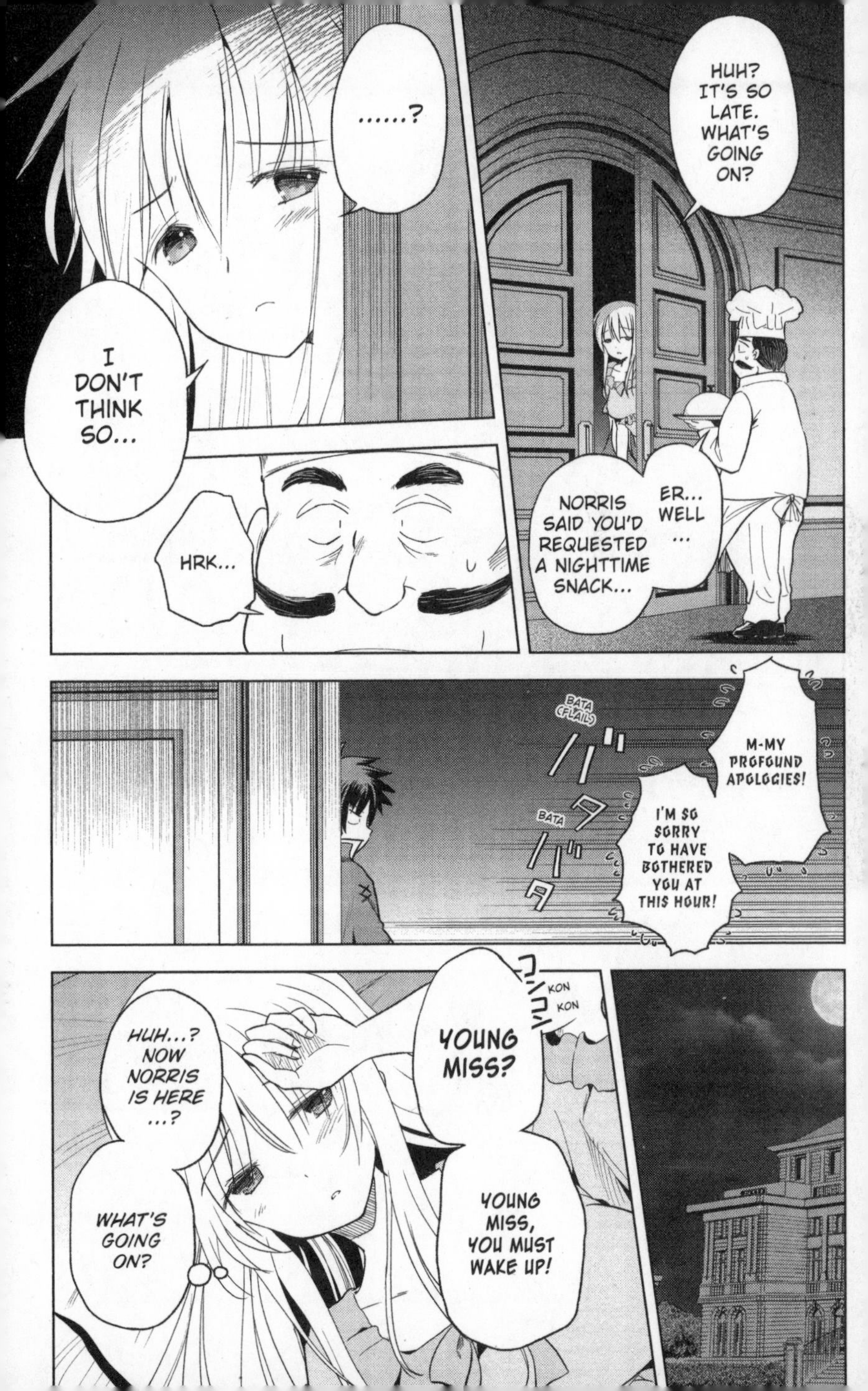
HUH? IT'S SO LATE. WHAT'S GOING ON?
ER... WELL ...
NORRIS SAID YOU'D REQUESTED A NIGHTTIME SNACK...
......?
I DON'T THINK SO...
HRK...
M-MY PROFOUND APOLOGIES!
I'M SO SORRY TO HAVE BOTHERED YOU AT THIS HOUR!
BATA (FLAILS)
BATA
KON
KON
YOUNG MISS?
YOUNG MISS, YOU MUST WAKE UP!
HUH...? NOW NORRIS IS HERE ...?
WHAT'S GOING ON?

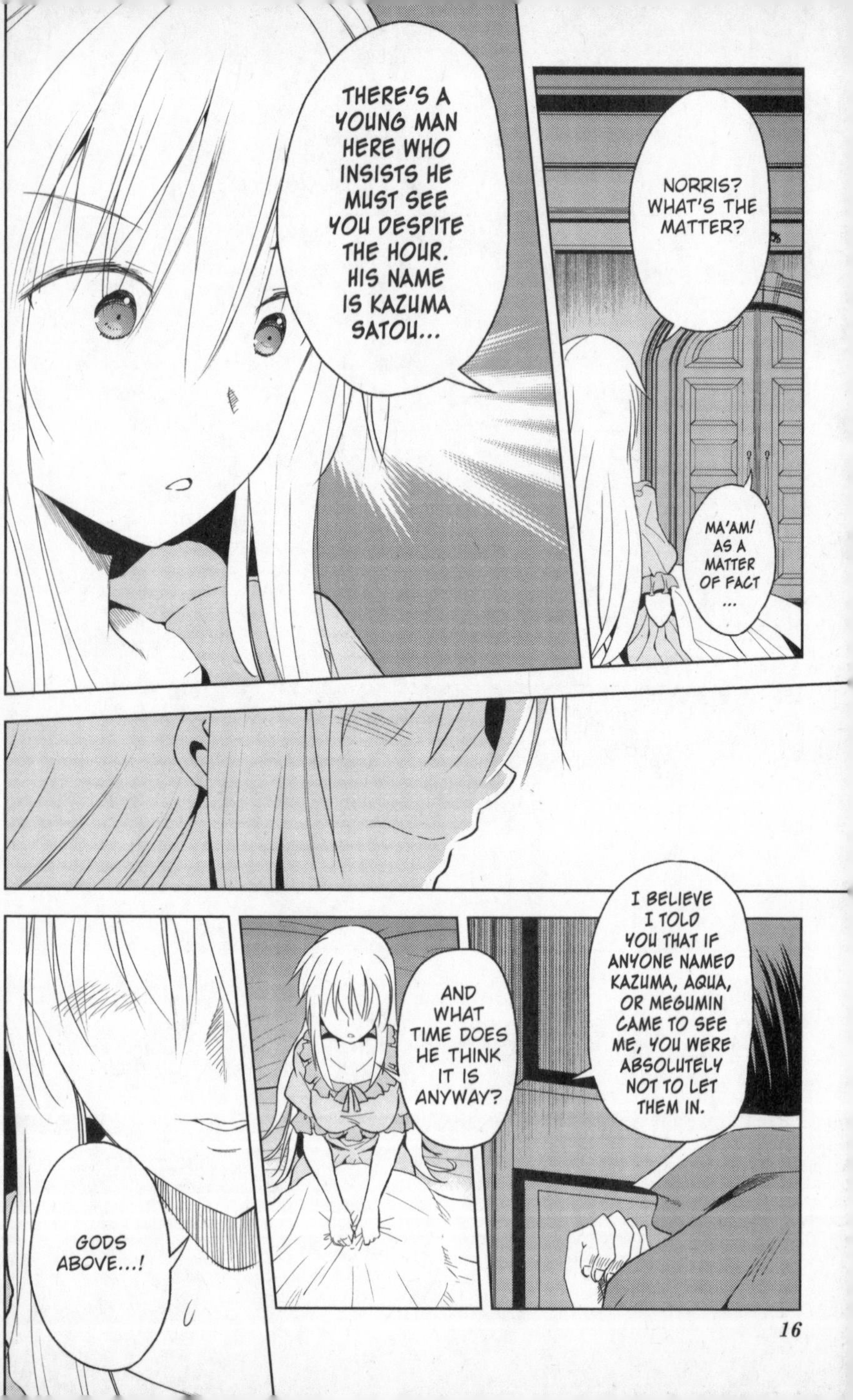
NORRIS? WHAT'S THE MATTER?
MA'AM! AS A MATTER OF FACT...
THERE'S A YOUNG MAN HERE WHO INSISTS HE MUST SEE YOU DESPITE THE HOUR. HIS NAME IS KAZUMA SATOU...
I BELIEVE I TOLD YOU THAT IF ANYONE NAMED KAZUMA, AQUA, OR MEGUMIN CAME TO SEE ME, YOU WERE ABSOLUTELY NOT TO LET THEM IN.
AND WHAT TIME DOES HE THINK IT IS ANYWAY?
GODS ABOVE...!

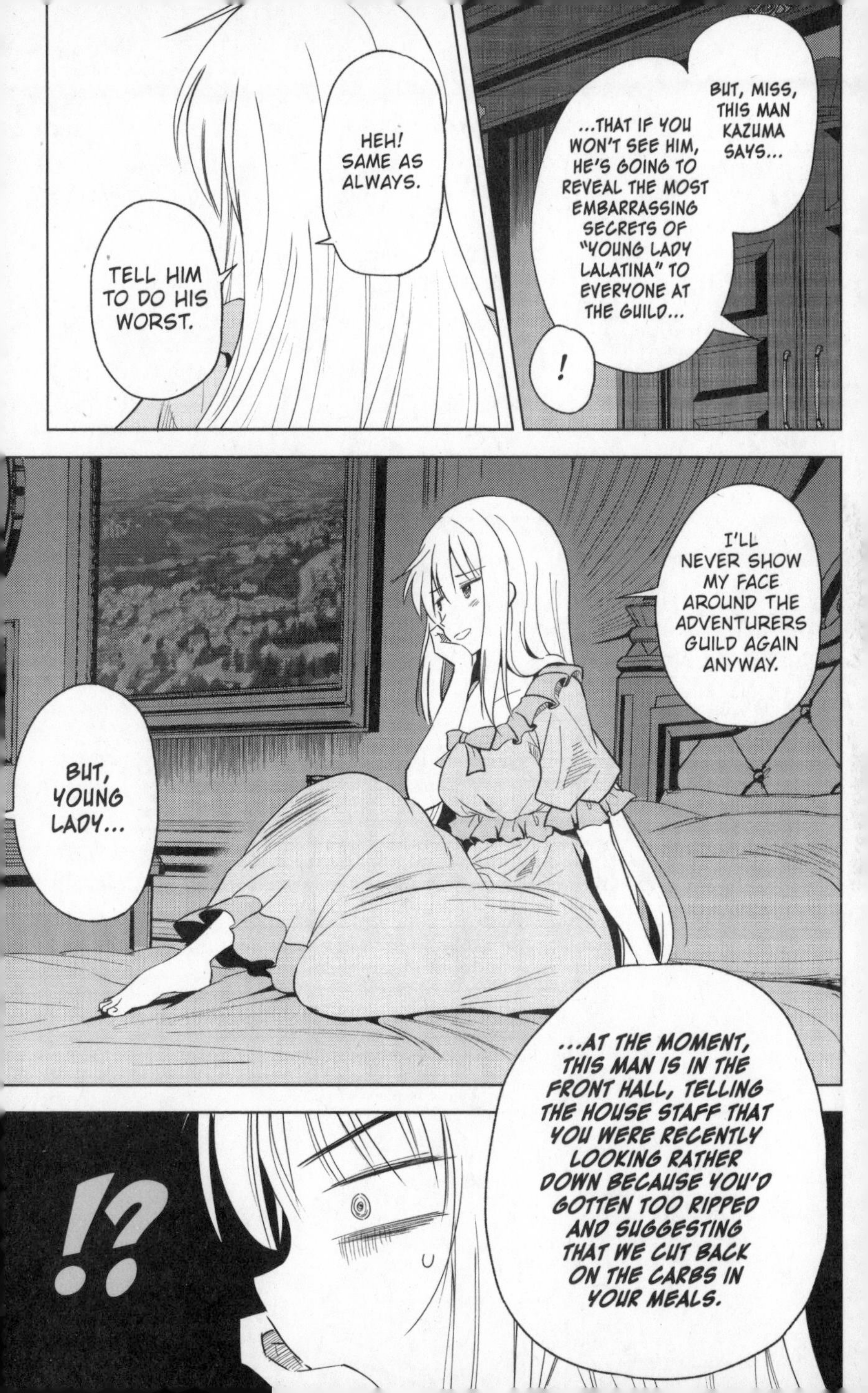

BUT, MISS, THIS MAN KAZUMA SAYS...
...THAT IF YOU WON'T SEE HIM, HE'S GOING TO REVEAL THE MOST EMBARRASSING SECRETS OF "YOUNG LADY LALATINA" TO EVERYONE AT THE GUILD...
!
HEH! SAME AS ALWAYS.
TELL HIM TO DO HIS WORST.
I'LL NEVER SHOW MY FACE AROUND THE ADVENTURERS GUILD AGAIN ANYWAY.
BUT, YOUNG LADY...
...AT THE MOMENT, THIS MAN IS IN THE FRONT HALL, TELLING THE HOUSE STAFF THAT YOU WERE RECENTLY LOOKING RATHER DOWN BECAUSE YOU'D GOTTEN TOO RIPPED AND SUGGESTING THAT WE CUT BACK ON THE CARBS IN YOUR MEALS.
!?

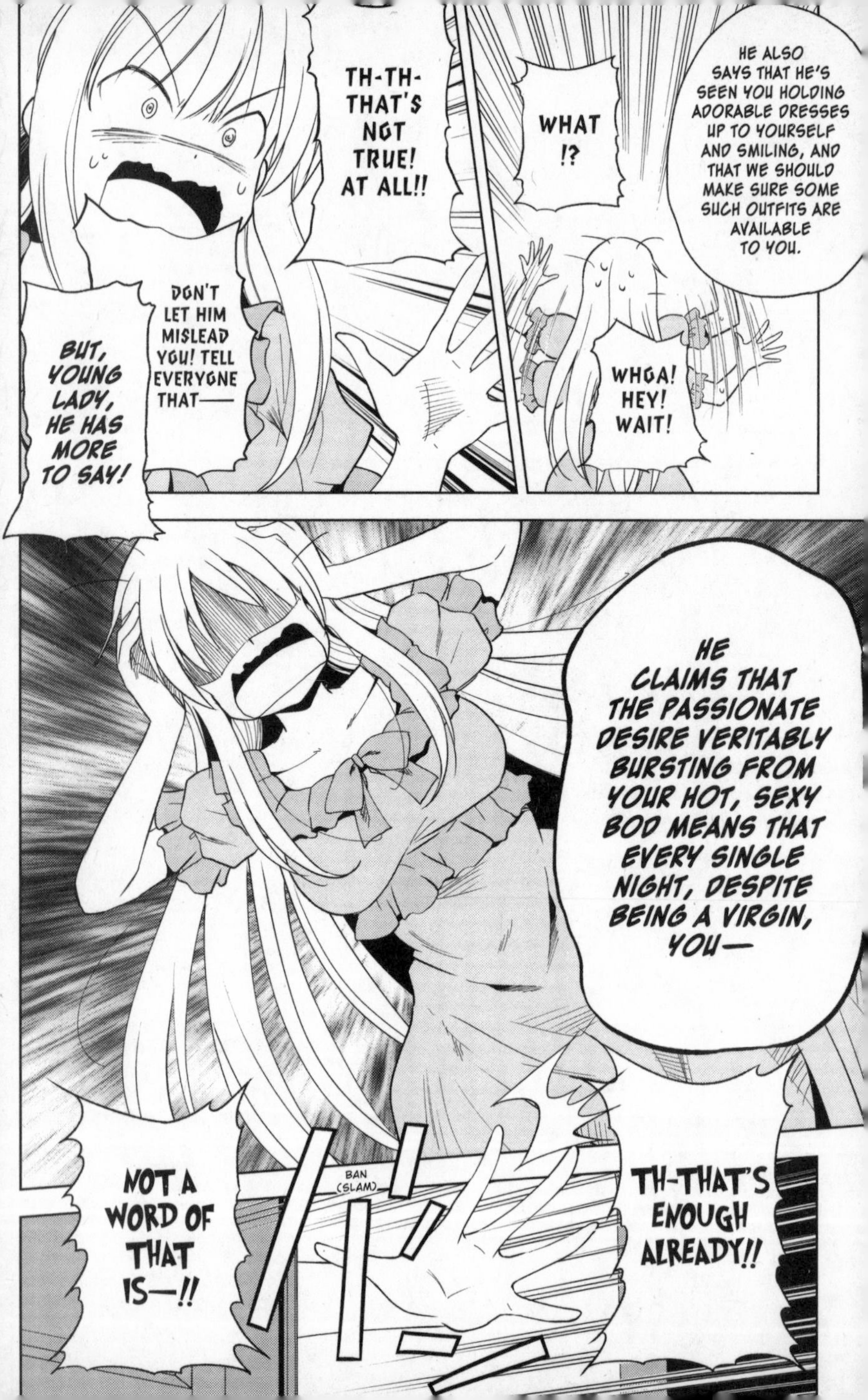
HE ALSO SAYS THAT HE'S SEEN YOU HOLDING ADORABLE DRESSES UP TO YOURSELF AND SMILING, AND THAT WE SHOULD MAKE SURE SOME SUCH OUTFITS ARE AVAILABLE TO YOU.
WHAT!?
WHOA! HEY! WAIT!
TH-TH-THAT'S NOT TRUE! AT ALL!!
DON'T LET HIM MISLEAD YOU! TELL EVERYONE THAT——
BUT, YOUNG LADY, HE HAS MORE TO SAY!
HE CLAIMS THAT THE PASSIONATE DESIRE VERITABLY BURSTING FROM YOUR HOT, SEXY BOD MEANS THAT EVERY SINGLE NIGHT, DESPITE BEING A VIRGIN, YOU—
TH-THAT'S ENOUGH ALREADY!!
BAN (SLAM)
NOT A WORD OF THAT IS—!!

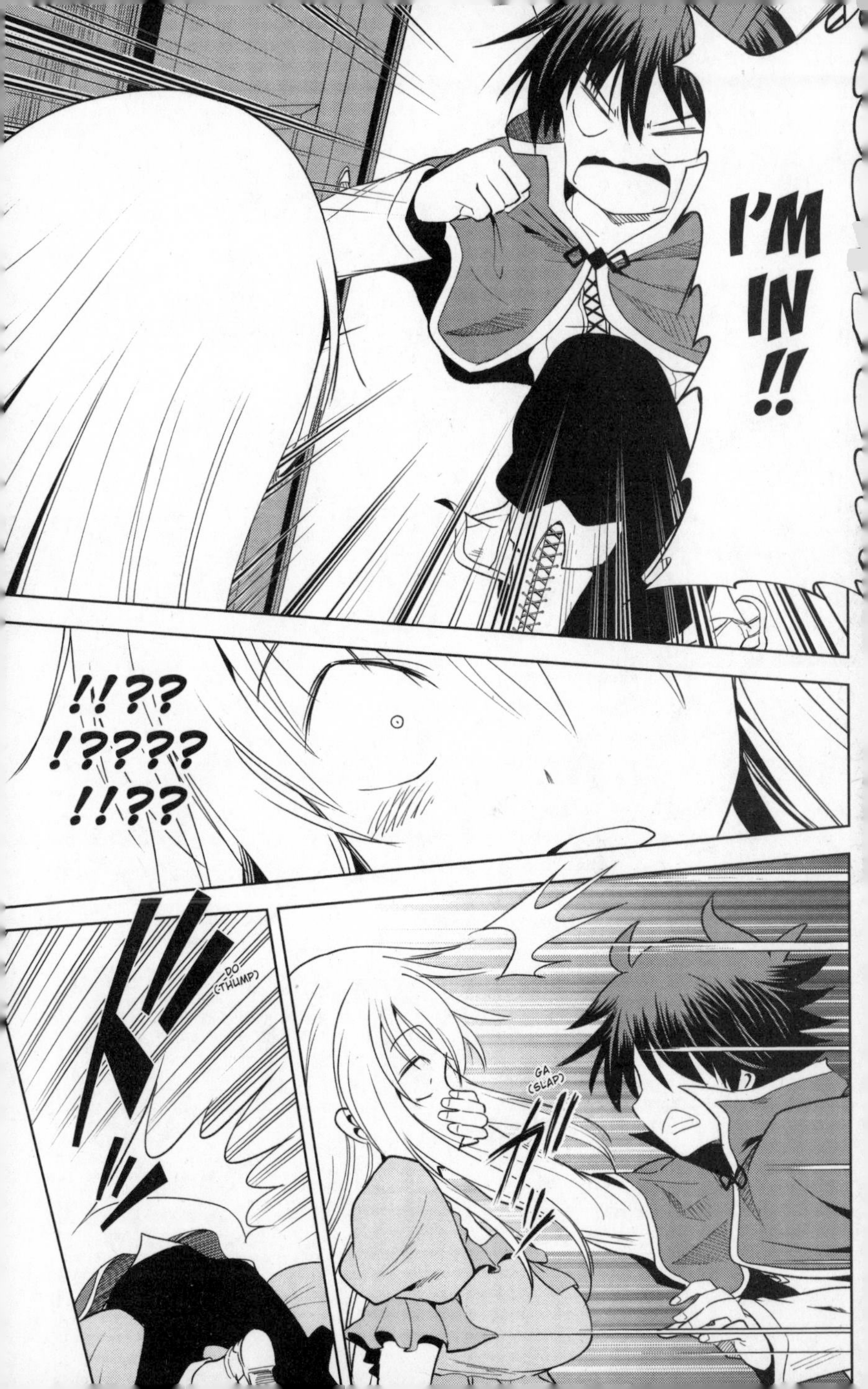
I'M IN!!
!!??
!????
!!??
GA (SLAP)
DO (THUMP)

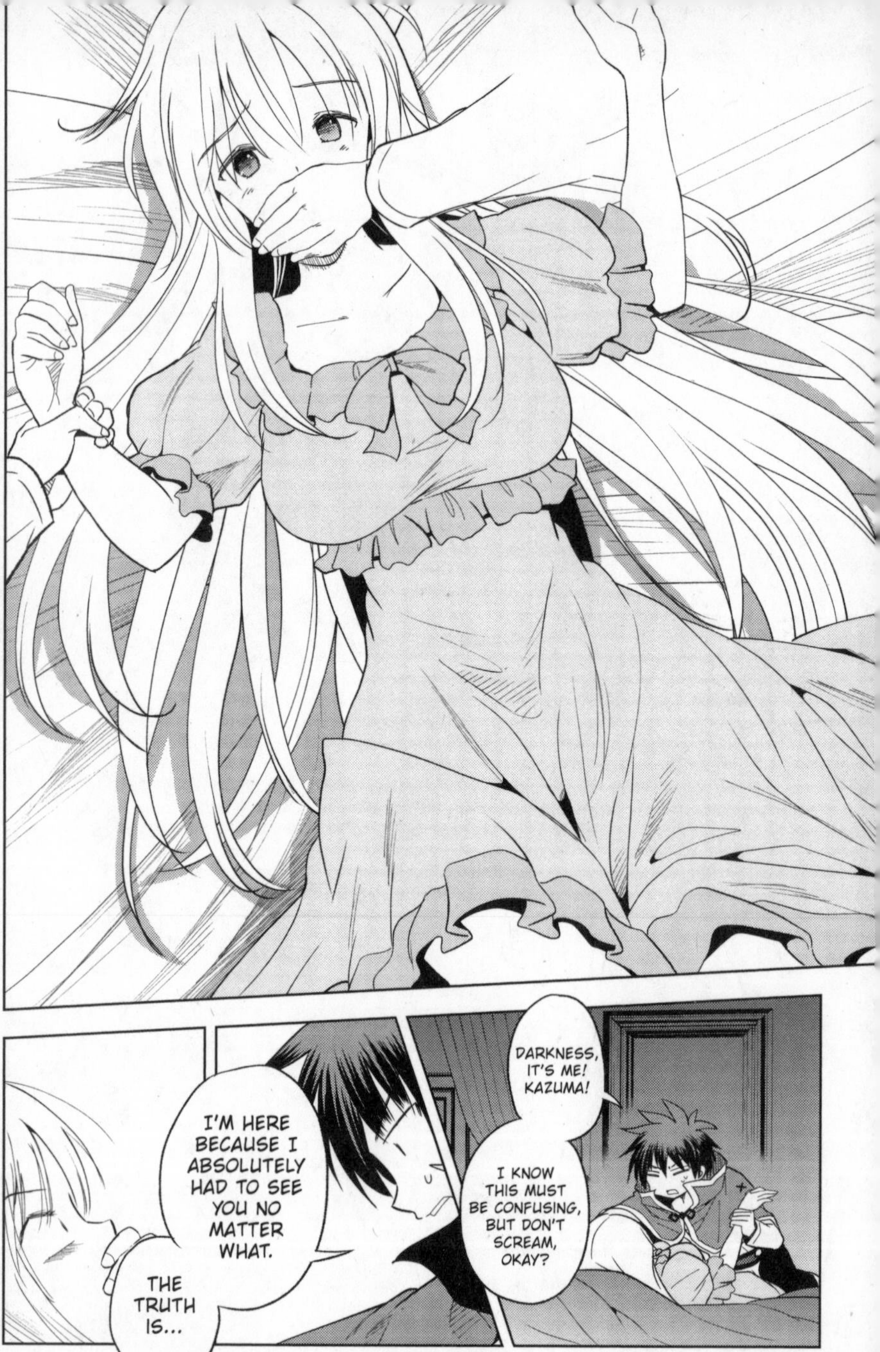
DARKNESS, IT'S ME! KAZUMA!
I KNOW THIS MUST BE CONFUSING, BUT DON'T SCREAM, OKAY?
I'M HERE BECAUSE I ABSOLUTELY HAD TO SEE YOU NO MATTER WHAT.
THE TRUTH IS...

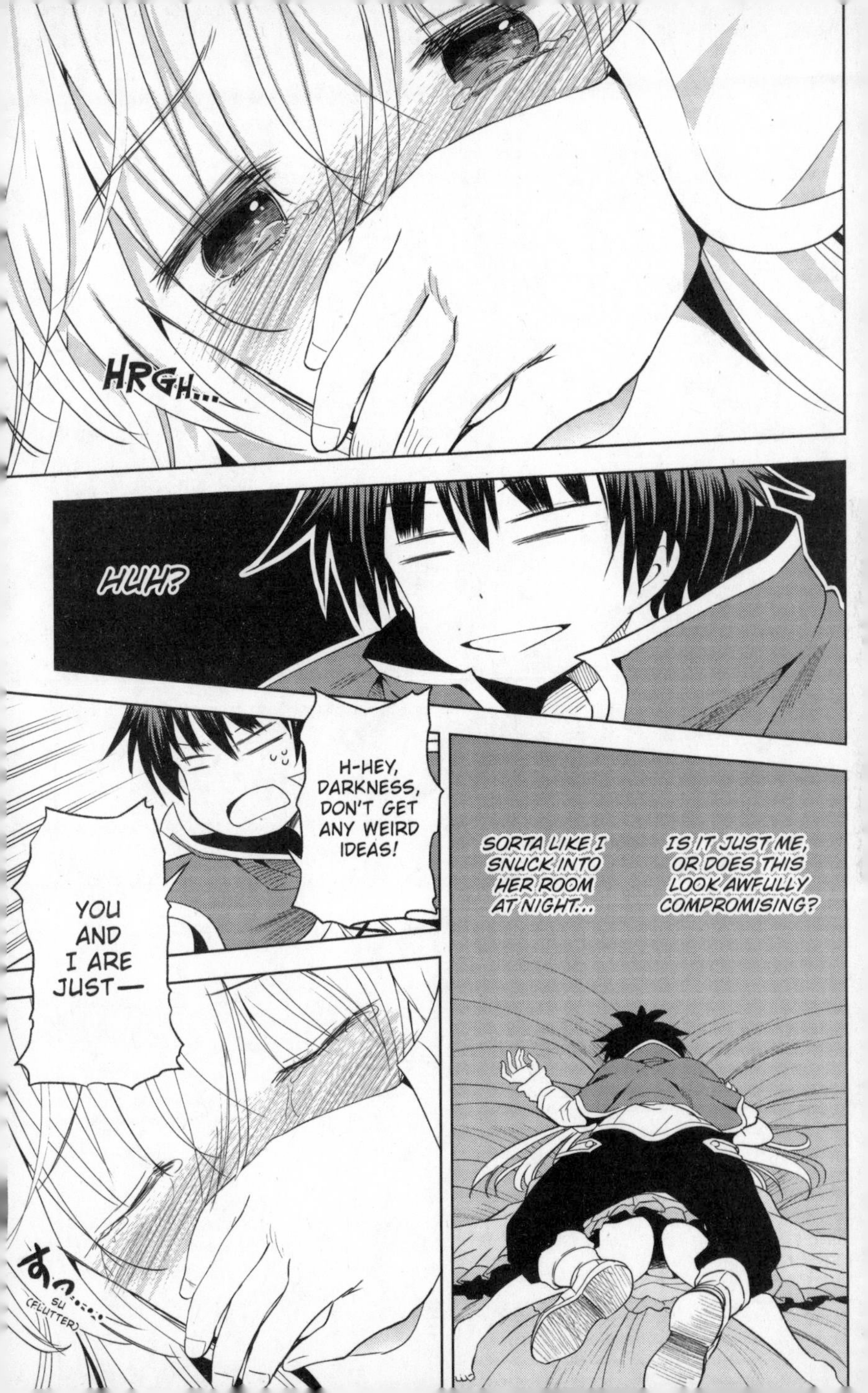
HRGH...
HUH?
H-HEY, DARKNESS, DON'T GET ANY WEIRD IDEAS!
YOU AND I ARE JUST—
IS IT JUST ME, OR DOES THIS LOOK AWFULLY COMPROMISING?
SORTA LIKE I SNUCK INTO HER ROOM AT NIGHT...
すっ
SU (FLUTTER)

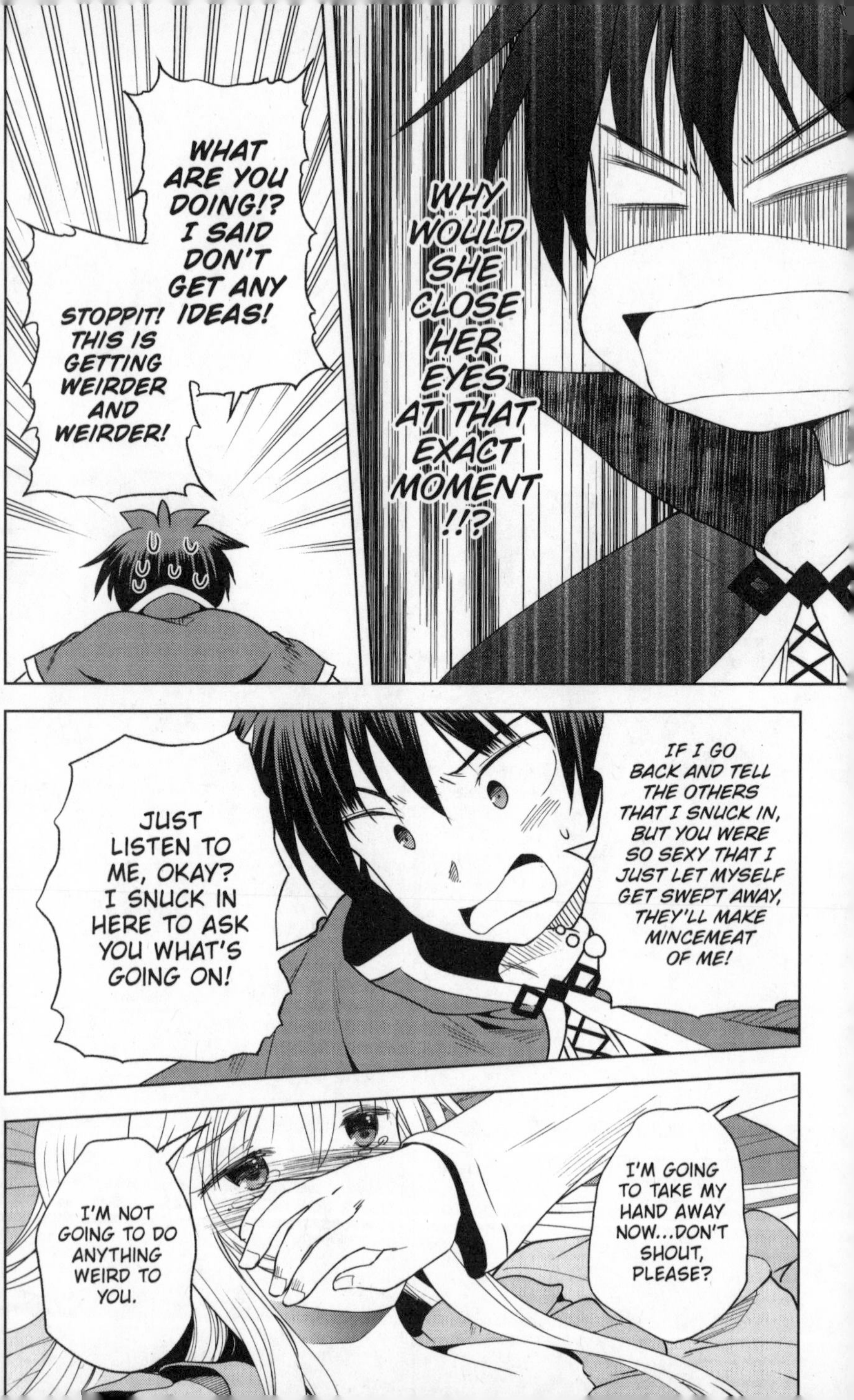
WHY WOULD SHE CLOSE HER EYES AT THAT EXACT MOMENT!!?
WHAT ARE YOU DOING!? I SAID DON'T GET ANY IDEAS!
STOPPIT! THIS IS GETTING WEIRDER AND WEIRDER!
IF I GO BACK AND TELL THE OTHERS THAT I SNUCK IN, BUT YOU WERE SO SEXY THAT I JUST LET MYSELF GET SWEPT AWAY, THEY'LL MAKE MINCEMEAT OF ME!
JUST LISTEN TO ME, OKAY? I SNUCK IN HERE TO ASK YOU WHAT'S GOING ON!
I'M GOING TO TAKE MY HAND AWAY NOW...DON'T SHOUT, PLEASE?
I'M NOT GOING TO DO ANYTHING WEIRD TO YOU.

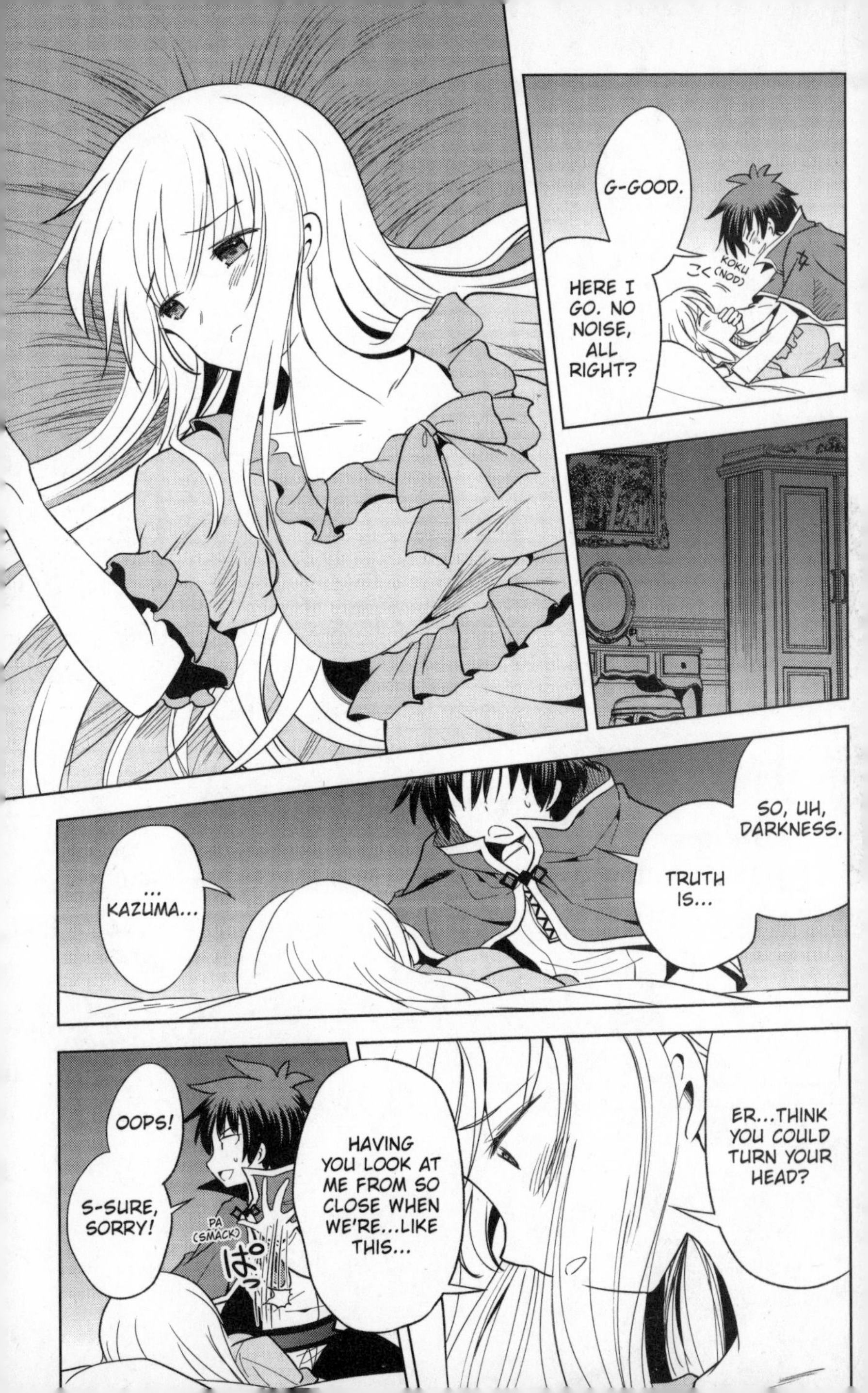
G-GOOD.
KOKU (NOD)
こく
HERE I GO. NO NOISE, ALL RIGHT?
SO, UH, DARKNESS.
TRUTH IS...
...KAZUMA...
ER...THINK YOU COULD TURN YOUR HEAD?
HAVING YOU LOOK AT ME FROM SO CLOSE WHEN WE'RE...LIKE THIS...
OOPS!
PA (SMACK)
ぱっ
S-SURE, SORRY!

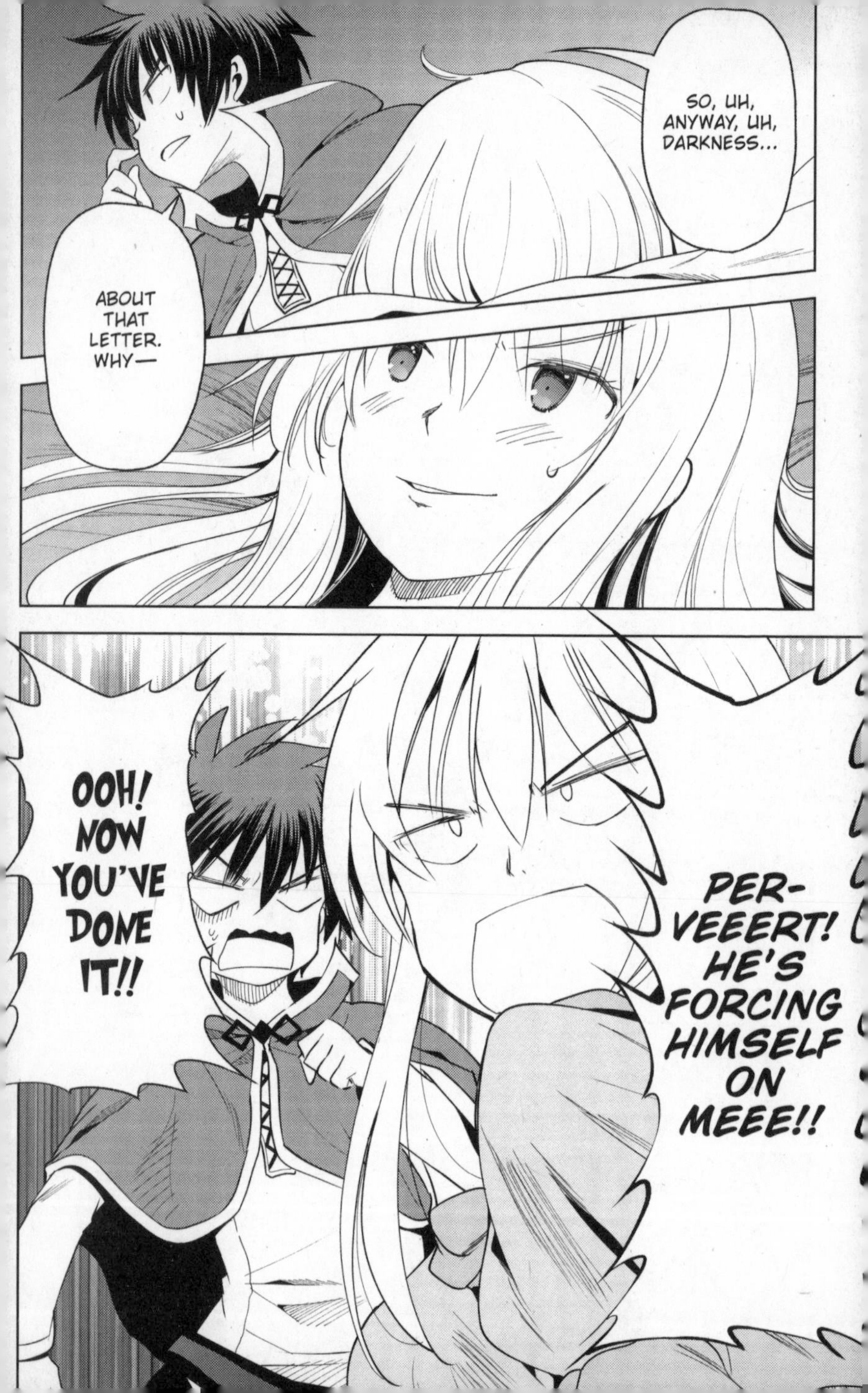
SO, UH, ANYWAY, UH, DARKNESS...
ABOUT THAT LETTER. WHY—
PER-VEEERT! HE'S FORCING HIMSELF ON MEEE!!
OOH! NOW YOU'VE DONE IT!!

GOD'S
BLESSING
ON THIS
WONDERFUL
WORLD!

13

13

GOD'S
BLESSING
ON THIS
WONDERFUL
WORLD!

CHAPTER 75

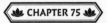

ONE LAST NIGHT WITH THIS NOBLE GIRL! ②

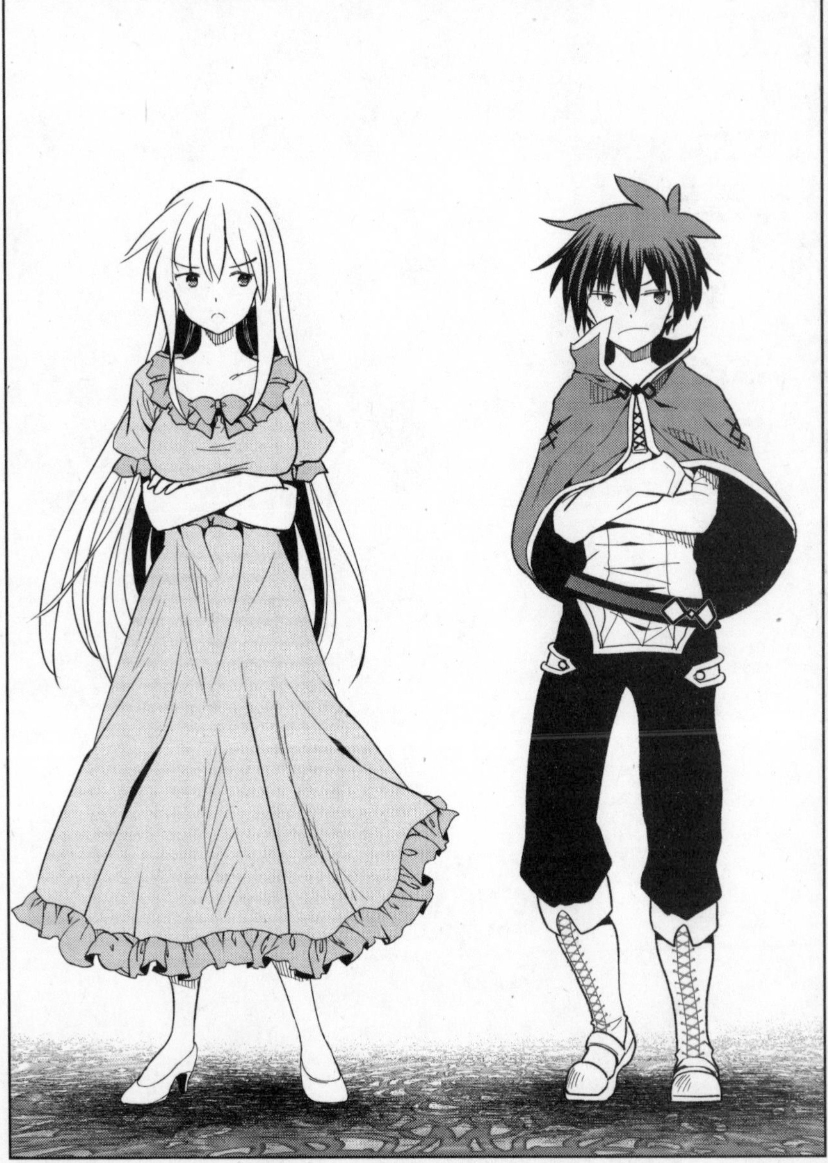

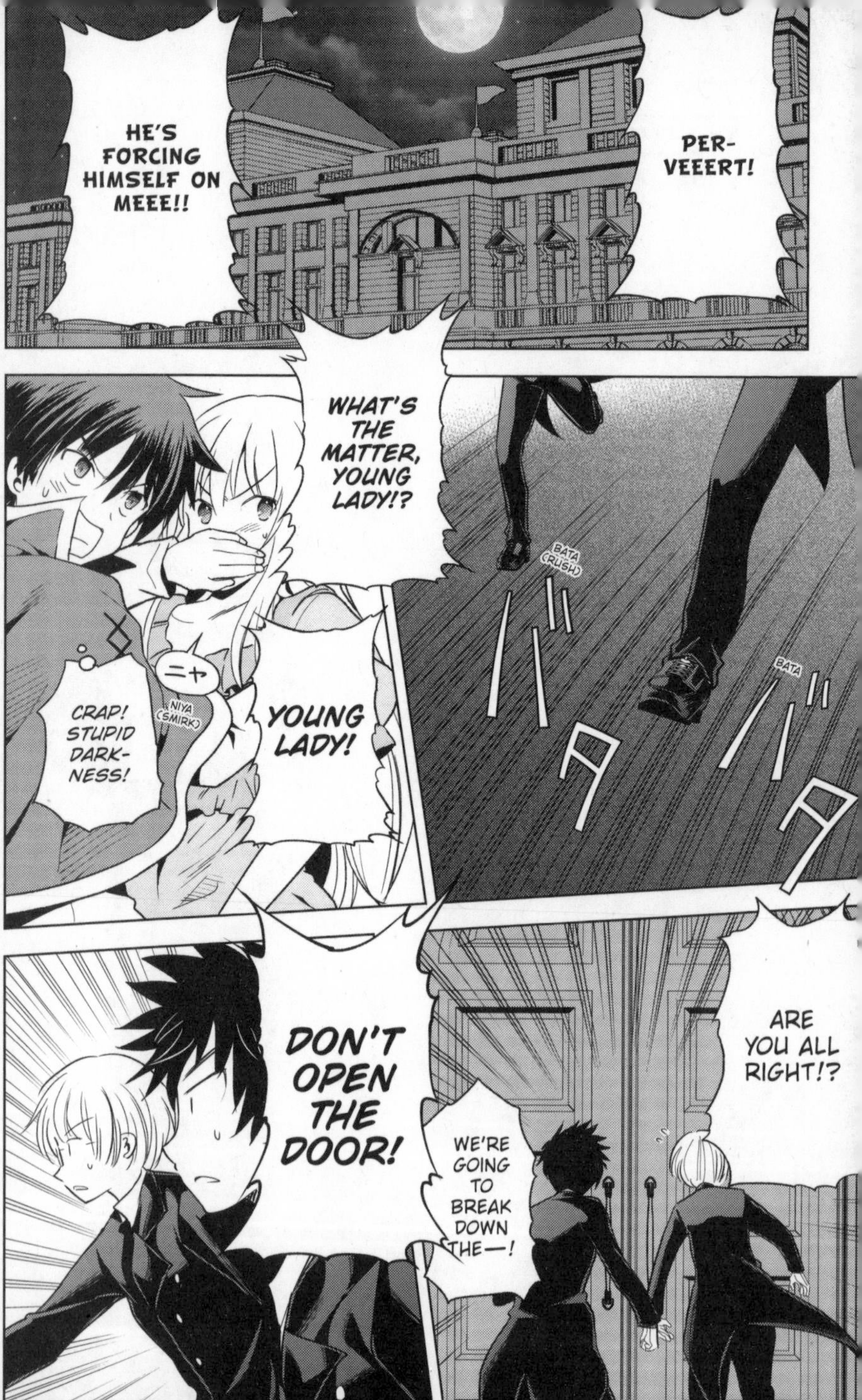
PER-VEEERT!
HE'S FORCING HIMSELF ON MEEE!!
BATA (RUSH)
バタ
BATA
バタ
WHAT'S THE MATTER, YOUNG LADY!?
YOUNG LADY!
ニヤ
NIYA (SMIRK)
CRAP! STUPID DARK-NESS!
ARE YOU ALL RIGHT!?
WE'RE GOING TO BREAK DOWN THE—!
DON'T OPEN THE DOOR!

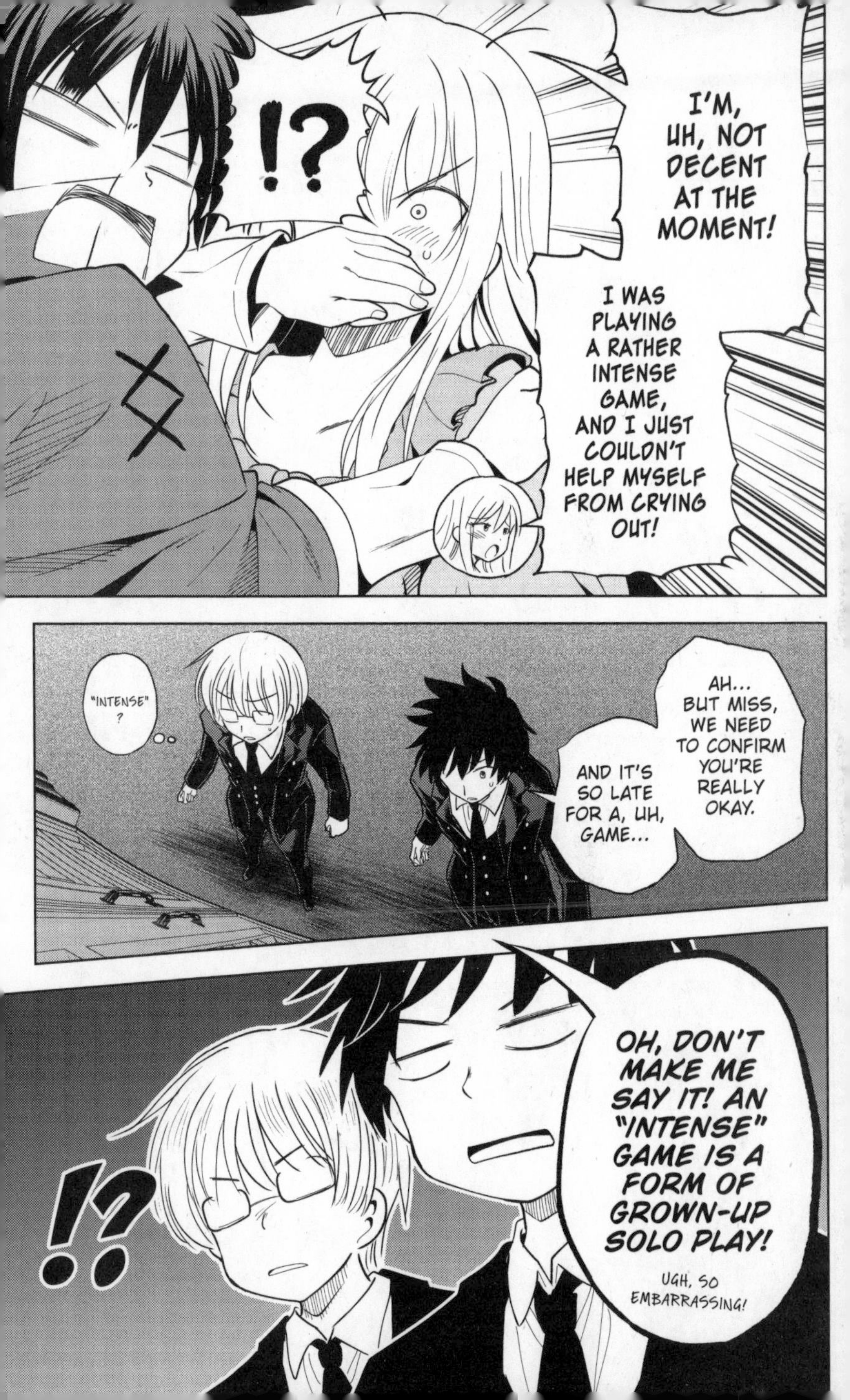
I'M, UH, NOT DECENT AT THE MOMENT!
I WAS PLAYING A RATHER INTENSE GAME, AND I JUST COULDN'T HELP MYSELF FROM CRYING OUT!
AH... BUT MISS, WE NEED TO CONFIRM YOU'RE REALLY OKAY.
AND IT'S SO LATE FOR A, UH, GAME...
"INTENSE"?
OH, DON'T MAKE ME SAY IT! AN "INTENSE" GAME IS A FORM OF GROWN-UP SOLO PLAY!
UGH, SO EMBARRASSING!
!?
!?

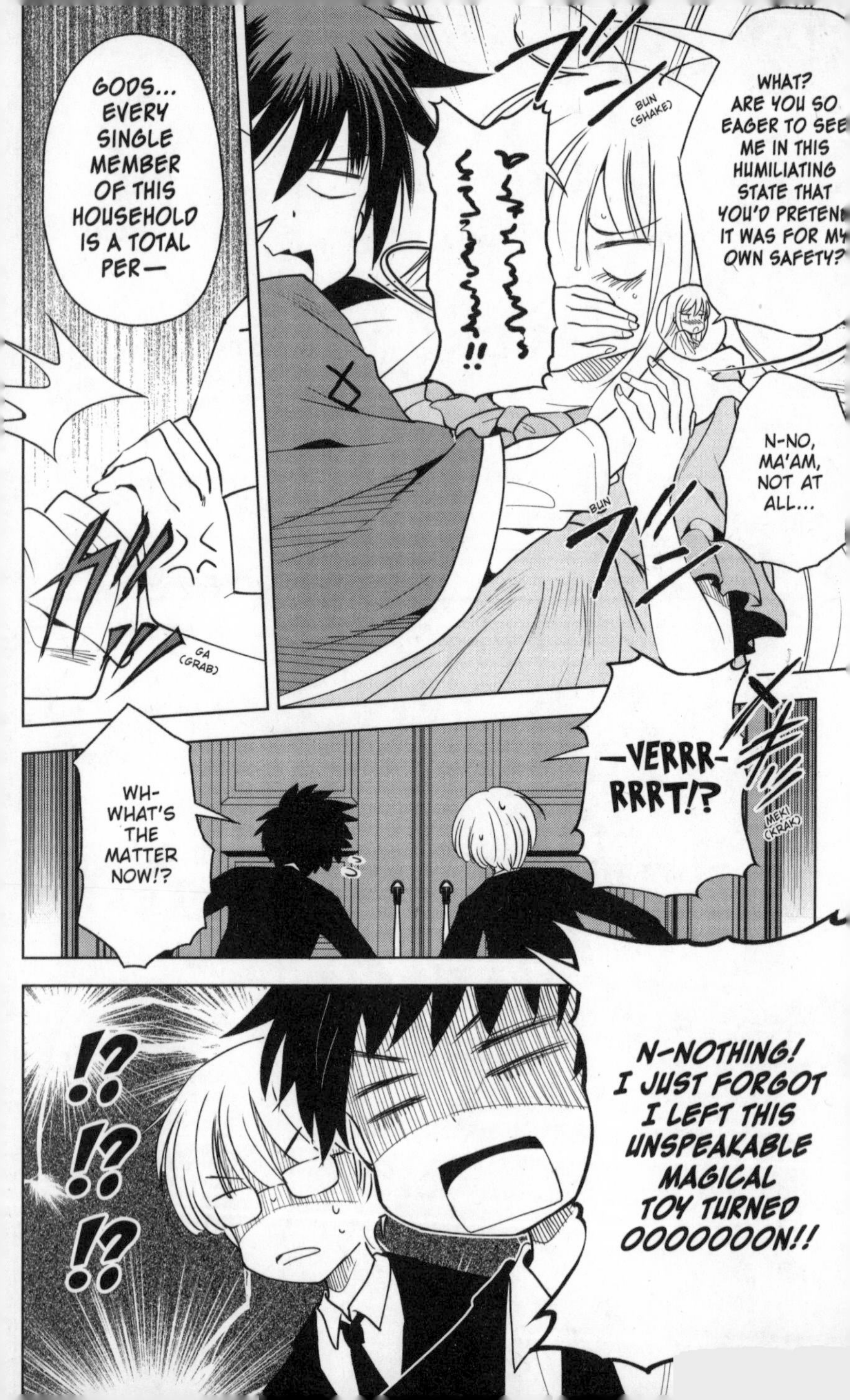
BUN (SHAKE)
WHAT? ARE YOU SO EAGER TO SEE ME IN THIS HUMILIATING STATE THAT YOU'D PRETEN IT WAS FOR MY OWN SAFETY?
N-NO, MA'AM, NOT AT ALL...
BUN
GODS... EVERY SINGLE MEMBER OF THIS HOUSEHOLD IS A TOTAL PER—
GA (GRAB)
—VERRR-RRRT!?
MEKI (KRAK)
WH-WHAT'S THE MATTER NOW!?
N-NOTHING! I JUST FORGOT I LEFT THIS UNSPEAKABLE MAGICAL TOY TURNED OOOOOOON!!
!? !? !?

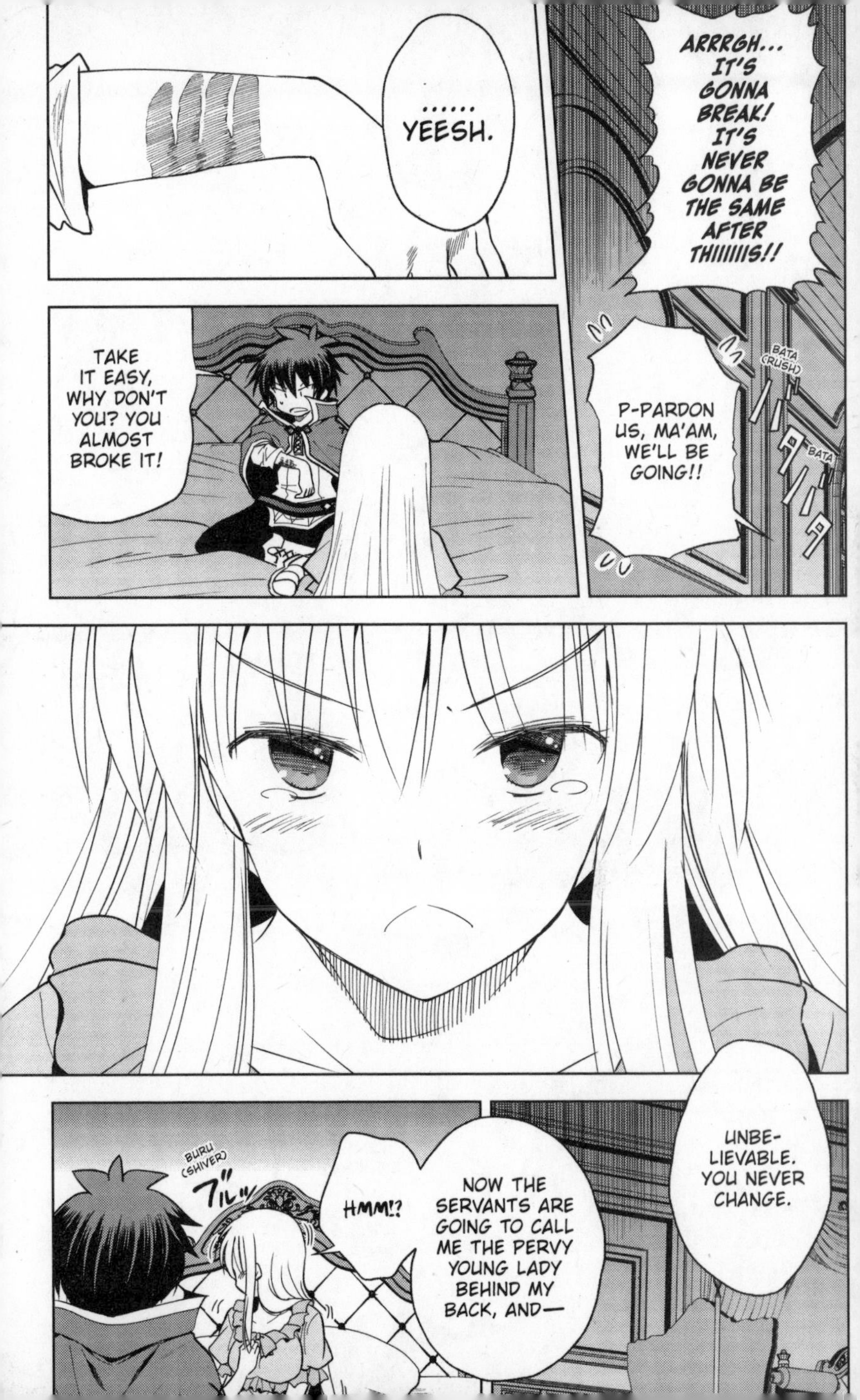
ARRRGH... IT'S GONNA BREAK! IT'S NEVER GONNA BE THE SAME AFTER THIIIIIIS!!
...... YEESH.
BATA (RUSH)
BATA
P-PARDON US, MA'AM, WE'LL BE GOING!!
TAKE IT EASY, WHY DON'T YOU? YOU ALMOST BROKE IT!
UNBE-LIEVABLE. YOU NEVER CHANGE.
NOW THE SERVANTS ARE GOING TO CALL ME THE PERVY YOUNG LADY BEHIND MY BACK, AND—
HMM!?
BURU (SHIVER)
ブルッ

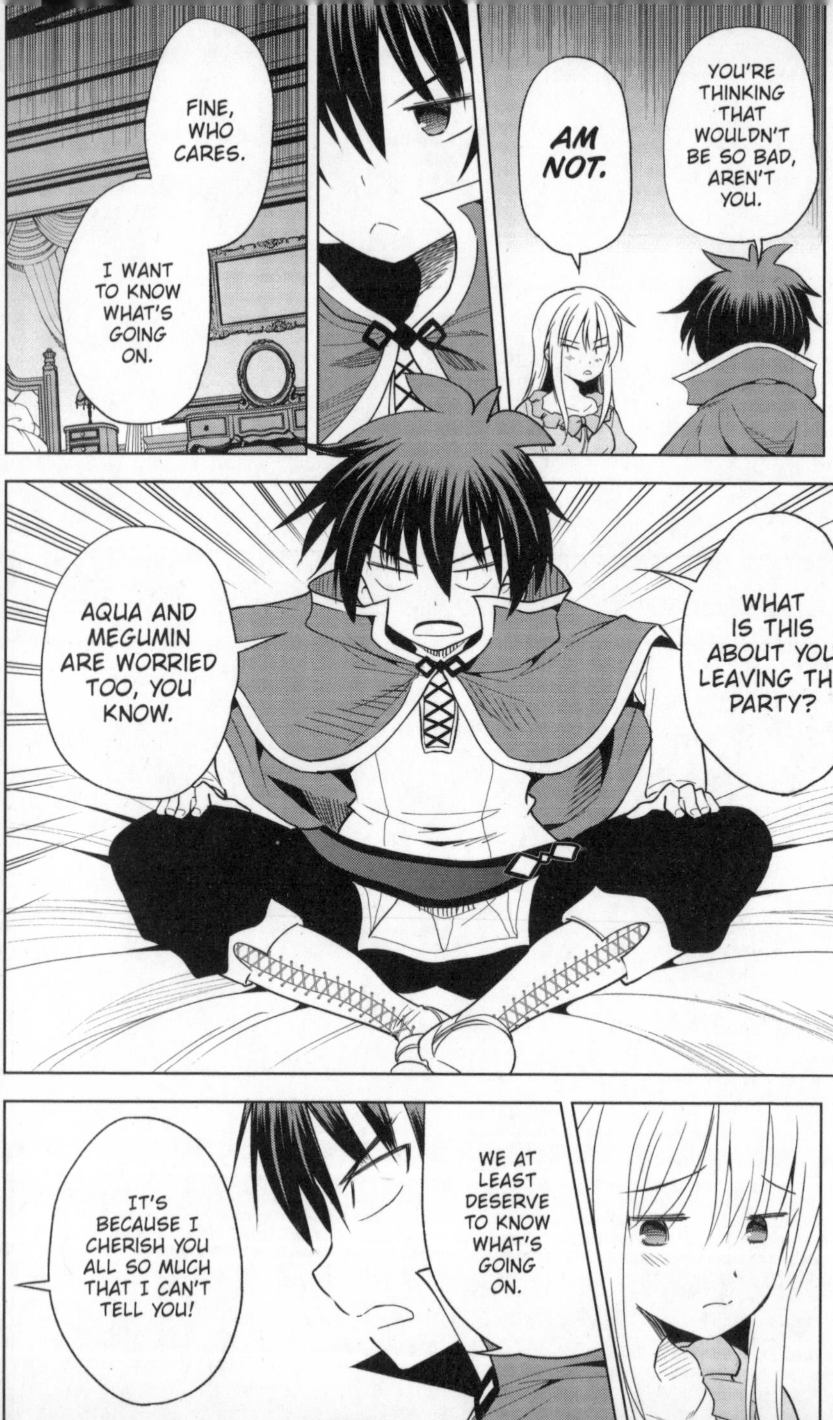
YOU'RE THINKING THAT WOULDN'T BE SO BAD, AREN'T YOU.
AM NOT.
FINE, WHO CARES.
I WANT TO KNOW WHAT'S GOING ON.
WHAT IS THIS ABOUT YOU LEAVING THE PARTY?
AQUA AND MEGUMIN ARE WORRIED TOO, YOU KNOW.
WE AT LEAST DESERVE TO KNOW WHAT'S GOING ON.
IT'S BECAUSE I CHERISH YOU ALL SO MUCH THAT I CAN'T TELL YOU!

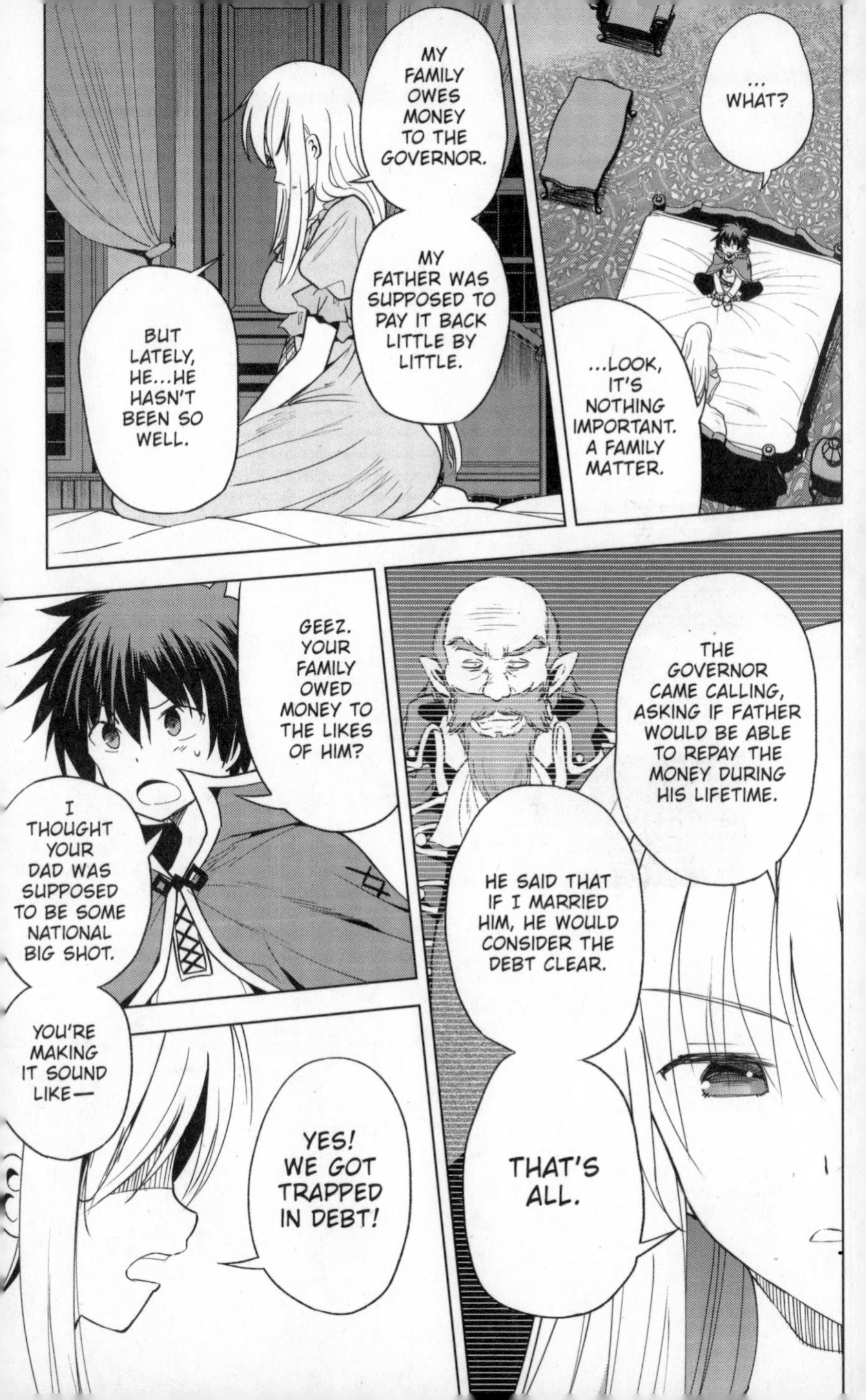
...WHAT?
...LOOK, IT'S NOTHING IMPORTANT. A FAMILY MATTER.
MY FAMILY OWES MONEY TO THE GOVERNOR.
MY FATHER WAS SUPPOSED TO PAY IT BACK LITTLE BY LITTLE.
BUT LATELY, HE...HE HASN'T BEEN SO WELL.
THE GOVERNOR CAME CALLING, ASKING IF FATHER WOULD BE ABLE TO REPAY THE MONEY DURING HIS LIFETIME.
HE SAID THAT IF I MARRIED HIM, HE WOULD CONSIDER THE DEBT CLEAR.
THAT'S ALL.
GEEZ. YOUR FAMILY OWED MONEY TO THE LIKES OF HIM?
I THOUGHT YOUR DAD WAS SUPPOSED TO BE SOME NATIONAL BIG SHOT.
YOU'RE MAKING IT SOUND LIKE—
YES! WE GOT TRAPPED IN DEBT!

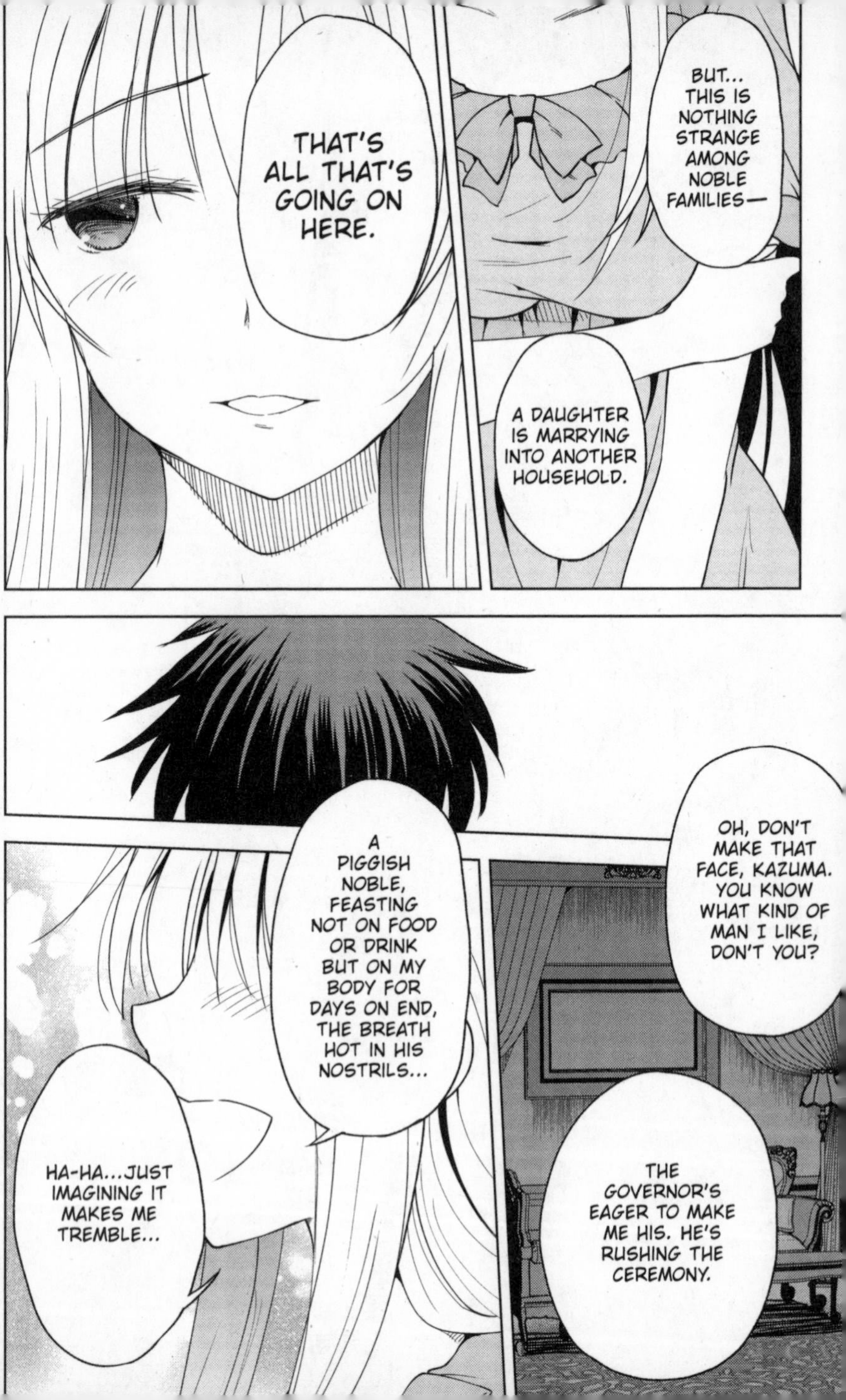
BUT... THIS IS NOTHING STRANGE AMONG NOBLE FAMILIES—
A DAUGHTER IS MARRYING INTO ANOTHER HOUSEHOLD.
THAT'S ALL THAT'S GOING ON HERE.
OH, DON'T MAKE THAT FACE, KAZUMA. YOU KNOW WHAT KIND OF MAN I LIKE, DON'T YOU?
THE GOVERNOR'S EAGER TO MAKE ME HIS. HE'S RUSHING THE CEREMONY.
A PIGGISH NOBLE, FEASTING NOT ON FOOD OR DRINK BUT ON MY BODY FOR DAYS ON END, THE BREATH HOT IN HIS NOSTRILS...
HA-HA...JUST IMAGINING IT MAKES ME TREMBLE...

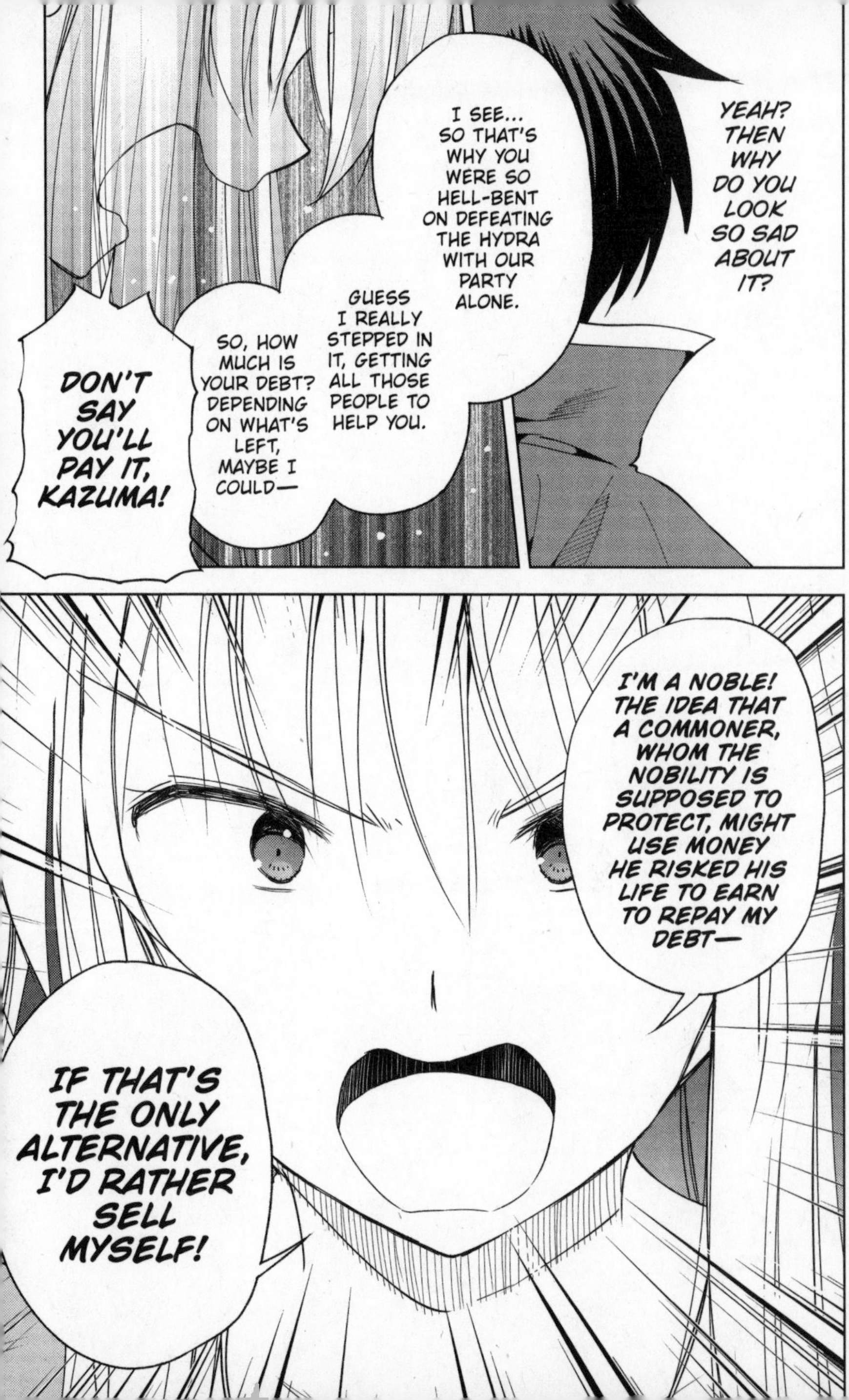
YEAH? THEN WHY DO YOU LOOK SO SAD ABOUT IT?
I SEE... SO THAT'S WHY YOU WERE SO HELL-BENT ON DEFEATING THE HYDRA WITH OUR PARTY ALONE.
GUESS I REALLY STEPPED IN IT, GETTING ALL THOSE PEOPLE TO HELP YOU.
SO, HOW MUCH IS YOUR DEBT? DEPENDING ON WHAT'S LEFT, MAYBE I COULD—
DON'T SAY YOU'LL PAY IT, KAZUMA!
I'M A NOBLE! THE IDEA THAT A COMMONER, WHOM THE NOBILITY IS SUPPOSED TO PROTECT, MIGHT USE MONEY HE RISKED HIS LIFE TO EARN TO REPAY MY DEBT—
IF THAT'S THE ONLY ALTERNATIVE, I'D RATHER SELL MYSELF!

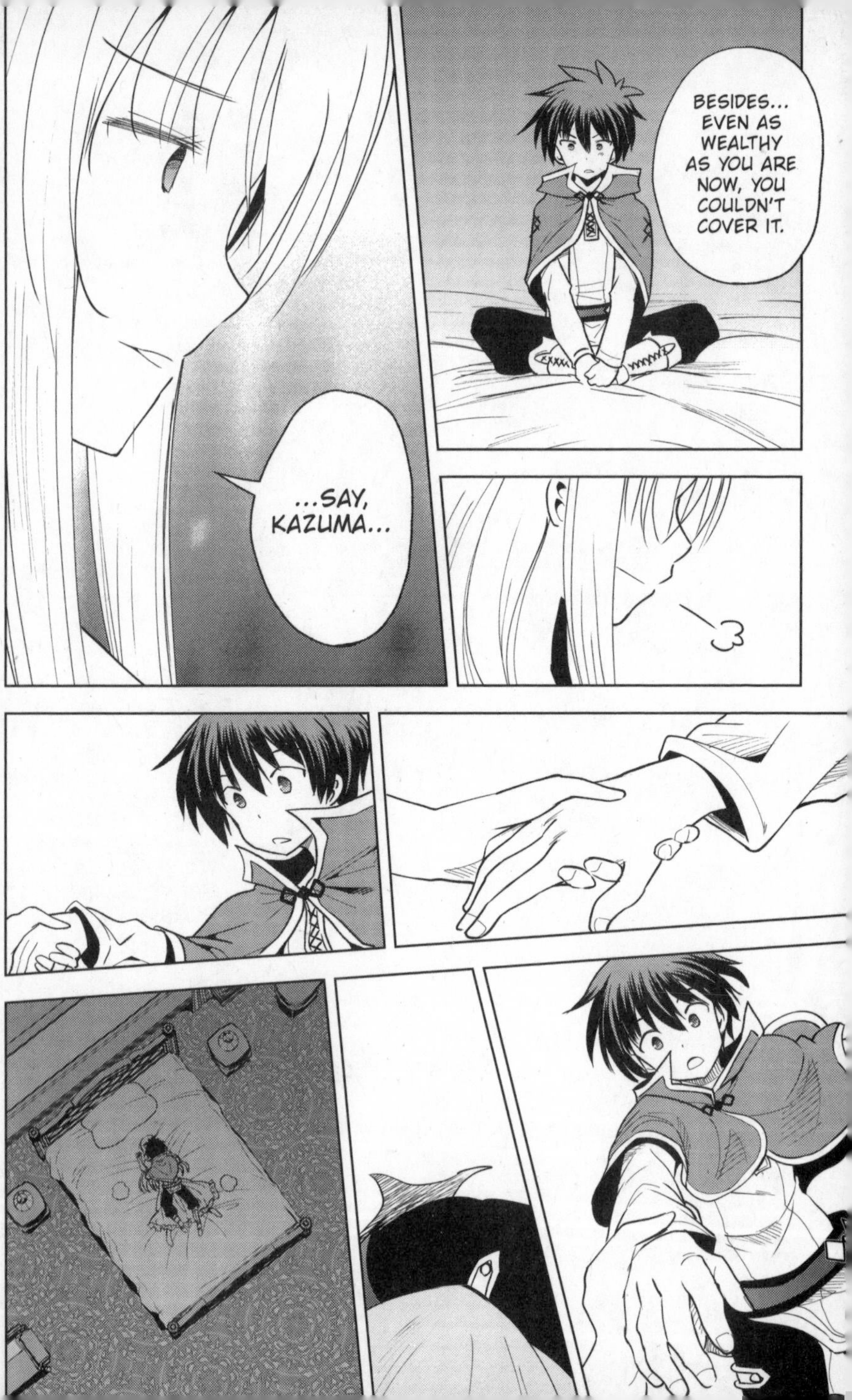
BESIDES... EVEN AS WEALTHY AS YOU ARE NOW, YOU COULDN'T COVER IT.
...SAY, KAZUMA...

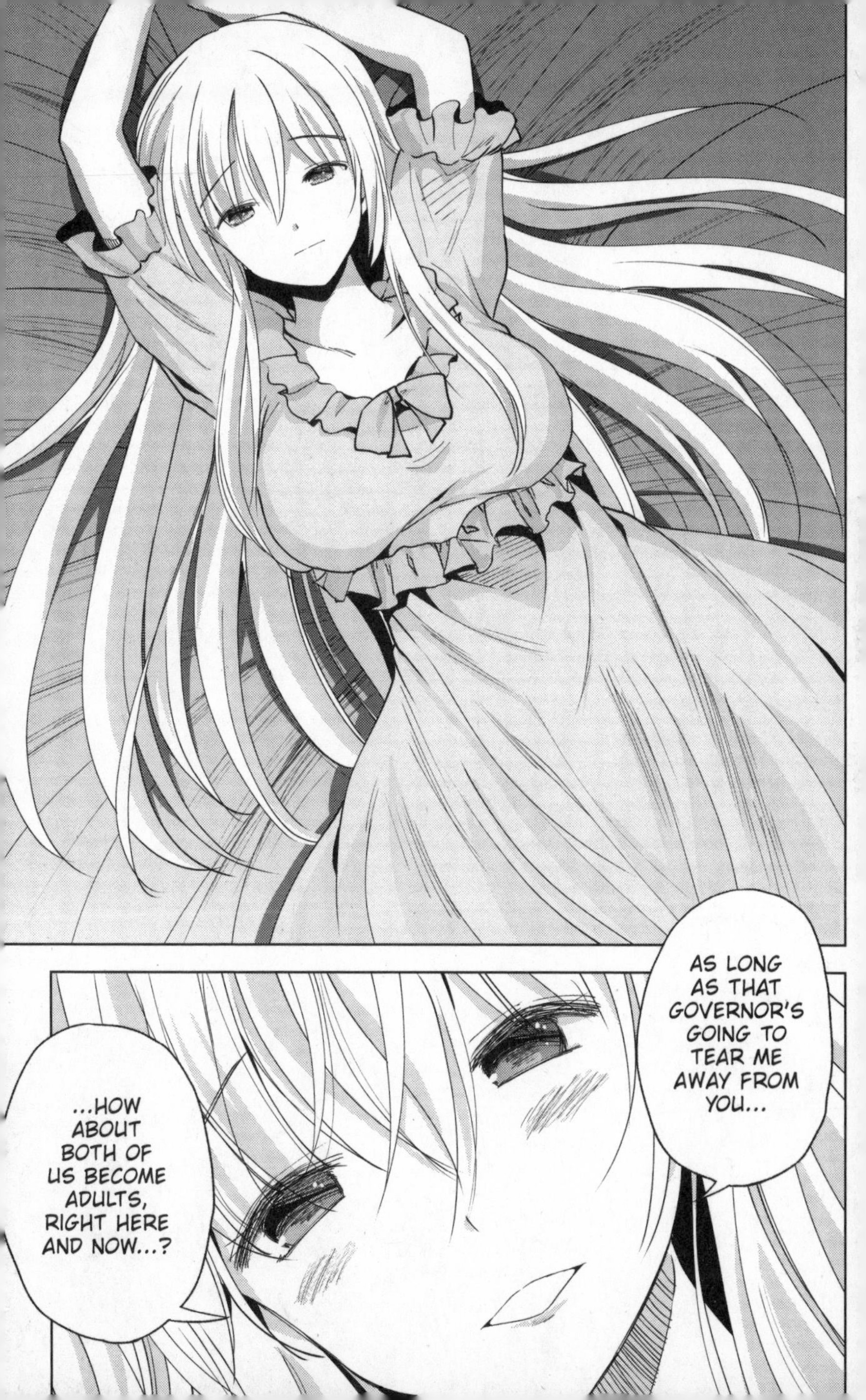
AS LONG AS THAT GOVERNOR'S GOING TO TEAR ME AWAY FROM YOU...
...HOW ABOUT BOTH OF US BECOME ADULTS, RIGHT HERE AND NOW...?

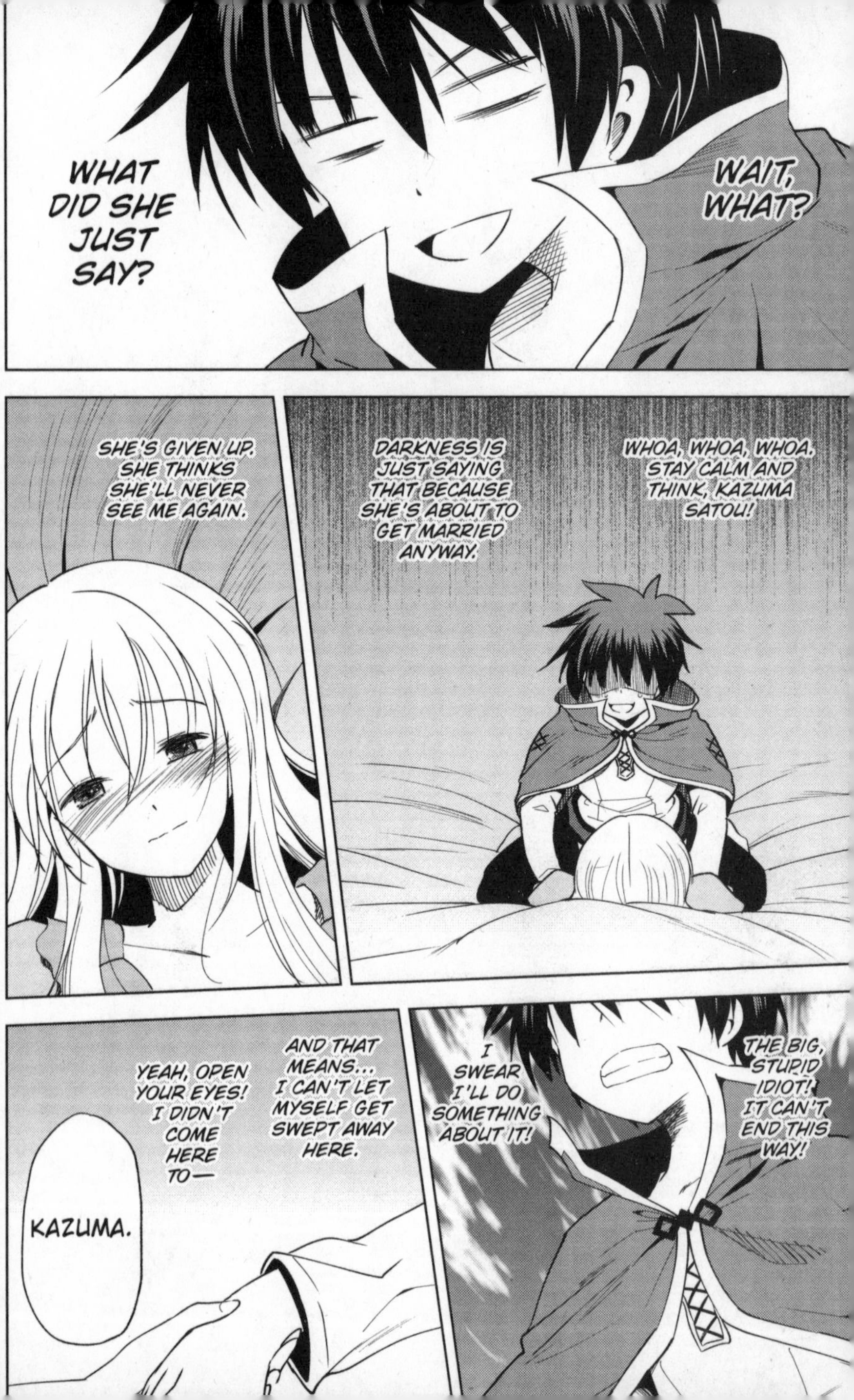
WAIT, WHAT?
WHAT DID SHE JUST SAY?
WHOA, WHOA, WHOA. STAY CALM AND THINK, KAZUMA SATOU!
DARKNESS IS JUST SAYING THAT BECAUSE SHE'S ABOUT TO GET MARRIED ANYWAY.
SHE'S GIVEN UP. SHE THINKS SHE'LL NEVER SEE ME AGAIN.
THE BIG, STUPID IDIOT! IT CAN'T END THIS WAY!
I SWEAR I'LL DO SOMETHING ABOUT IT!
AND THAT MEANS... I CAN'T LET MYSELF GET SWEPT AWAY HERE.
YEAH, OPEN YOUR EYES! I DIDN'T COME HERE TO—
KAZUMA.

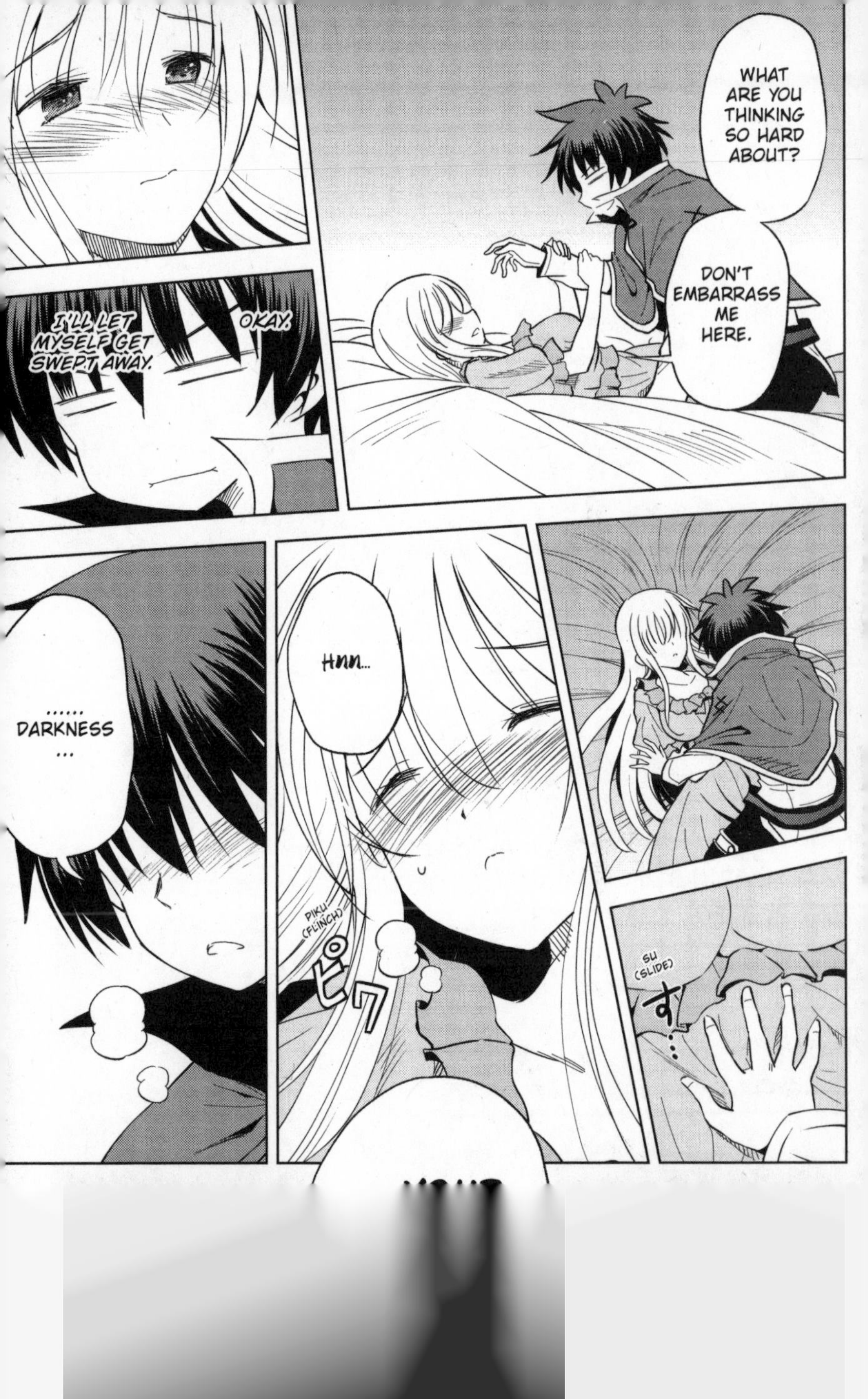
WHAT ARE YOU THINKING SO HARD ABOUT?
DON'T EMBARRASS ME HERE.
OKAY.
I'LL LET MYSELF GET SWEPT AWAY.
SU (SLIDE)
す…
Hnn...
PIKU (FLINCH)
ピク
......DARKNESS...

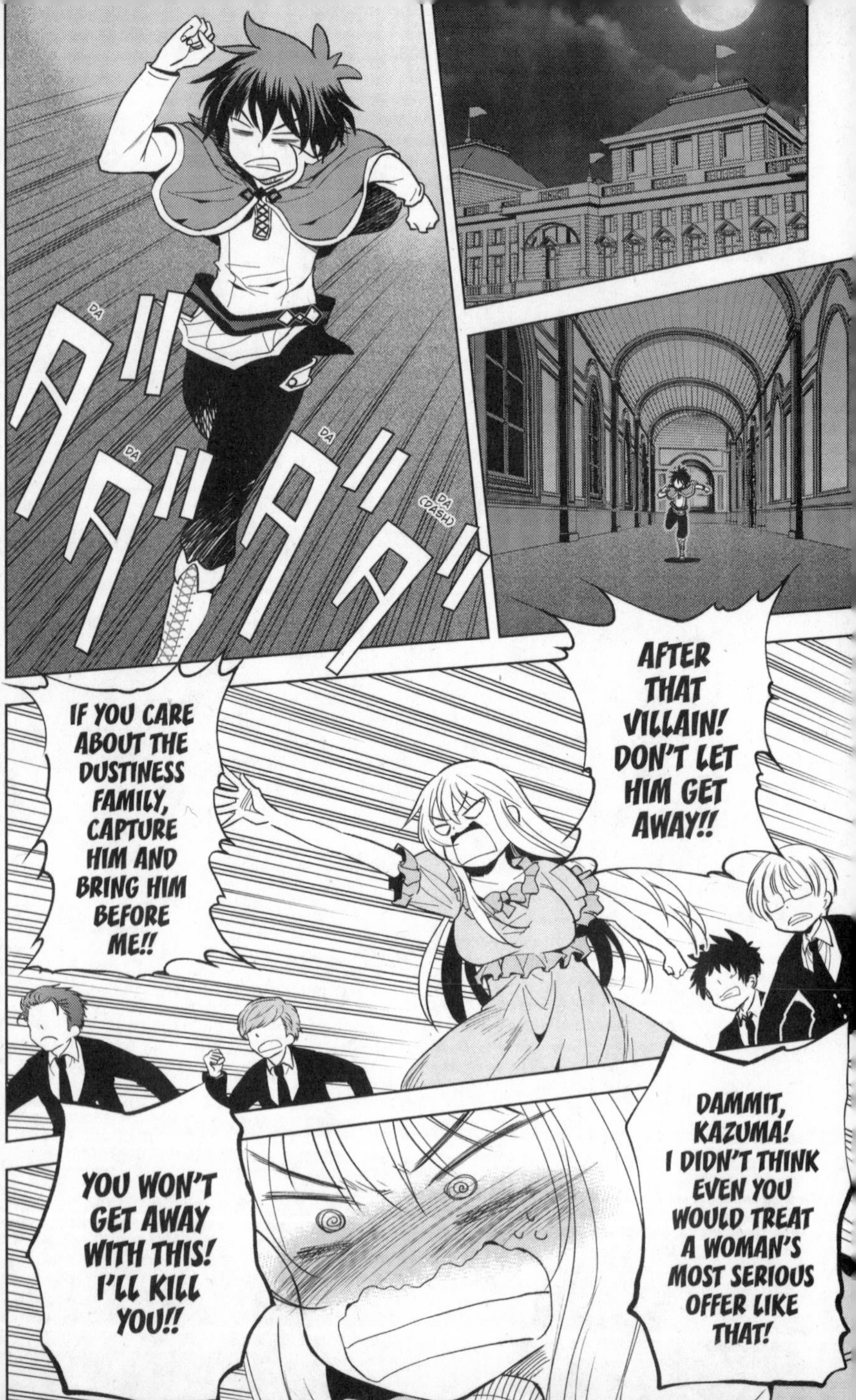
DA
DA
DA
DA (DASH)
AFTER THAT VILLAIN! DON'T LET HIM GET AWAY!!
IF YOU CARE ABOUT THE DUSTINESS FAMILY, CAPTURE HIM AND BRING HIM BEFORE ME!!
DAMMIT, KAZUMA! I DIDN'T THINK EVEN YOU WOULD TREAT A WOMAN'S MOST SERIOUS OFFER LIKE THAT!
YOU WON'T GET AWAY WITH THIS! I'LL KILL YOU!!

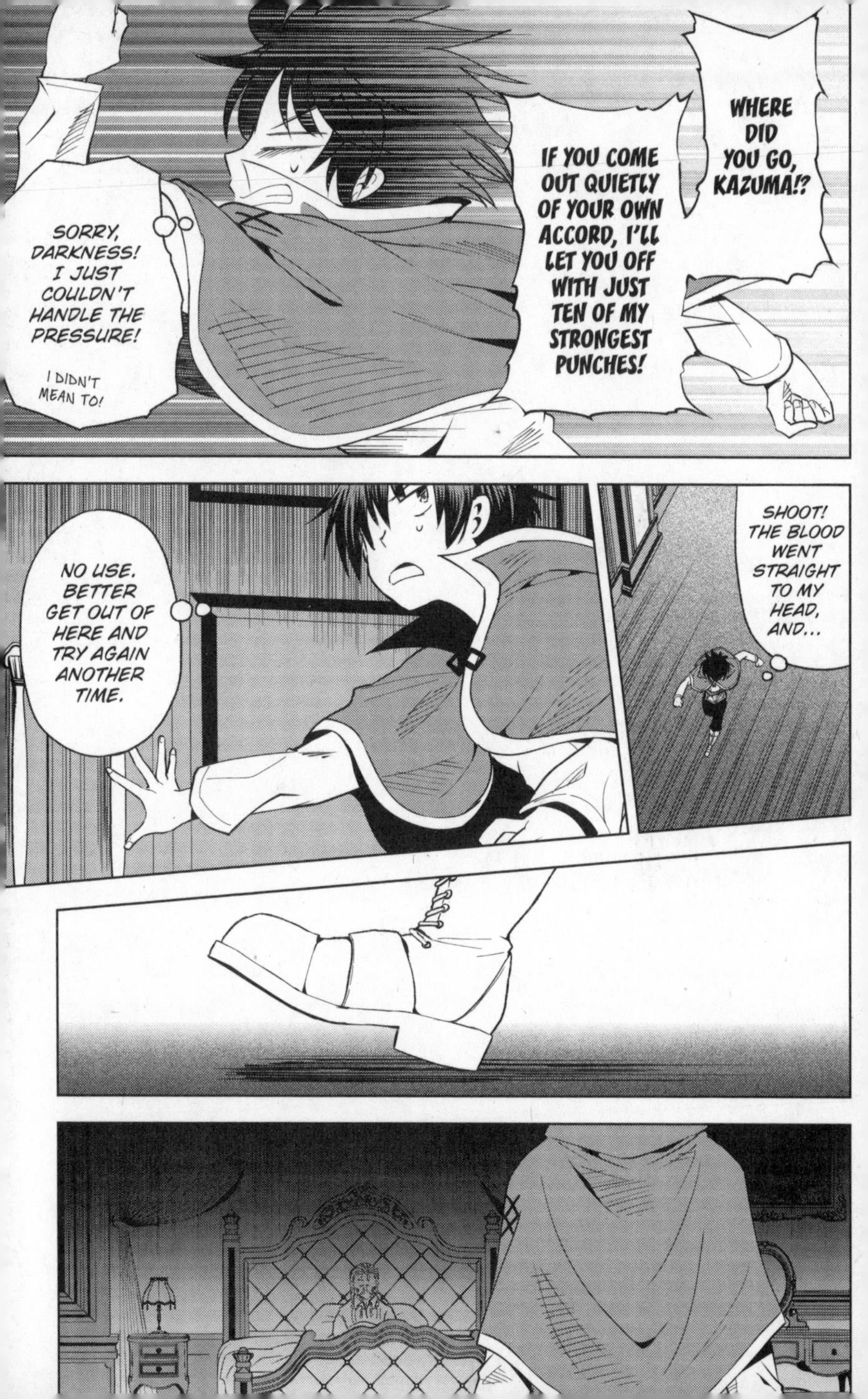
WHERE DID YOU GO, KAZUMA!?
IF YOU COME OUT QUIETLY OF YOUR OWN ACCORD, I'LL LET YOU OFF WITH JUST TEN OF MY STRONGEST PUNCHES!
SORRY, DARKNESS! I JUST COULDN'T HANDLE THE PRESSURE!
I DIDN'T MEAN TO!
SHOOT! THE BLOOD WENT STRAIGHT TO MY HEAD, AND...
NO USE. BETTER GET OUT OF HERE AND TRY AGAIN ANOTHER TIME.

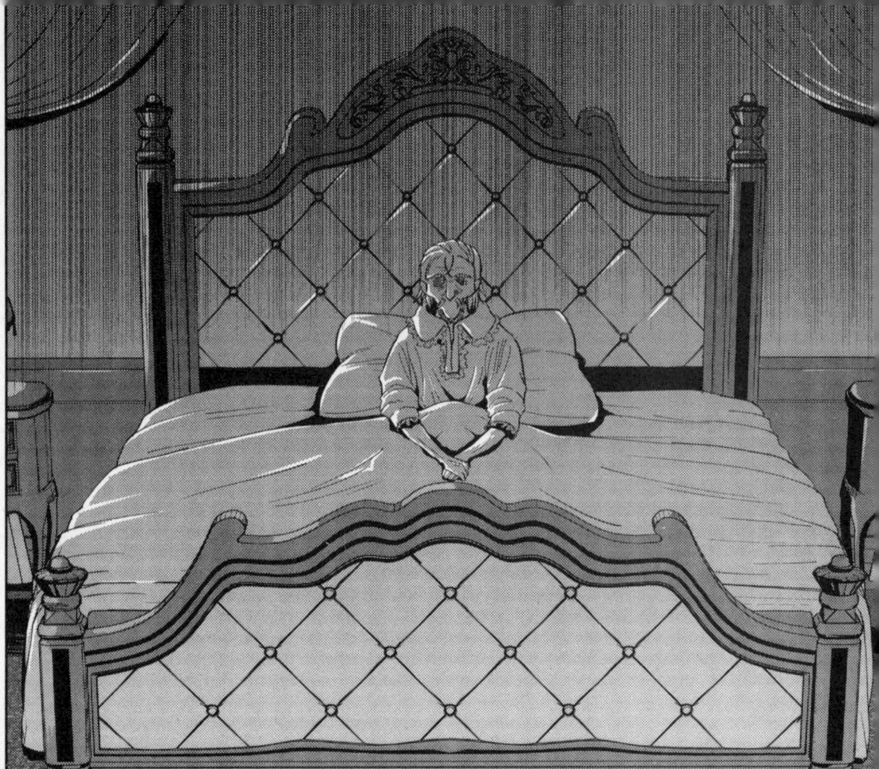

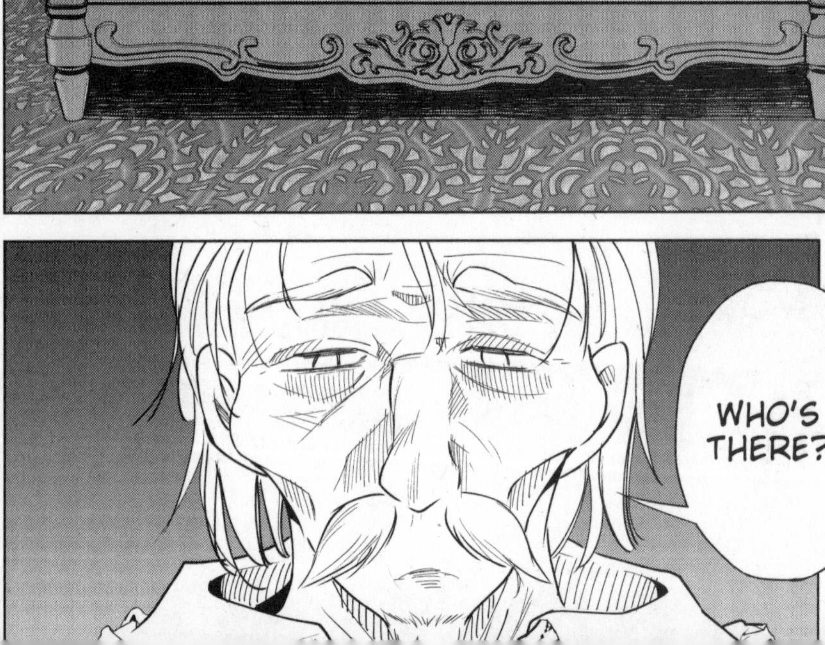
WHO'S THERE?

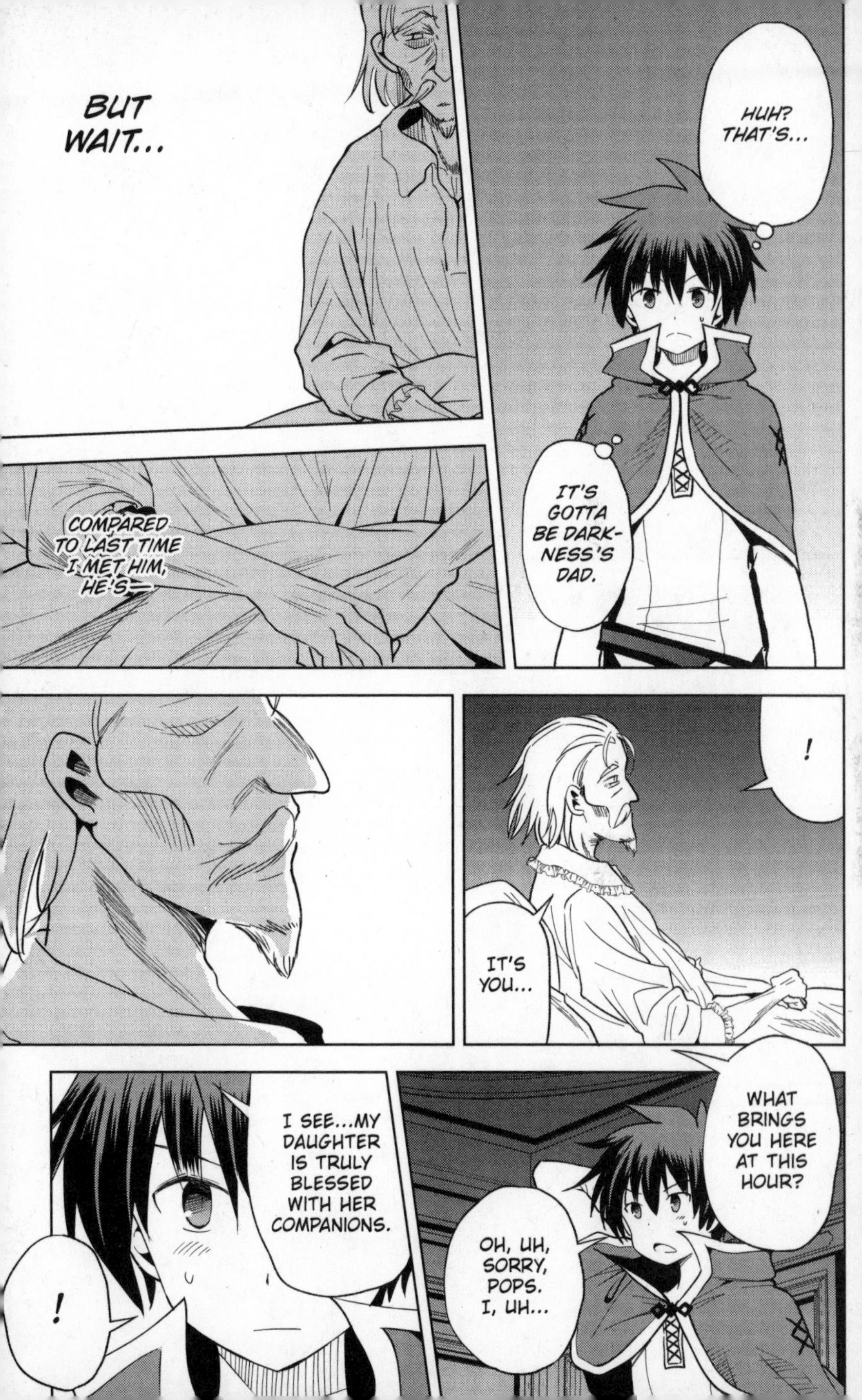
HUH? THAT'S...
IT'S GOTTA BE DARKNESS'S DAD.
BUT WAIT...
COMPARED TO LAST TIME I MET HIM, HE'S—
!
IT'S YOU...
WHAT BRINGS YOU HERE AT THIS HOUR?
OH, UH, SORRY, POPS. I, UH...
I SEE...MY DAUGHTER IS TRULY BLESSED WITH HER COMPANIONS.
!

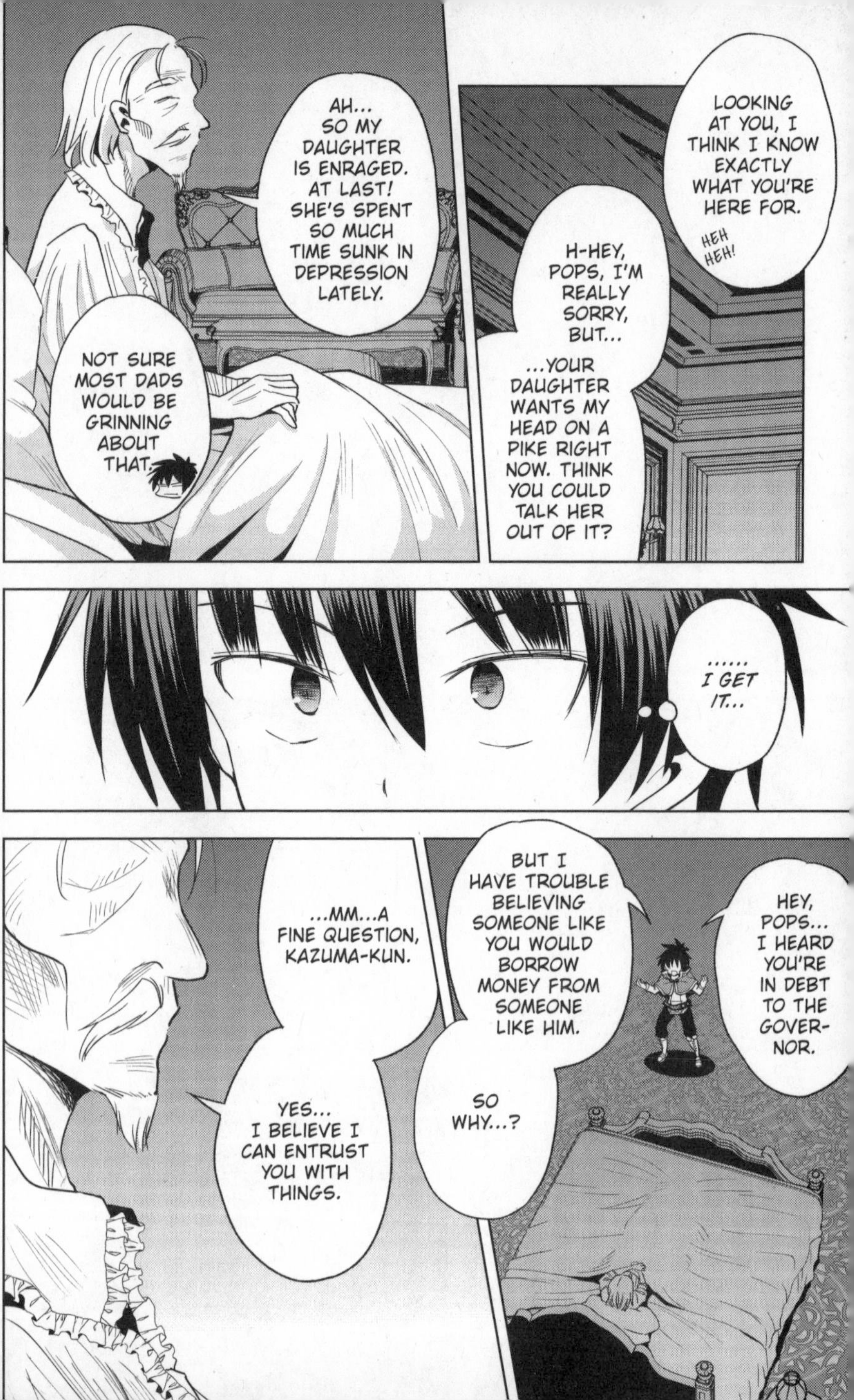
LOOKING AT YOU, I THINK I KNOW EXACTLY WHAT YOU'RE HERE FOR.
HEH HEH!
H-HEY, POPS, I'M REALLY SORRY, BUT...
...YOUR DAUGHTER WANTS MY HEAD ON A PIKE RIGHT NOW. THINK YOU COULD TALK HER OUT OF IT?
AH... SO MY DAUGHTER IS ENRAGED. AT LAST! SHE'S SPENT SO MUCH TIME SUNK IN DEPRESSION LATELY.
NOT SURE MOST DADS WOULD BE GRINNING ABOUT THAT.
...... I GET IT...
HEY, POPS... I HEARD YOU'RE IN DEBT TO THE GOVER-NOR.
BUT I HAVE TROUBLE BELIEVING SOMEONE LIKE YOU WOULD BORROW MONEY FROM SOMEONE LIKE HIM.
SO WHY...?
...MM...A FINE QUESTION, KAZUMA-KUN.
YES... I BELIEVE I CAN ENTRUST YOU WITH THINGS.

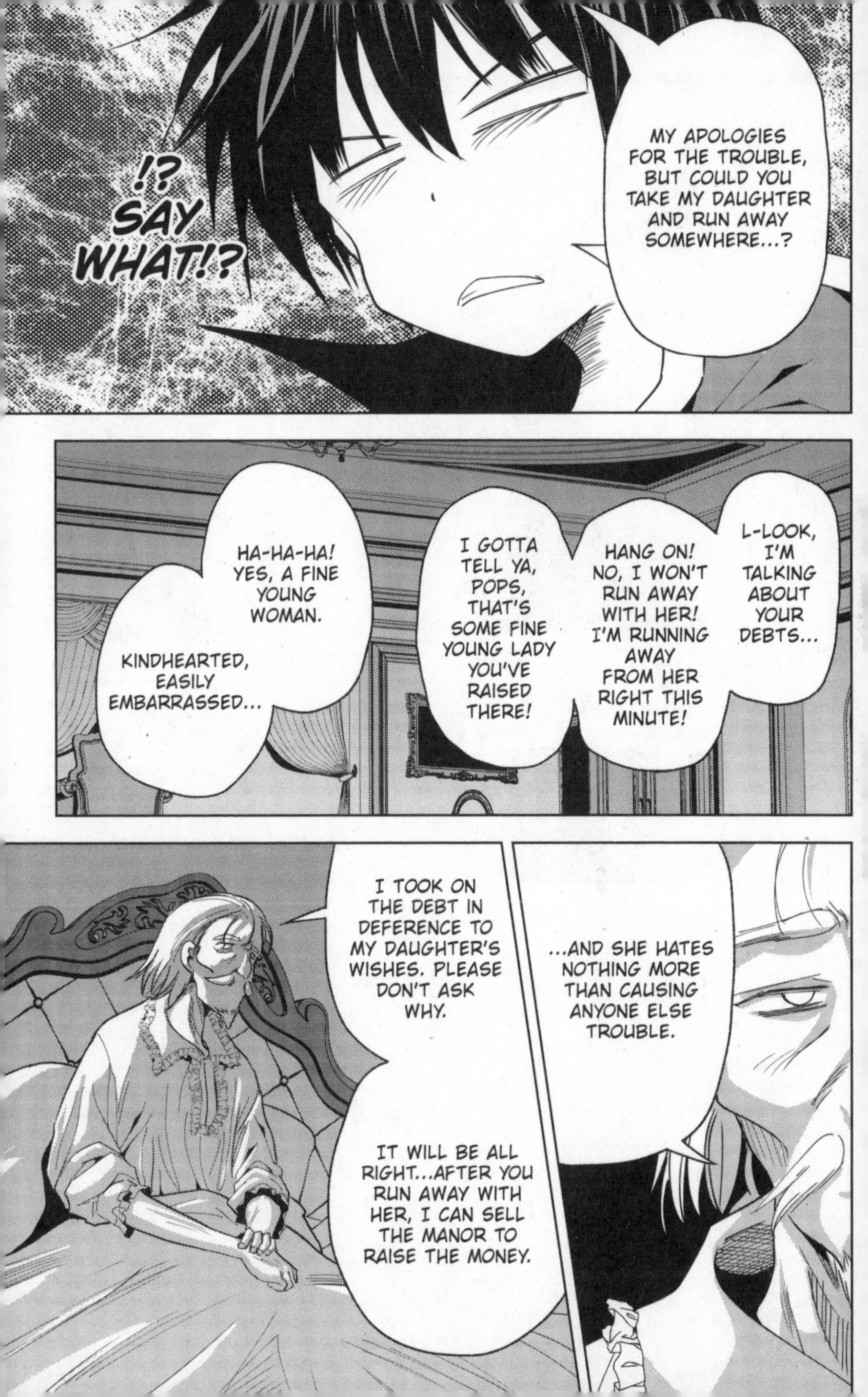
MY APOLOGIES FOR THE TROUBLE, BUT COULD YOU TAKE MY DAUGHTER AND RUN AWAY SOMEWHERE...?
!? SAY WHAT!?
L-LOOK, I'M TALKING ABOUT YOUR DEBTS...
HANG ON! NO, I WON'T RUN AWAY WITH HER! I'M RUNNING AWAY FROM HER RIGHT THIS MINUTE!
I GOTTA TELL YA, POPS, THAT'S SOME FINE YOUNG LADY YOU'VE RAISED THERE!
HA-HA-HA! YES, A FINE YOUNG WOMAN.
KINDHEARTED, EASILY EMBARRASSED...
I TOOK ON THE DEBT IN DEFERENCE TO MY DAUGHTER'S WISHES. PLEASE DON'T ASK WHY.
...AND SHE HATES NOTHING MORE THAN CAUSING ANYONE ELSE TROUBLE.
IT WILL BE ALL RIGHT...AFTER YOU RUN AWAY WITH HER, I CAN SELL THE MANOR TO RAISE THE MONEY.

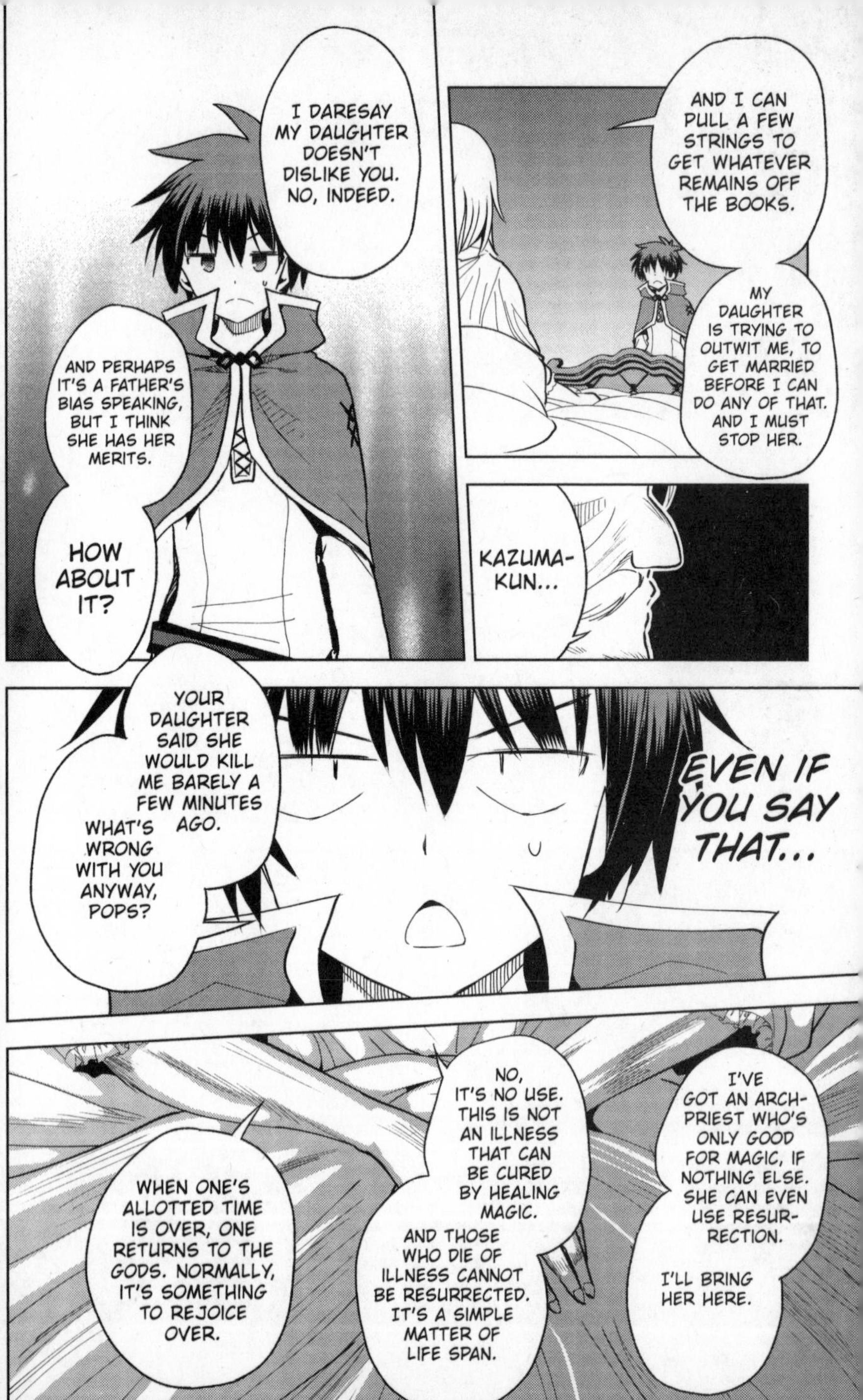
AND I CAN PULL A FEW STRINGS TO GET WHATEVER REMAINS OFF THE BOOKS.
MY DAUGHTER IS TRYING TO OUTWIT ME, TO GET MARRIED BEFORE I CAN DO ANY OF THAT. AND I MUST STOP HER.
KAZUMA-KUN...
I DARESAY MY DAUGHTER DOESN'T DISLIKE YOU. NO, INDEED.
AND PERHAPS IT'S A FATHER'S BIAS SPEAKING, BUT I THINK SHE HAS HER MERITS.
HOW ABOUT IT?
EVEN IF YOU SAY THAT...
YOUR DAUGHTER SAID SHE WOULD KILL ME BARELY A FEW MINUTES AGO.
WHAT'S WRONG WITH YOU ANYWAY, POPS?
I'VE GOT AN ARCH-PRIEST WHO'S ONLY GOOD FOR MAGIC, IF NOTHING ELSE. SHE CAN EVEN USE RESUR-RECTION.
I'LL BRING HER HERE.
NO, IT'S NO USE. THIS IS NOT AN ILLNESS THAT CAN BE CURED BY HEALING MAGIC.
AND THOSE WHO DIE OF ILLNESS CANNOT BE RESURRECTED. IT'S A SIMPLE MATTER OF LIFE SPAN.
WHEN ONE'S ALLOTTED TIME IS OVER, ONE RETURNS TO THE GODS. NORMALLY, IT'S SOMETHING TO REJOICE OVER.

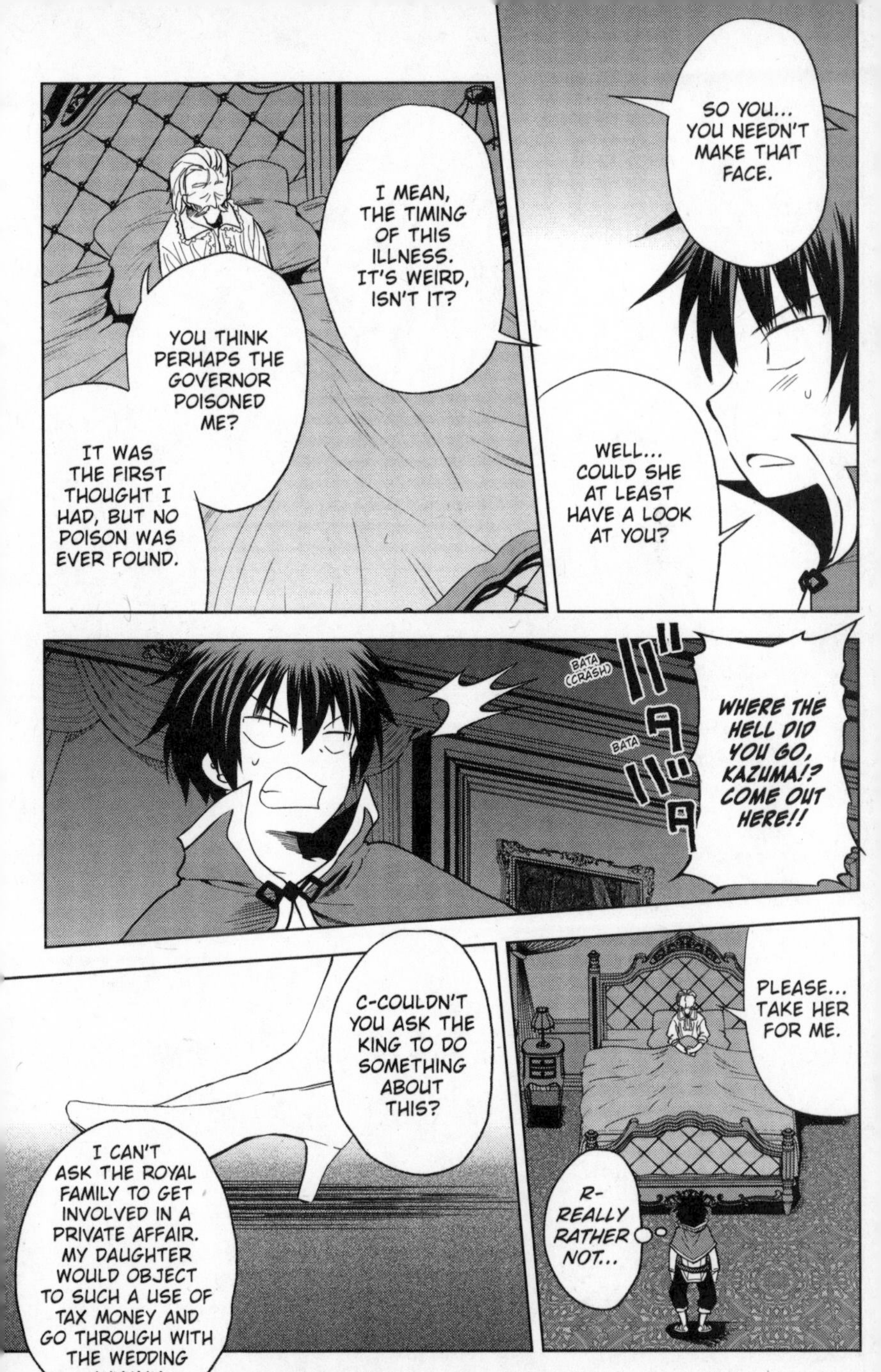
SO YOU... YOU NEEDN'T MAKE THAT FACE.
WELL... COULD SHE AT LEAST HAVE A LOOK AT YOU?
I MEAN, THE TIMING OF THIS ILLNESS. IT'S WEIRD, ISN'T IT?
YOU THINK PERHAPS THE GOVERNOR POISONED ME?
IT WAS THE FIRST THOUGHT I HAD, BUT NO POISON WAS EVER FOUND.
WHERE THE HELL DID YOU GO, KAZUMA!? COME OUT HERE!!
BATA (CRASH)
BATA
C-COULDN'T YOU ASK THE KING TO DO SOMETHING ABOUT THIS?
I CAN'T ASK THE ROYAL FAMILY TO GET INVOLVED IN A PRIVATE AFFAIR. MY DAUGHTER WOULD OBJECT TO SUCH A USE OF TAX MONEY AND GO THROUGH WITH THE WEDDING ANYWAY.
PLEASE... TAKE HER FOR ME.
R-REALLY RATHER NOT...

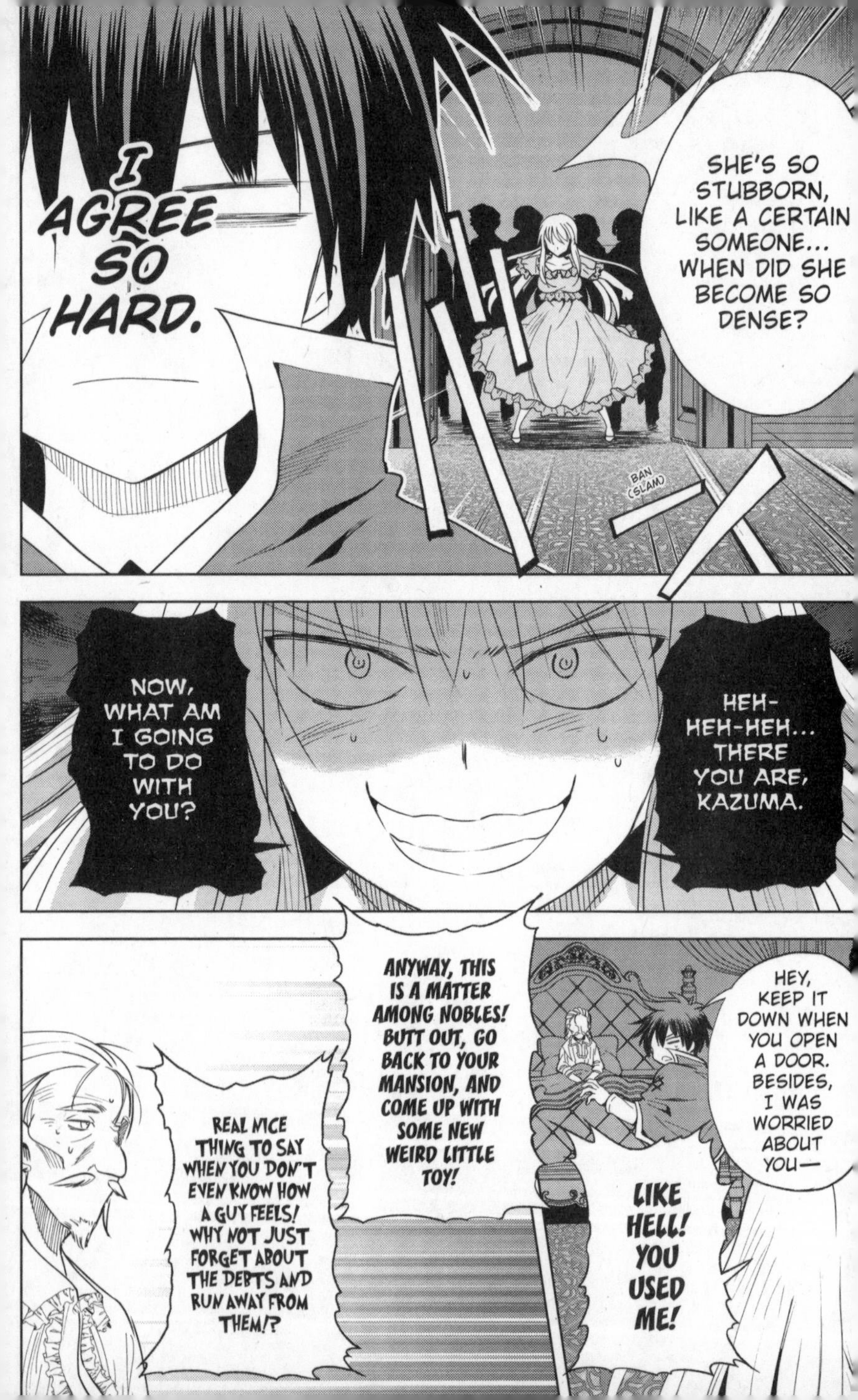
SHE'S SO STUBBORN, LIKE A CERTAIN SOMEONE... WHEN DID SHE BECOME SO DENSE?
BAN (SLAM)
I AGREE SO HARD.
HEH-HEH-HEH... THERE YOU ARE, KAZUMA.
NOW, WHAT AM I GOING TO DO WITH YOU?
HEY, KEEP IT DOWN WHEN YOU OPEN A DOOR. BESIDES, I WAS WORRIED ABOUT YOU—
LIKE HELL! YOU USED ME!
ANYWAY, THIS IS A MATTER AMONG NOBLES! BUTT OUT, GO BACK TO YOUR MANSION, AND COME UP WITH SOME NEW WEIRD LITTLE TOY!
REAL NICE THING TO SAY WHEN YOU DON'T EVEN KNOW HOW A GUY FEELS! WHY NOT JUST FORGET ABOUT THE DEBTS AND RUN AWAY FROM THEM!?

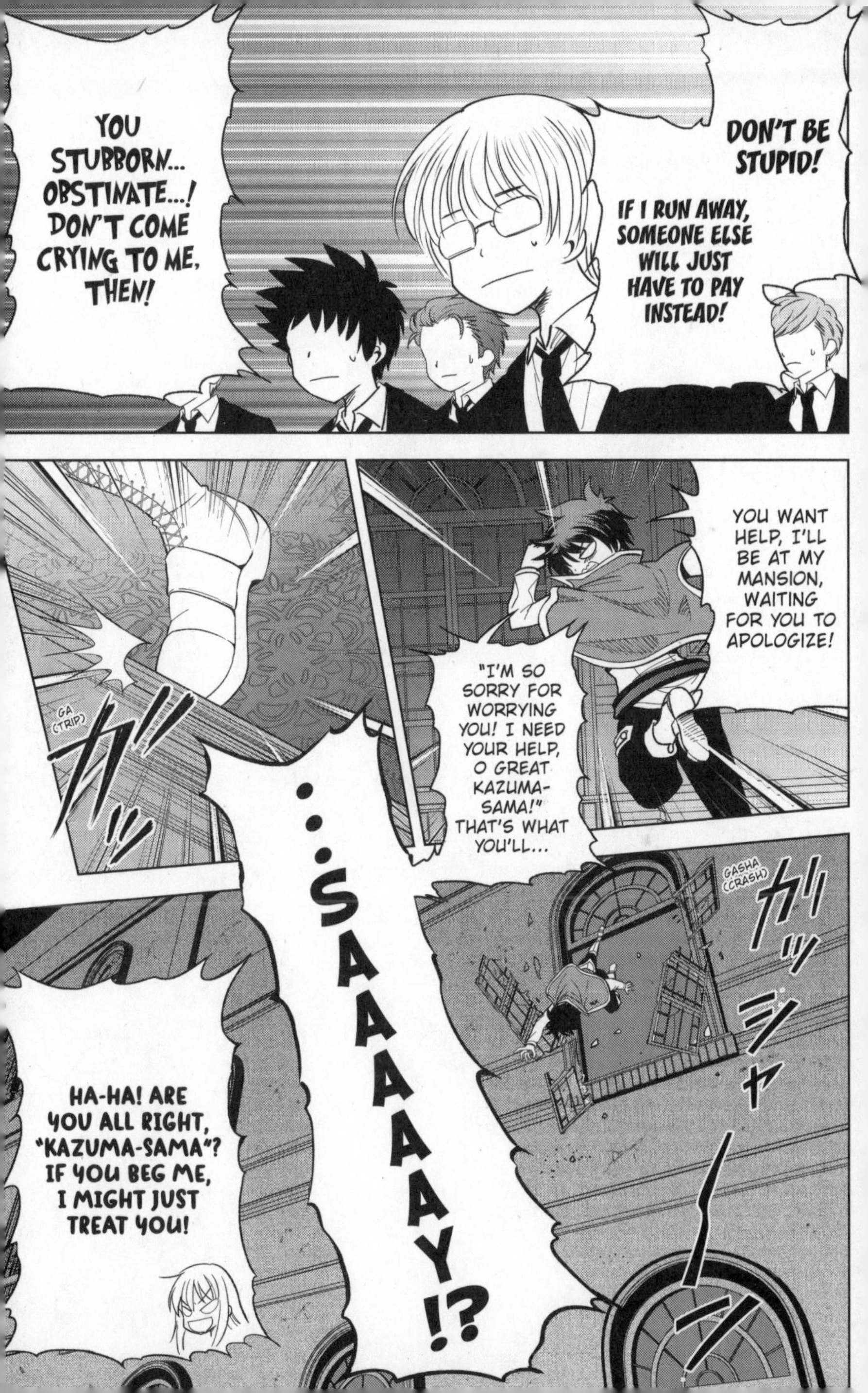
DON'T BE STUPID!
IF I RUN AWAY, SOMEONE ELSE WILL JUST HAVE TO PAY INSTEAD!
YOU STUBBORN... OBSTINATE...! DON'T COME CRYING TO ME, THEN!
YOU WANT HELP, I'LL BE AT MY MANSION, WAITING FOR YOU TO APOLOGIZE!
"I'M SO SORRY FOR WORRYING YOU! I NEED YOUR HELP, O GREAT KAZUMA-SAMA!" THAT'S WHAT YOU'LL...
GA (TRIP)
...SAAAAAY!?
GASHA (CRASH)
HA-HA! ARE YOU ALL RIGHT, "KAZUMA-SAMA"? IF YOU BEG ME, I MIGHT JUST TREAT YOU!

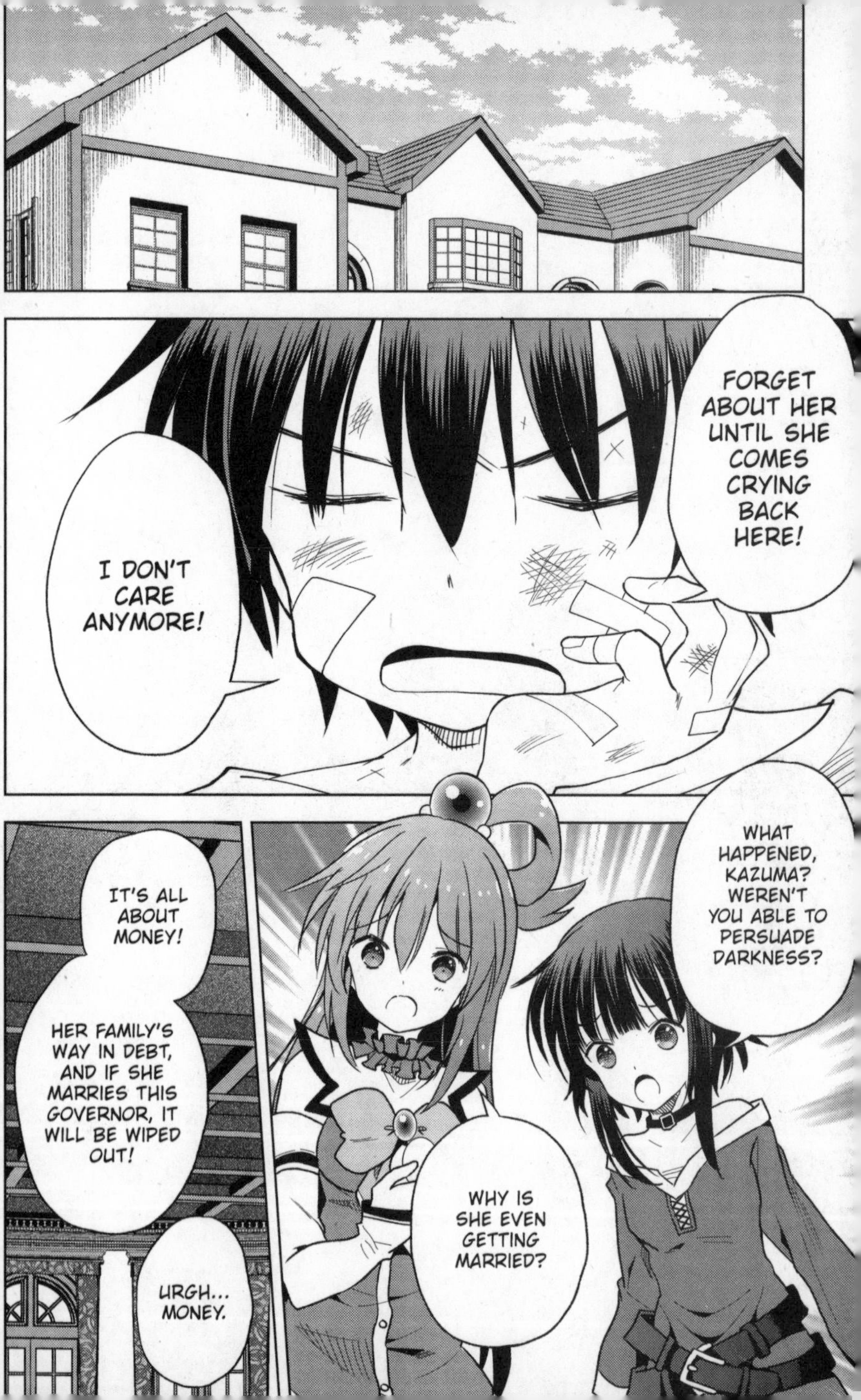
FORGET ABOUT HER UNTIL SHE COMES CRYING BACK HERE!
I DON'T CARE ANYMORE!
WHAT HAPPENED, KAZUMA? WEREN'T YOU ABLE TO PERSUADE DARKNESS?
WHY IS SHE EVEN GETTING MARRIED?
IT'S ALL ABOUT MONEY!
HER FAMILY'S WAY IN DEBT, AND IF SHE MARRIES THIS GOVERNOR, IT WILL BE WIPED OUT!
URGH... MONEY.

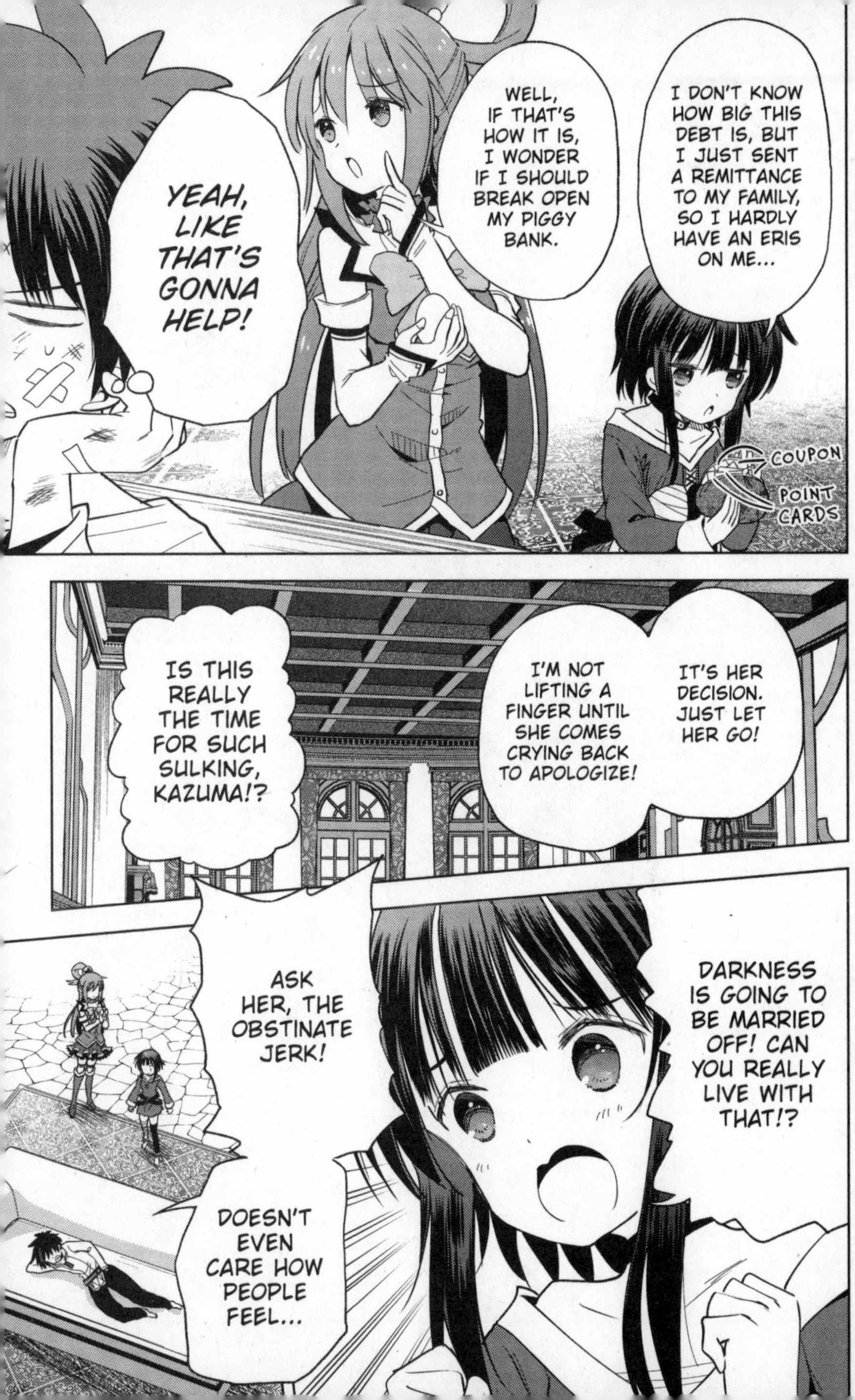
I DON'T KNOW HOW BIG THIS DEBT IS, BUT I JUST SENT A REMITTANCE TO MY FAMILY, SO I HARDLY HAVE AN ERIS ON ME...
WELL, IF THAT'S HOW IT IS, I WONDER IF I SHOULD BREAK OPEN MY PIGGY BANK.
COUPON
POINT CARDS
YEAH, LIKE THAT'S GONNA HELP!
IT'S HER DECISION. JUST LET HER GO!
I'M NOT LIFTING A FINGER UNTIL SHE COMES CRYING BACK TO APOLOGIZE!
IS THIS REALLY THE TIME FOR SUCH SULKING, KAZUMA!?
DARKNESS IS GOING TO BE MARRIED OFF! CAN YOU REALLY LIVE WITH THAT!?
ASK HER, THE OBSTINATE JERK!
DOESN'T EVEN CARE HOW PEOPLE FEEL...

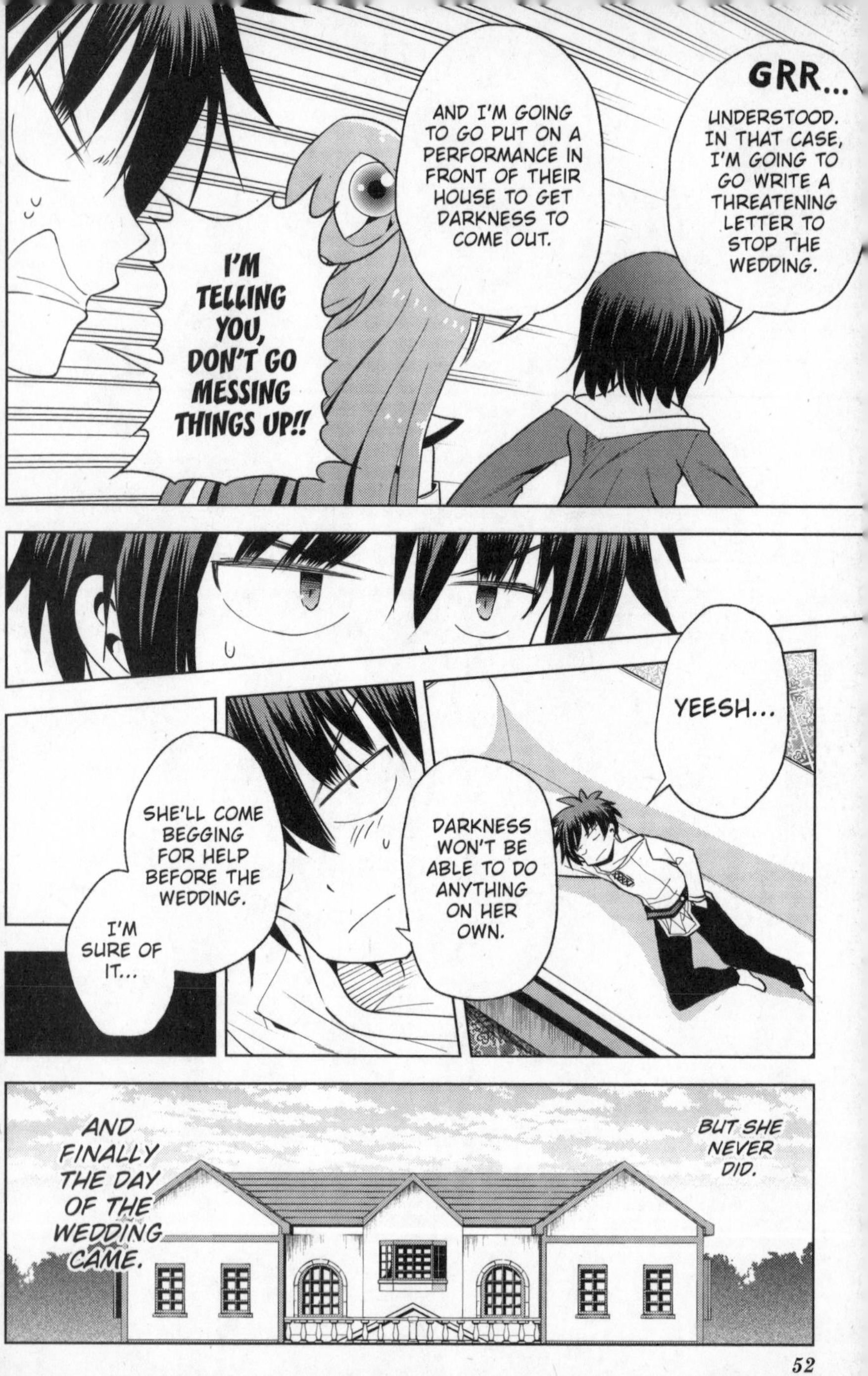
GRR...
UNDERSTOOD. IN THAT CASE, I'M GOING TO GO WRITE A THREATENING LETTER TO STOP THE WEDDING.
AND I'M GOING TO GO PUT ON A PERFORMANCE IN FRONT OF THEIR HOUSE TO GET DARKNESS TO COME OUT.
I'M TELLING YOU, DON'T GO MESSING THINGS UP!!
YEESH...
DARKNESS WON'T BE ABLE TO DO ANYTHING ON HER OWN.
SHE'LL COME BEGGING FOR HELP BEFORE THE WEDDING.
I'M SURE OF IT...
BUT SHE NEVER DID.
AND FINALLY THE DAY OF THE WEDDING CAME.

GOD'S
BLESSING
ON THIS
WONDERFUL
WORLD!

13

13

GOD'S
BLESSING
ON THIS
WONDERFUL
WORLD!

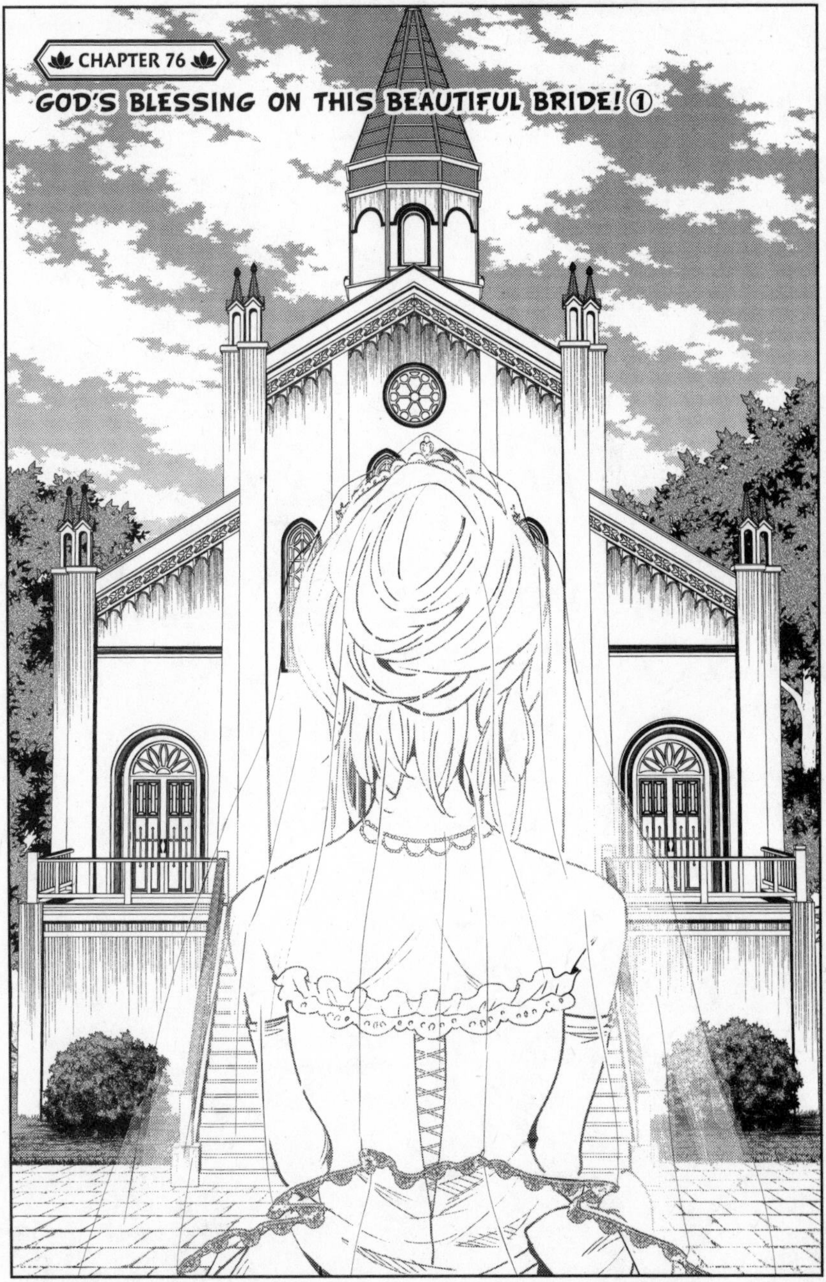
CHAPTER 76
GOD'S BLESSING ON THIS BEAUTIFUL BRIDE! ①

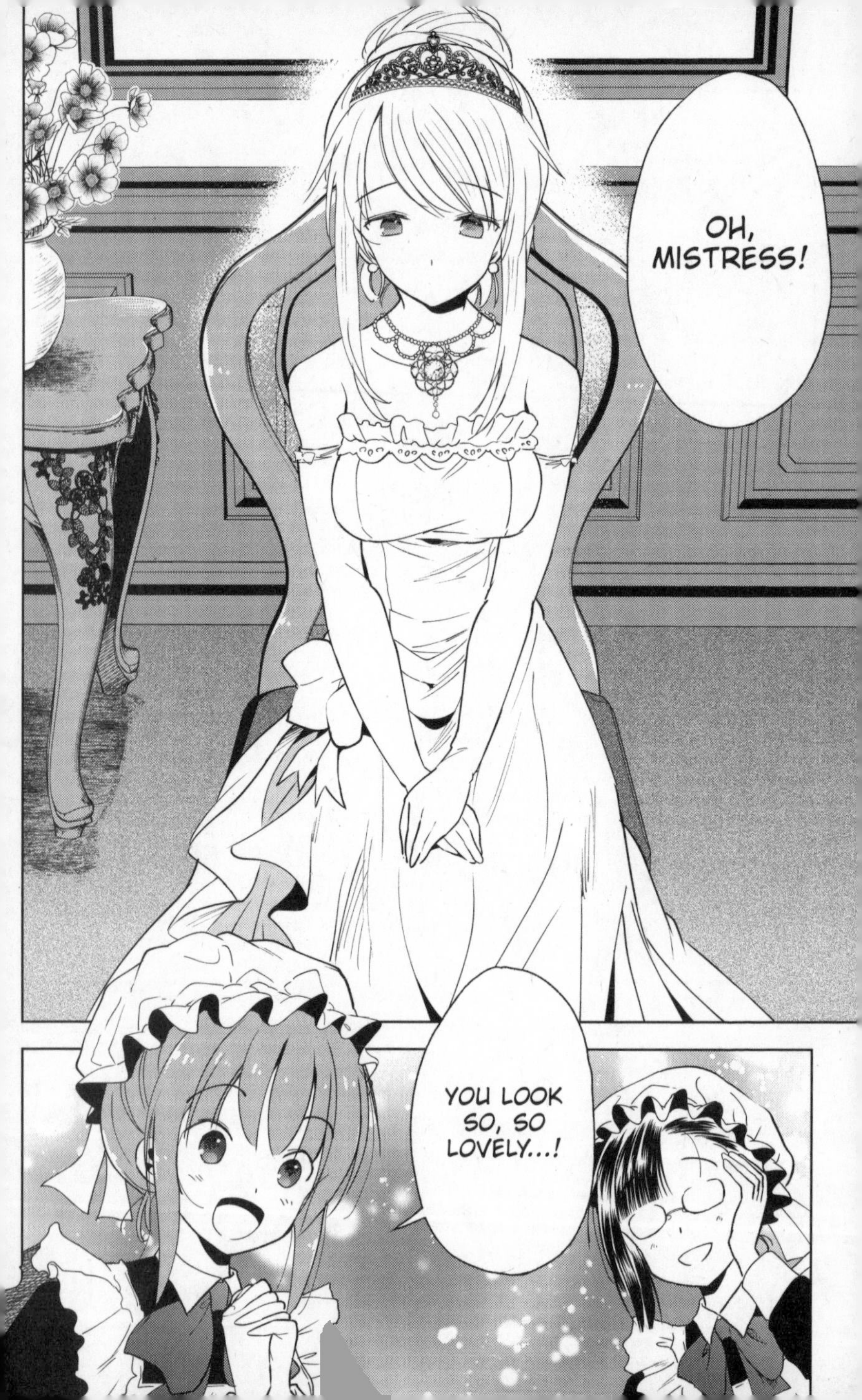
OH, MISTRESS!
YOU LOOK SO, SO LOVELY...!

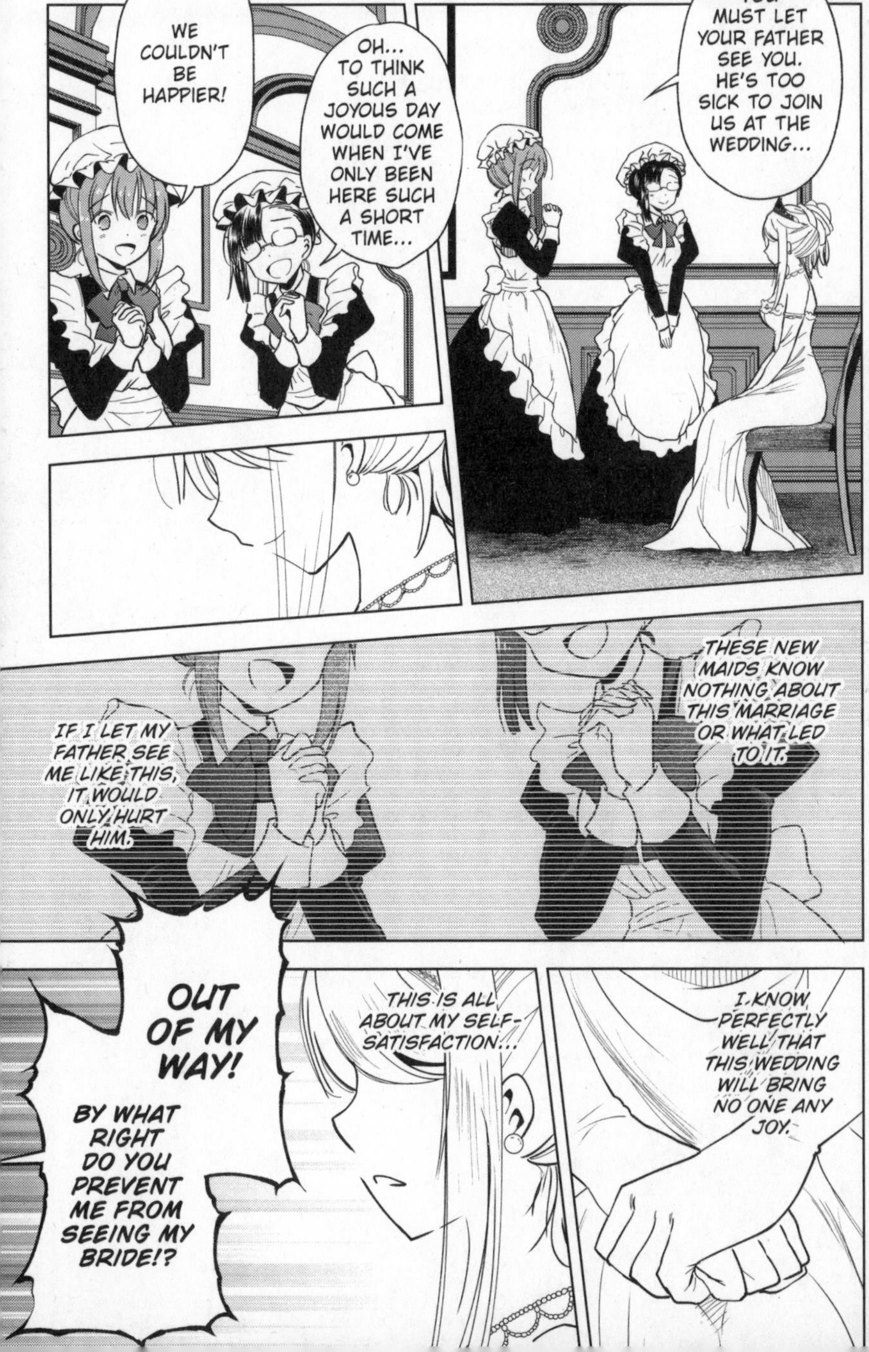
YOU MUST LET YOUR FATHER SEE YOU. HE'S TOO SICK TO JOIN US AT THE WEDDING...
OH... TO THINK SUCH A JOYOUS DAY WOULD COME WHEN I'VE ONLY BEEN HERE SUCH A SHORT TIME...
WE COULDN'T BE HAPPIER!
THESE NEW MAIDS KNOW NOTHING ABOUT THIS MARRIAGE OR WHAT LED TO IT.
IF I LET MY FATHER SEE ME LIKE THIS, IT WOULD ONLY HURT HIM.
I KNOW PERFECTLY WELL THAT THIS WEDDING WILL BRING NO ONE ANY JOY.
THIS IS ALL ABOUT MY SELF-SATISFACTION...
OUT OF MY WAY!
BY WHAT RIGHT DO YOU PREVENT ME FROM SEEING MY BRIDE!?

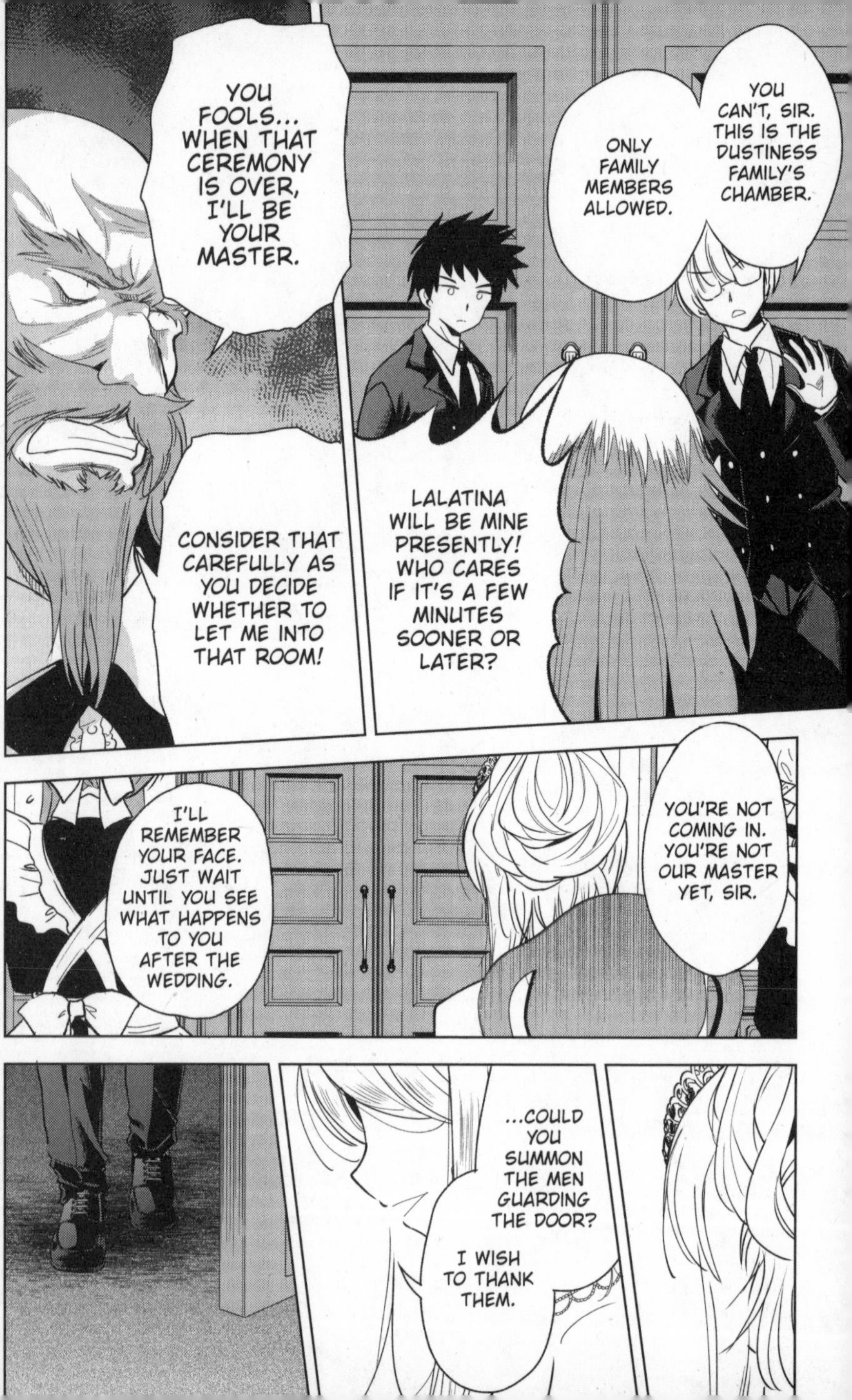
YOU CAN'T, SIR. THIS IS THE DUSTINESS FAMILY'S CHAMBER.
ONLY FAMILY MEMBERS ALLOWED.
LALATINA WILL BE MINE PRESENTLY! WHO CARES IF IT'S A FEW MINUTES SOONER OR LATER?
YOU FOOLS... WHEN THAT CEREMONY IS OVER, I'LL BE YOUR MASTER.
CONSIDER THAT CAREFULLY AS YOU DECIDE WHETHER TO LET ME INTO THAT ROOM!
YOU'RE NOT COMING IN. YOU'RE NOT OUR MASTER YET, SIR.
I'LL REMEMBER YOUR FACE. JUST WAIT UNTIL YOU SEE WHAT HAPPENS TO YOU AFTER THE WEDDING.
...COULD YOU SUMMON THE MEN GUARDING THE DOOR?
I WISH TO THANK THEM.

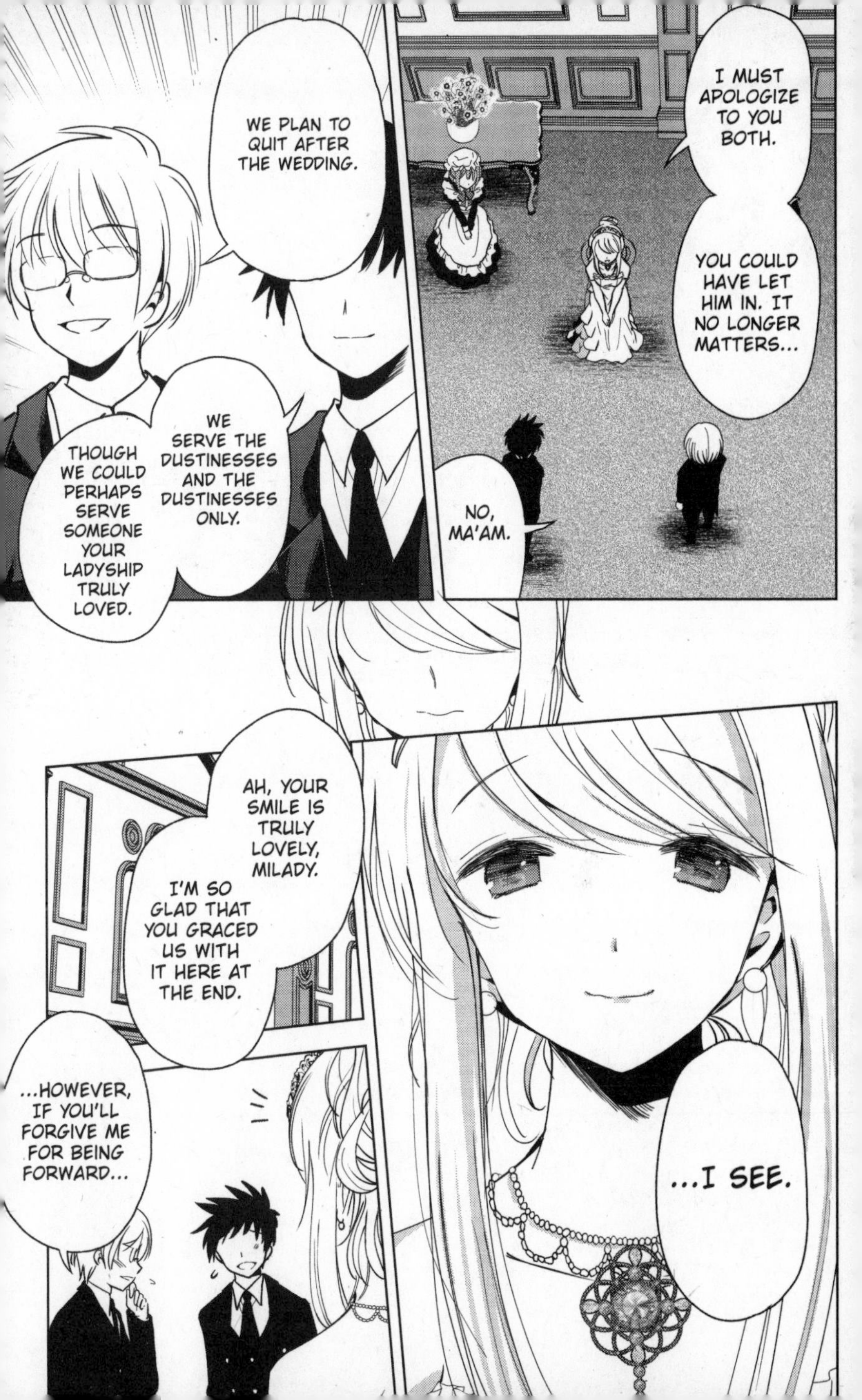
I MUST APOLOGIZE TO YOU BOTH.
YOU COULD HAVE LET HIM IN. IT NO LONGER MATTERS...
NO, MA'AM.
WE PLAN TO QUIT AFTER THE WEDDING.
WE SERVE THE DUSTINESSES AND THE DUSTINESSES ONLY.
THOUGH WE COULD PERHAPS SERVE SOMEONE YOUR LADYSHIP TRULY LOVED.
...I SEE.
AH, YOUR SMILE IS TRULY LOVELY, MILADY.
I'M SO GLAD THAT YOU GRACED US WITH IT HERE AT THE END.
...HOWEVER, IF YOU'LL FORGIVE ME FOR BEING FORWARD...

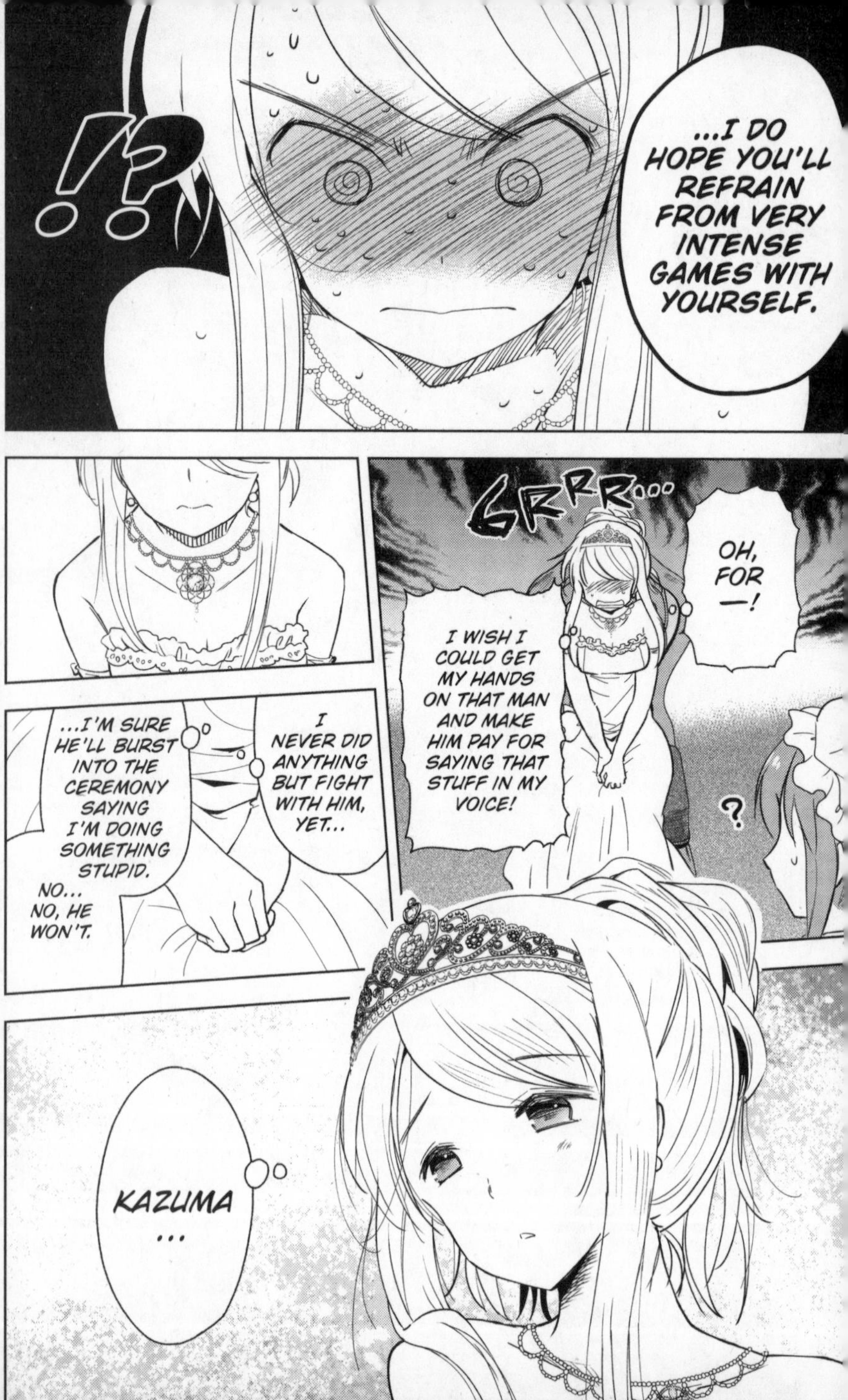
...I DO HOPE YOU'LL REFRAIN FROM VERY INTENSE GAMES WITH YOURSELF.
!?
OH, FOR—!
GRRR...
I WISH I COULD GET MY HANDS ON THAT MAN AND MAKE HIM PAY FOR SAYING THAT STUFF IN MY VOICE!
?
I NEVER DID ANYTHING BUT FIGHT WITH HIM, YET...
...I'M SURE HE'LL BURST INTO THE CEREMONY SAYING I'M DOING SOMETHING STUPID.
NO... NO, HE WON'T.
KAZUMA...

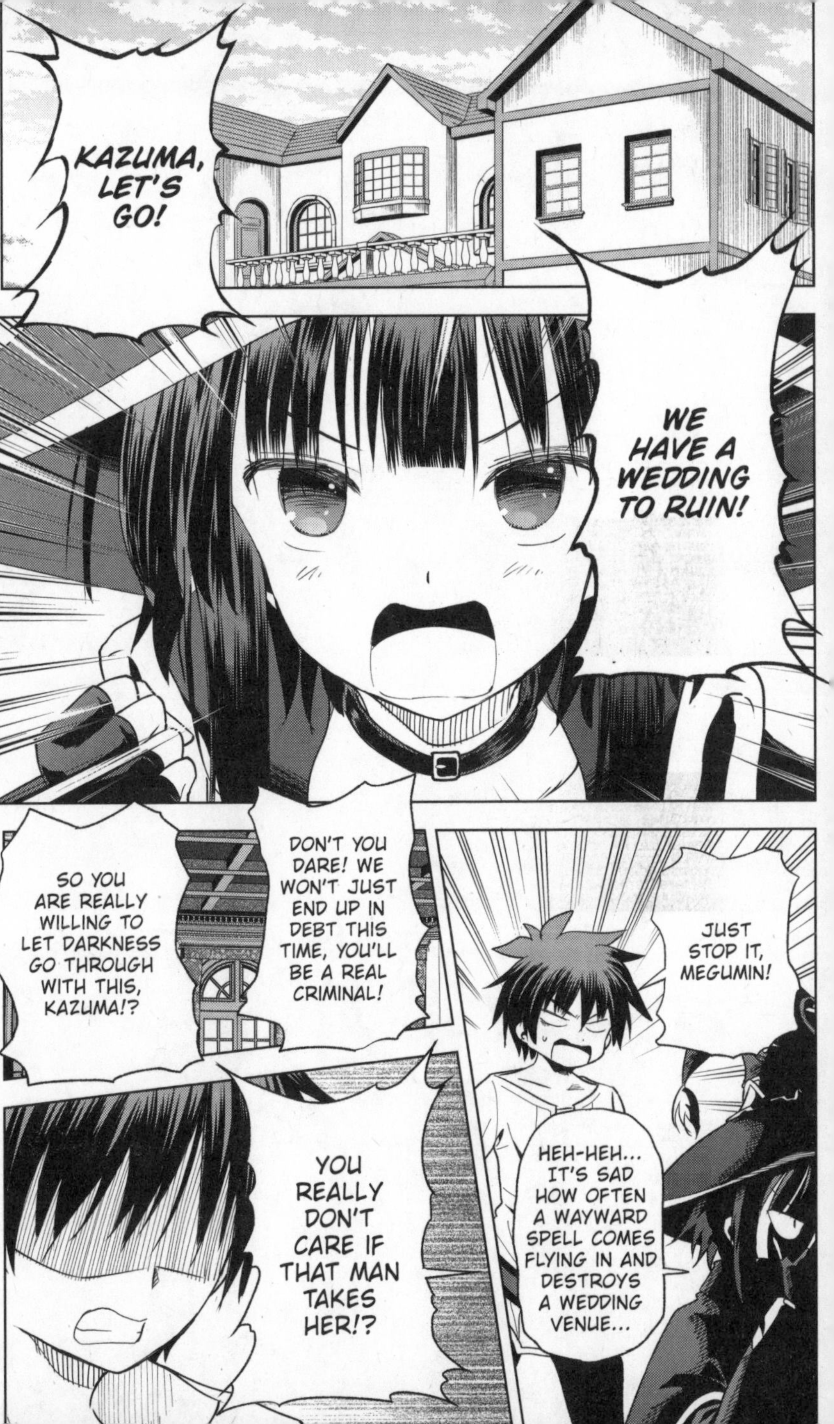
KAZUMA, LET'S GO!
WE HAVE A WEDDING TO RUIN!
JUST STOP IT, MEGUMIN!
HEH-HEH... IT'S SAD HOW OFTEN A WAYWARD SPELL COMES FLYING IN AND DESTROYS A WEDDING VENUE...
DON'T YOU DARE! WE WON'T JUST END UP IN DEBT THIS TIME, YOU'LL BE A REAL CRIMINAL!
SO YOU ARE REALLY WILLING TO LET DARKNESS GO THROUGH WITH THIS, KAZUMA!?
YOU REALLY DON'T CARE IF THAT MAN TAKES HER!?

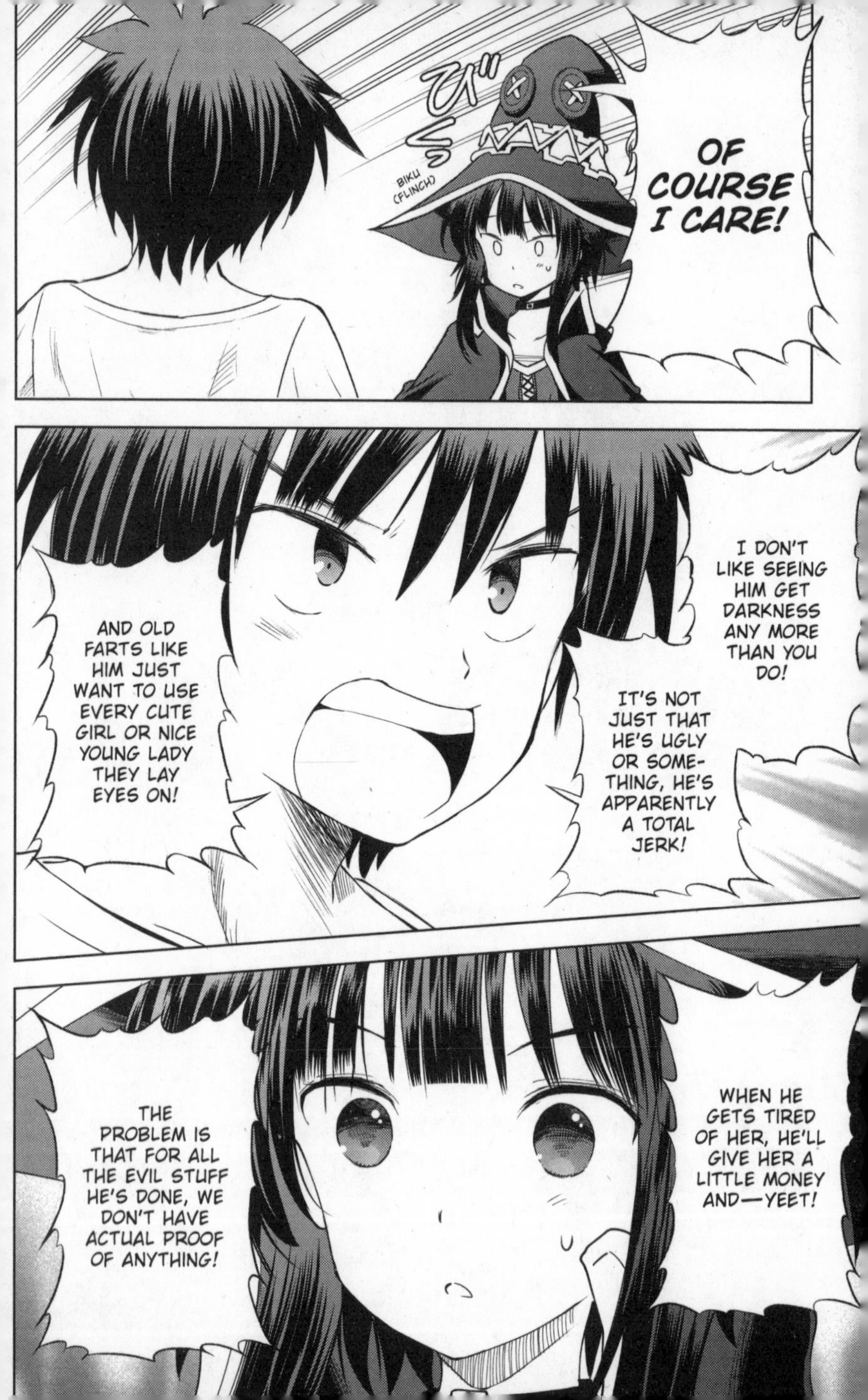

OF COURSE I CARE!
びく
BIKU (FLINCH)
I DON'T LIKE SEEING HIM GET DARKNESS ANY MORE THAN YOU DO!
IT'S NOT JUST THAT HE'S UGLY OR SOME-THING, HE'S APPARENTLY A TOTAL JERK!
AND OLD FARTS LIKE HIM JUST WANT TO USE EVERY CUTE GIRL OR NICE YOUNG LADY THEY LAY EYES ON!
WHEN HE GETS TIRED OF HER, HE'LL GIVE HER A LITTLE MONEY AND—YEET!
THE PROBLEM IS THAT FOR ALL THE EVIL STUFF HE'S DONE, WE DON'T HAVE ACTUAL PROOF OF ANYTHING!

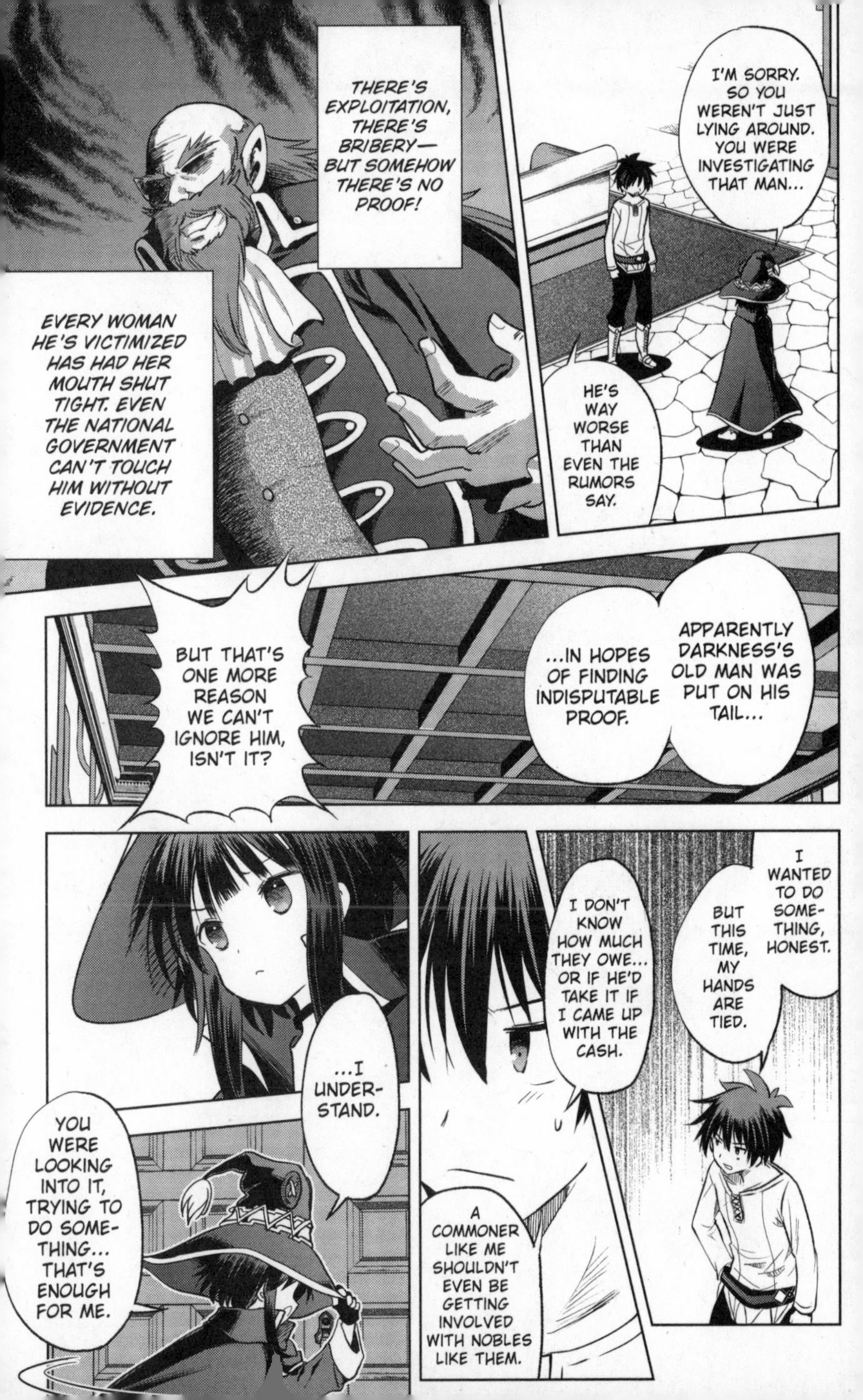
I'M SORRY. SO YOU WEREN'T JUST LYING AROUND. YOU WERE INVESTIGATING THAT MAN...
HE'S WAY WORSE THAN EVEN THE RUMORS SAY.
THERE'S EXPLOITATION, THERE'S BRIBERY—BUT SOMEHOW THERE'S NO PROOF!
EVERY WOMAN HE'S VICTIMIZED HAS HAD HER MOUTH SHUT TIGHT. EVEN THE NATIONAL GOVERNMENT CAN'T TOUCH HIM WITHOUT EVIDENCE.
APPARENTLY DARKNESS'S OLD MAN WAS PUT ON HIS TAIL...
...IN HOPES OF FINDING INDISPUTABLE PROOF.
BUT THAT'S ONE MORE REASON WE CAN'T IGNORE HIM, ISN'T IT?
I WANTED TO DO SOMETHING, HONEST.
BUT THIS TIME, MY HANDS ARE TIED.
I DON'T KNOW HOW MUCH THEY OWE... OR IF HE'D TAKE IT IF I CAME UP WITH THE CASH.
A COMMONER LIKE ME SHOULDN'T EVEN BE GETTING INVOLVED WITH NOBLES LIKE THEM.
...I UNDERSTAND.
YOU WERE LOOKING INTO IT, TRYING TO DO SOMETHING... THAT'S ENOUGH FOR ME.

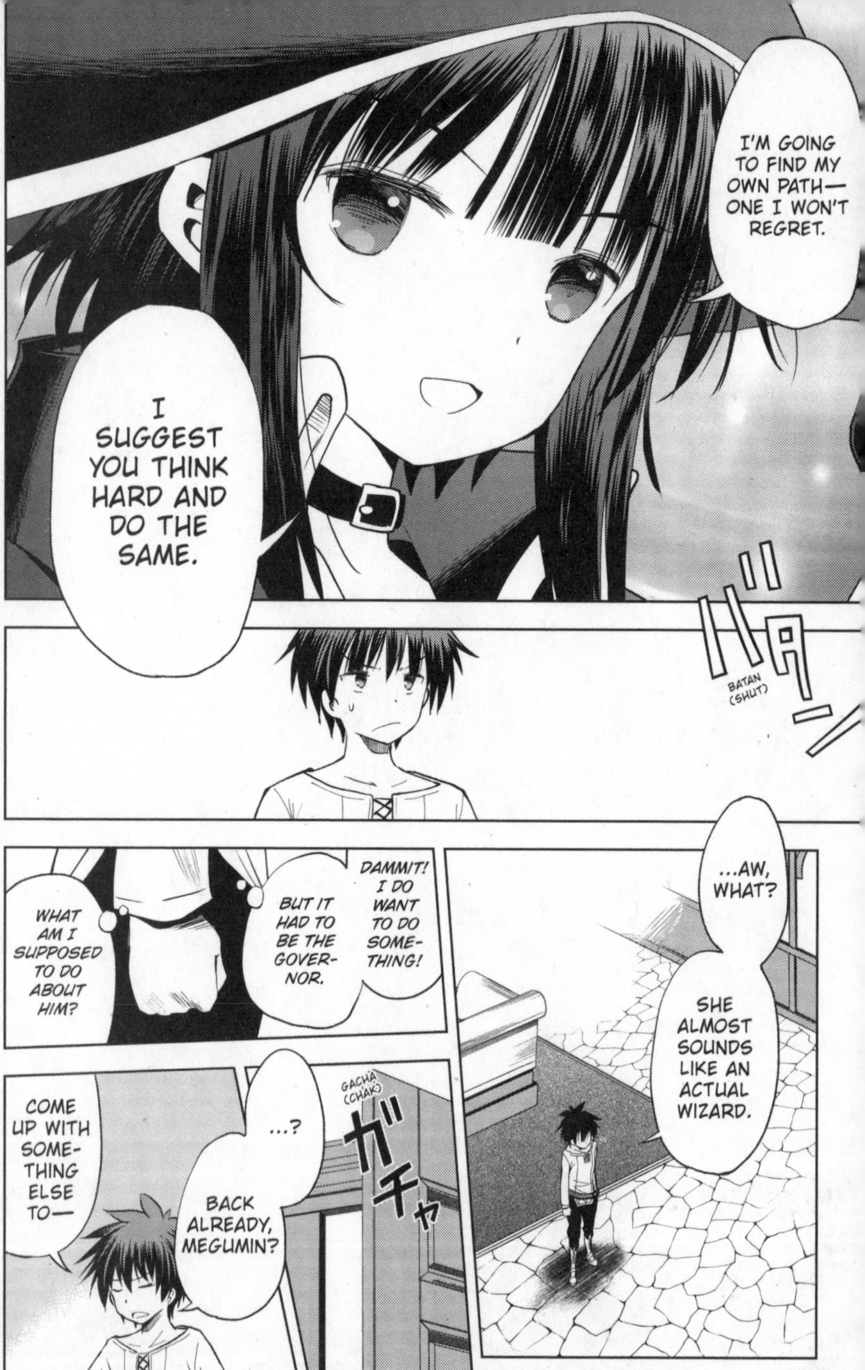
I'M GOING TO FIND MY OWN PATH—ONE I WON'T REGRET.
I SUGGEST YOU THINK HARD AND DO THE SAME.
BATAN (SHUT)
...AW, WHAT?
SHE ALMOST SOUNDS LIKE AN ACTUAL WIZARD.
DAMMIT! I DO WANT TO DO SOME-THING!
BUT IT HAD TO BE THE GOVER-NOR.
WHAT AM I SUPPOSED TO DO ABOUT HIM?
COME UP WITH SOME-THING ELSE TO—
GACHA (CHAK)
...?
BACK ALREADY, MEGUMIN?

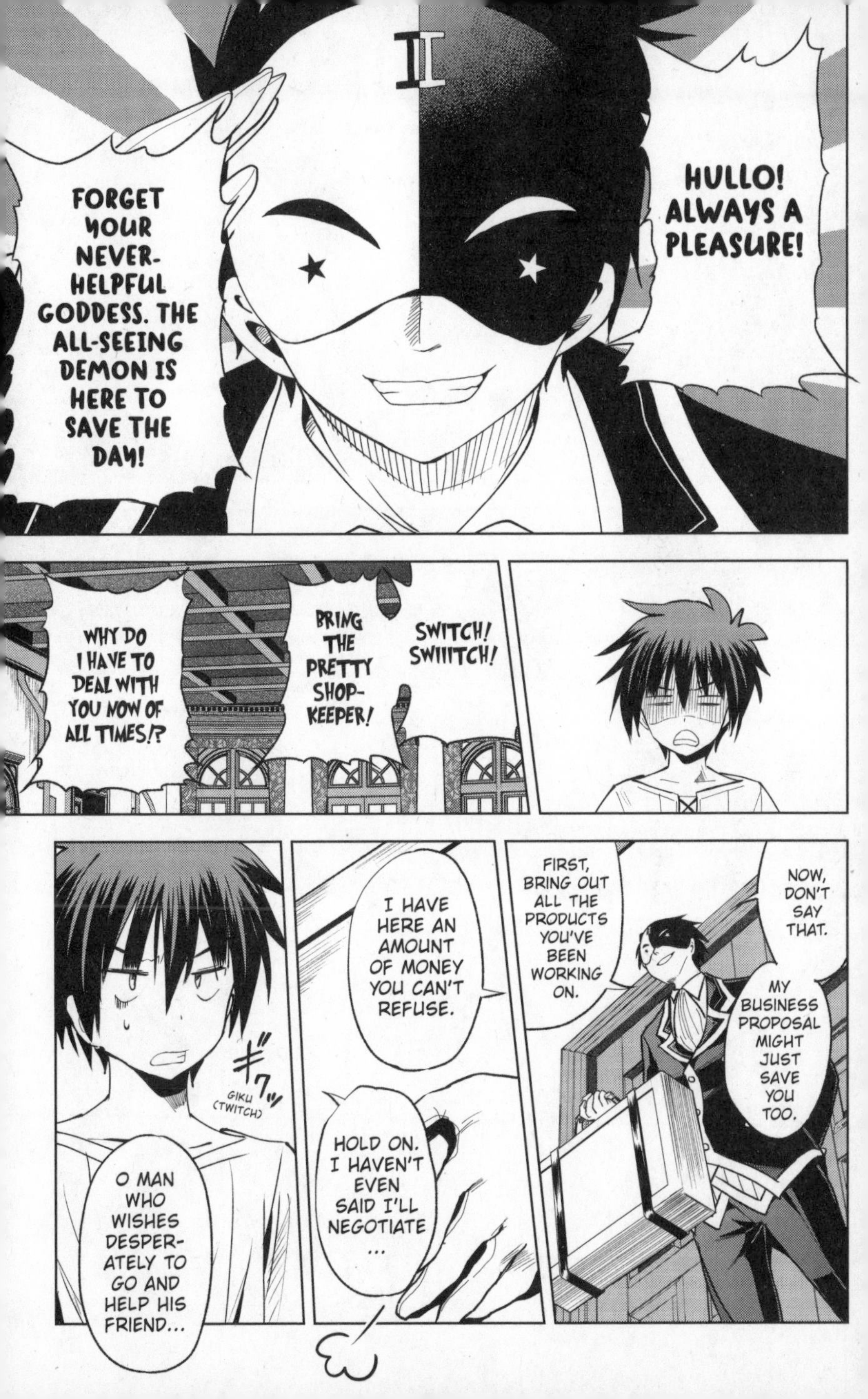
HULLO! ALWAYS A PLEASURE!
FORGET YOUR NEVER-HELPFUL GODDESS. THE ALL-SEEING DEMON IS HERE TO SAVE THE DAY!
SWITCH! SWIIITCH!
BRING THE PRETTY SHOPKEEPER!
WHY DO I HAVE TO DEAL WITH YOU NOW OF ALL TIMES!?
NOW, DON'T SAY THAT.
MY BUSINESS PROPOSAL MIGHT JUST SAVE YOU TOO.
FIRST, BRING OUT ALL THE PRODUCTS YOU'VE BEEN WORKING ON.
I HAVE HERE AN AMOUNT OF MONEY YOU CAN'T REFUSE.
HOLD ON. I HAVEN'T EVEN SAID I'LL NEGOTIATE...
ギクッ
GIKU (TWITCH)
O MAN WHO WISHES DESPERATELY TO GO AND HELP HIS FRIEND...

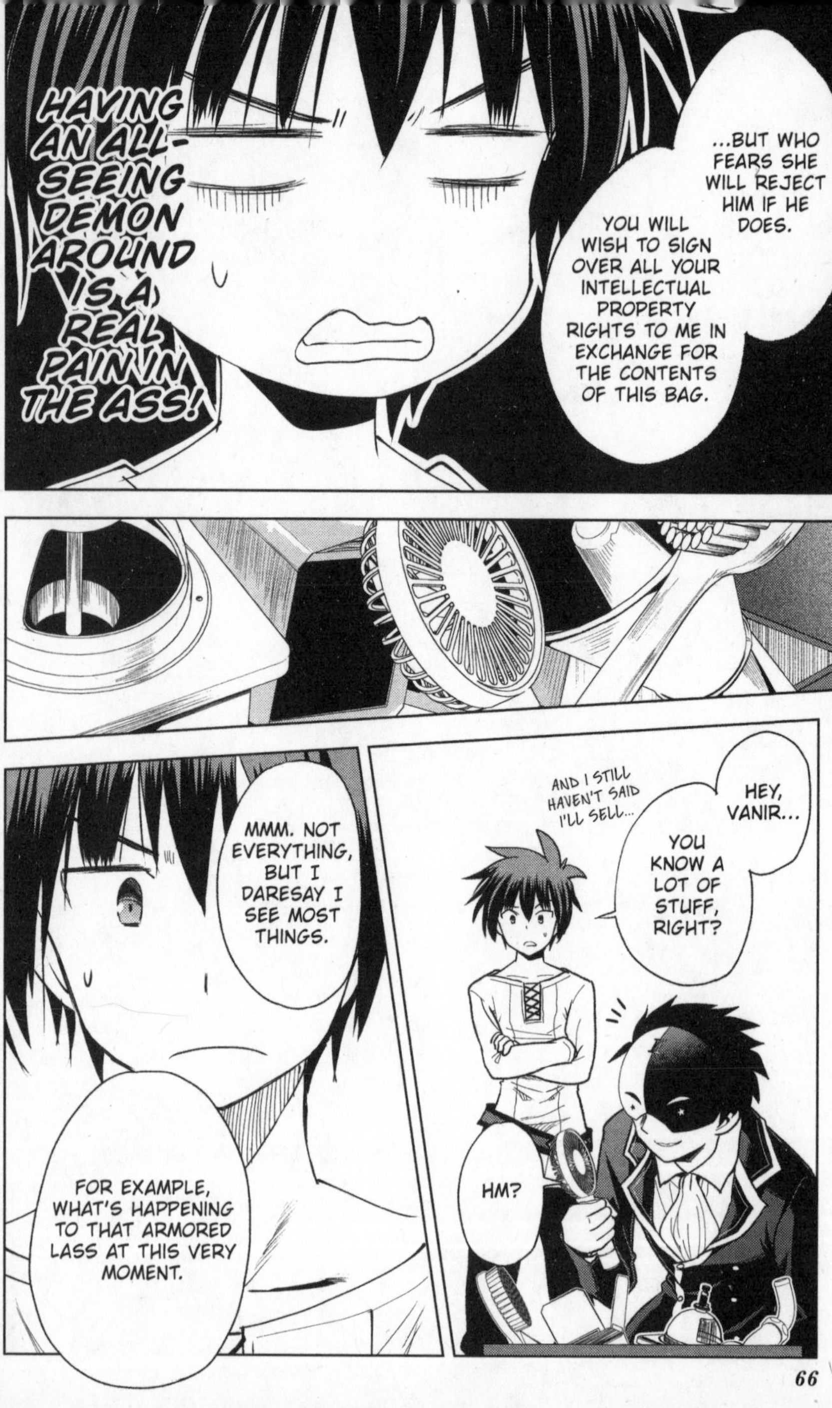
...BUT WHO FEARS SHE WILL REJECT HIM IF HE DOES.
YOU WILL WISH TO SIGN OVER ALL YOUR INTELLECTUAL PROPERTY RIGHTS TO ME IN EXCHANGE FOR THE CONTENTS OF THIS BAG.
HAVING AN ALL-SEEING DEMON AROUND IS A REAL PAIN IN THE ASS!
HEY, VANIR...
YOU KNOW A LOT OF STUFF, RIGHT?
AND I STILL HAVEN'T SAID I'LL SELL...
HM?
MMM. NOT EVERYTHING, BUT I DARESAY I SEE MOST THINGS.
FOR EXAMPLE, WHAT'S HAPPENING TO THAT ARMORED LASS AT THIS VERY MOMENT.

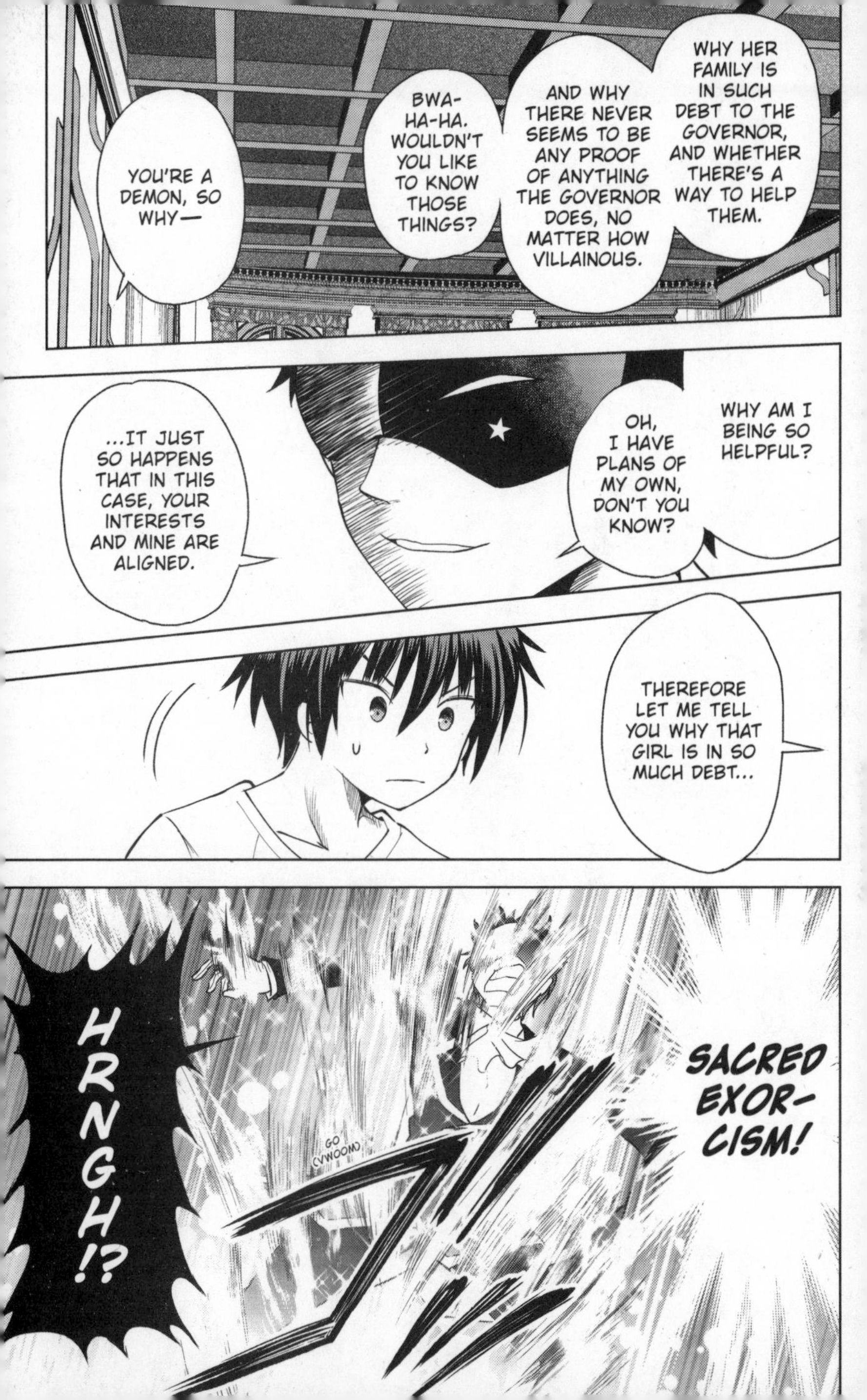
WHY HER FAMILY IS IN SUCH DEBT TO THE GOVERNOR, AND WHETHER THERE'S A WAY TO HELP THEM.
AND WHY THERE NEVER SEEMS TO BE ANY PROOF OF ANYTHING THE GOVERNOR DOES, NO MATTER HOW VILLAINOUS.
BWA-HA-HA. WOULDN'T YOU LIKE TO KNOW THOSE THINGS?
YOU'RE A DEMON, SO WHY—
WHY AM I BEING SO HELPFUL?
OH, I HAVE PLANS OF MY OWN, DON'T YOU KNOW?
...IT JUST SO HAPPENS THAT IN THIS CASE, YOUR INTERESTS AND MINE ARE ALIGNED.
THEREFORE LET ME TELL YOU WHY THAT GIRL IS IN SO MUCH DEBT...
SACRED EXORCISM!
GO (VWOOM)
HRNGH!?

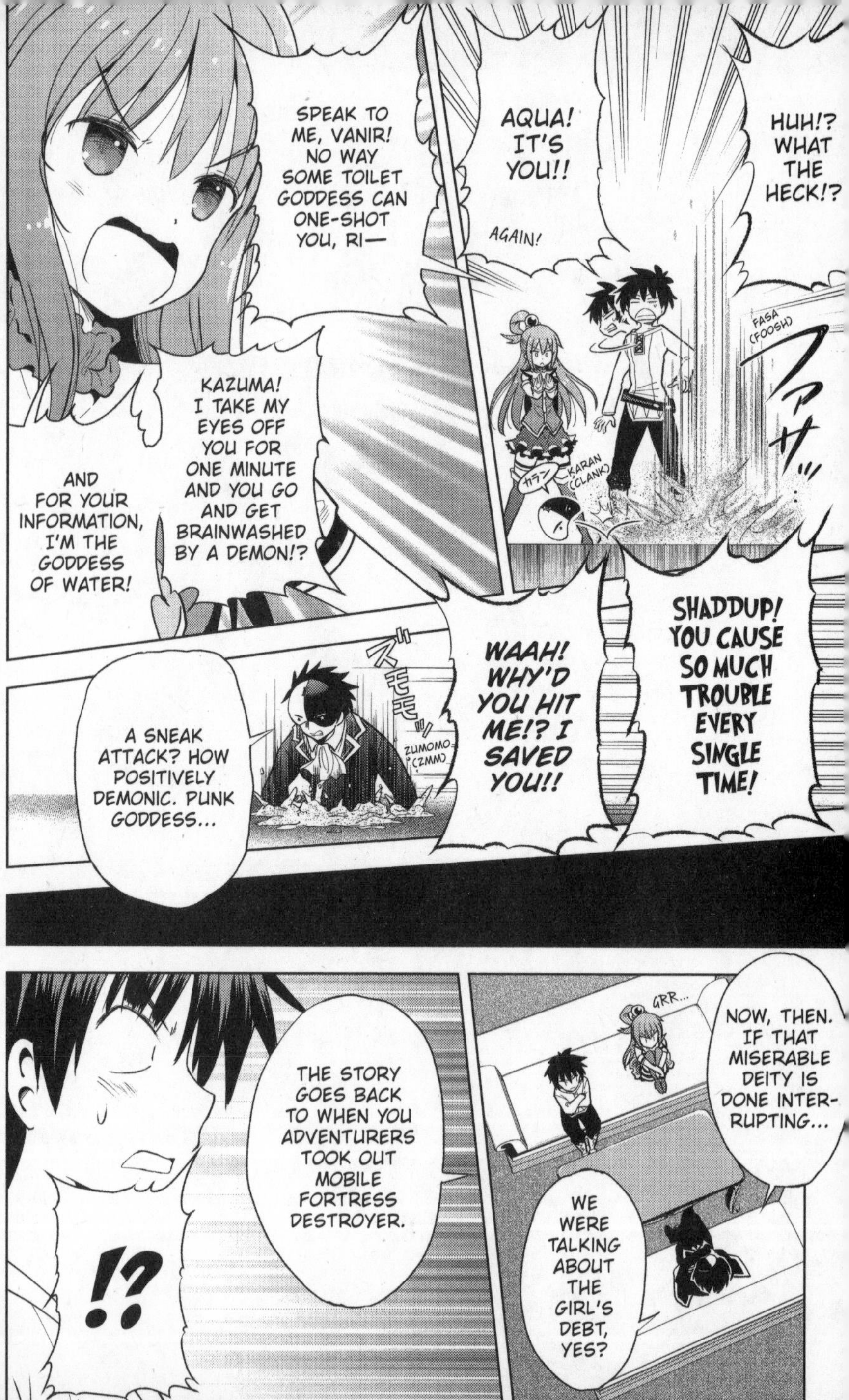
HUH!? WHAT THE HECK!?
AQUA! IT'S YOU!!
AGAIN!
FASA (FOOSH)
KARAN (CLANK)
SPEAK TO ME, VANIR! NO WAY SOME TOILET GODDESS CAN ONE-SHOT YOU, RI—
KAZUMA! I TAKE MY EYES OFF YOU FOR ONE MINUTE AND YOU GO AND GET BRAINWASHED BY A DEMON!?
AND FOR YOUR INFORMATION, I'M THE GODDESS OF WATER!
SHADDUP! YOU CAUSE SO MUCH TROUBLE EVERY SINGLE TIME!
WAAH! WHY'D YOU HIT ME!? I SAVED YOU!!
ZUMOMO (ZMM)
A SNEAK ATTACK? HOW POSITIVELY DEMONIC. PUNK GODDESS...
GRR...
NOW, THEN. IF THAT MISERABLE DEITY IS DONE INTER-RUPTING...
WE WERE TALKING ABOUT THE GIRL'S DEBT, YES?
THE STORY GOES BACK TO WHEN YOU ADVENTURERS TOOK OUT MOBILE FORTRESS DESTROYER.
!?

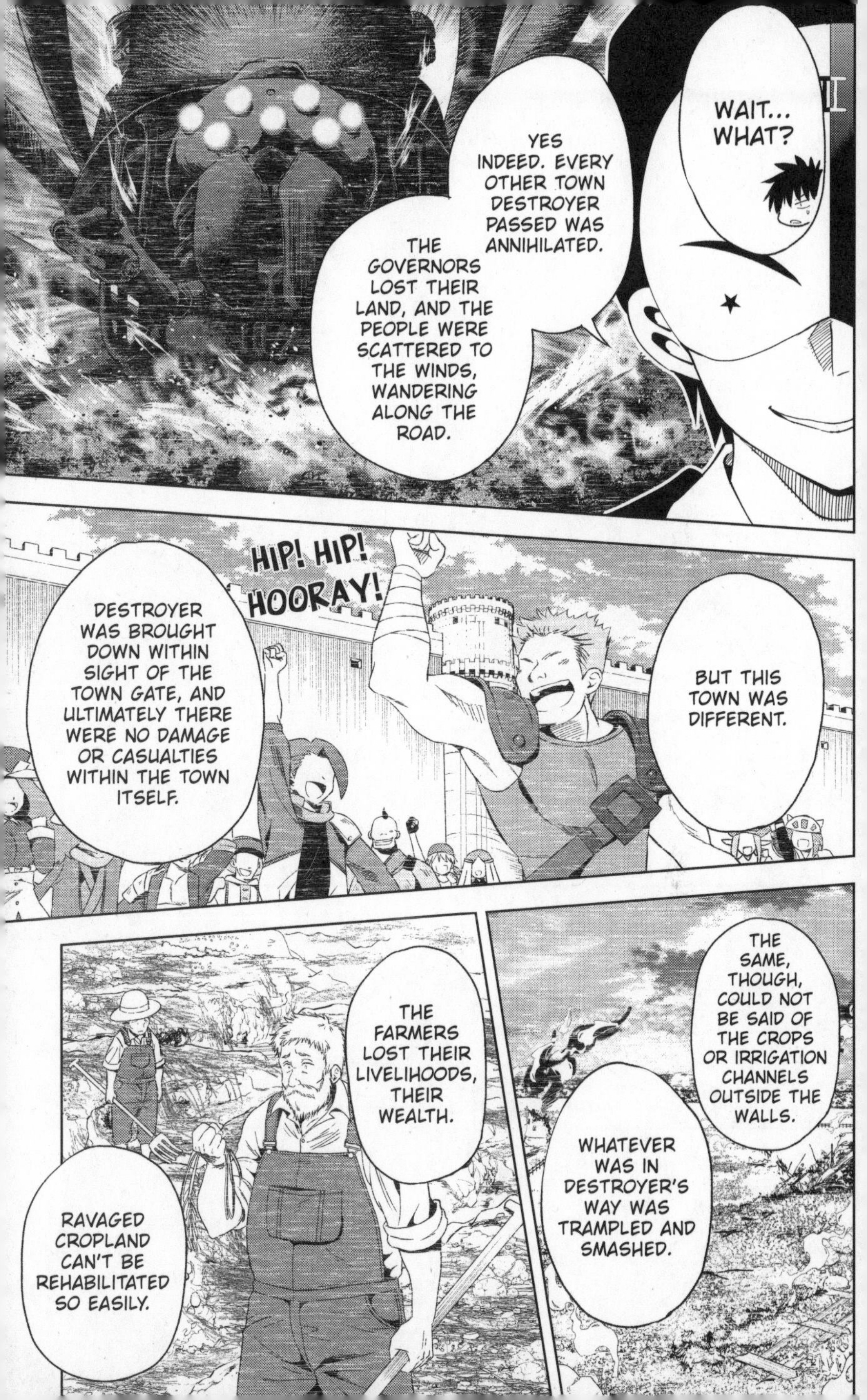
WAIT... WHAT?
YES INDEED. EVERY OTHER TOWN DESTROYER PASSED WAS ANNIHILATED.
THE GOVERNORS LOST THEIR LAND, AND THE PEOPLE WERE SCATTERED TO THE WINDS, WANDERING ALONG THE ROAD.
BUT THIS TOWN WAS DIFFERENT.
HIP! HIP! HOORAY!
DESTROYER WAS BROUGHT DOWN WITHIN SIGHT OF THE TOWN GATE, AND ULTIMATELY THERE WERE NO DAMAGE OR CASUALTIES WITHIN THE TOWN ITSELF.
THE SAME, THOUGH, COULD NOT BE SAID OF THE CROPS OR IRRIGATION CHANNELS OUTSIDE THE WALLS.
WHATEVER WAS IN DESTROYER'S WAY WAS TRAMPLED AND SMASHED.
THE FARMERS LOST THEIR LIVELIHOODS, THEIR WEALTH.
RAVAGED CROPLAND CAN'T BE REHABILITATED SO EASILY.

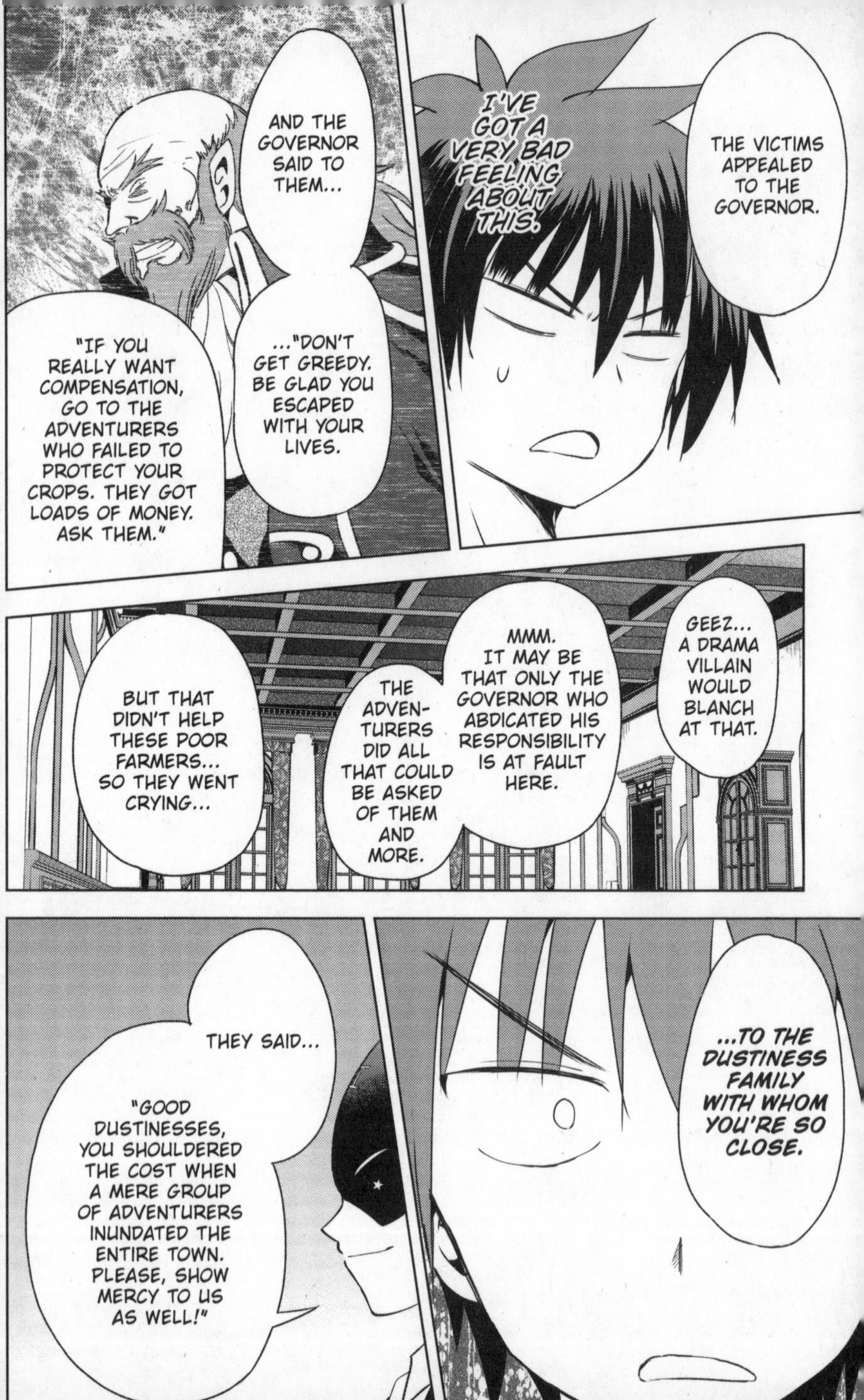
THE VICTIMS APPEALED TO THE GOVERNOR.
I'VE GOT A VERY BAD FEELING ABOUT THIS.
AND THE GOVERNOR SAID TO THEM...
..."DON'T GET GREEDY. BE GLAD YOU ESCAPED WITH YOUR LIVES.
"IF YOU REALLY WANT COMPENSATION, GO TO THE ADVENTURERS WHO FAILED TO PROTECT YOUR CROPS. THEY GOT LOADS OF MONEY. ASK THEM."
GEEZ... A DRAMA VILLAIN WOULD BLANCH AT THAT.
MMM. IT MAY BE THAT ONLY THE GOVERNOR WHO ABDICATED HIS RESPONSIBILITY IS AT FAULT HERE.
THE ADVEN-TURERS DID ALL THAT COULD BE ASKED OF THEM AND MORE.
BUT THAT DIDN'T HELP THESE POOR FARMERS... SO THEY WENT CRYING...
...TO THE DUSTINESS FAMILY WITH WHOM YOU'RE SO CLOSE.
THEY SAID...
"GOOD DUSTINESSES, YOU SHOULDERED THE COST WHEN A MERE GROUP OF ADVENTURERS INUNDATED THE ENTIRE TOWN. PLEASE, SHOW MERCY TO US AS WELL!"

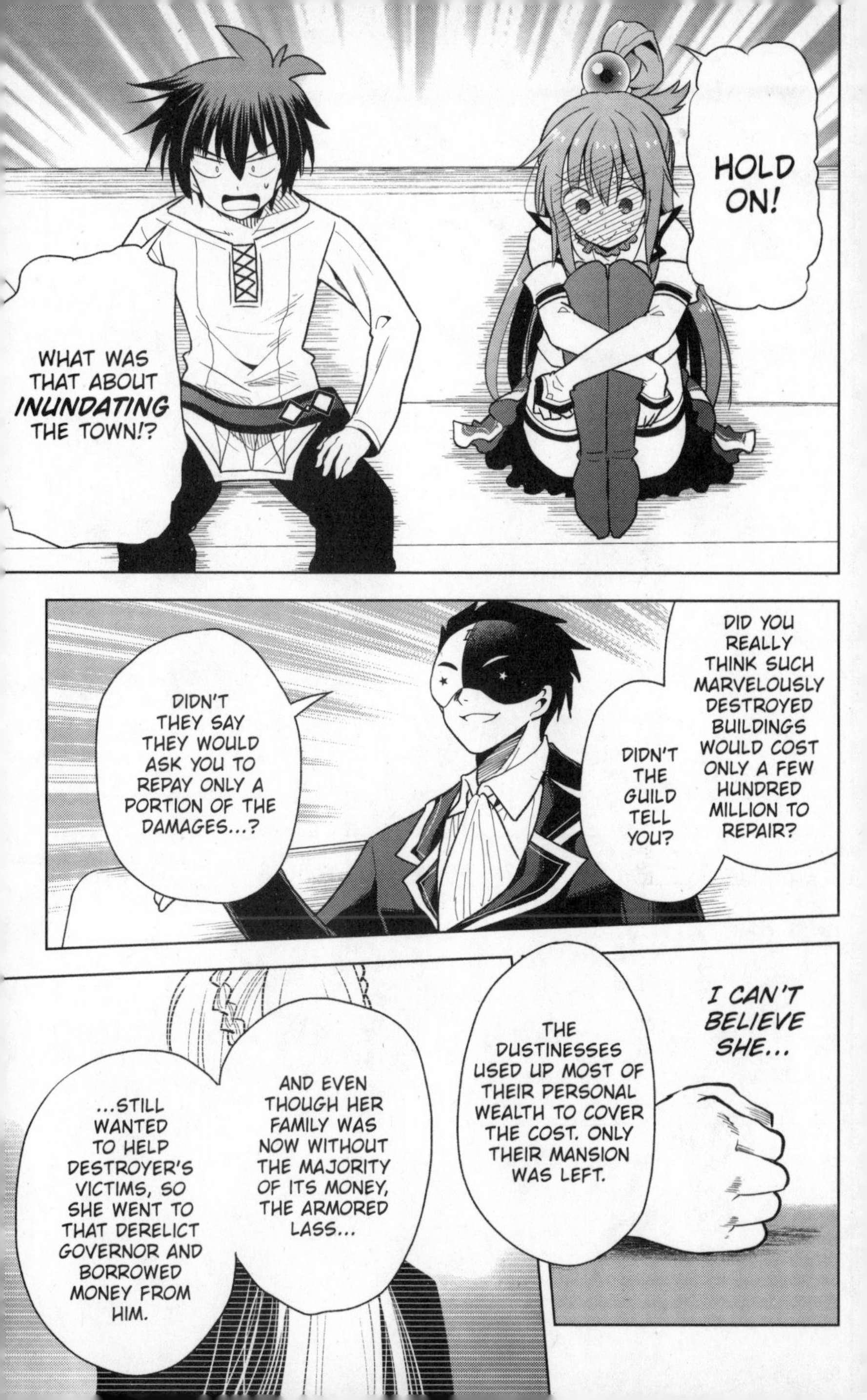
HOLD ON!
WHAT WAS THAT ABOUT *INUNDATING* THE TOWN!?
DID YOU REALLY THINK SUCH MARVELOUSLY DESTROYED BUILDINGS WOULD COST ONLY A FEW HUNDRED MILLION TO REPAIR?
DIDN'T THE GUILD TELL YOU?
DIDN'T THEY SAY THEY WOULD ASK YOU TO REPAY ONLY A PORTION OF THE DAMAGES...?
I CAN'T BELIEVE SHE...
THE DUSTINESSES USED UP MOST OF THEIR PERSONAL WEALTH TO COVER THE COST. ONLY THEIR MANSION WAS LEFT.
AND EVEN THOUGH HER FAMILY WAS NOW WITHOUT THE MAJORITY OF ITS MONEY, THE ARMORED LASS...
...STILL WANTED TO HELP DESTROYER'S VICTIMS, SO SHE WENT TO THAT DERELICT GOVERNOR AND BORROWED MONEY FROM HIM.

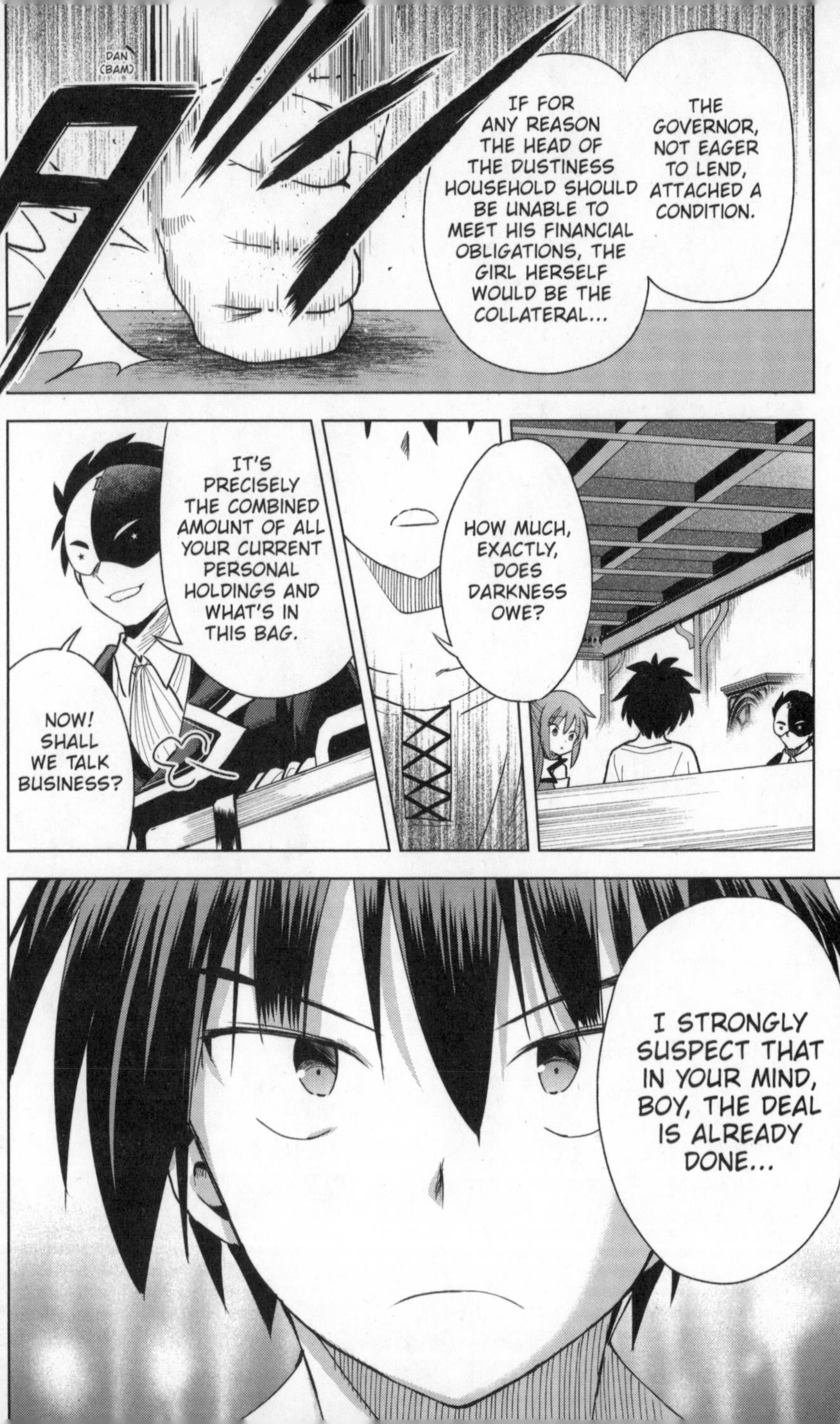
THE GOVERNOR, NOT EAGER TO LEND, ATTACHED A CONDITION.
IF FOR ANY REASON THE HEAD OF THE DUSTINESS HOUSEHOLD SHOULD BE UNABLE TO MEET HIS FINANCIAL OBLIGATIONS, THE GIRL HERSELF WOULD BE THE COLLATERAL...
DAN (BAM)
HOW MUCH, EXACTLY, DOES DARKNESS OWE?
IT'S PRECISELY THE COMBINED AMOUNT OF ALL YOUR CURRENT PERSONAL HOLDINGS AND WHAT'S IN THIS BAG.
NOW! SHALL WE TALK BUSINESS?
I STRONGLY SUSPECT THAT IN YOUR MIND, BOY, THE DEAL IS ALREADY DONE...

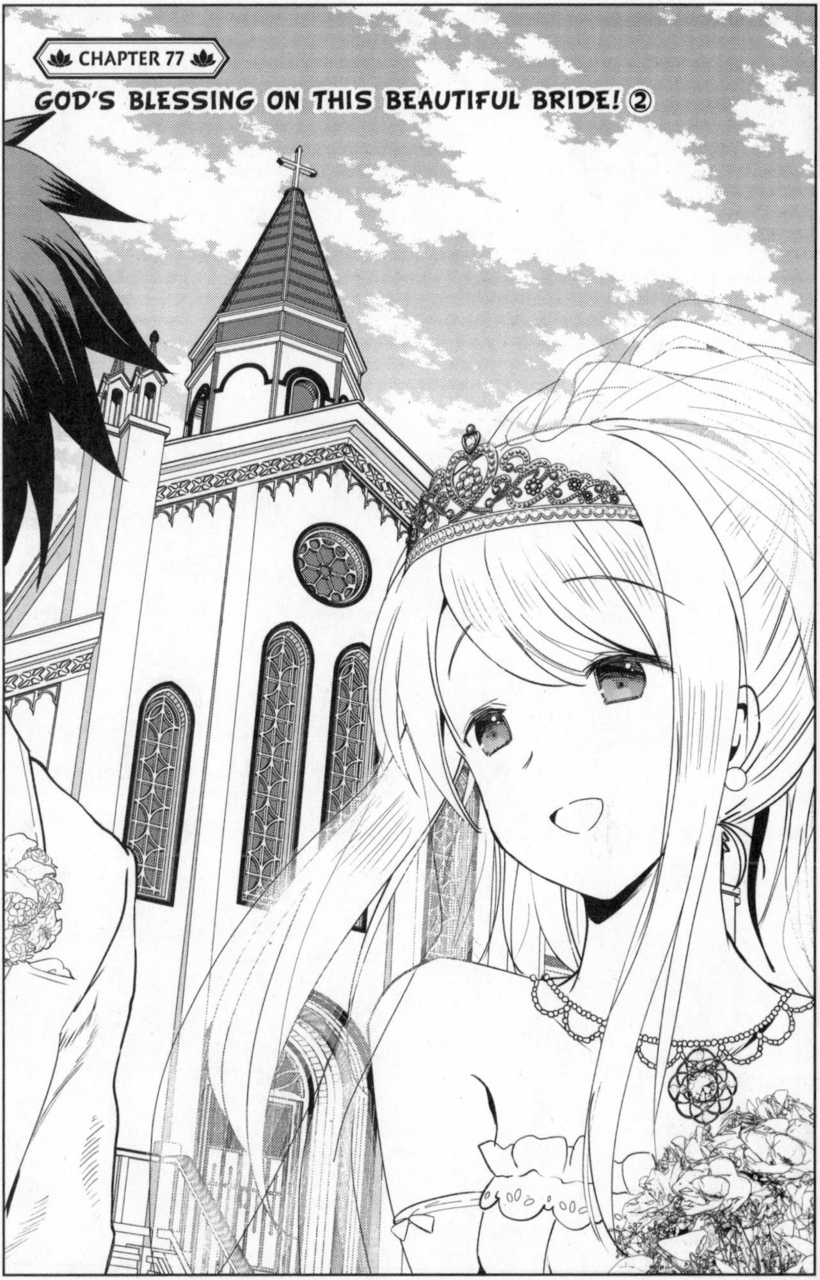
CHAPTER 77
GOD'S BLESSING ON THIS BEAUTIFUL BRIDE! ②

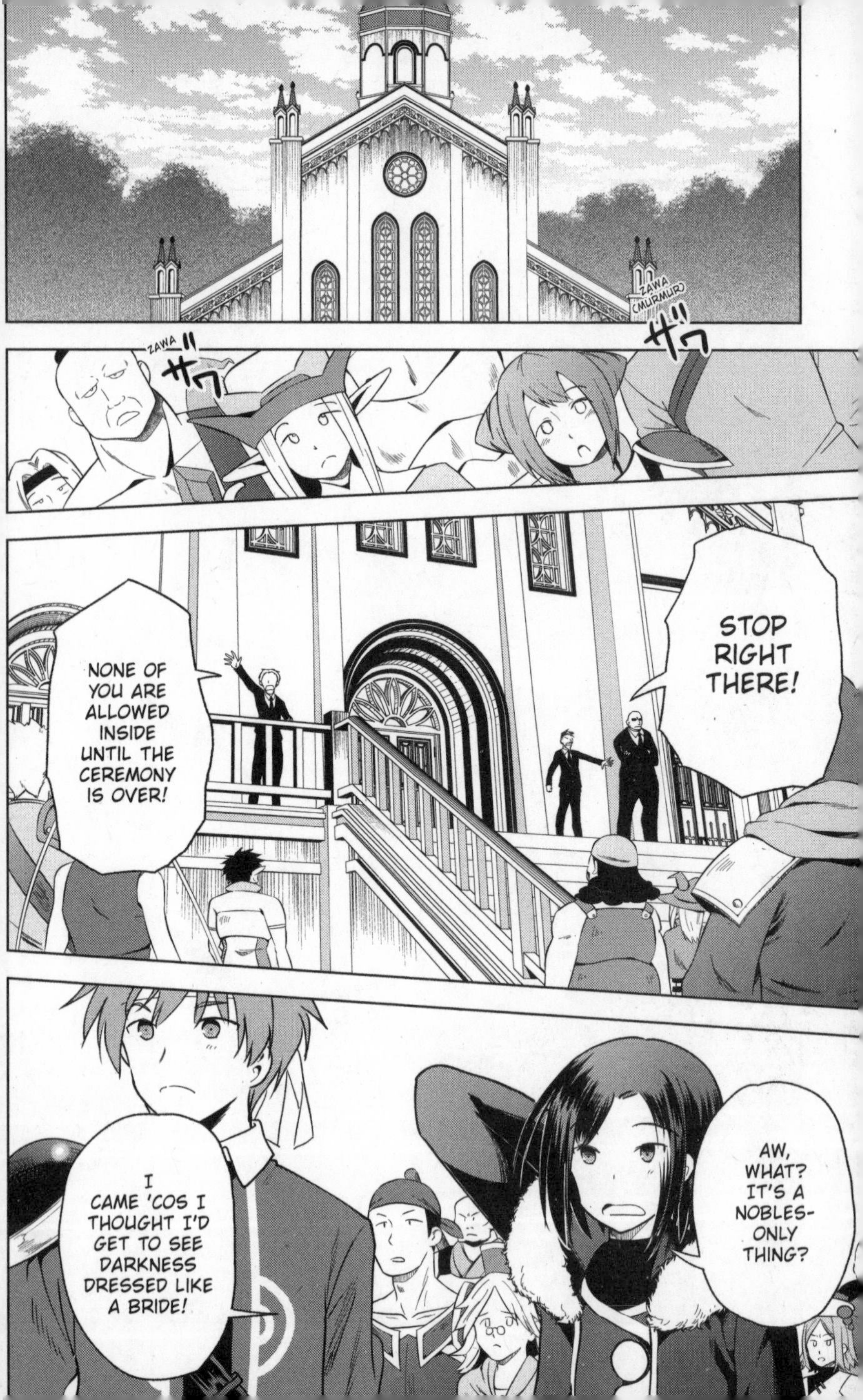
ZAWA (MURMUR)
ザワ
ZAWA
ザワ
STOP RIGHT THERE!
NONE OF YOU ARE ALLOWED INSIDE UNTIL THE CEREMONY IS OVER!
AW, WHAT? IT'S A NOBLES-ONLY THING?
I CAME 'COS I THOUGHT I'D GET TO SEE DARKNESS DRESSED LIKE A BRIDE!

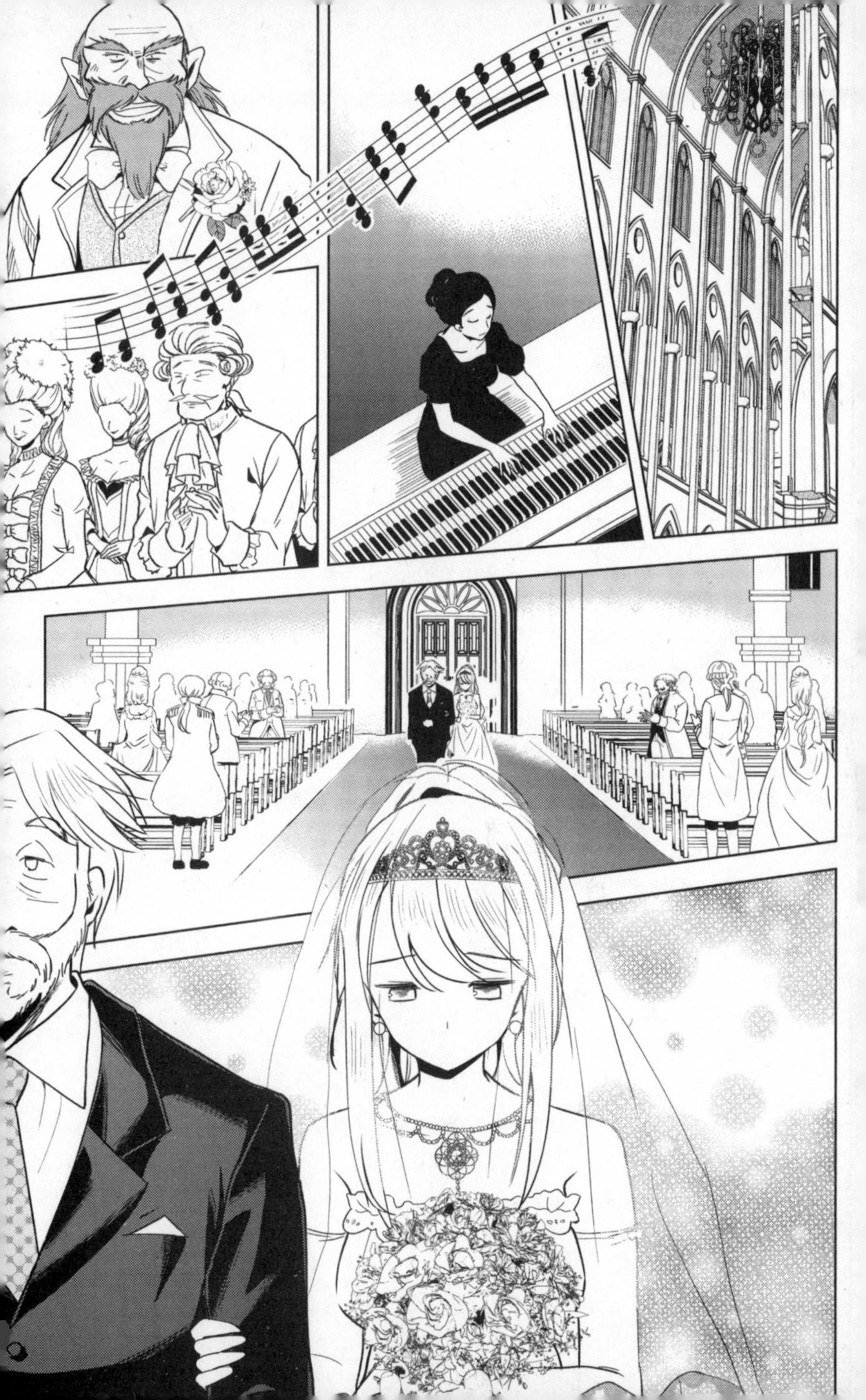

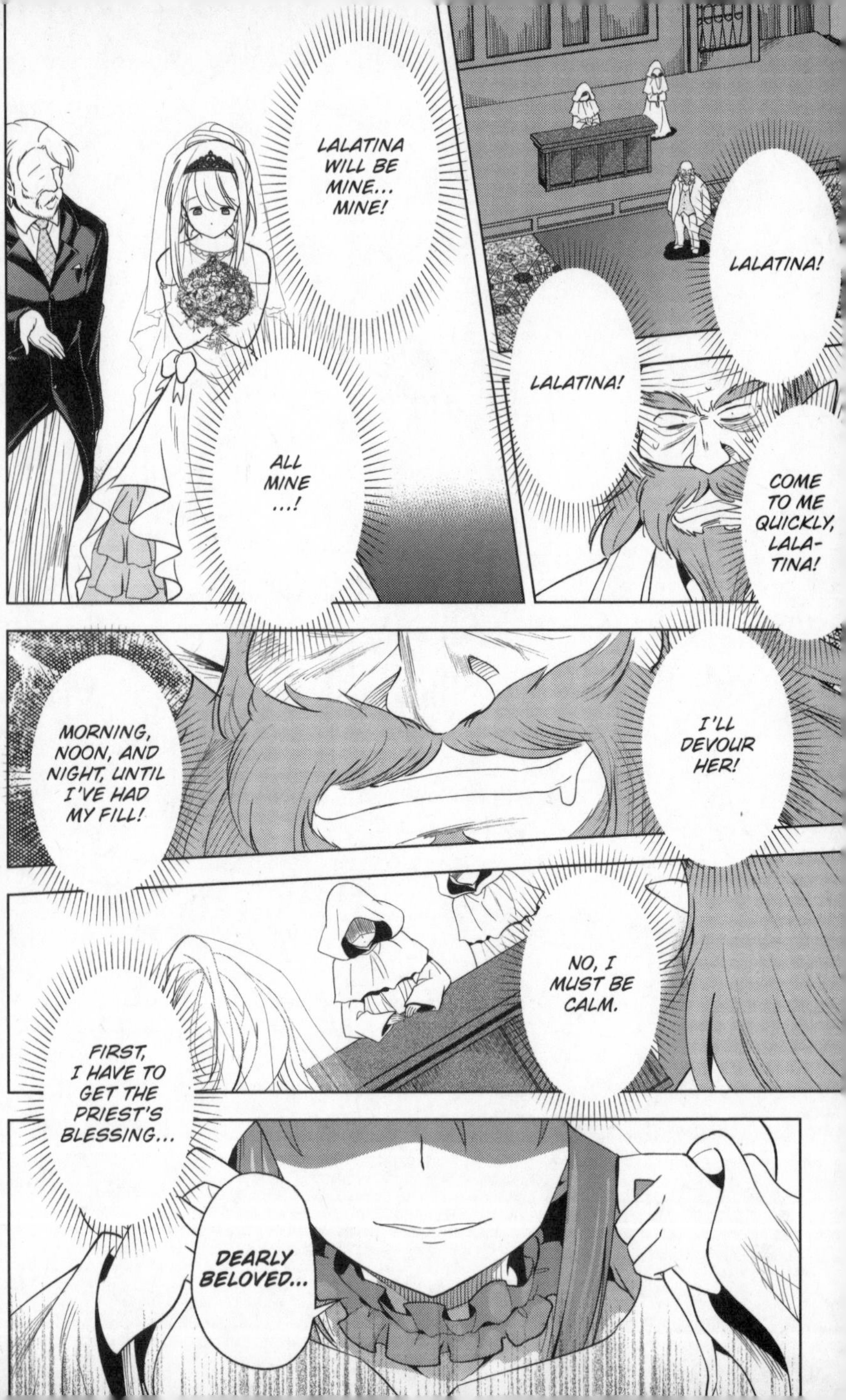
LALATINA!
LALATINA!
COME TO ME QUICKLY, LALA-TINA!
LALATINA WILL BE MINE... MINE!
ALL MINE ...!
I'LL DEVOUR HER!
MORNING, NOON, AND NIGHT, UNTIL I'VE HAD MY FILL!
NO, I MUST BE CALM.
FIRST, I HAVE TO GET THE PRIEST'S BLESSING...
DEARLY BELOVED...

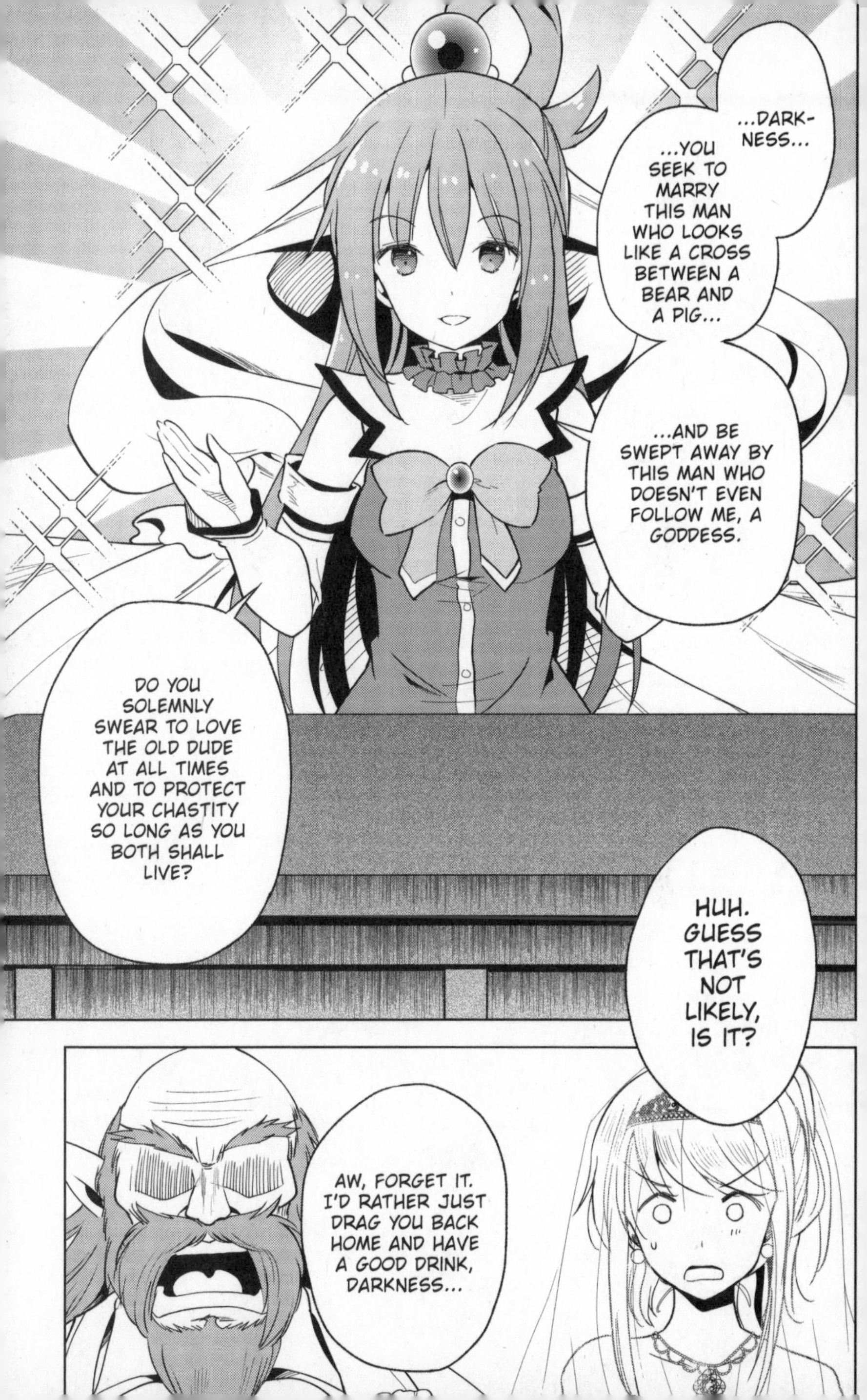
...DARKNESS...
...YOU SEEK TO MARRY THIS MAN WHO LOOKS LIKE A CROSS BETWEEN A BEAR AND A PIG...
...AND BE SWEPT AWAY BY THIS MAN WHO DOESN'T EVEN FOLLOW ME, A GODDESS.
DO YOU SOLEMNLY SWEAR TO LOVE THE OLD DUDE AT ALL TIMES AND TO PROTECT YOUR CHASTITY SO LONG AS YOU BOTH SHALL LIVE?
HUH. GUESS THAT'S NOT LIKELY, IS IT?
AW, FORGET IT. I'D RATHER JUST DRAG YOU BACK HOME AND HAVE A GOOD DRINK, DARKNESS...

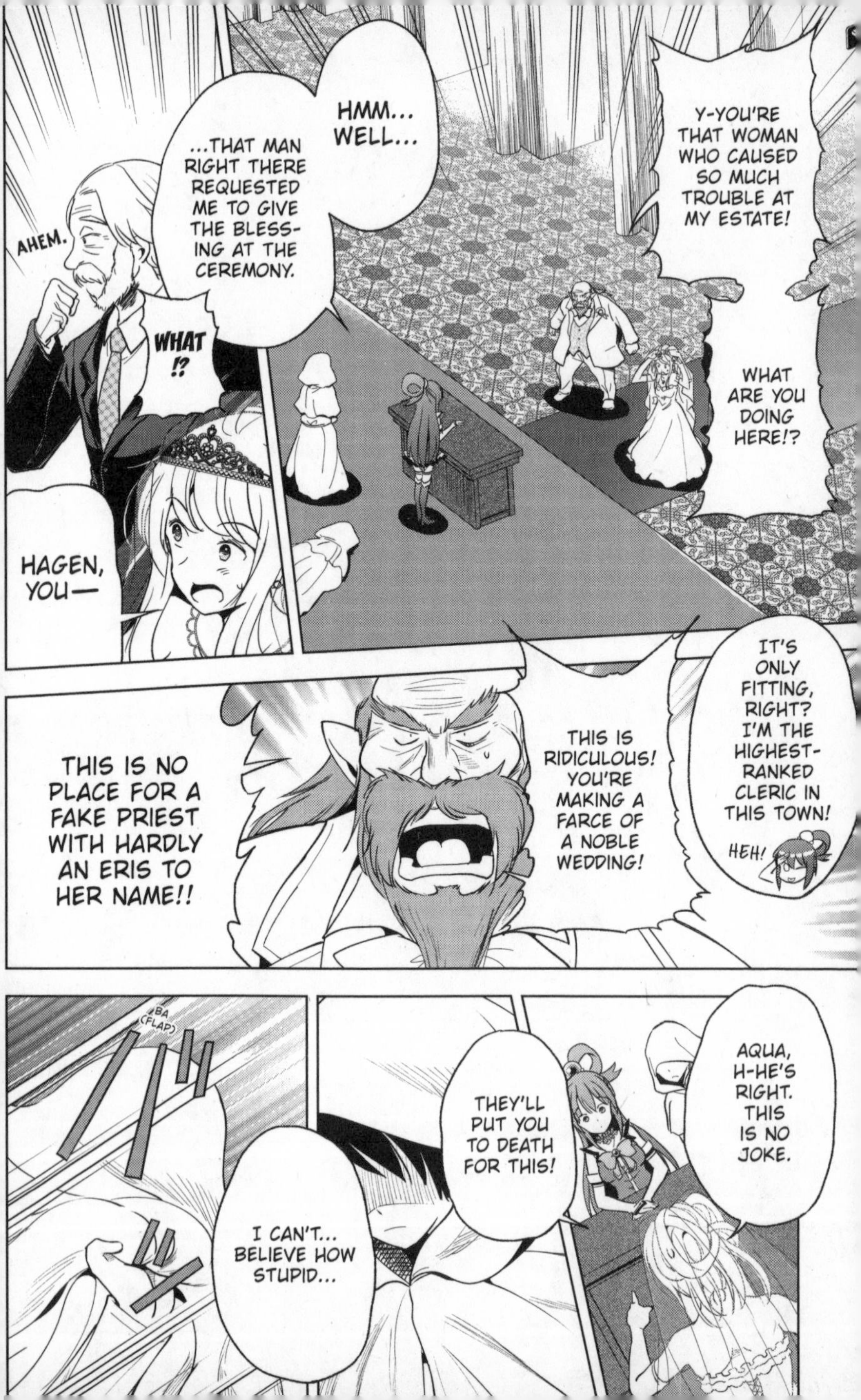
Y-YOU'RE THAT WOMAN WHO CAUSED SO MUCH TROUBLE AT MY ESTATE!
WHAT ARE YOU DOING HERE!?
HMM... WELL...
...THAT MAN RIGHT THERE REQUESTED ME TO GIVE THE BLESS-ING AT THE CEREMONY.
WHAT!?
AHEM.
HAGEN, YOU—
IT'S ONLY FITTING, RIGHT? I'M THE HIGHEST-RANKED CLERIC IN THIS TOWN!
HEH!
THIS IS RIDICULOUS! YOU'RE MAKING A FARCE OF A NOBLE WEDDING!
THIS IS NO PLACE FOR A FAKE PRIEST WITH HARDLY AN ERIS TO HER NAME!!
AQUA, H-HE'S RIGHT. THIS IS NO JOKE.
THEY'LL PUT YOU TO DEATH FOR THIS!
I CAN'T... BELIEVE HOW STUPID...
BA (FLAP)

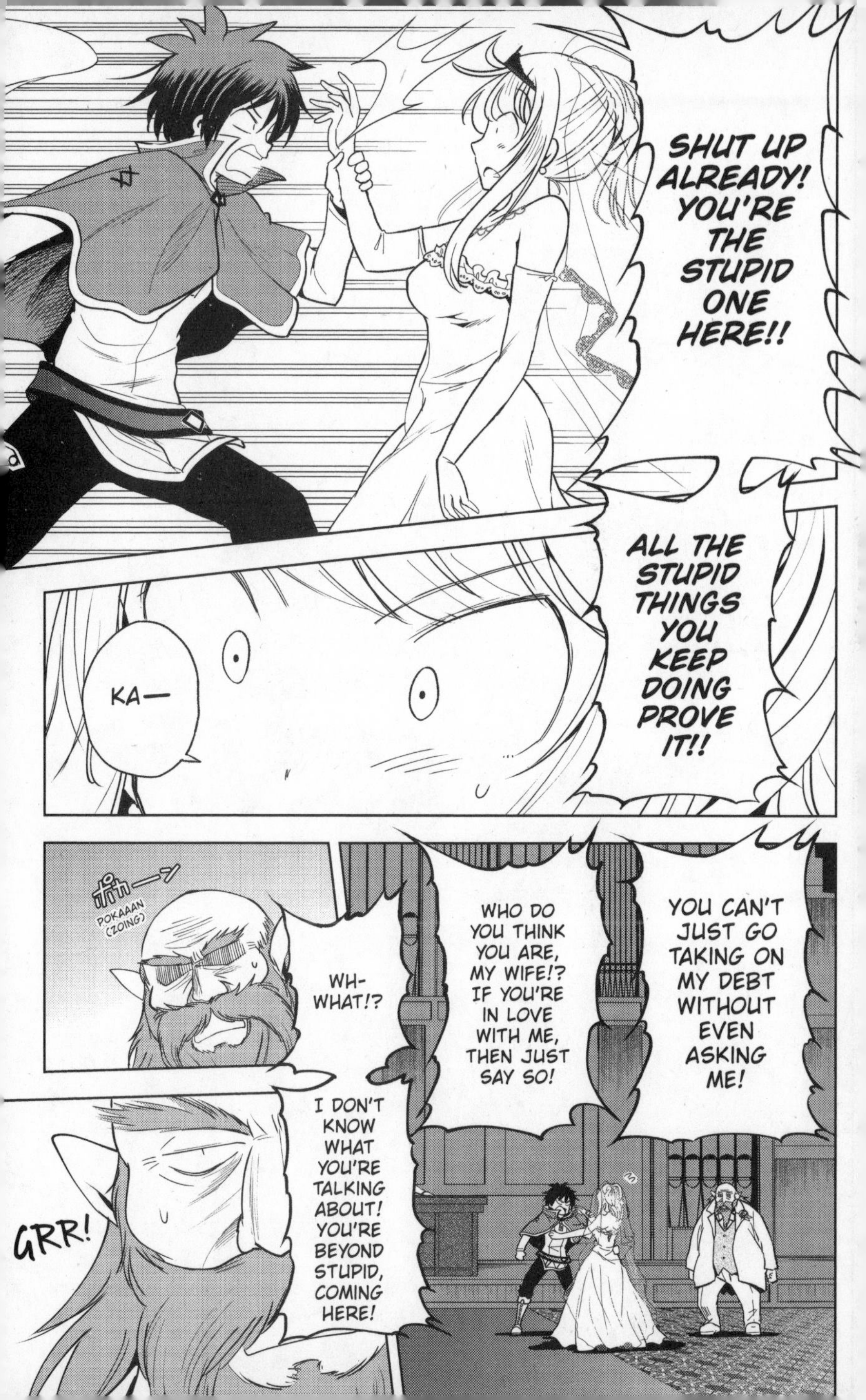
SHUT UP ALREADY! YOU'RE THE STUPID ONE HERE!!
ALL THE STUPID THINGS YOU KEEP DOING PROVE IT!!
KA—
YOU CAN'T JUST GO TAKING ON MY DEBT WITHOUT EVEN ASKING ME!
WHO DO YOU THINK YOU ARE, MY WIFE!? IF YOU'RE IN LOVE WITH ME, THEN JUST SAY SO!
ポカーン
POKAAAN (ZOING)
WH- WHAT!?
I DON'T KNOW WHAT YOU'RE TALKING ABOUT! YOU'RE BEYOND STUPID, COMING HERE!
GRR!

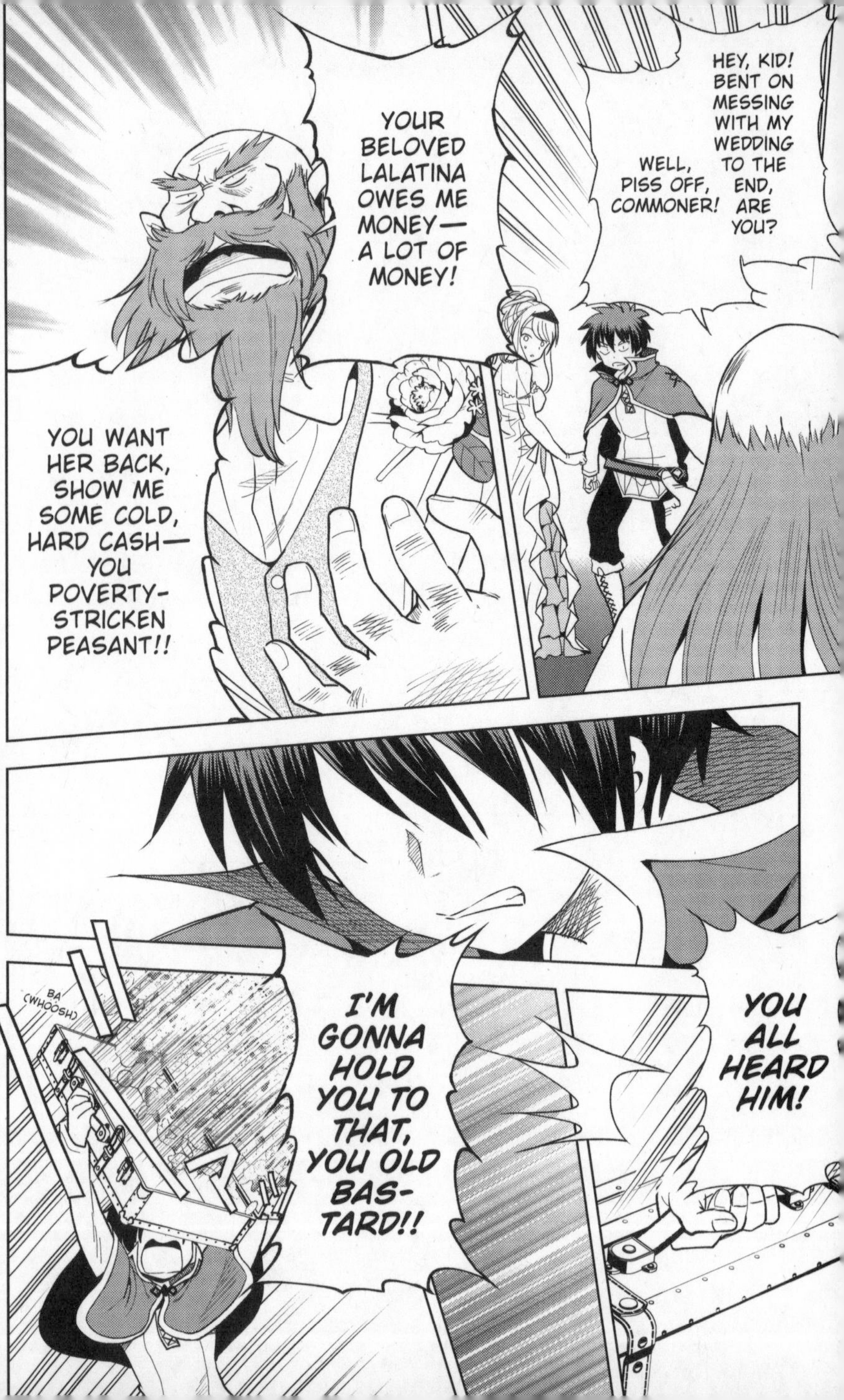
HEY, KID! BENT ON MESSING WITH MY WEDDING TO THE END, ARE YOU?
WELL, PISS OFF, COMMONER!
YOUR BELOVED LALATINA OWES ME MONEY— A LOT OF MONEY!
YOU WANT HER BACK, SHOW ME SOME COLD, HARD CASH— YOU POVERTY-STRICKEN PEASANT!!
YOU ALL HEARD HIM!
I'M GONNA HOLD YOU TO THAT, YOU OLD BAS-TARD!!
BA (WHOOSH)

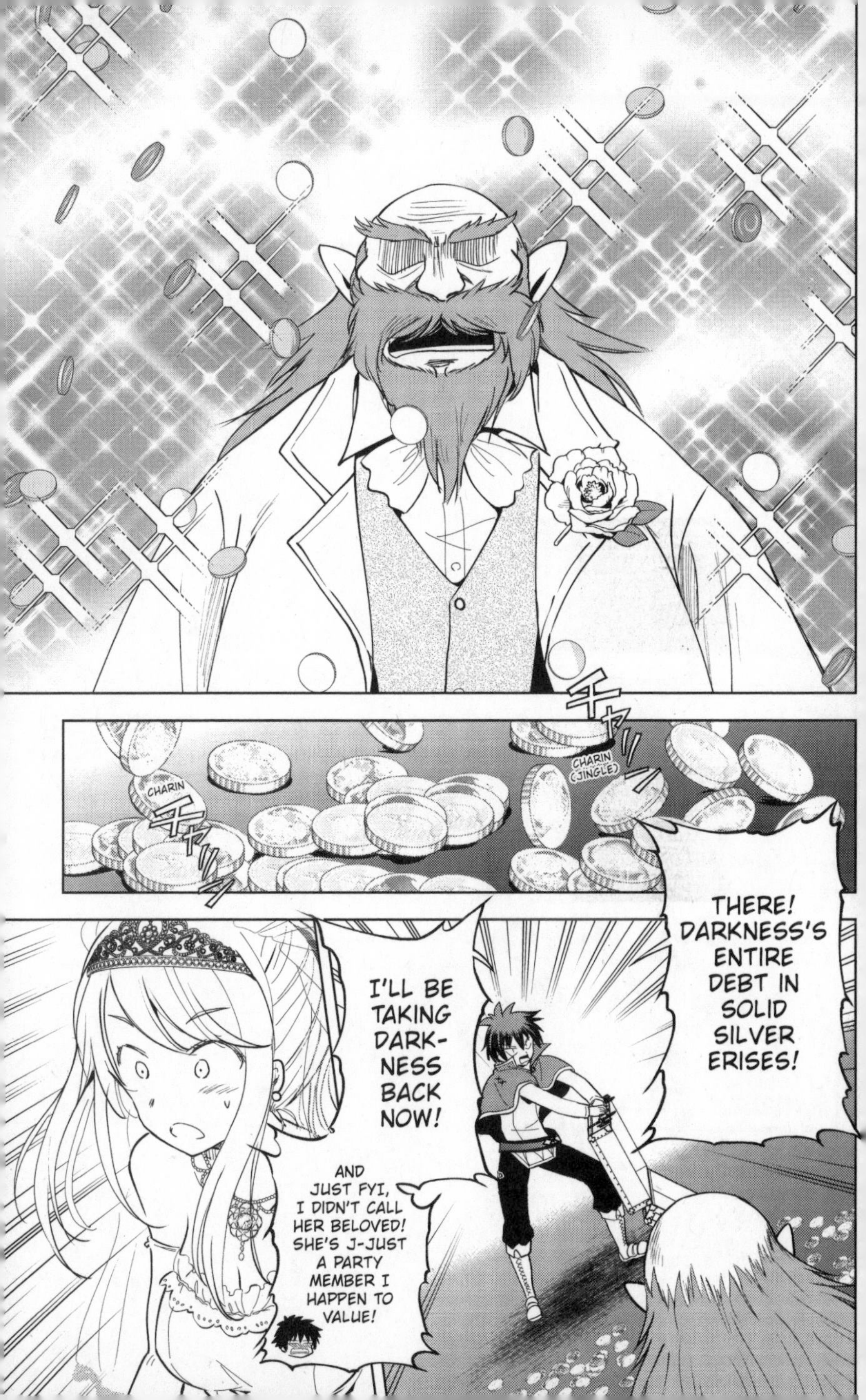

チャリン
CHARIN (JINGLE)
CHARIN
チャリン
THERE! DARKNESS'S ENTIRE DEBT IN SOLID SILVER ERISES!
I'LL BE TAKING DARKNESS BACK NOW!
AND JUST FYI, I DIDN'T CALL HER BELOVED! SHE'S J-JUST A PARTY MEMBER I HAPPEN TO VALUE!

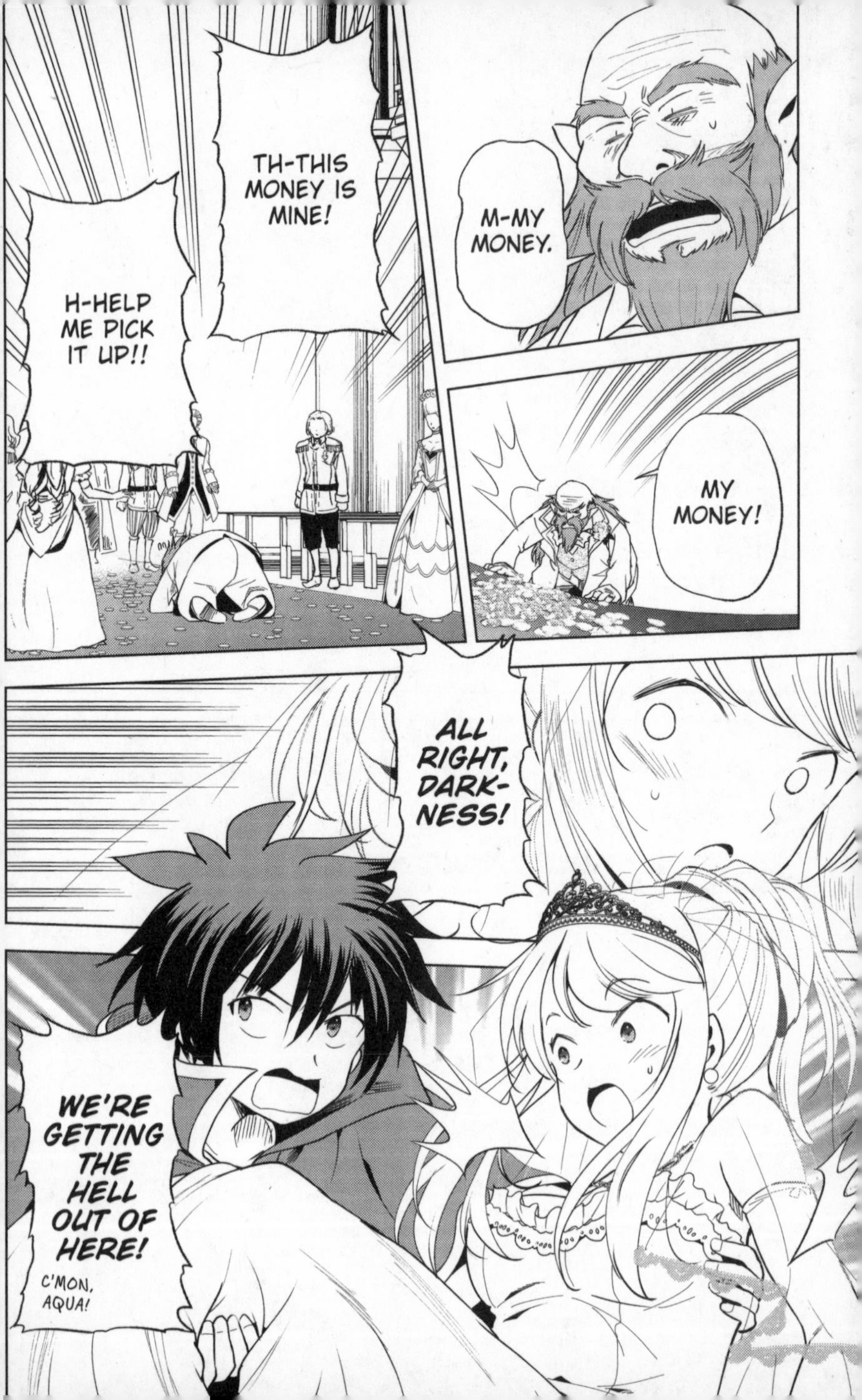
M-MY MONEY.
MY MONEY!
TH-THIS MONEY IS MINE!
H-HELP ME PICK IT UP!!
ALL RIGHT, DARKNESS!
WE'RE GETTING THE HELL OUT OF HERE!
C'MON, AQUA!

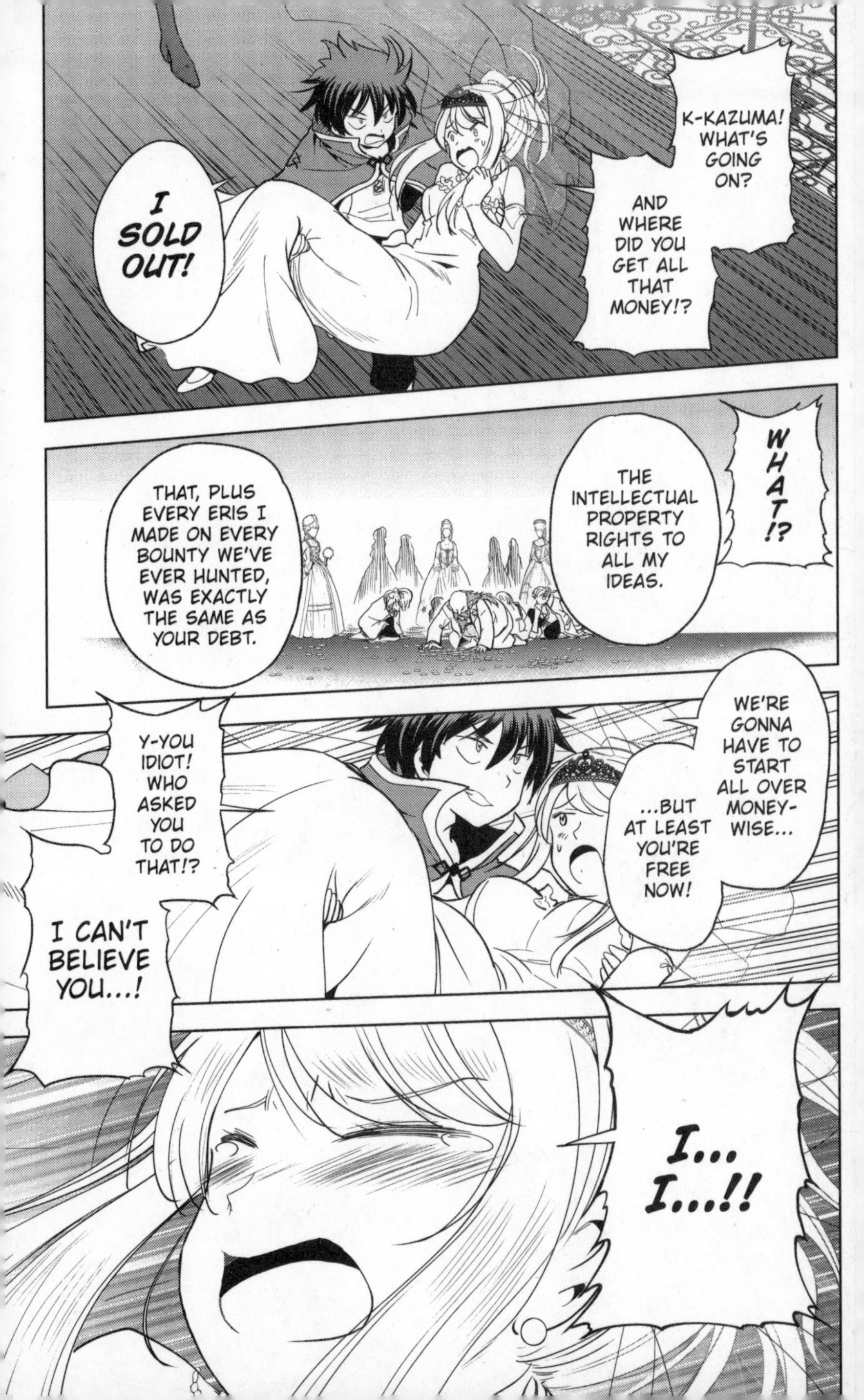
K-KAZUMA! WHAT'S GOING ON?
AND WHERE DID YOU GET ALL THAT MONEY!?
I SOLD OUT!
WHAT!?
THE INTELLECTUAL PROPERTY RIGHTS TO ALL MY IDEAS.
THAT, PLUS EVERY ERIS I MADE ON EVERY BOUNTY WE'VE EVER HUNTED, WAS EXACTLY THE SAME AS YOUR DEBT.
WE'RE GONNA HAVE TO START ALL OVER MONEY-WISE...
...BUT AT LEAST YOU'RE FREE NOW!
Y-YOU IDIOT! WHO ASKED YOU TO DO THAT!?
I CAN'T BELIEVE YOU...!
I... I...!!

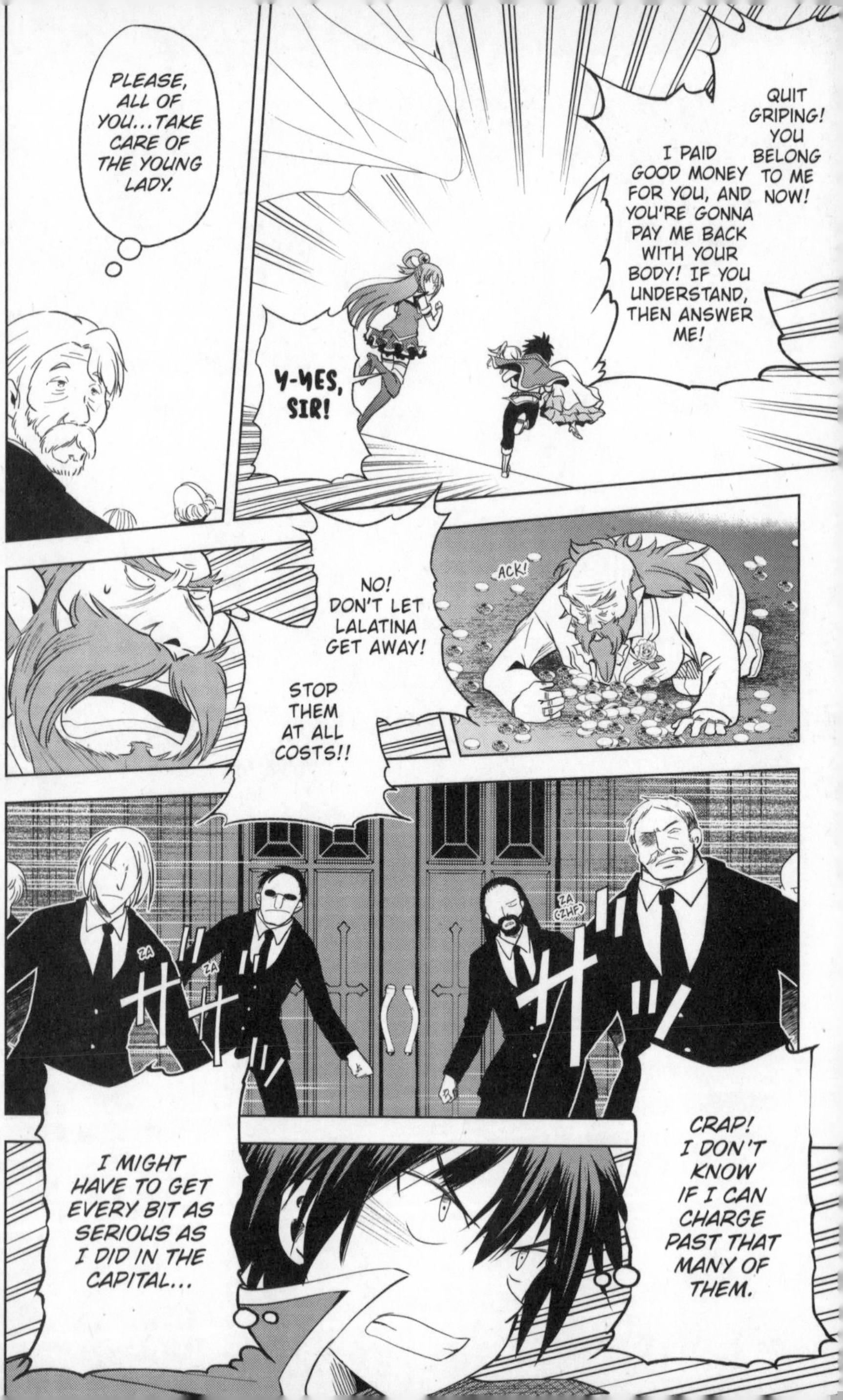
QUIT GRIPING! YOU BELONG TO ME NOW!
I PAID GOOD MONEY FOR YOU, AND YOU'RE GONNA PAY ME BACK WITH YOUR BODY! IF YOU UNDERSTAND, THEN ANSWER ME!
Y-YES, SIR!
PLEASE, ALL OF YOU...TAKE CARE OF THE YOUNG LADY.
ACK!
NO! DON'T LET LALATINA GET AWAY!
STOP THEM AT ALL COSTS!!
ZA (ZHF)
ZA
ZA
CRAP! I DON'T KNOW IF I CAN CHARGE PAST THAT MANY OF THEM.
I MIGHT HAVE TO GET EVERY BIT AS SERIOUS AS I DID IN THE CAPITAL...

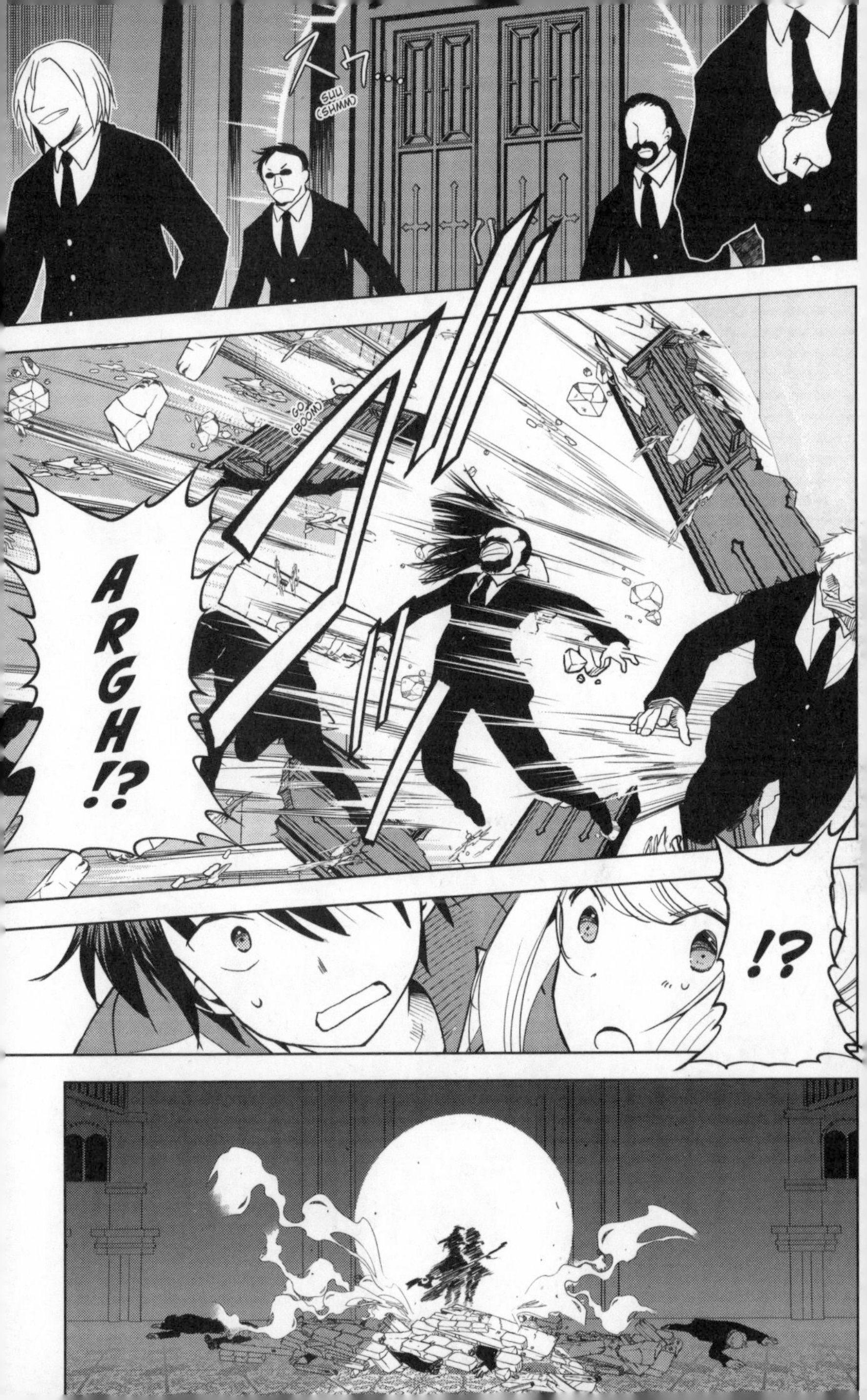

SUU (SHMM)
GO (BOOM)
ARGH!?
!?

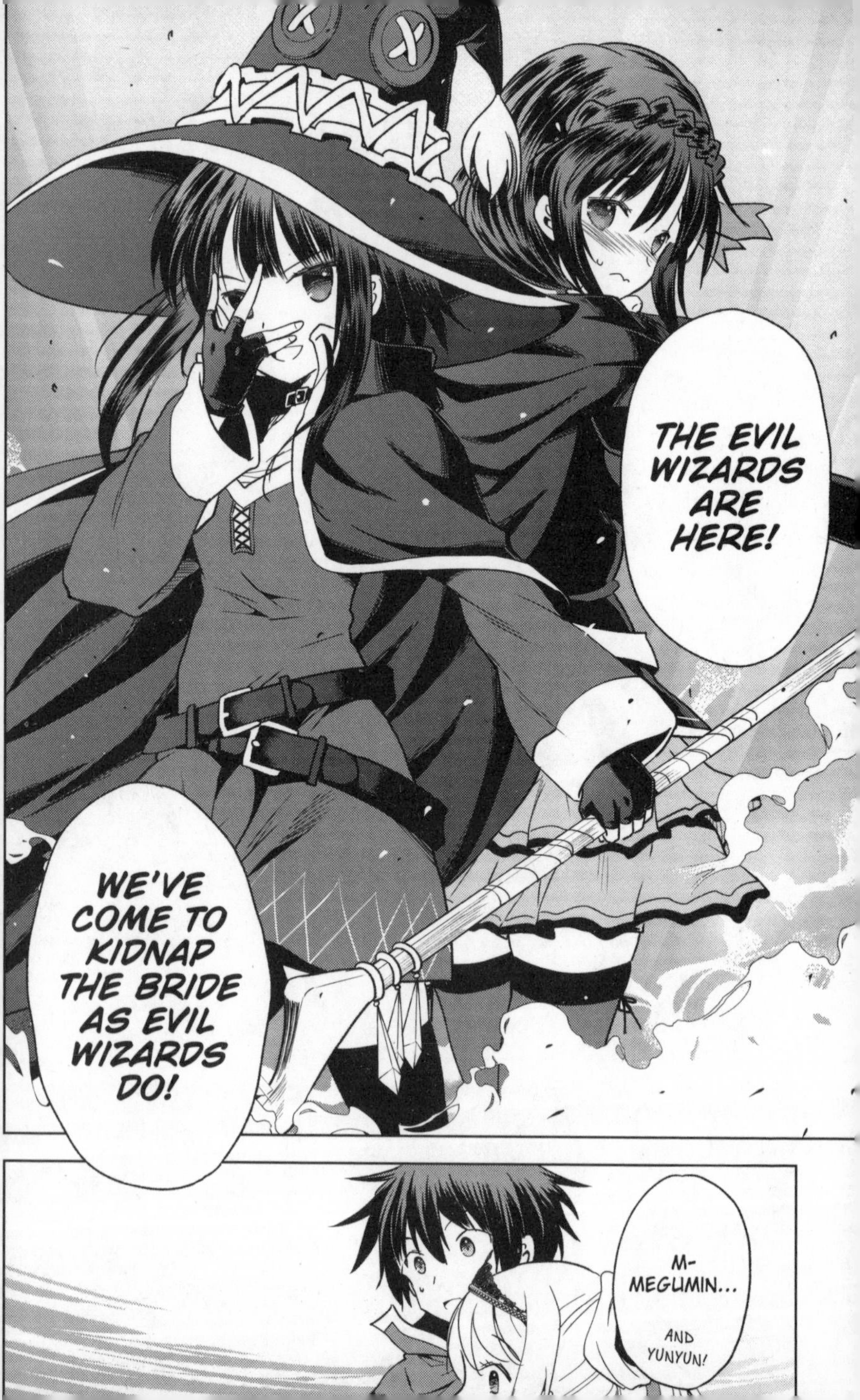
THE EVIL WIZARDS ARE HERE!
WE'VE COME TO KIDNAP THE BRIDE AS EVIL WIZARDS DO!
M-MEGUMIN...
AND YUNYUN!

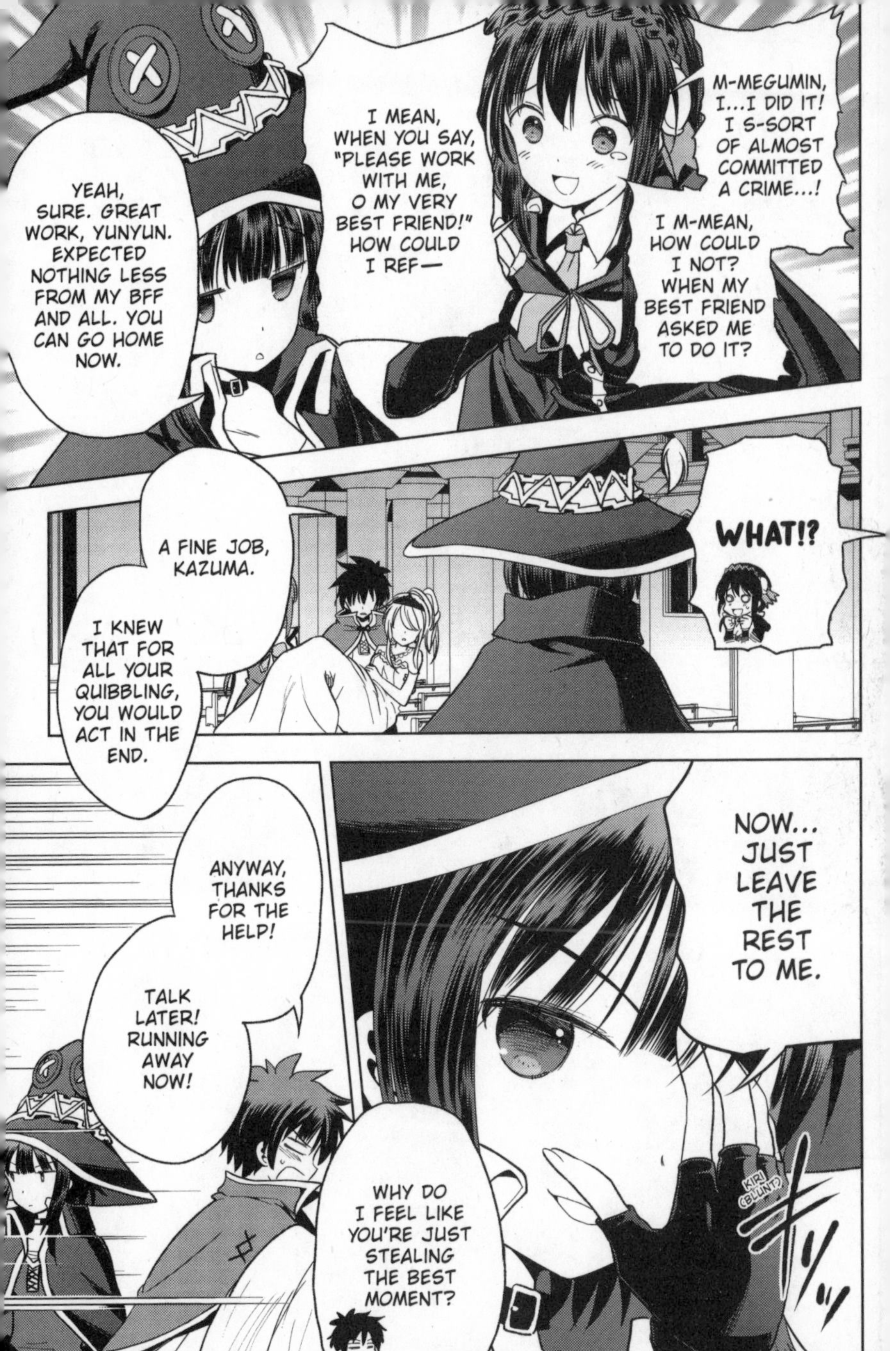
M-MEGUMIN, I...I DID IT! I S-SORT OF ALMOST COMMITTED A CRIME...!
I M-MEAN, HOW COULD I NOT? WHEN MY BEST FRIEND ASKED ME TO DO IT?
I MEAN, WHEN YOU SAY, "PLEASE WORK WITH ME, O MY VERY BEST FRIEND!" HOW COULD I REF—
YEAH, SURE. GREAT WORK, YUNYUN. EXPECTED NOTHING LESS FROM MY BFF AND ALL. YOU CAN GO HOME NOW.
WHAT!?
A FINE JOB, KAZUMA.
I KNEW THAT FOR ALL YOUR QUIBBLING, YOU WOULD ACT IN THE END.
NOW... JUST LEAVE THE REST TO ME.
KIRI (BLUNT)
ANYWAY, THANKS FOR THE HELP!
TALK LATER! RUNNING AWAY NOW!
WHY DO I FEEL LIKE YOU'RE JUST STEALING THE BEST MOMENT?

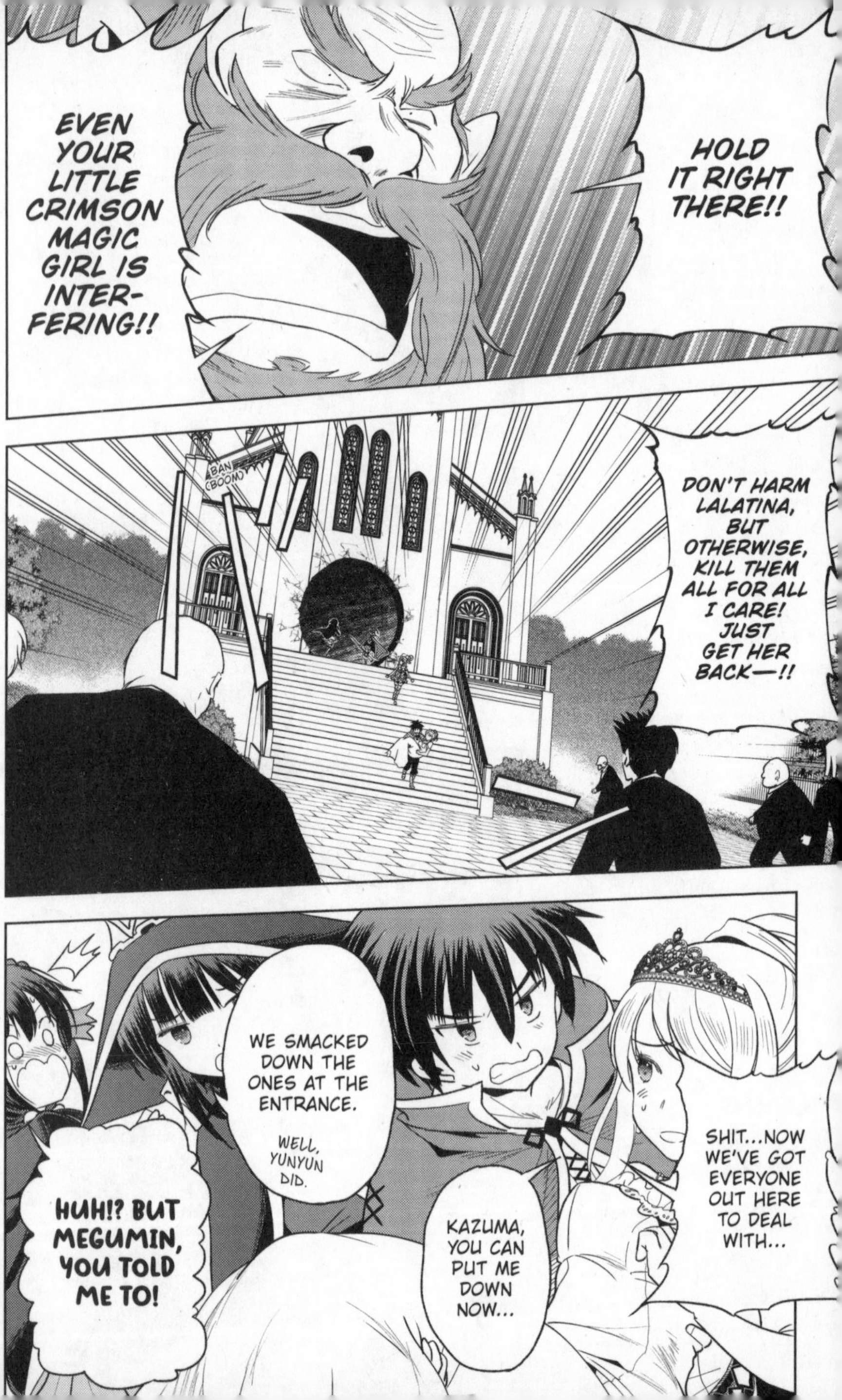
HOLD IT RIGHT THERE!!
EVEN YOUR LITTLE CRIMSON MAGIC GIRL IS INTER-FERING!!
DON'T HARM LALATINA, BUT OTHERWISE, KILL THEM ALL FOR ALL I CARE! JUST GET HER BACK—!!
BAN (BOOM)
SHIT...NOW WE'VE GOT EVERYONE OUT HERE TO DEAL WITH...
KAZUMA, YOU CAN PUT ME DOWN NOW...
WE SMACKED DOWN THE ONES AT THE ENTRANCE.
WELL, YUNYUN DID.
HUH!? BUT MEGUMIN, YOU TOLD ME TO!

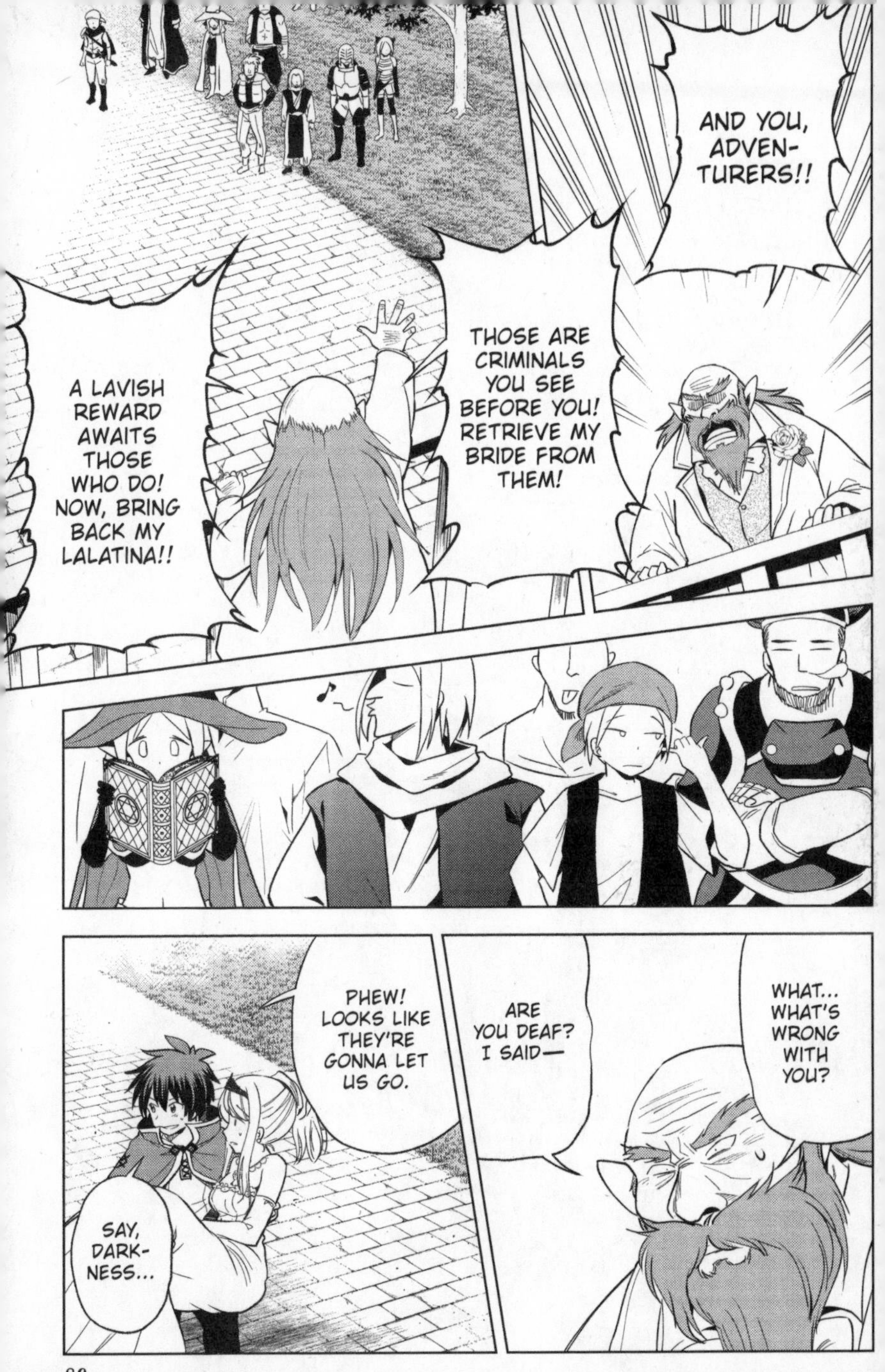
AND YOU, ADVENTURERS!!
THOSE ARE CRIMINALS YOU SEE BEFORE YOU! RETRIEVE MY BRIDE FROM THEM!
A LAVISH REWARD AWAITS THOSE WHO DO! NOW, BRING BACK MY LALATINA!!
WHAT... WHAT'S WRONG WITH YOU?
ARE YOU DEAF? I SAID—
PHEW! LOOKS LIKE THEY'RE GONNA LET US GO.
SAY, DARKNESS...

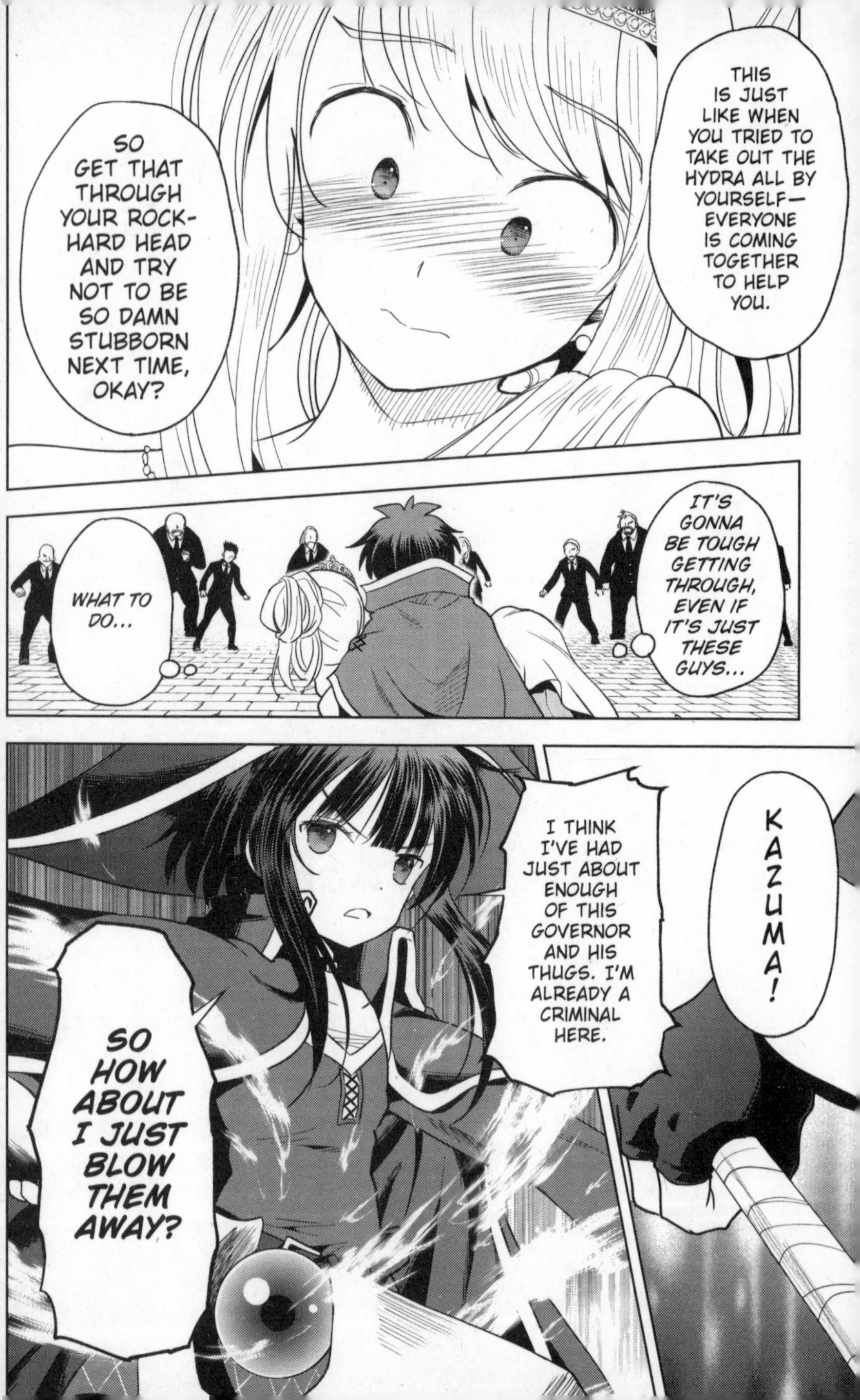
THIS IS JUST LIKE WHEN YOU TRIED TO TAKE OUT THE HYDRA ALL BY YOURSELF—EVERYONE IS COMING TOGETHER TO HELP YOU.
SO GET THAT THROUGH YOUR ROCK-HARD HEAD AND TRY NOT TO BE SO DAMN STUBBORN NEXT TIME, OKAY?
IT'S GONNA BE TOUGH GETTING THROUGH, EVEN IF IT'S JUST THESE GUYS...
WHAT TO DO...
KAZUMA!
I THINK I'VE HAD JUST ABOUT ENOUGH OF THIS GOVERNOR AND HIS THUGS. I'M ALREADY A CRIMINAL HERE.
SO HOW ABOUT I JUST BLOW THEM AWAY?

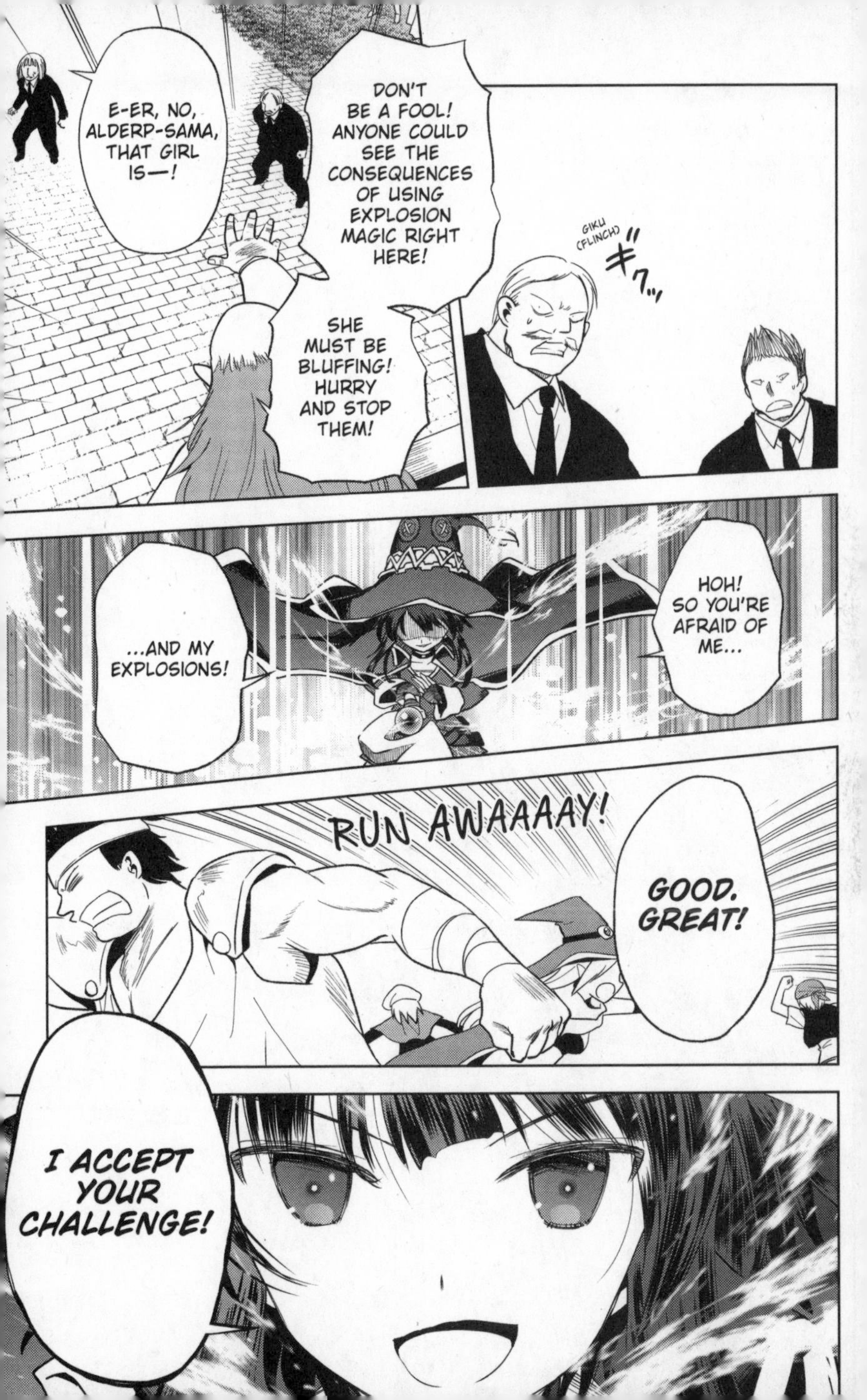
E-ER, NO, ALDERP-SAMA, THAT GIRL IS—!
DON'T BE A FOOL! ANYONE COULD SEE THE CONSEQUENCES OF USING EXPLOSION MAGIC RIGHT HERE!
SHE MUST BE BLUFFING! HURRY AND STOP THEM!
GIKU (FLINCH)
HOH! SO YOU'RE AFRAID OF ME…
…AND MY EXPLOSIONS!
GOOD. GREAT!
RUN AWAAAAY!
I ACCEPT YOUR CHALLENGE!

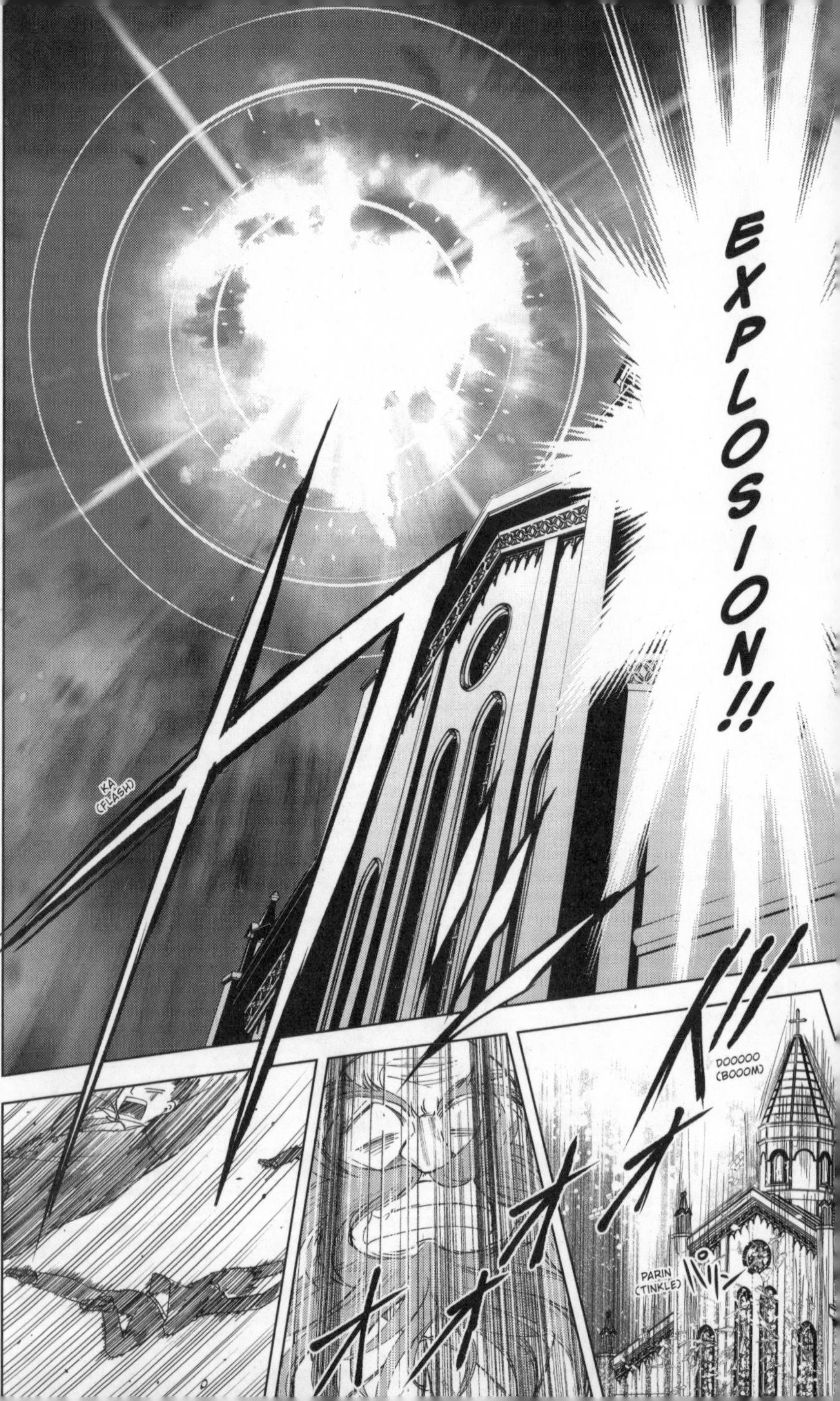
EXPLOSION!!
KA (FLASH)
DOOOOO (BOOOM)
PARIN (TINKLE)

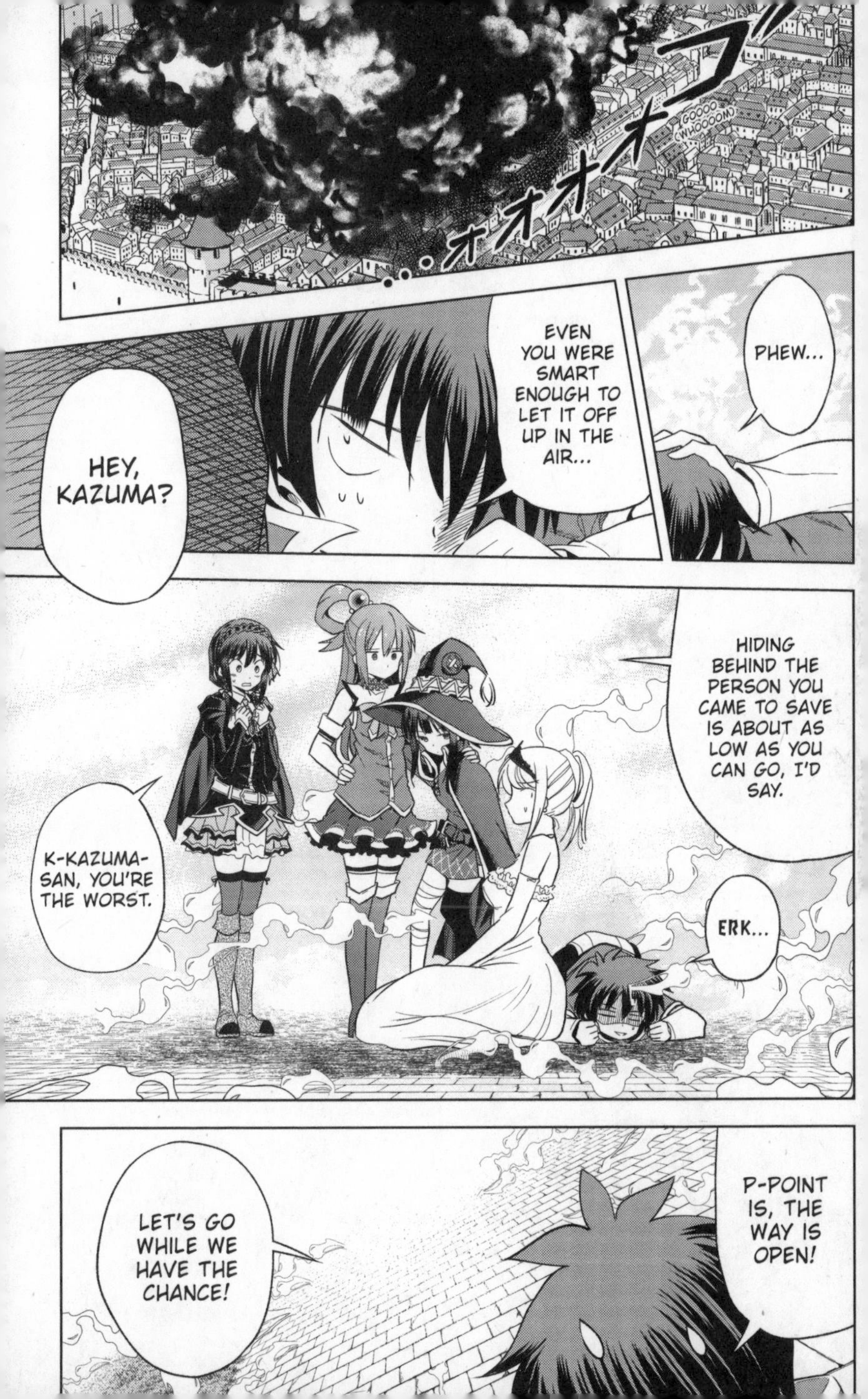
GOOOO (WHOOOOM)
PHEW...
EVEN YOU WERE SMART ENOUGH TO LET IT OFF UP IN THE AIR...
HEY, KAZUMA?
HIDING BEHIND THE PERSON YOU CAME TO SAVE IS ABOUT AS LOW AS YOU CAN GO, I'D SAY.
ERK...
K-KAZUMA-SAN, YOU'RE THE WORST.
P-POINT IS, THE WAY IS OPEN!
LET'S GO WHILE WE HAVE THE CHANCE!

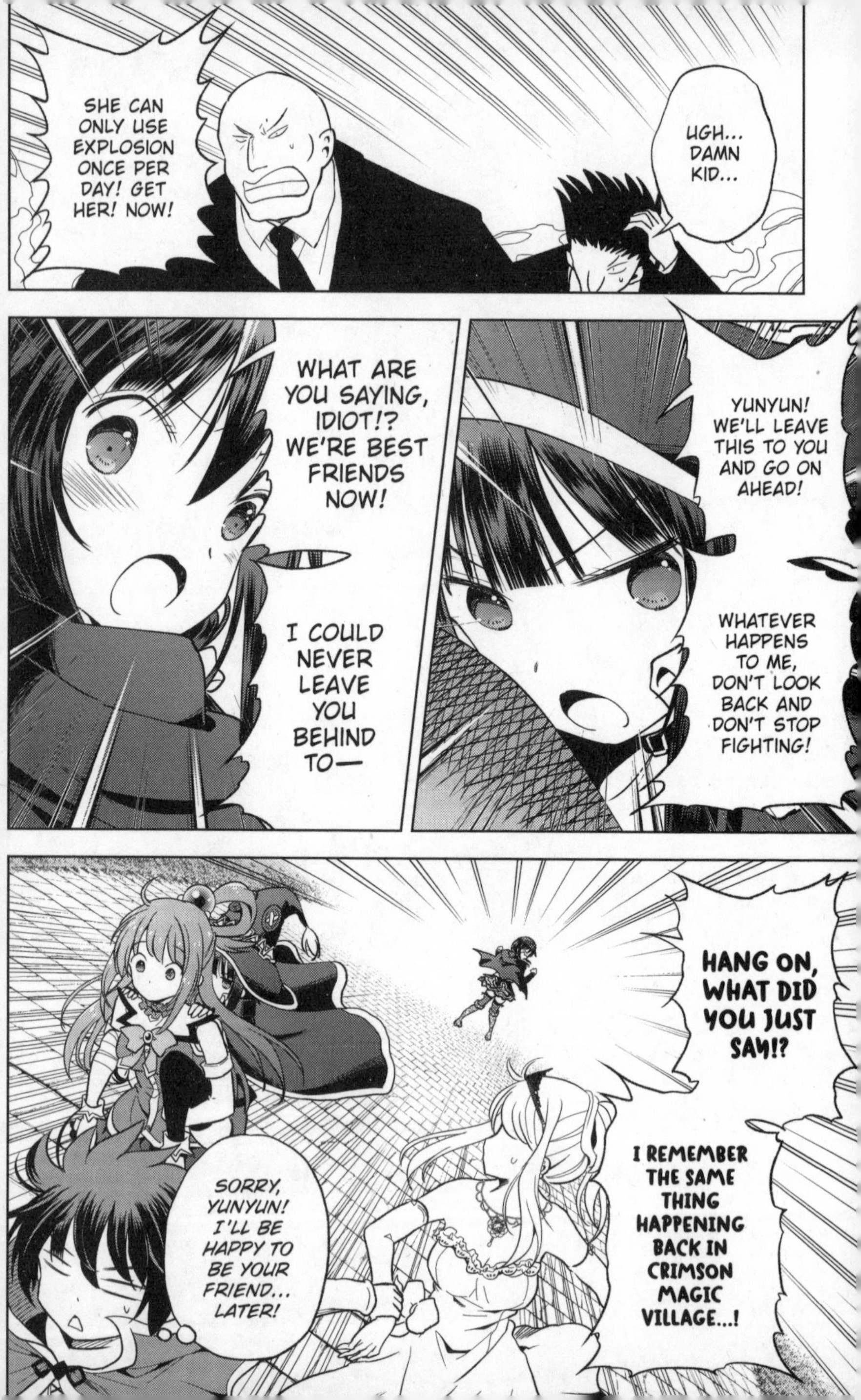
UGH... DAMN KID...
SHE CAN ONLY USE EXPLOSION ONCE PER DAY! GET HER! NOW!
YUNYUN! WE'LL LEAVE THIS TO YOU AND GO ON AHEAD!
WHATEVER HAPPENS TO ME, DON'T LOOK BACK AND DON'T STOP FIGHTING!
WHAT ARE YOU SAYING, IDIOT!? WE'RE BEST FRIENDS NOW!
I COULD NEVER LEAVE YOU BEHIND TO—
HANG ON, WHAT DID YOU JUST SAY!?
I REMEMBER THE SAME THING HAPPENING BACK IN CRIMSON MAGIC VILLAGE...!
SORRY, YUNYUN! I'LL BE HAPPY TO BE YOUR FRIEND... LATER!

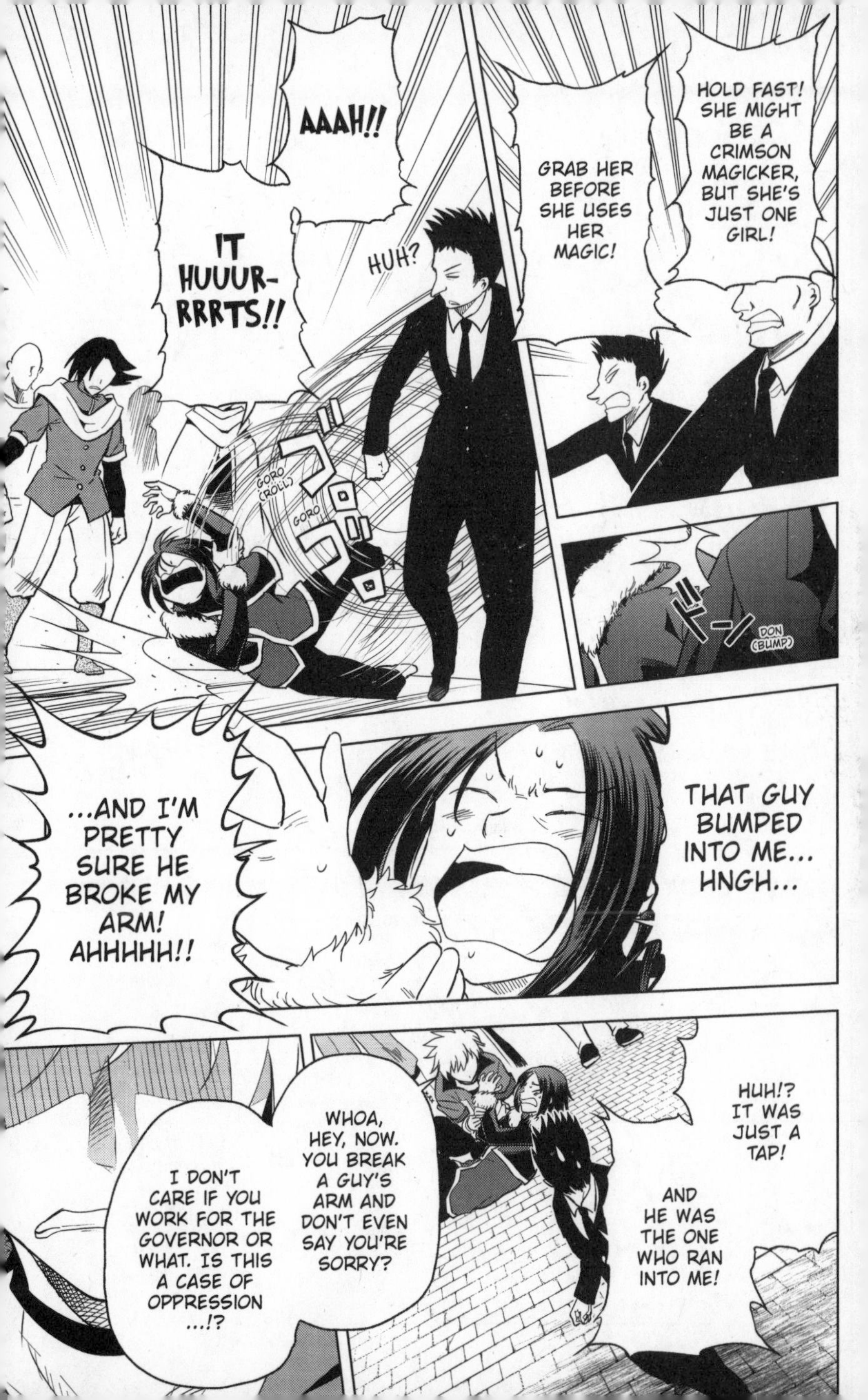
HOLD FAST! SHE MIGHT BE A CRIMSON MAGICKER, BUT SHE'S JUST ONE GIRL!
GRAB HER BEFORE SHE USES HER MAGIC!
DON (BUMP)
HUH?
AAAH!!
IT HUUUR-RRRTS!!
GORO (ROLL)
GORO
THAT GUY BUMPED INTO ME... HNGH...
...AND I'M PRETTY SURE HE BROKE MY ARM! AHHHHH!!
HUH!? IT WAS JUST A TAP!
AND HE WAS THE ONE WHO RAN INTO ME!
WHOA, HEY, NOW. YOU BREAK A GUY'S ARM AND DON'T EVEN SAY YOU'RE SORRY?
I DON'T CARE IF YOU WORK FOR THE GOVERNOR OR WHAT. IS THIS A CASE OF OPPRESSION ...!?

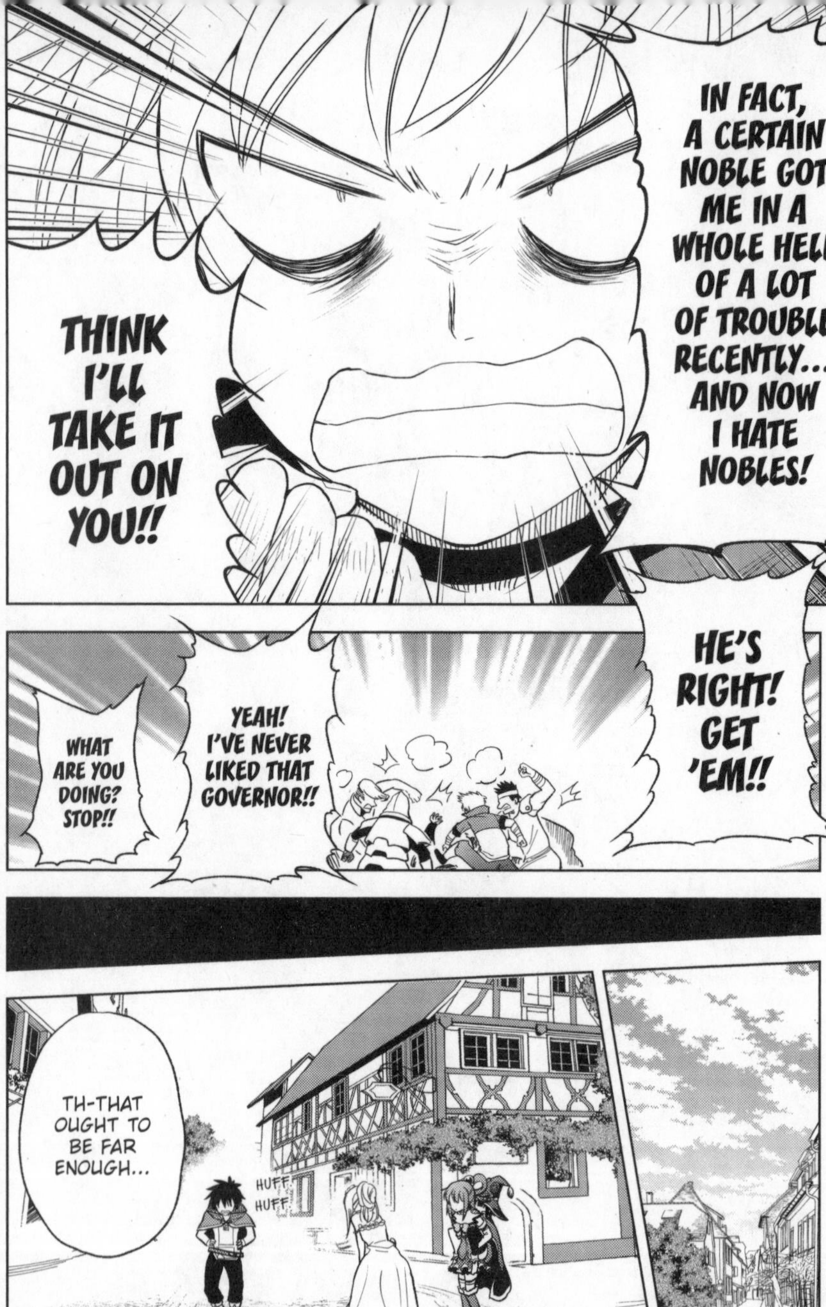
IN FACT, A CERTAIN NOBLE GOT ME IN A WHOLE HELL OF A LOT OF TROUBLE RECENTLY... AND NOW I HATE NOBLES!
THINK I'LL TAKE IT OUT ON YOU!!
HE'S RIGHT! GET 'EM!!
YEAH! I'VE NEVER LIKED THAT GOVERNOR!!
WHAT ARE YOU DOING? STOP!!
TH-THAT OUGHT TO BE FAR ENOUGH...
HUFF HUFF

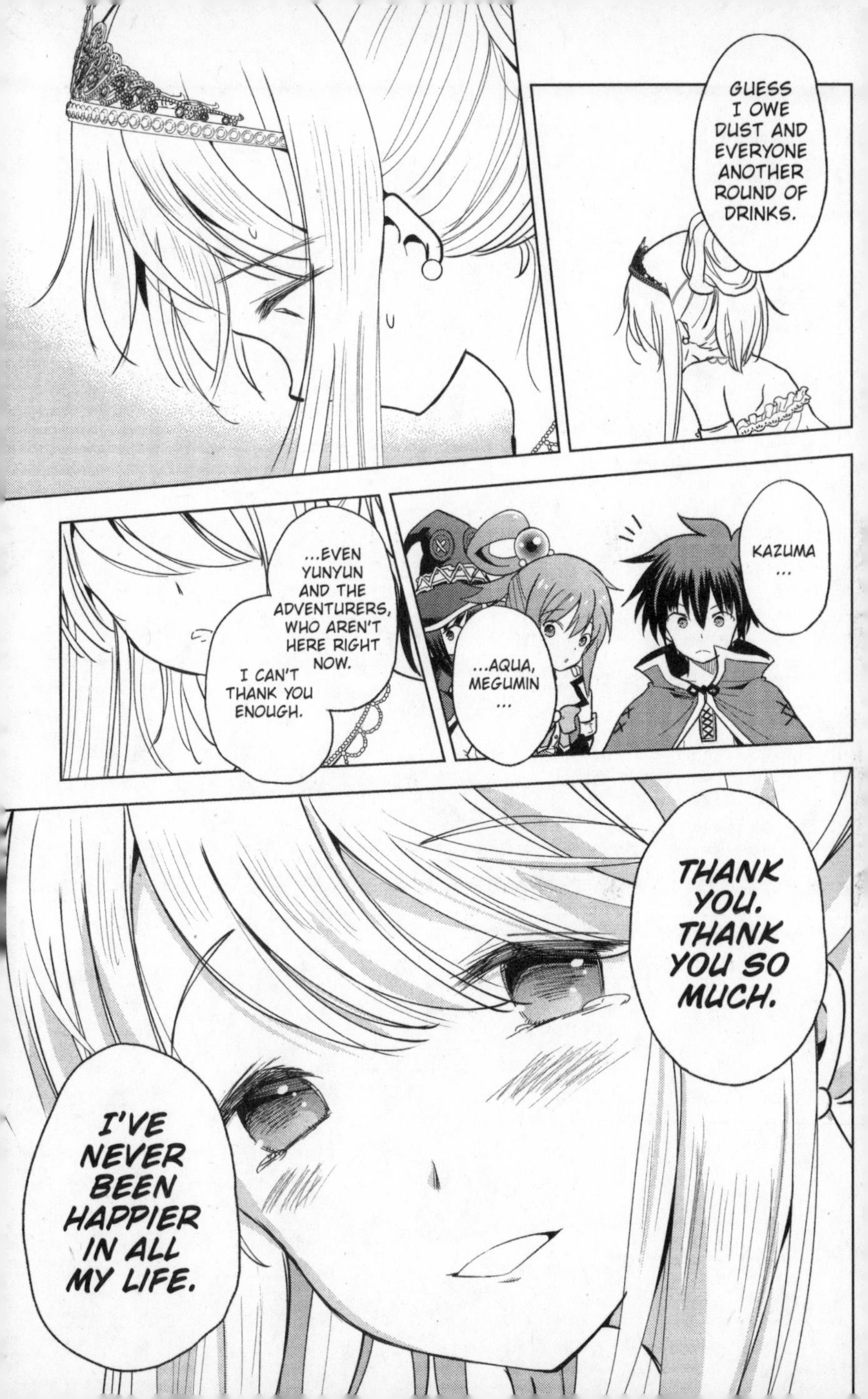
GUESS I OWE DUST AND EVERYONE ANOTHER ROUND OF DRINKS.
KAZUMA...
...AQUA, MEGUMIN...
...EVEN YUNYUN AND THE ADVENTURERS, WHO AREN'T HERE RIGHT NOW.
I CAN'T THANK YOU ENOUGH.
THANK YOU. THANK YOU SO MUCH.
I'VE NEVER BEEN HAPPIER IN ALL MY LIFE.

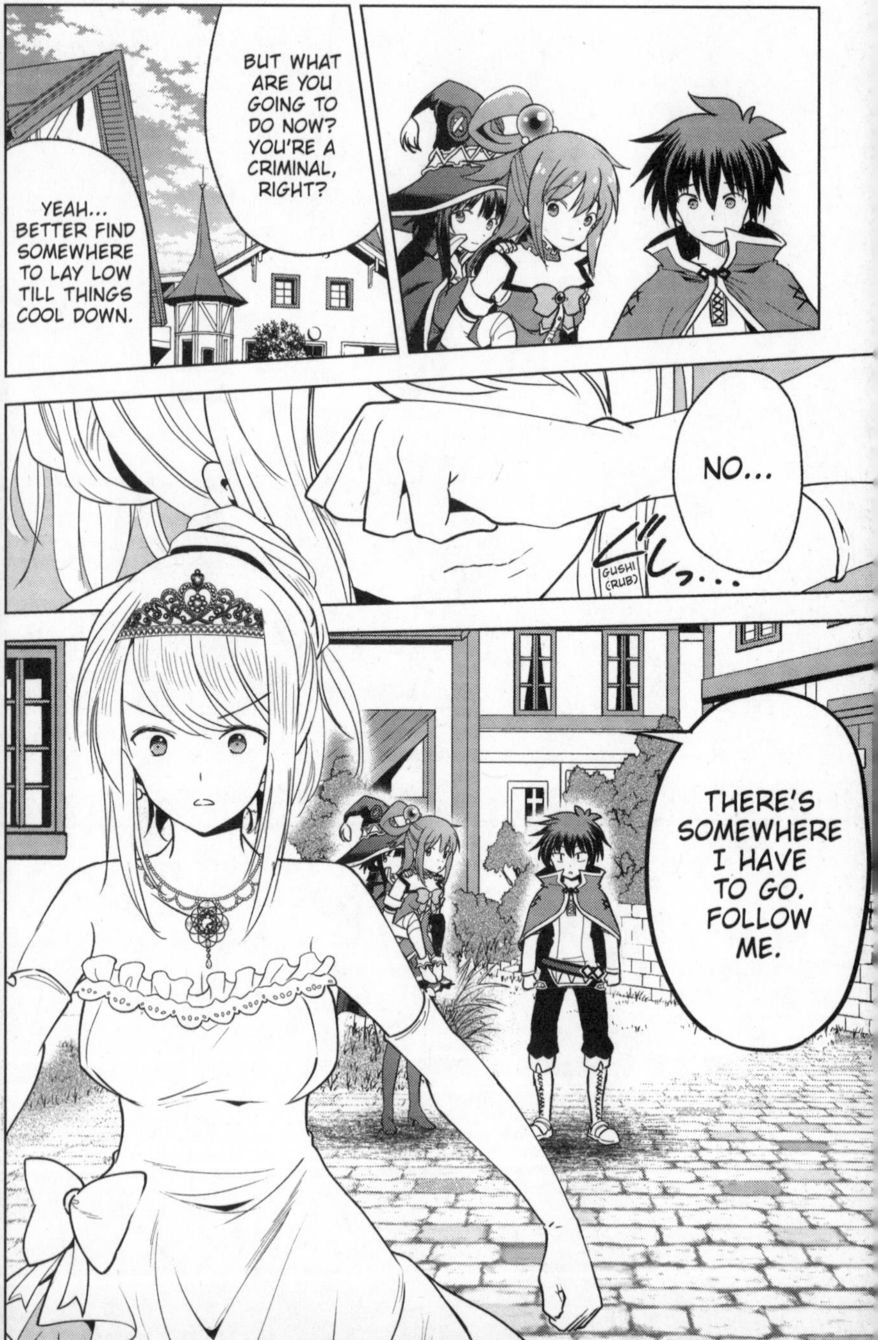
BUT WHAT ARE YOU GOING TO DO NOW? YOU'RE A CRIMINAL, RIGHT?
YEAH... BETTER FIND SOMEWHERE TO LAY LOW TILL THINGS COOL DOWN.
NO...
ぐしっ...
GUSHI (RUB)
THERE'S SOMEWHERE I HAVE TO GO. FOLLOW ME.

GOD'S
BLESSING
ON THIS
WONDERFUL
WORLD!

13

13

GOD'S
BLESSING
ON THIS
WONDERFUL
WORLD!

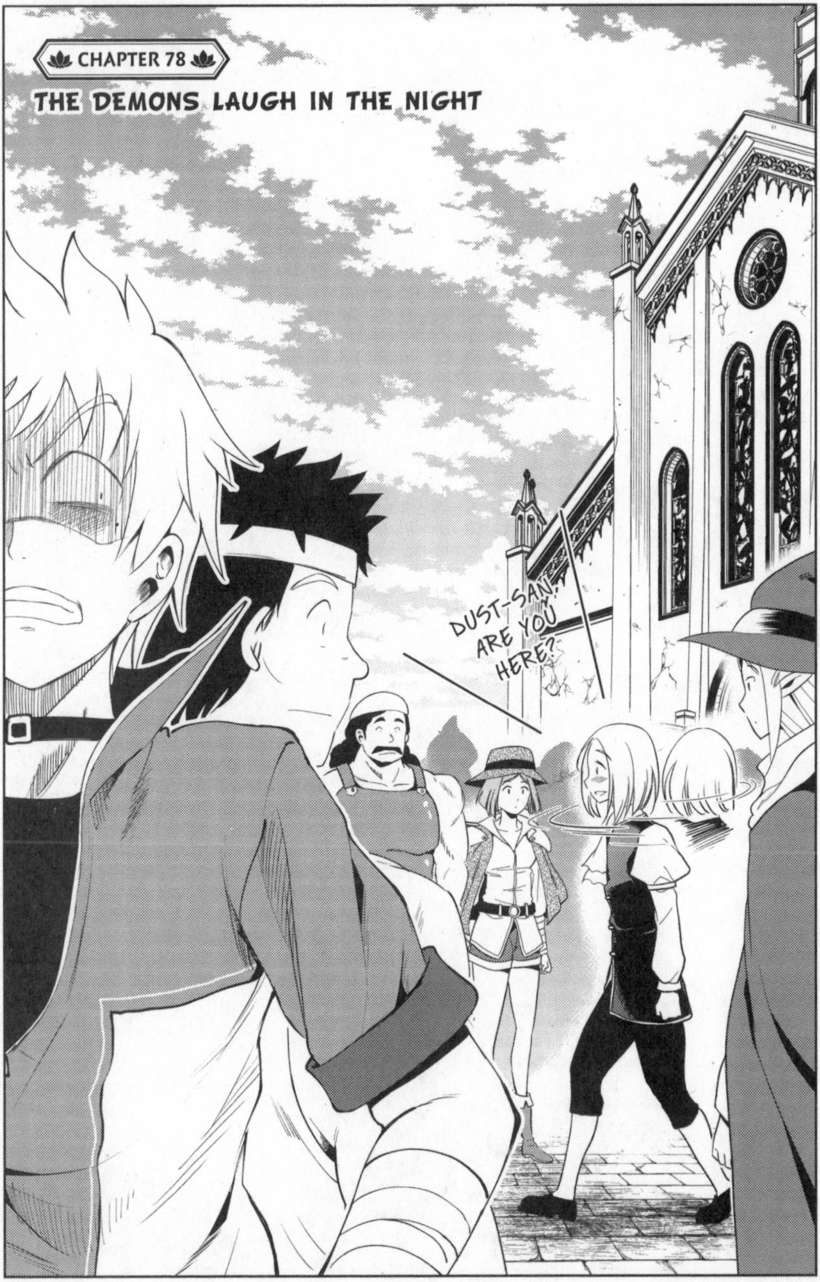
CHAPTER 78
THE DEMONS LAUGH IN THE NIGHT
DUST-SAN! ARE YOU HERE?

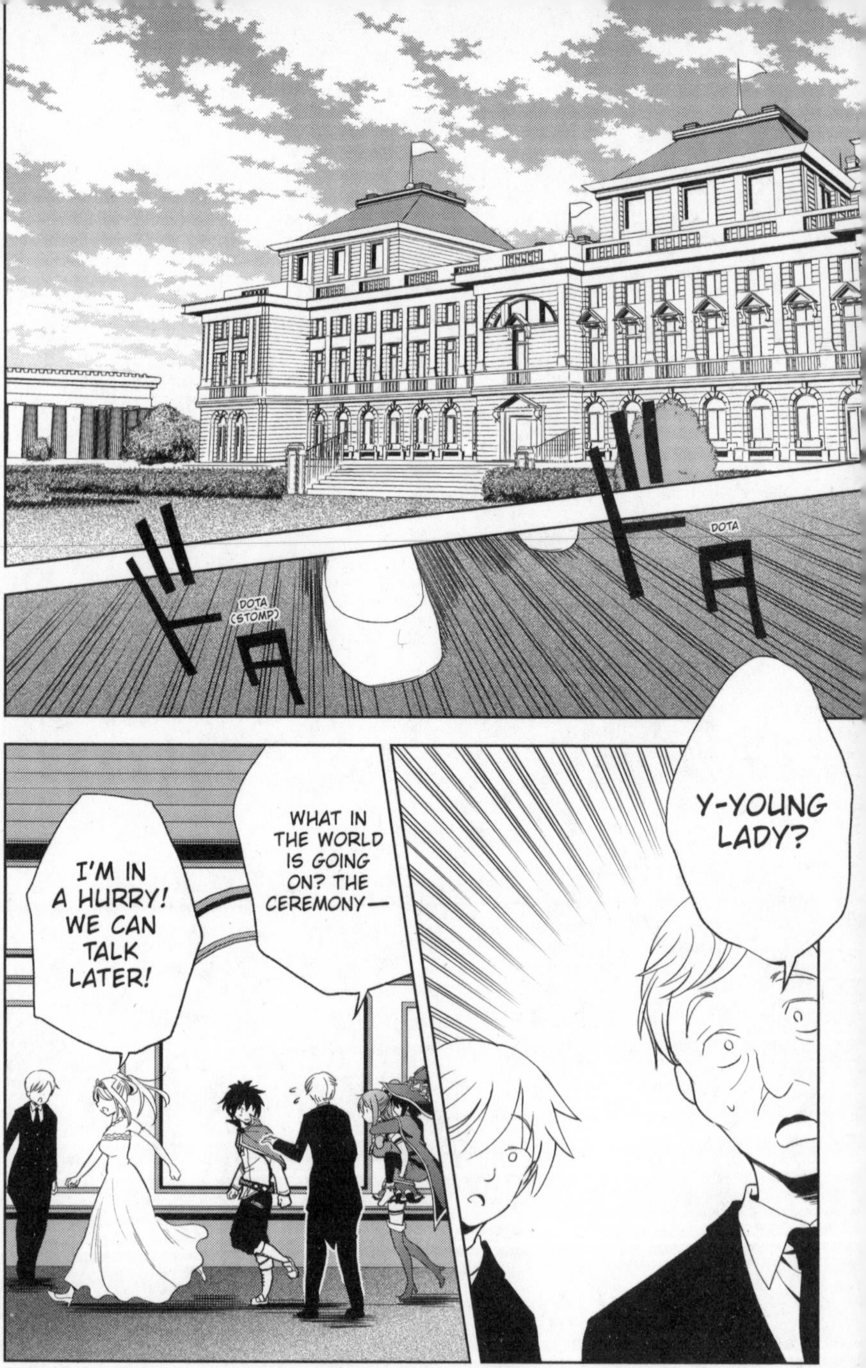
DOTA
DOTA (STOMP)
Y-YOUNG LADY?
WHAT IN THE WORLD IS GOING ON? THE CEREMONY—
I'M IN A HURRY! WE CAN TALK LATER!

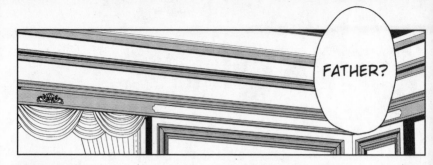

FATHER?

OH... LALATINA...

WHY ARE YOU HERE? I THOUGHT TODAY...

NO. ER...

FATHER, IT'S ME...

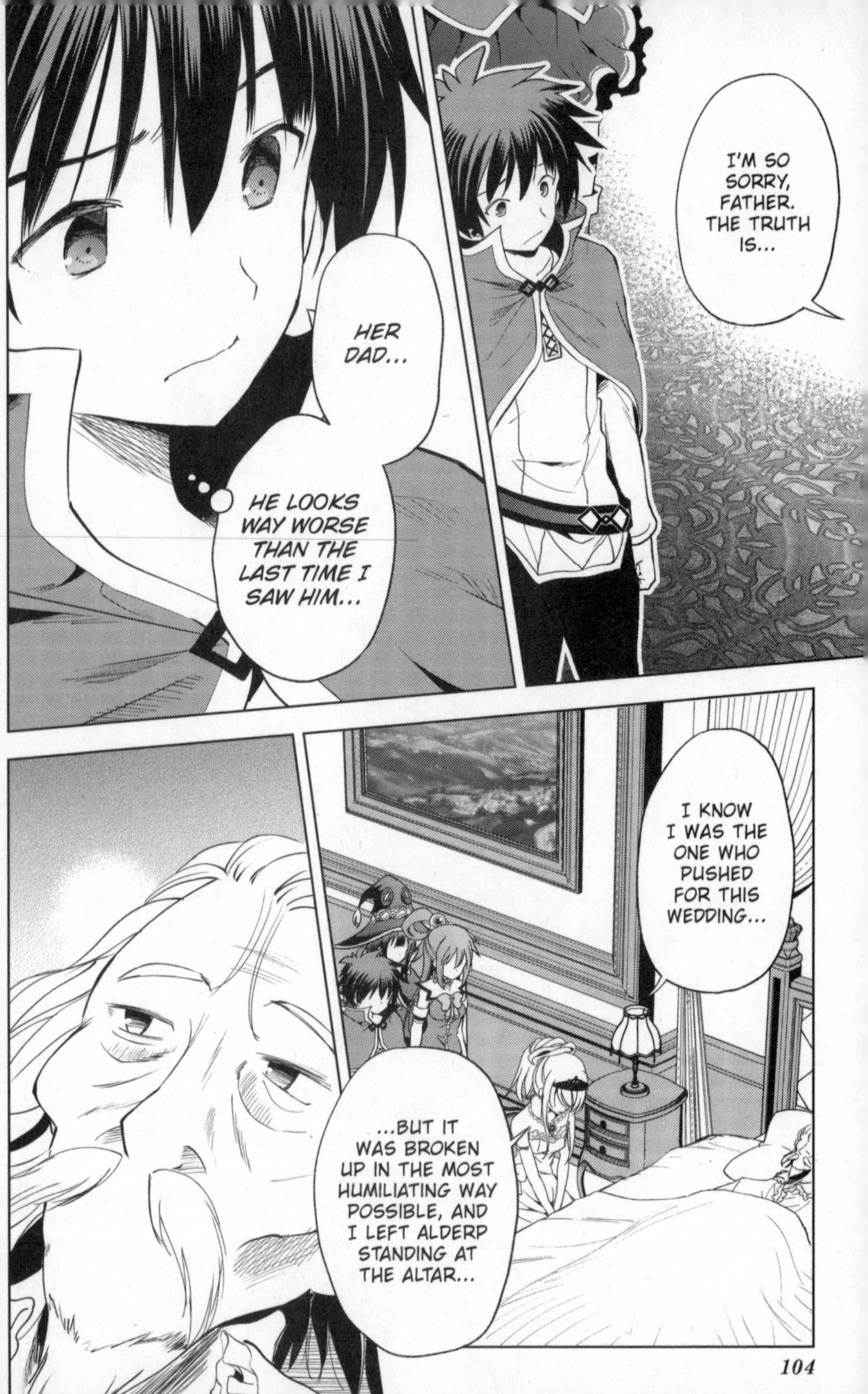
I'M SO SORRY, FATHER. THE TRUTH IS...
HER DAD...
HE LOOKS WAY WORSE THAN THE LAST TIME I SAW HIM...
I KNOW I WAS THE ONE WHO PUSHED FOR THIS WEDDING...
...BUT IT WAS BROKEN UP IN THE MOST HUMILIATING WAY POSSIBLE, AND I LEFT ALDERP STANDING AT THE ALTAR...

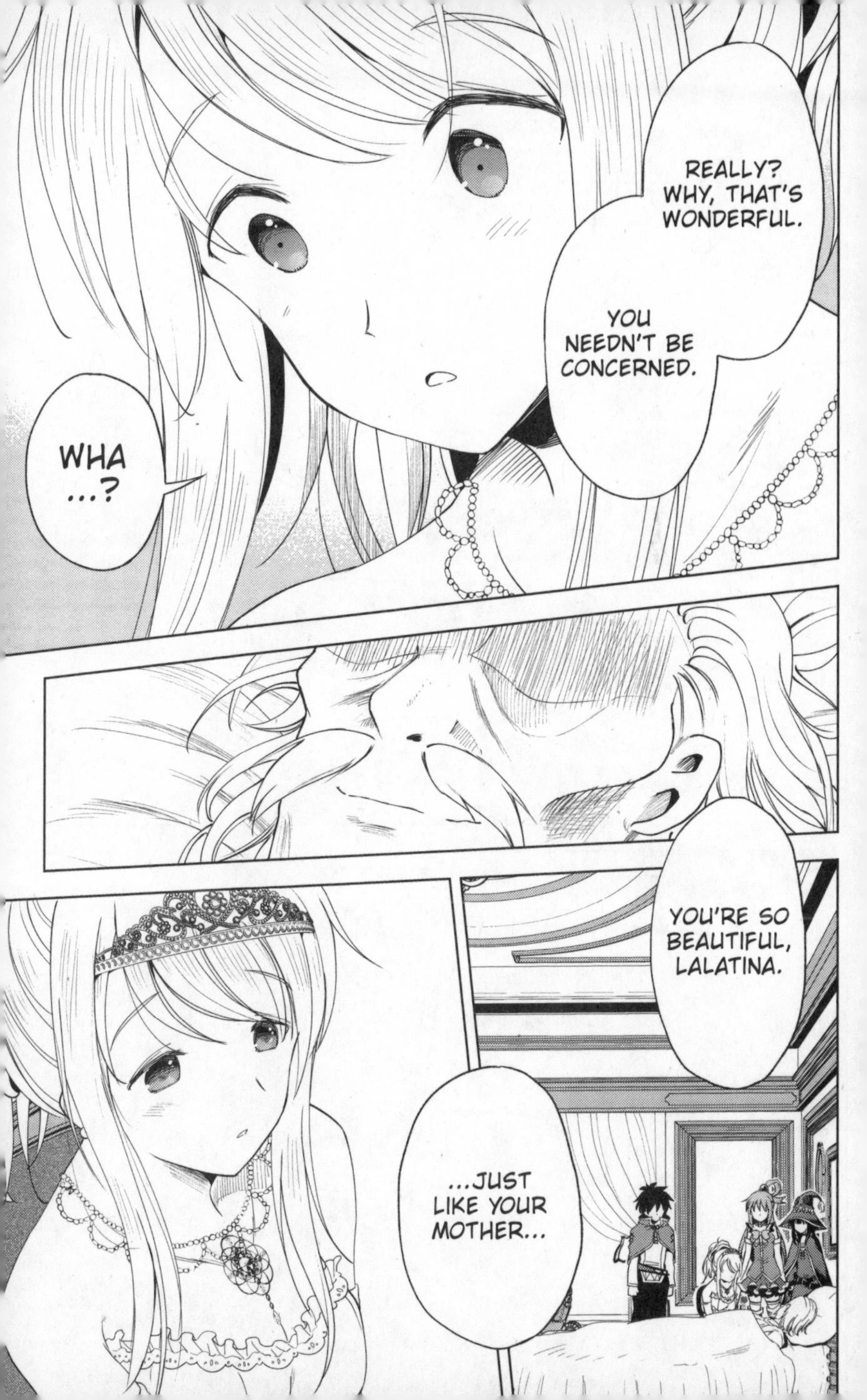
REALLY? WHY, THAT'S WONDERFUL.
YOU NEEDN'T BE CONCERNED.
WHA ...?
YOU'RE SO BEAUTIFUL, LALATINA.
...JUST LIKE YOUR MOTHER...

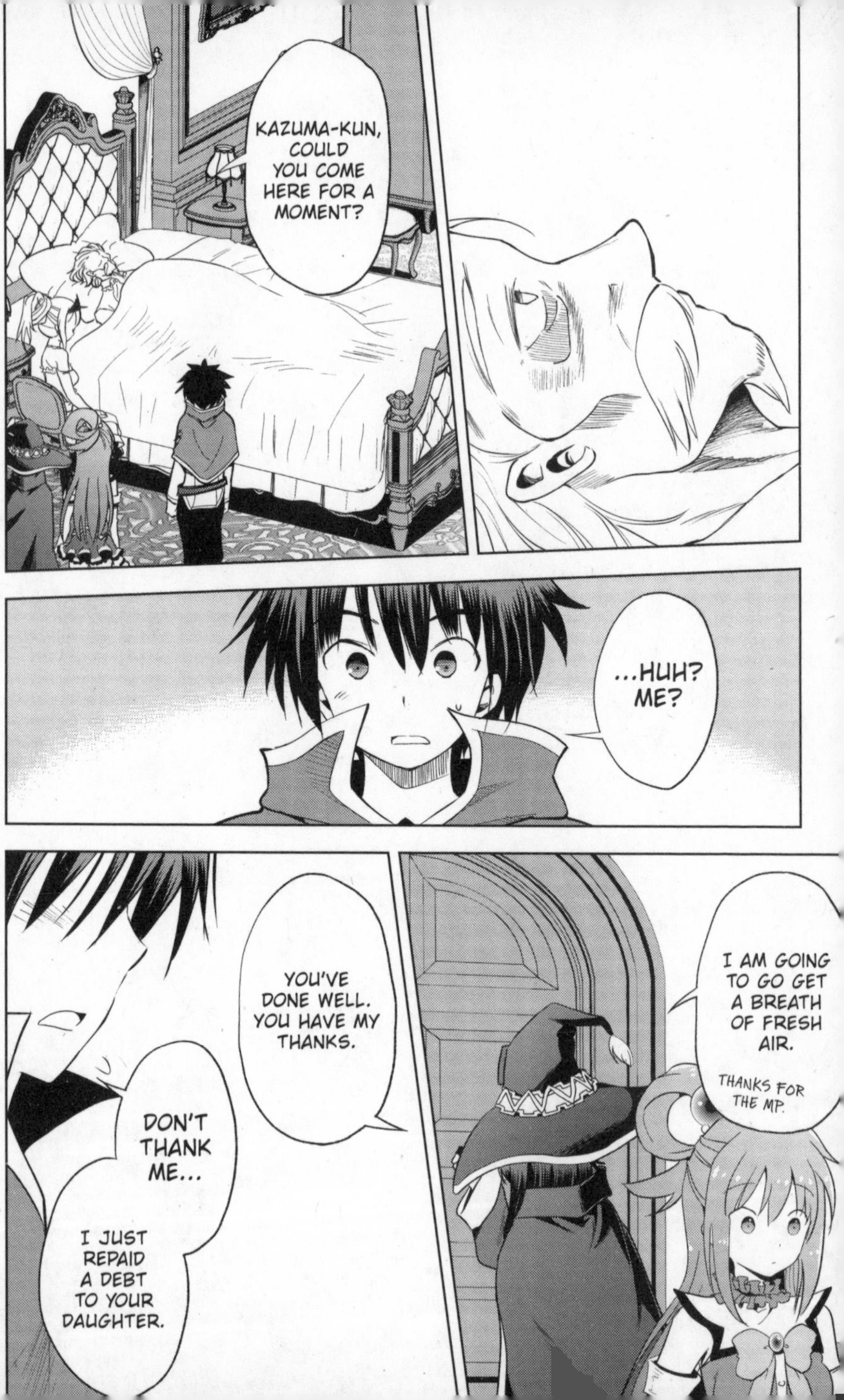
KAZUMA-KUN, COULD YOU COME HERE FOR A MOMENT?
...HUH? ME?
I AM GOING TO GO GET A BREATH OF FRESH AIR.
THANKS FOR THE MP.
YOU'VE DONE WELL. YOU HAVE MY THANKS.
DON'T THANK ME...
I JUST REPAID A DEBT TO YOUR DAUGHTER.

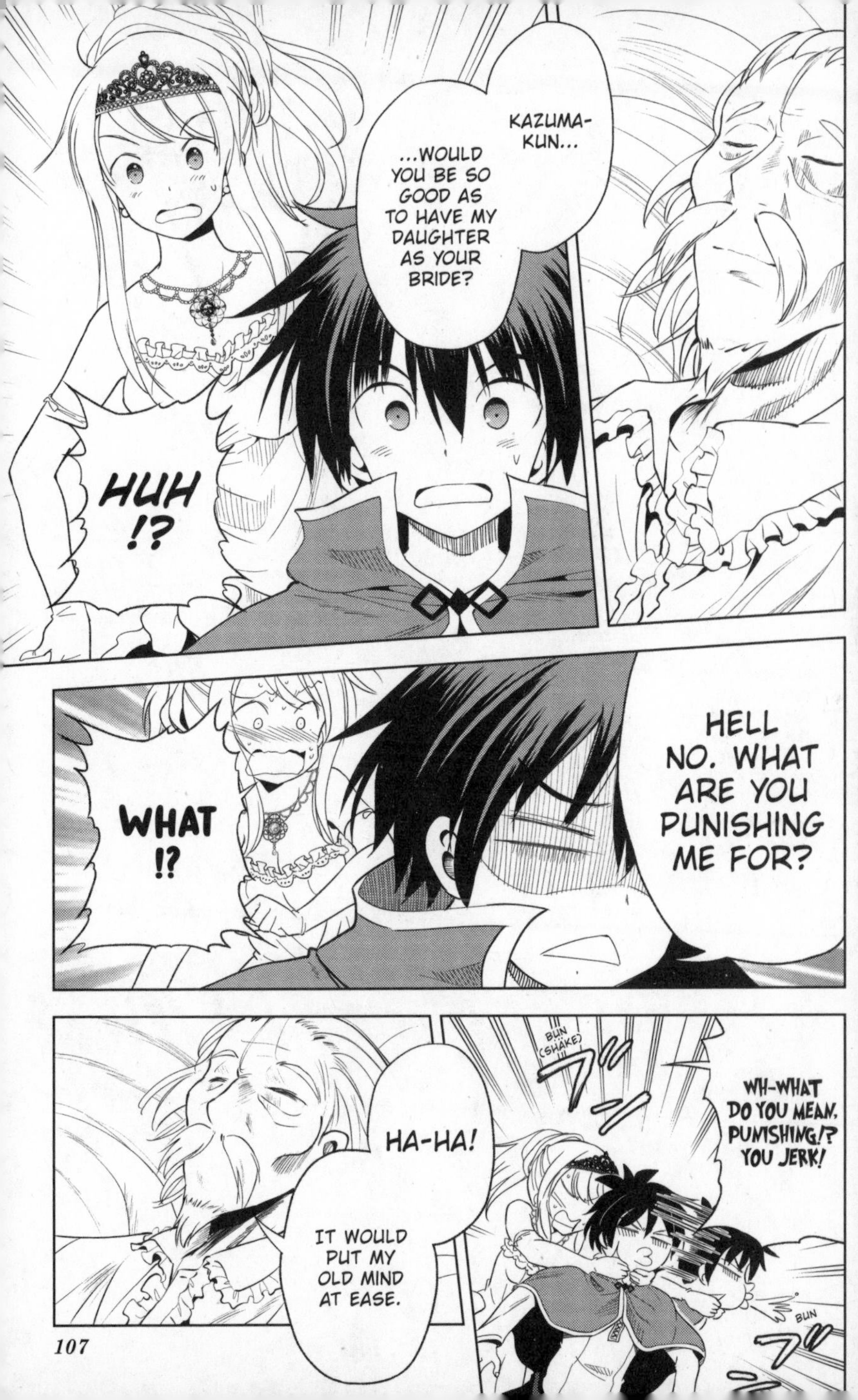
KAZUMA-KUN...
...WOULD YOU BE SO GOOD AS TO HAVE MY DAUGHTER AS YOUR BRIDE?
HUH !?
HELL NO. WHAT ARE YOU PUNISHING ME FOR?
WHAT !?
BUN (SHAKE)
WH-WHAT DO YOU MEAN, PUNISHING!? YOU JERK!
BUN
HA-HA!
IT WOULD PUT MY OLD MIND AT EASE.

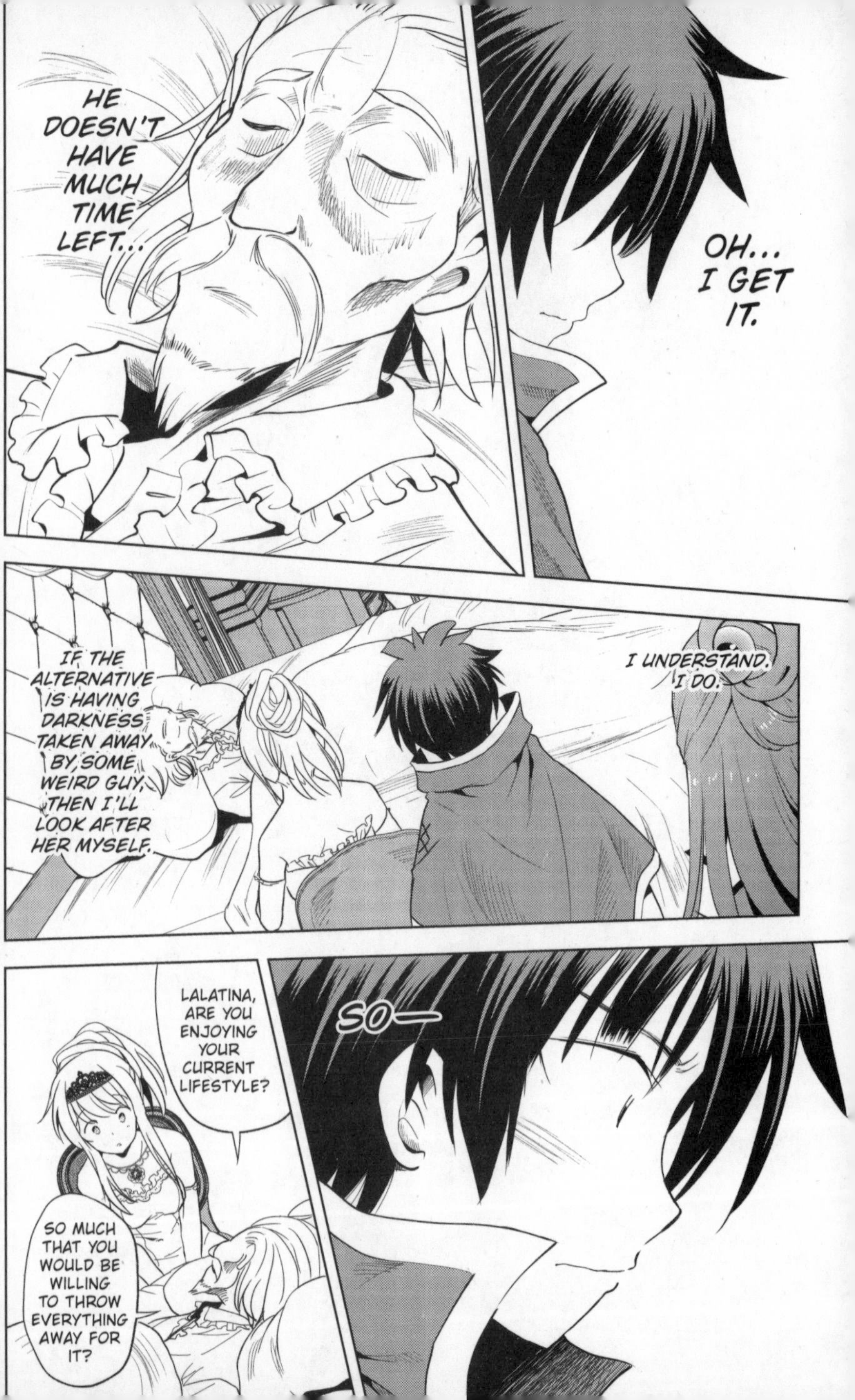
OH... I GET IT.
HE DOESN'T HAVE MUCH TIME LEFT...
I UNDERSTAND. I DO.
IF THE ALTERNATIVE IS HAVING DARKNESS TAKEN AWAY BY SOME WEIRD GUY, THEN I'LL LOOK AFTER HER MYSELF.
SO—
LALATINA, ARE YOU ENJOYING YOUR CURRENT LIFESTYLE?
SO MUCH THAT YOU WOULD BE WILLING TO THROW EVERYTHING AWAY FOR IT?

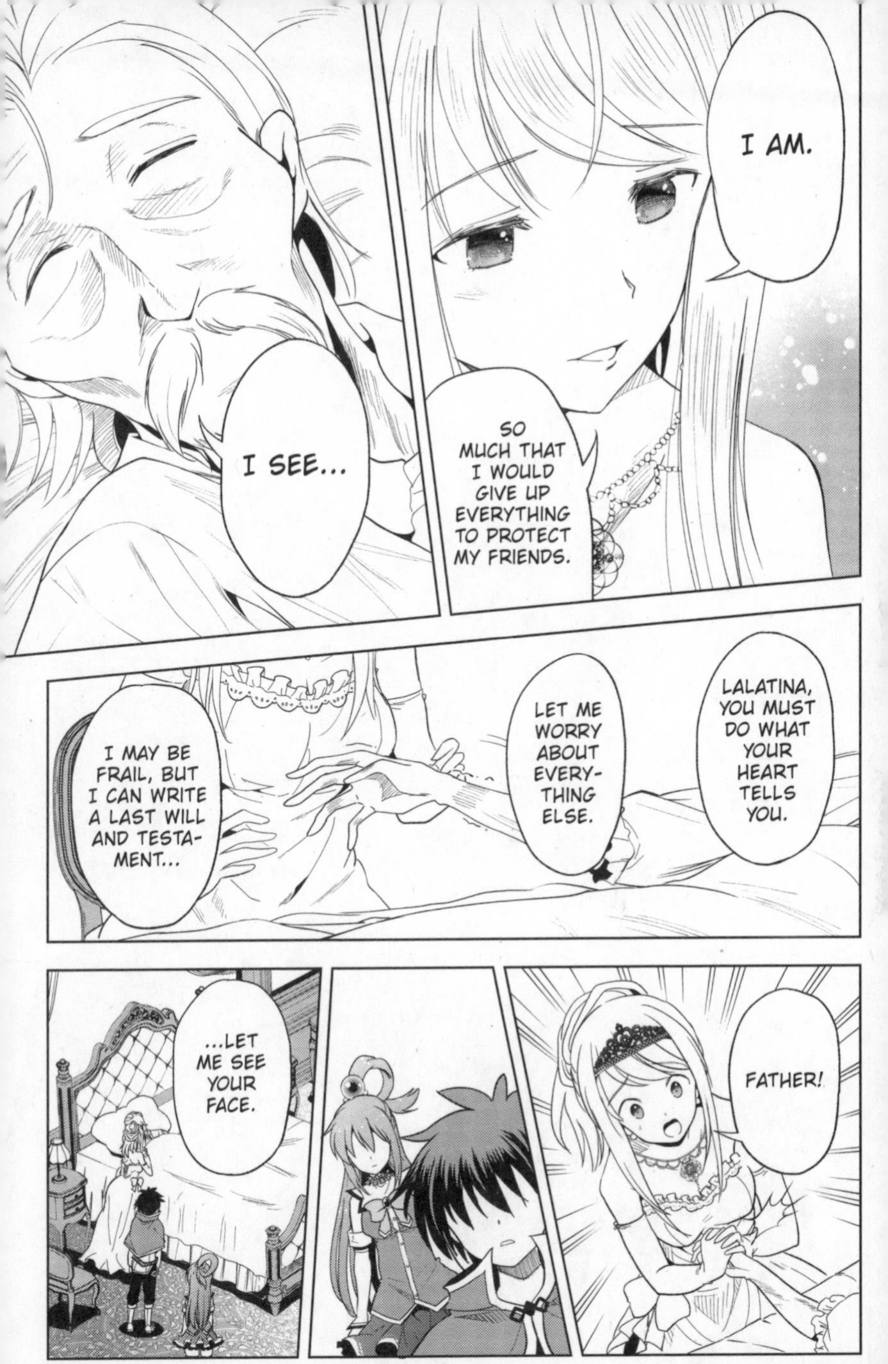
I AM.
SO MUCH THAT I WOULD GIVE UP EVERYTHING TO PROTECT MY FRIENDS.
I SEE...
LALATINA, YOU MUST DO WHAT YOUR HEART TELLS YOU.
LET ME WORRY ABOUT EVERY-THING ELSE.
I MAY BE FRAIL, BUT I CAN WRITE A LAST WILL AND TESTA-MENT...
FATHER!
...LET ME SEE YOUR FACE.

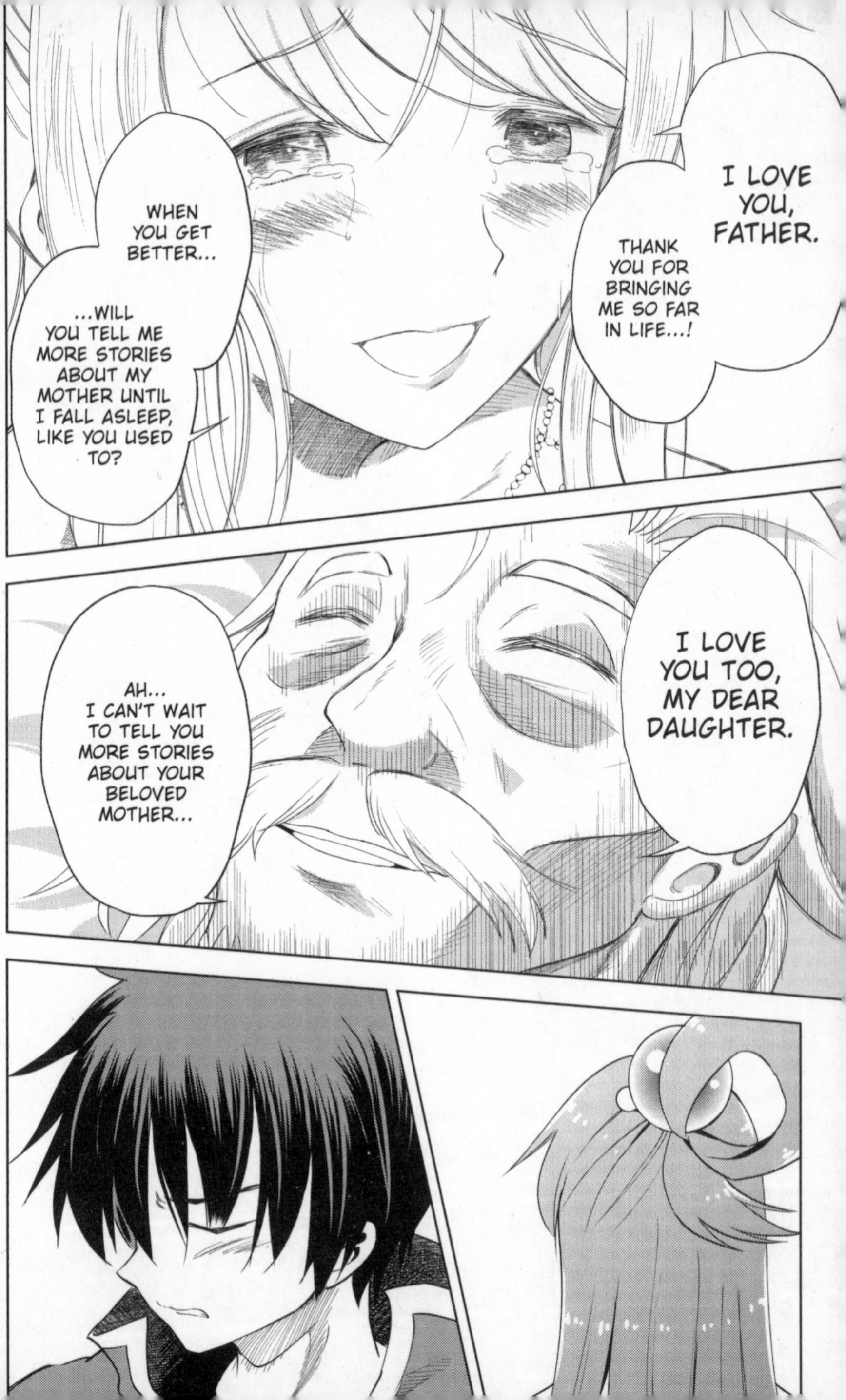
I LOVE YOU, FATHER.
THANK YOU FOR BRINGING ME SO FAR IN LIFE...!
WHEN YOU GET BETTER...
...WILL YOU TELL ME MORE STORIES ABOUT MY MOTHER UNTIL I FALL ASLEEP, LIKE YOU USED TO?
I LOVE YOU TOO, MY DEAR DAUGHTER.
AH... I CAN'T WAIT TO TELL YOU MORE STORIES ABOUT YOUR BELOVED MOTHER...

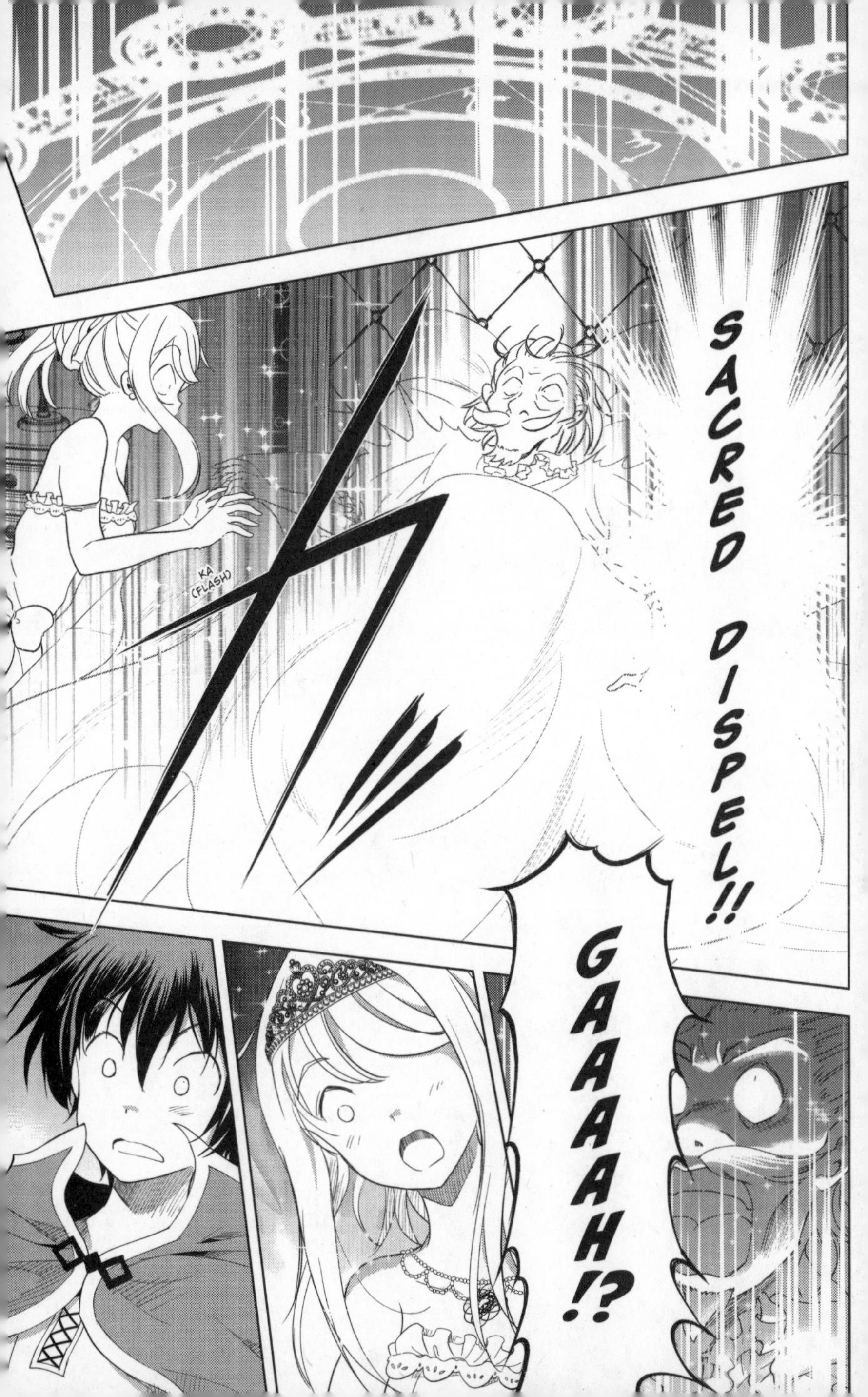
KA (FLASH)
SACRED DISPEL!!
GAAAAAH!?

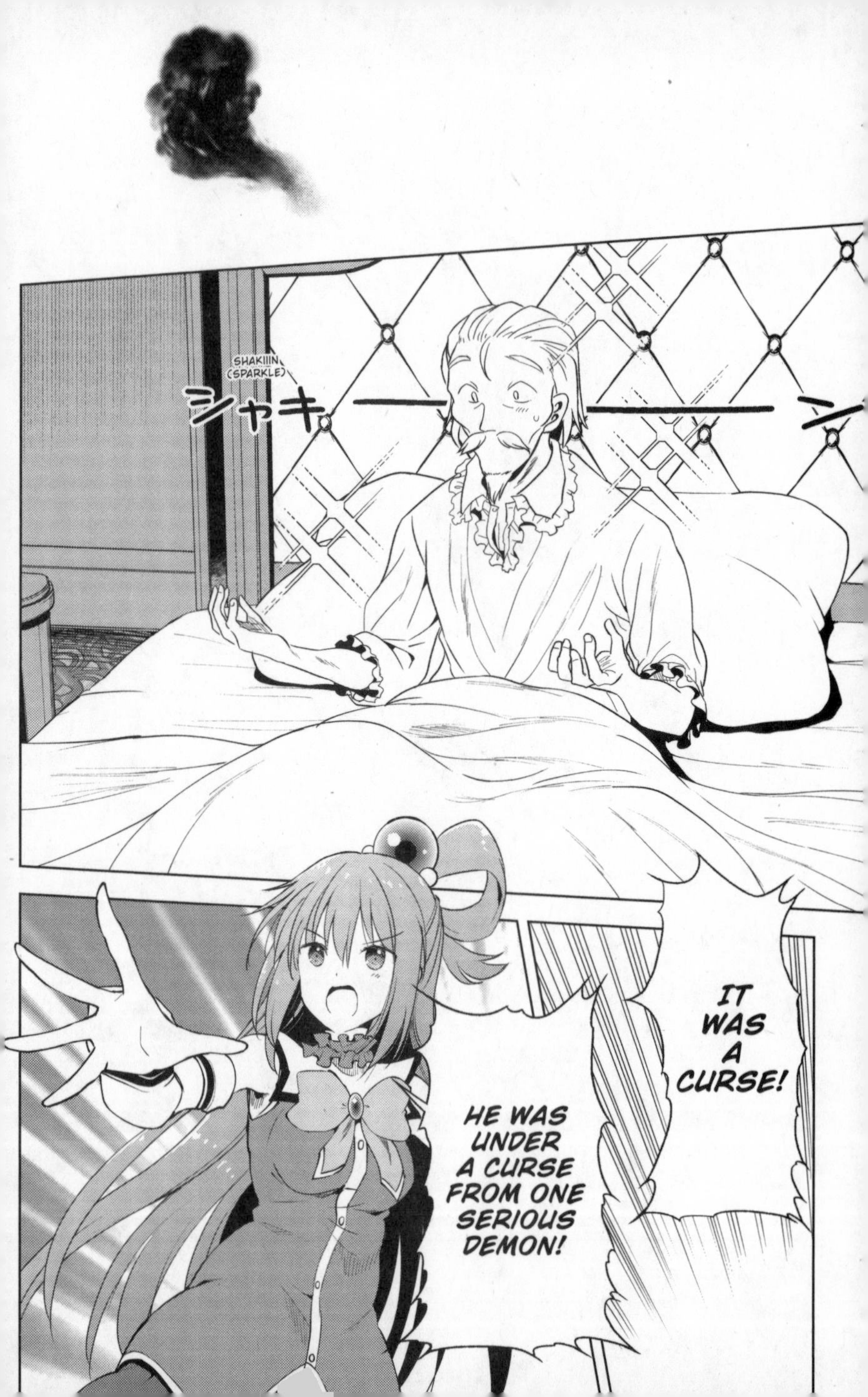
SHAKIIIN (SPARKLE)
シャキーーーン
IT WAS A CURSE!
HE WAS UNDER A CURSE FROM ONE SERIOUS DEMON!

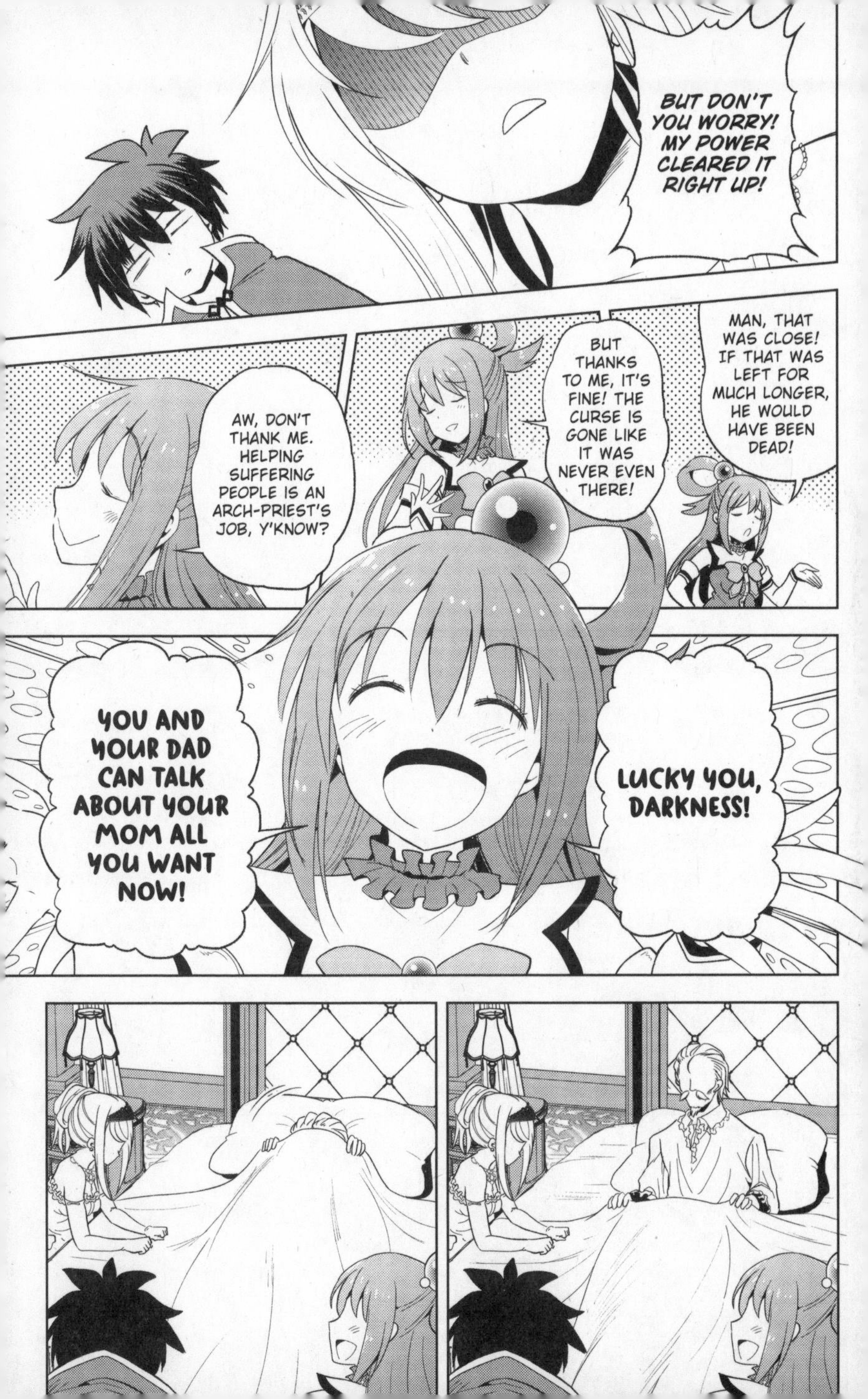
BUT DON'T YOU WORRY! MY POWER CLEARED IT RIGHT UP!
MAN, THAT WAS CLOSE! IF THAT WAS LEFT FOR MUCH LONGER, HE WOULD HAVE BEEN DEAD!
BUT THANKS TO ME, IT'S FINE! THE CURSE IS GONE LIKE IT WAS NEVER EVEN THERE!
AW, DON'T THANK ME. HELPING SUFFERING PEOPLE IS AN ARCH-PRIEST'S JOB, Y'KNOW?
LUCKY YOU, DARKNESS!
YOU AND YOUR DAD CAN TALK ABOUT YOUR MOM ALL YOU WANT NOW!

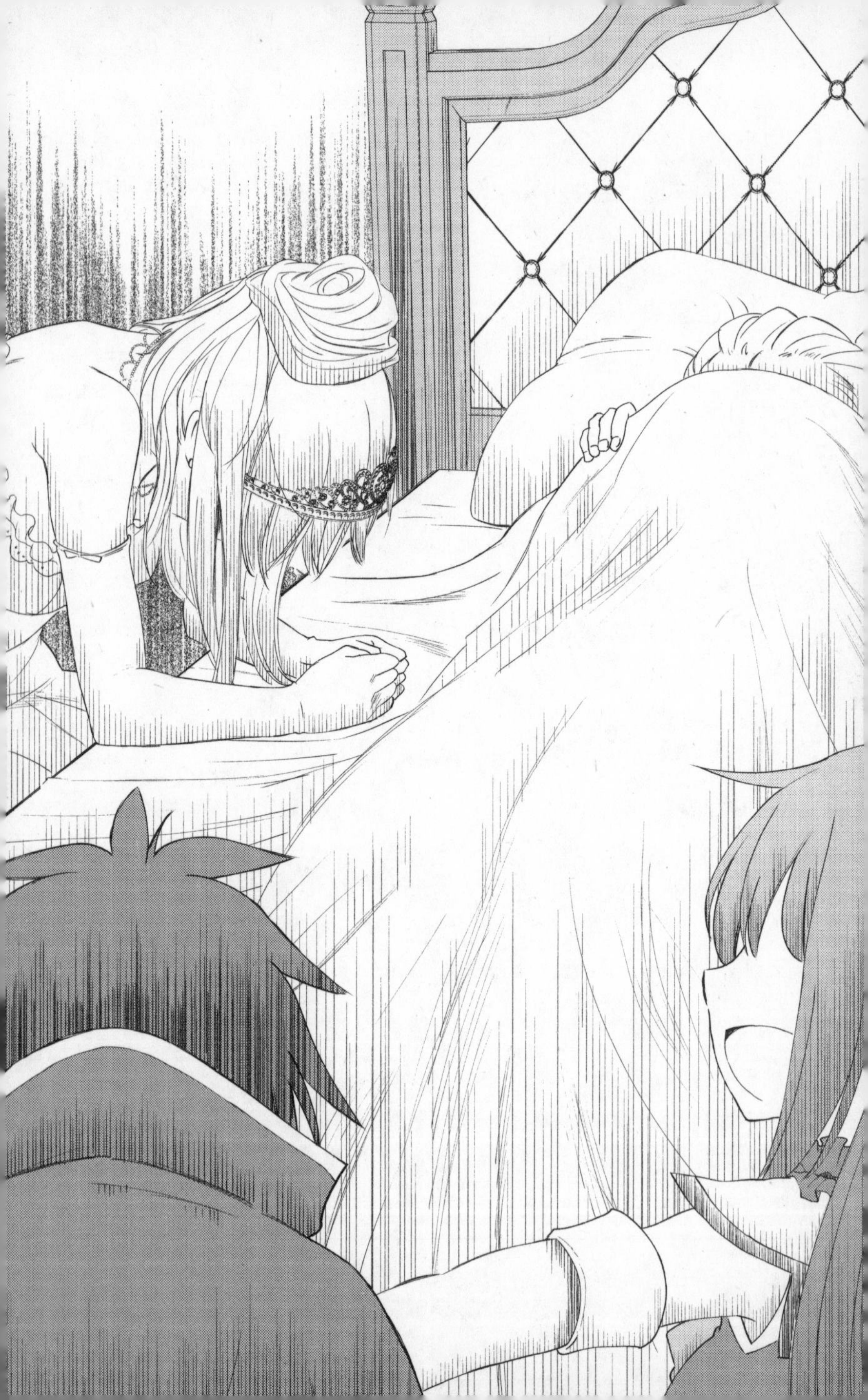

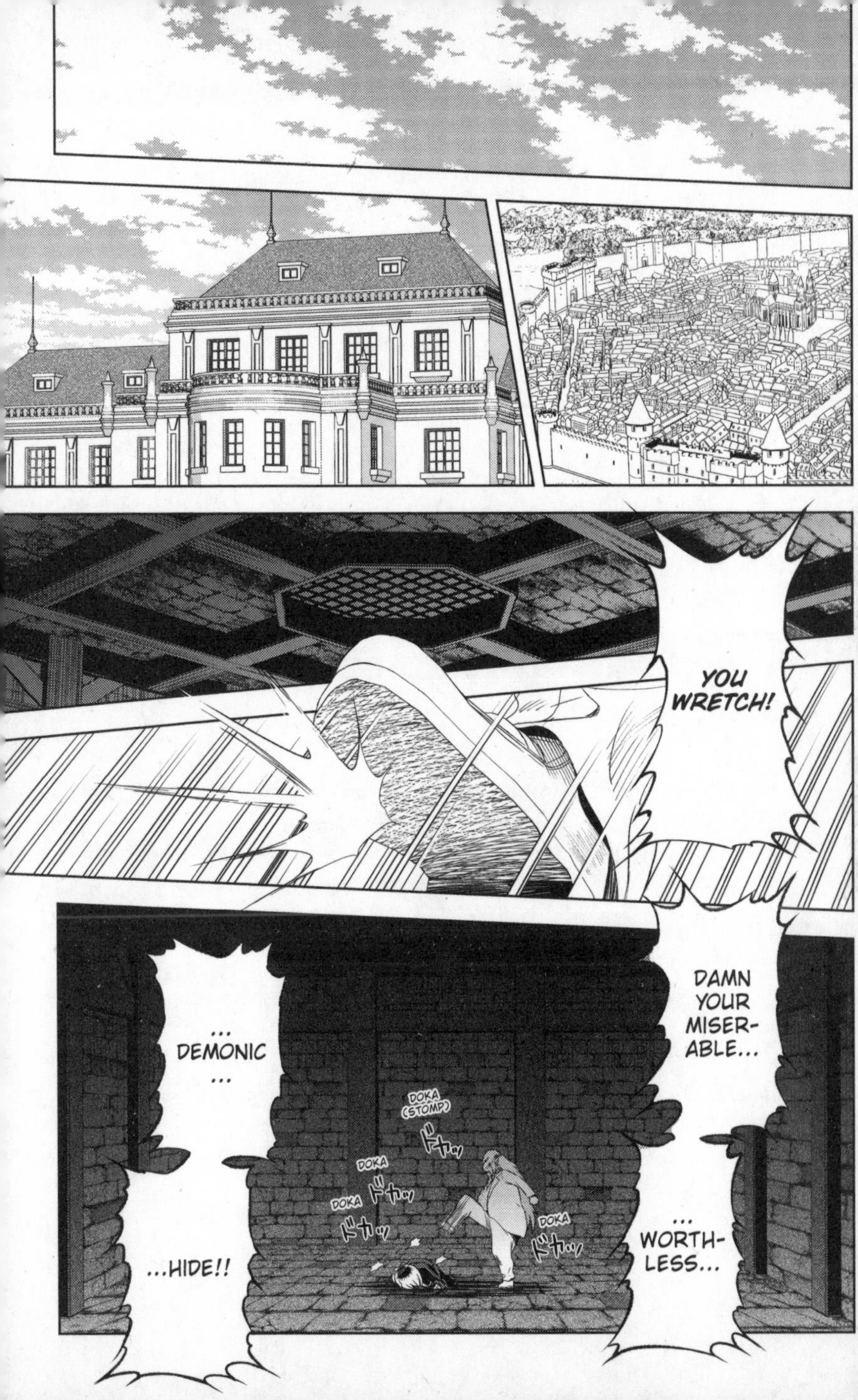
YOU WRETCH!
DAMN YOUR MISER-ABLE...
...WORTH-LESS...
DOKA (STOMP) ドカッ
DOKA ドカッ
DOKA ドカッ
DOKA ドカッ
...DEMONIC...
...HIDE!!

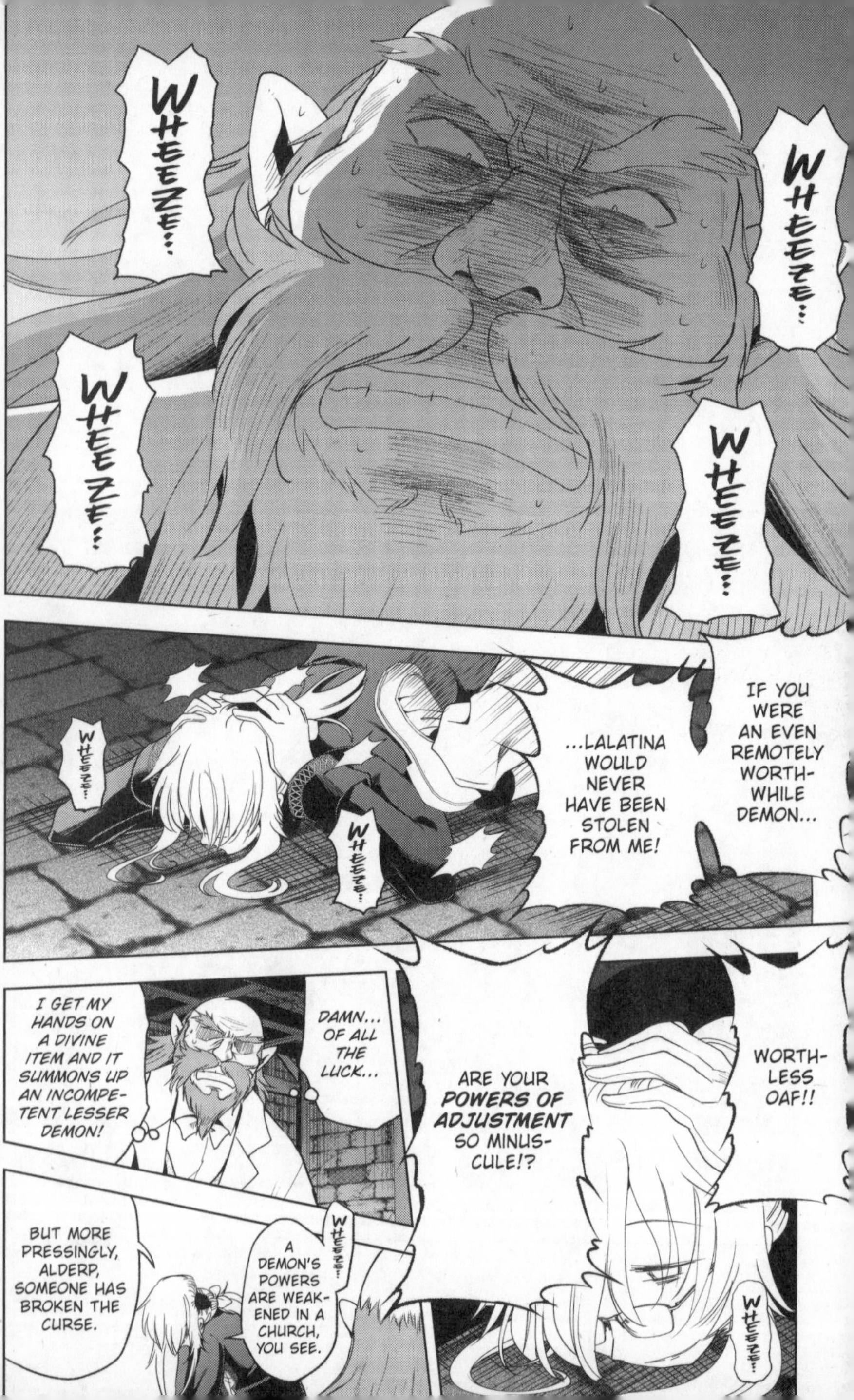

WHEEZE...
WHEEZE...
WHEEZE...
WHEEZE...
IF YOU WERE AN EVEN REMOTELY WORTHWHILE DEMON...
...LALATINA WOULD NEVER HAVE BEEN STOLEN FROM ME!
WHEEZE...
WHEEZE...
WORTHLESS OAF!!
ARE YOUR **POWERS OF ADJUSTMENT** SO MINUSCULE!?
WHEEZE...
DAMN... OF ALL THE LUCK...
I GET MY HANDS ON A DIVINE ITEM AND IT SUMMONS UP AN INCOMPETENT LESSER DEMON!
WHEEZE...
A DEMON'S POWERS ARE WEAKENED IN A CHURCH, YOU SEE.
BUT MORE PRESSINGLY, ALDERP, SOMEONE HAS BROKEN THE CURSE.

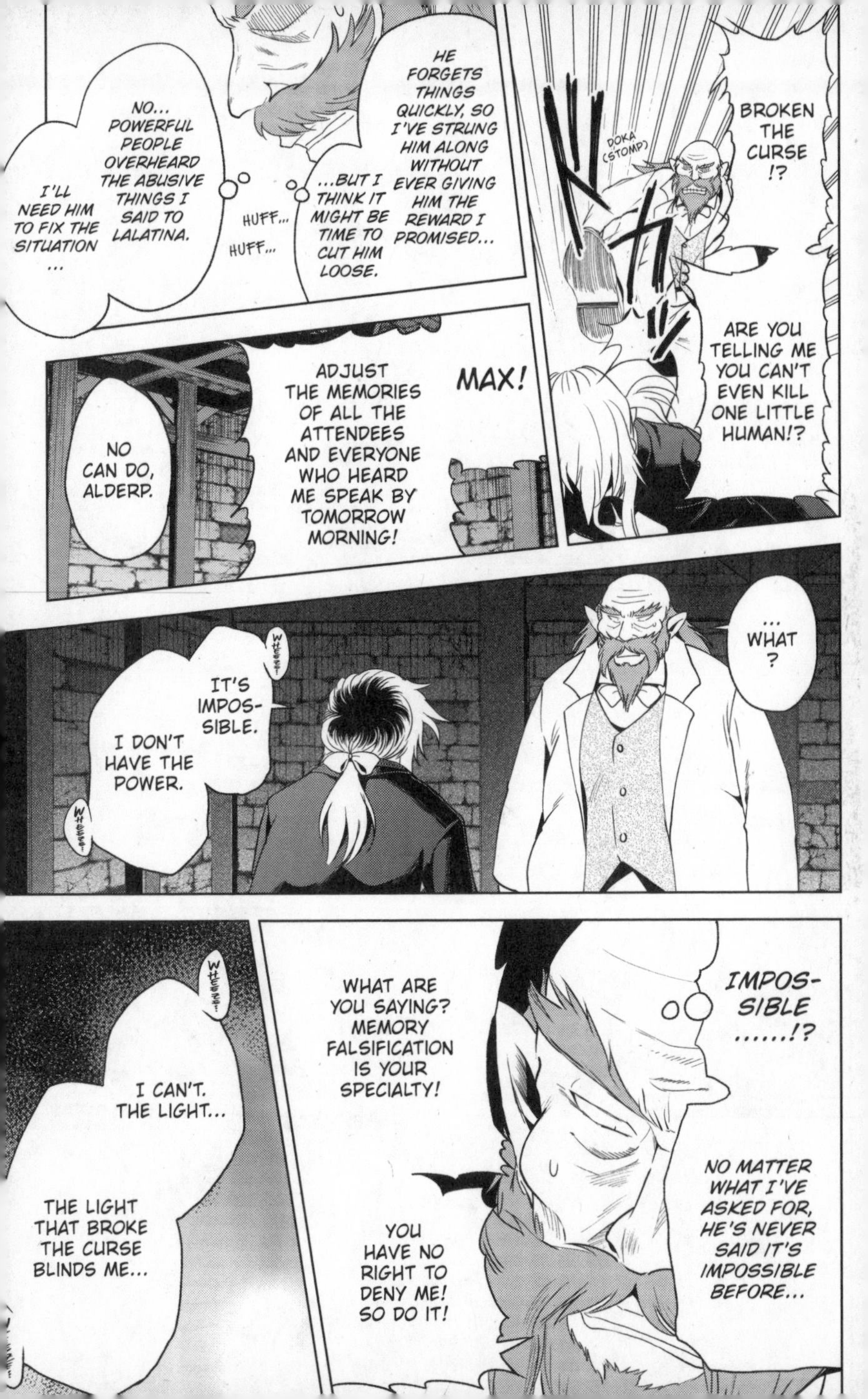
BROKEN THE CURSE!?
DOKA (STOMP)
ARE YOU TELLING ME YOU CAN'T EVEN KILL ONE LITTLE HUMAN!?
HE FORGETS THINGS QUICKLY, SO I'VE STRUNG HIM ALONG WITHOUT EVER GIVING HIM THE REWARD I PROMISED...
...BUT I THINK IT MIGHT BE TIME TO CUT HIM LOOSE.
HUFF...
HUFF...
NO... POWERFUL PEOPLE OVERHEARD THE ABUSIVE THINGS I SAID TO LALATINA.
I'LL NEED HIM TO FIX THE SITUATION...
MAX!
ADJUST THE MEMORIES OF ALL THE ATTENDEES AND EVERYONE WHO HEARD ME SPEAK BY TOMORROW MORNING!
NO CAN DO, ALDERP.
...WHAT?
WHEEZE...
IT'S IMPOSSIBLE.
I DON'T HAVE THE POWER.
WHEEZE...
IMPOSSIBLE......!?
WHAT ARE YOU SAYING? MEMORY FALSIFICATION IS YOUR SPECIALTY!
NO MATTER WHAT I'VE ASKED FOR, HE'S NEVER SAID IT'S IMPOSSIBLE BEFORE...
YOU HAVE NO RIGHT TO DENY ME! SO DO IT!
WHEEZE...
I CAN'T. THE LIGHT...
THE LIGHT THAT BROKE THE CURSE BLINDS ME...

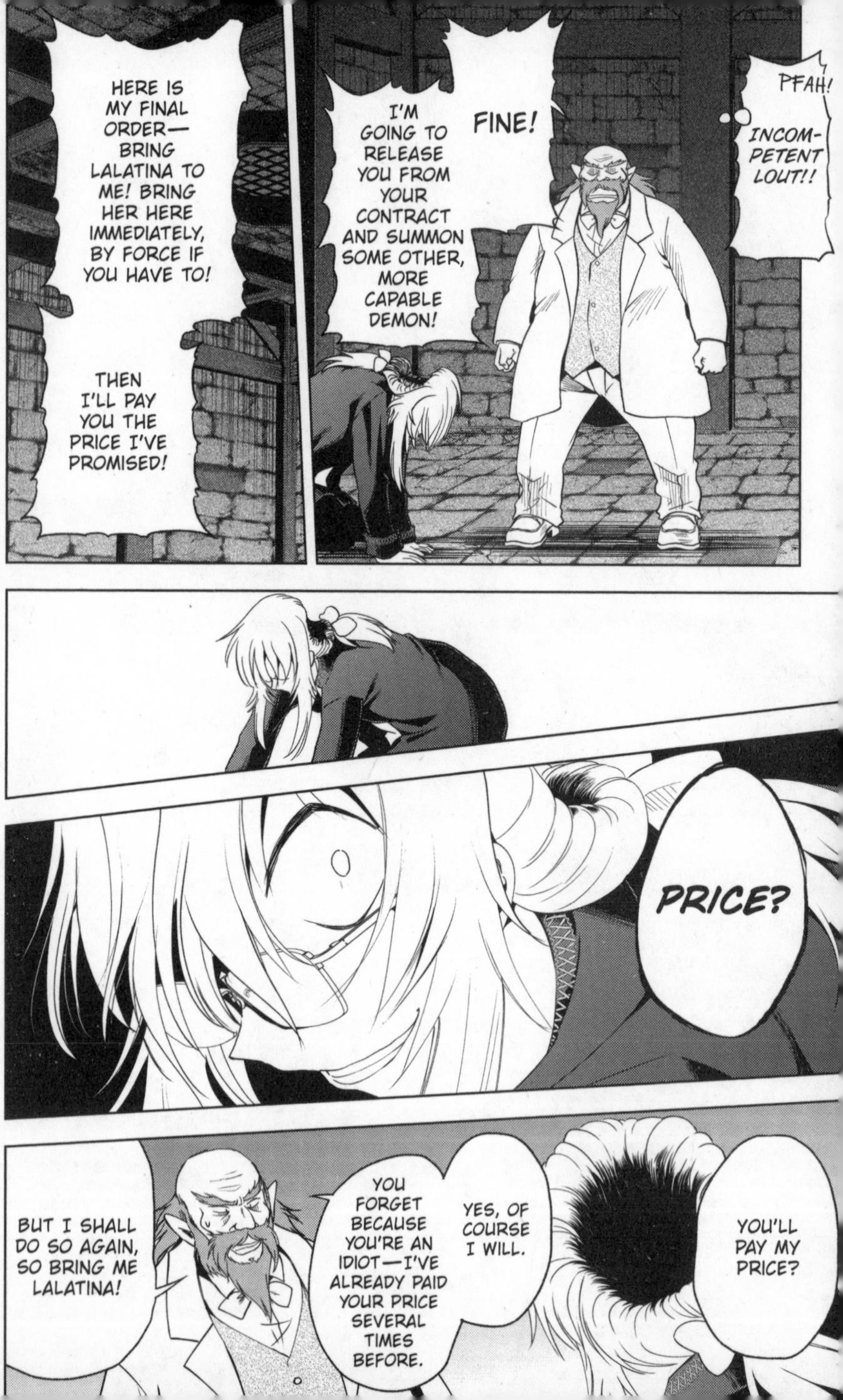
PFAH!
INCOMPETENT LOUT!!
FINE!
I'M GOING TO RELEASE YOU FROM YOUR CONTRACT AND SUMMON SOME OTHER, MORE CAPABLE DEMON!
HERE IS MY FINAL ORDER—BRING LALATINA TO ME! BRING HER HERE IMMEDIATELY, BY FORCE IF YOU HAVE TO!
THEN I'LL PAY YOU THE PRICE I'VE PROMISED!
PRICE?
YOU'LL PAY MY PRICE?
YES, OF COURSE I WILL.
YOU FORGET BECAUSE YOU'RE AN IDIOT—I'VE ALREADY PAID YOUR PRICE SEVERAL TIMES BEFORE.
BUT I SHALL DO SO AGAIN, SO BRING ME LALATINA!

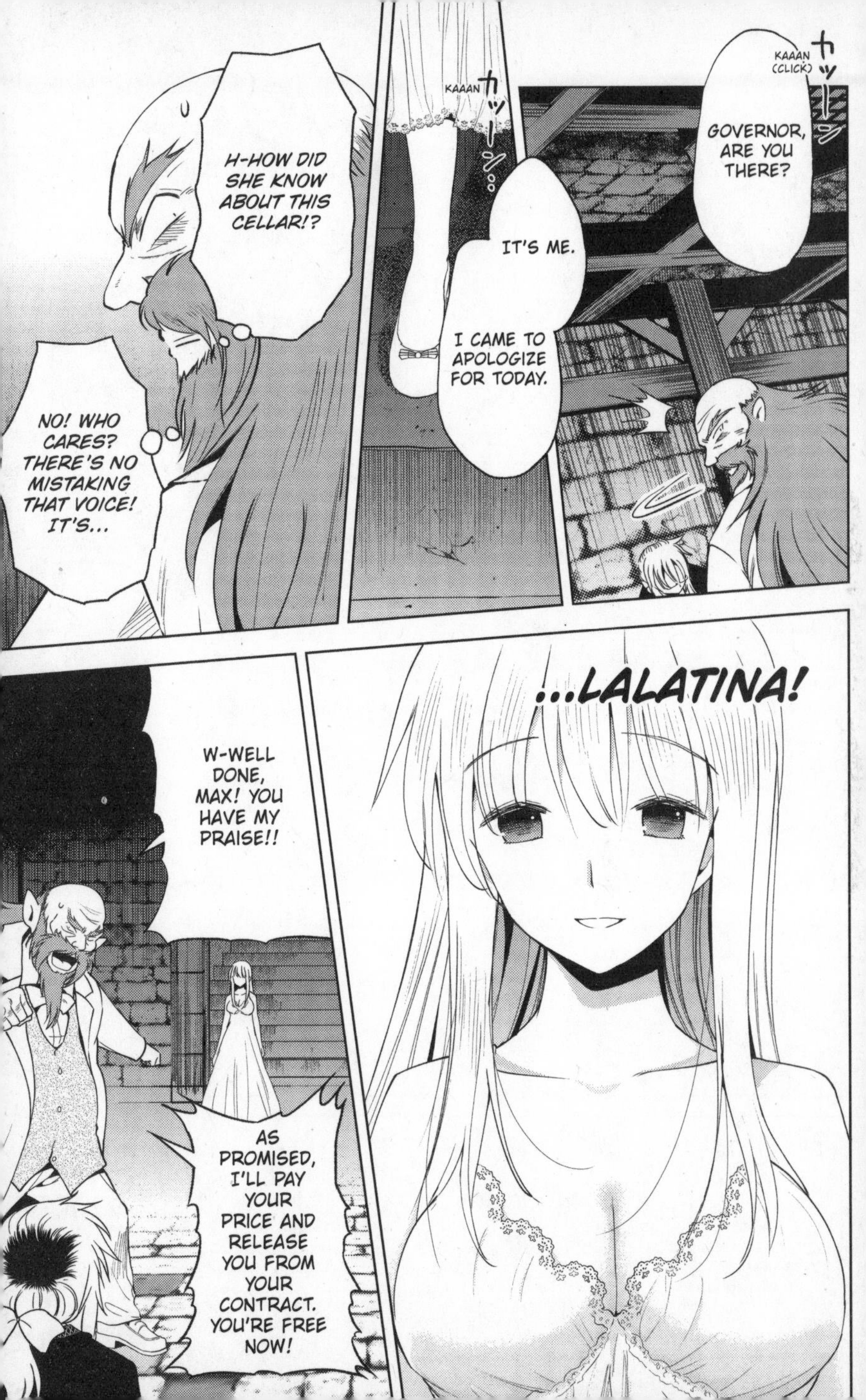
KAAAN (CLICK)
GOVERNOR, ARE YOU THERE?
KAAAN
IT'S ME.
I CAME TO APOLOGIZE FOR TODAY.
H-HOW DID SHE KNOW ABOUT THIS CELLAR!?
NO! WHO CARES? THERE'S NO MISTAKING THAT VOICE! IT'S...
...LALATINA!
W-WELL DONE, MAX! YOU HAVE MY PRAISE!!
AS PROMISED, I'LL PAY YOUR PRICE AND RELEASE YOU FROM YOUR CONTRACT. YOU'RE FREE NOW!

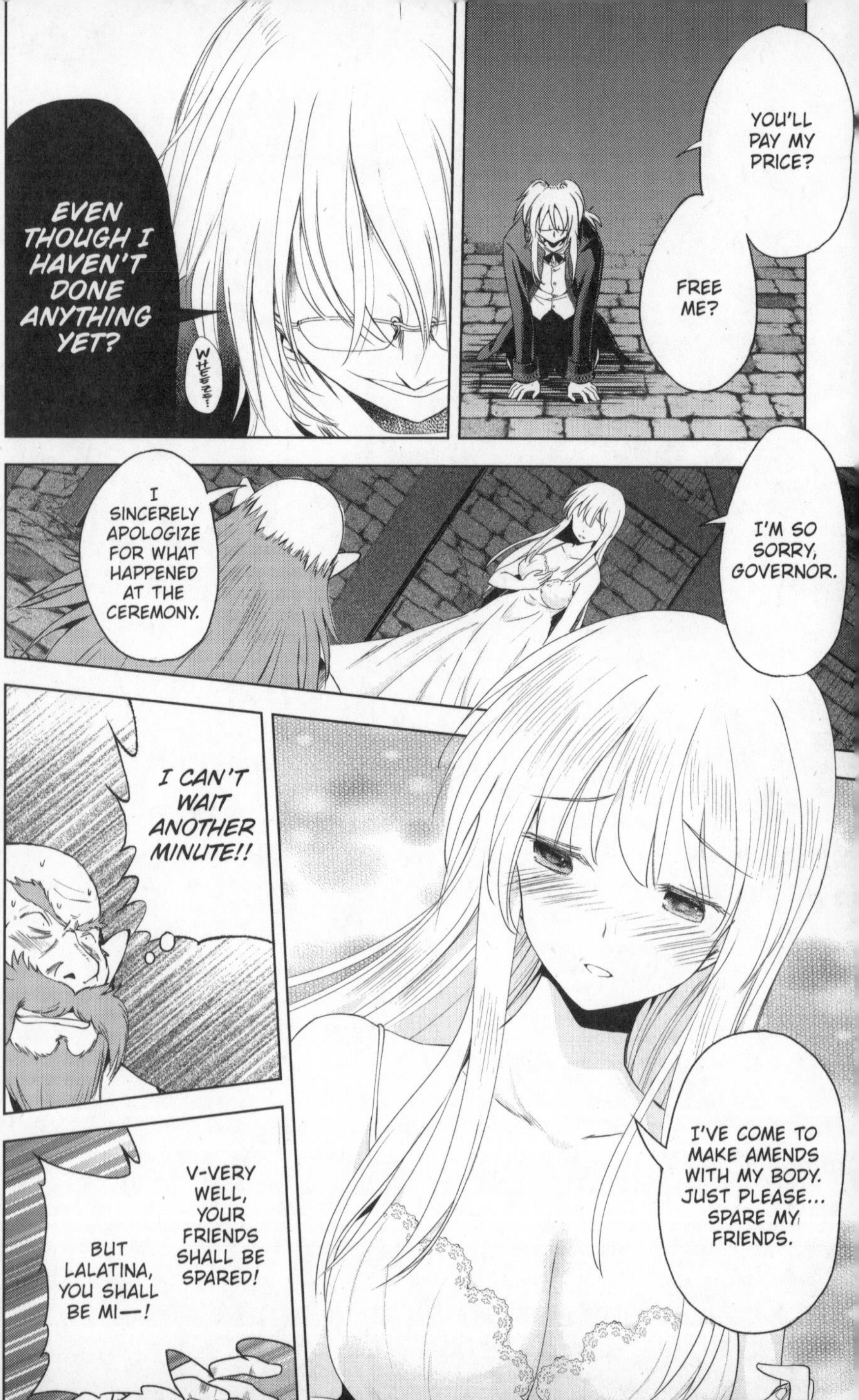
YOU'LL PAY MY PRICE?
FREE ME?
EVEN THOUGH I HAVEN'T DONE ANYTHING YET?
WHEEZE...
I'M SO SORRY, GOVERNOR.
I SINCERELY APOLOGIZE FOR WHAT HAPPENED AT THE CEREMONY.
I'VE COME TO MAKE AMENDS WITH MY BODY. JUST PLEASE... SPARE MY FRIENDS.
I CAN'T WAIT ANOTHER MINUTE!!
V-VERY WELL, YOUR FRIENDS SHALL BE SPARED!
BUT LALATINA, YOU SHALL BE MI—!

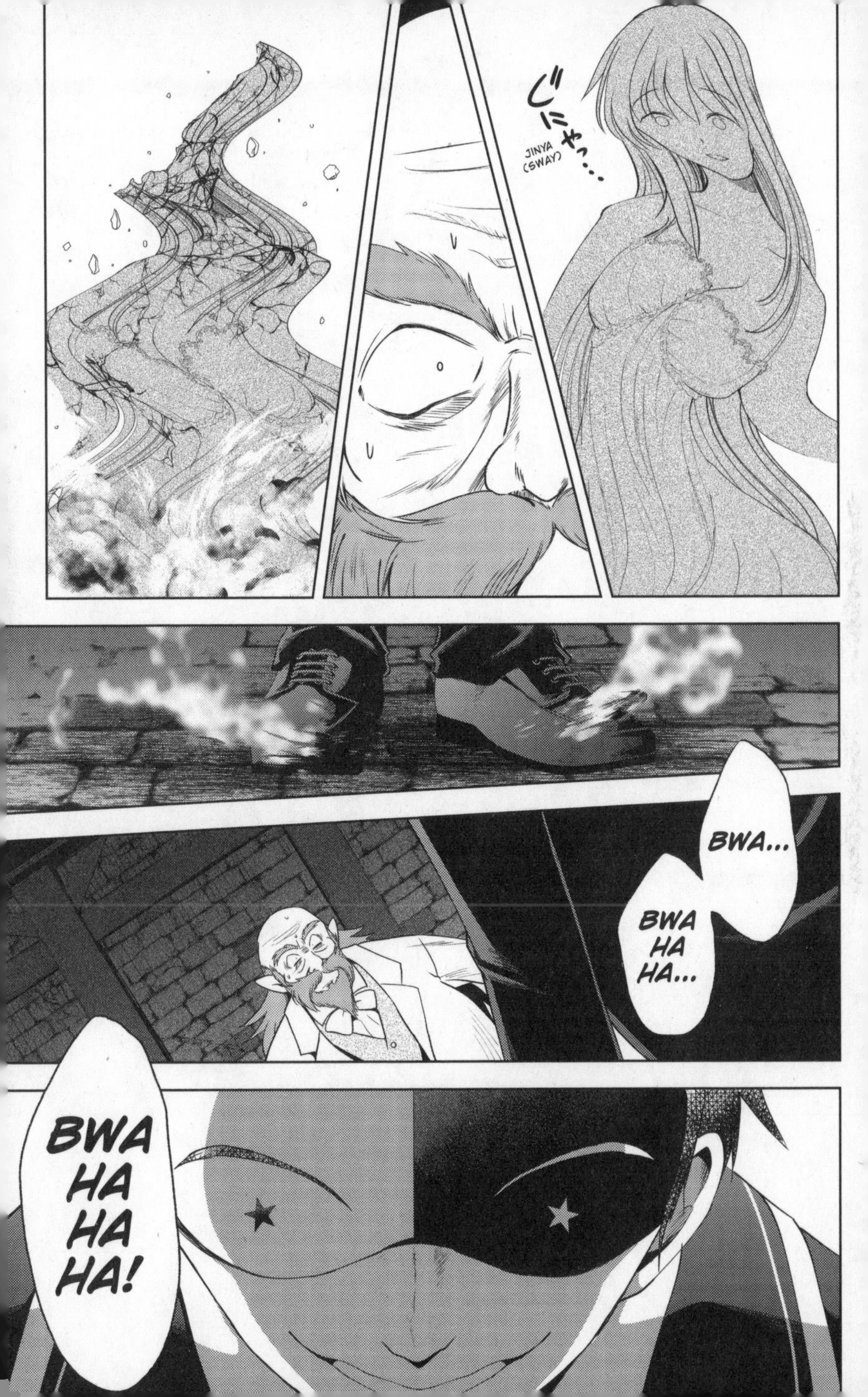
じにゃっ…
JINYA (SWAY)
BWA...
BWA HA HA...
BWA HA HA HA!

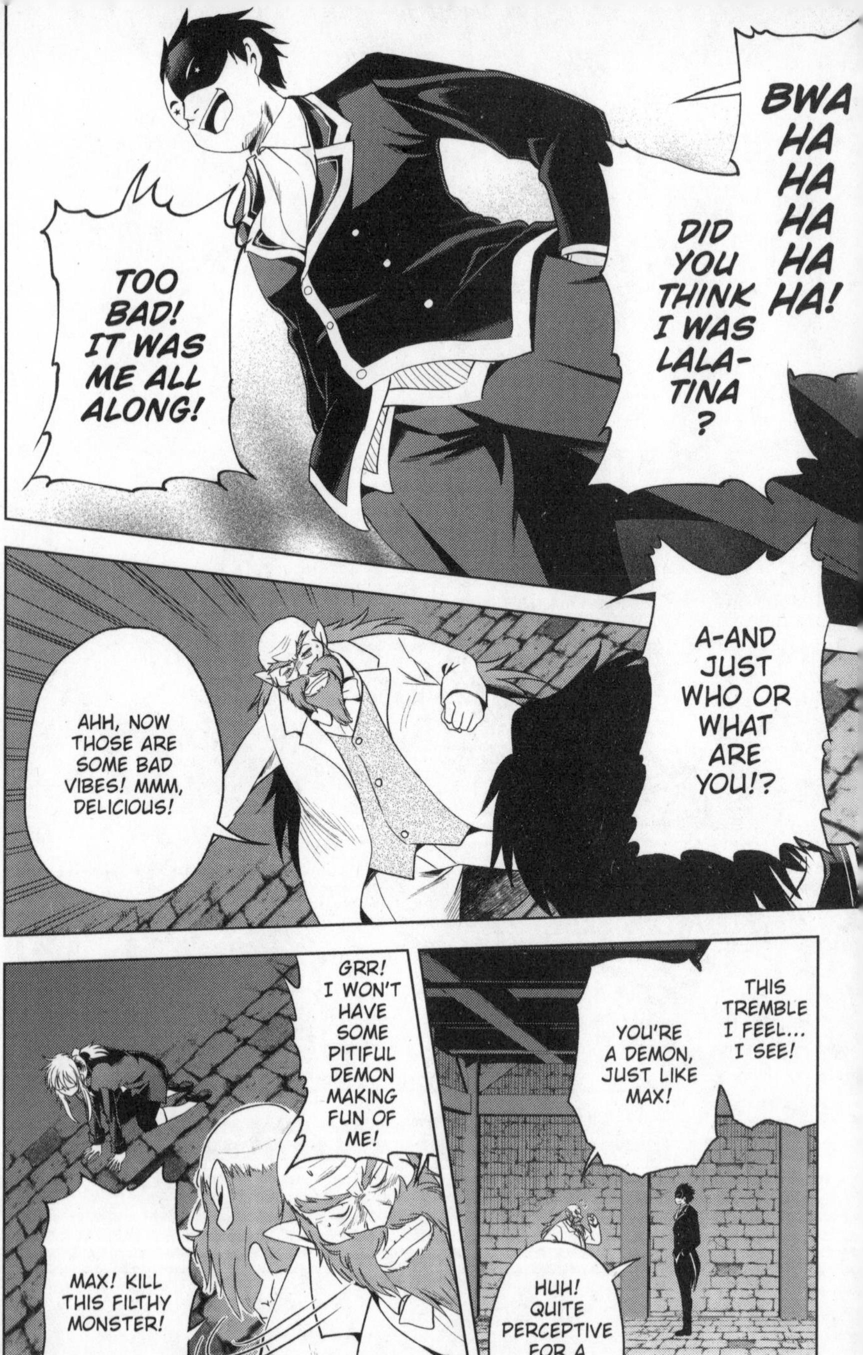
BWA HA HA HA HA HA!
DID YOU THINK I WAS LALA-TINA?
TOO BAD! IT WAS ME ALL ALONG!
A-AND JUST WHO OR WHAT ARE YOU!?
AHH, NOW THOSE ARE SOME BAD VIBES! MMM, DELICIOUS!
THIS TREMBLE I FEEL... I SEE!
YOU'RE A DEMON, JUST LIKE MAX!
HUH! QUITE PERCEPTIVE FOR A HUMAN.
GRR! I WON'T HAVE SOME PITIFUL DEMON MAKING FUN OF ME!
MAX! KILL THIS FILTHY MONSTER!

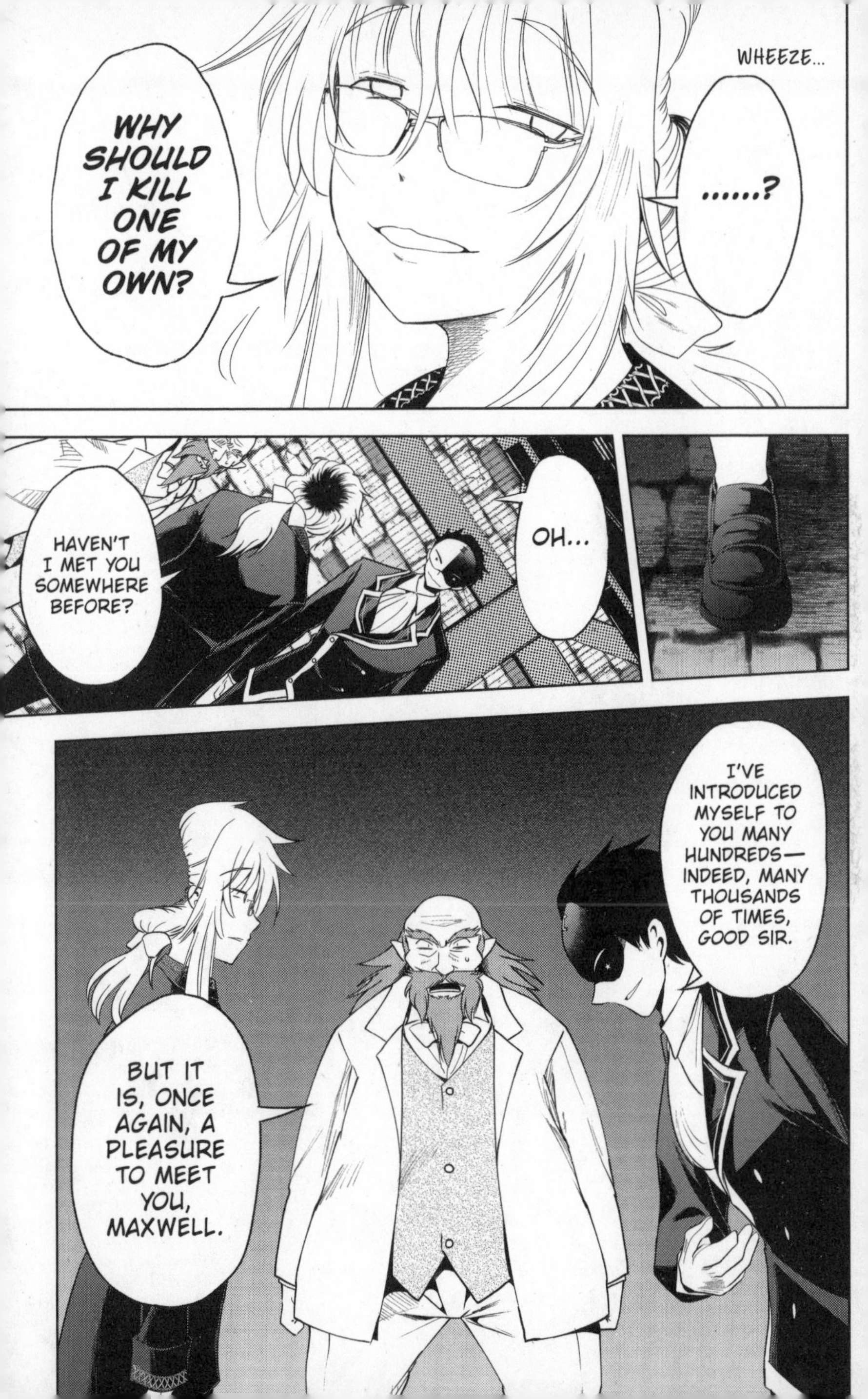
WHEEZE...
......?
WHY SHOULD I KILL ONE OF MY OWN?
OH...
HAVEN'T I MET YOU SOMEWHERE BEFORE?
I'VE INTRODUCED MYSELF TO YOU MANY HUNDREDS—INDEED, MANY THOUSANDS OF TIMES, GOOD SIR.
BUT IT IS, ONCE AGAIN, A PLEASURE TO MEET YOU, MAXWELL.

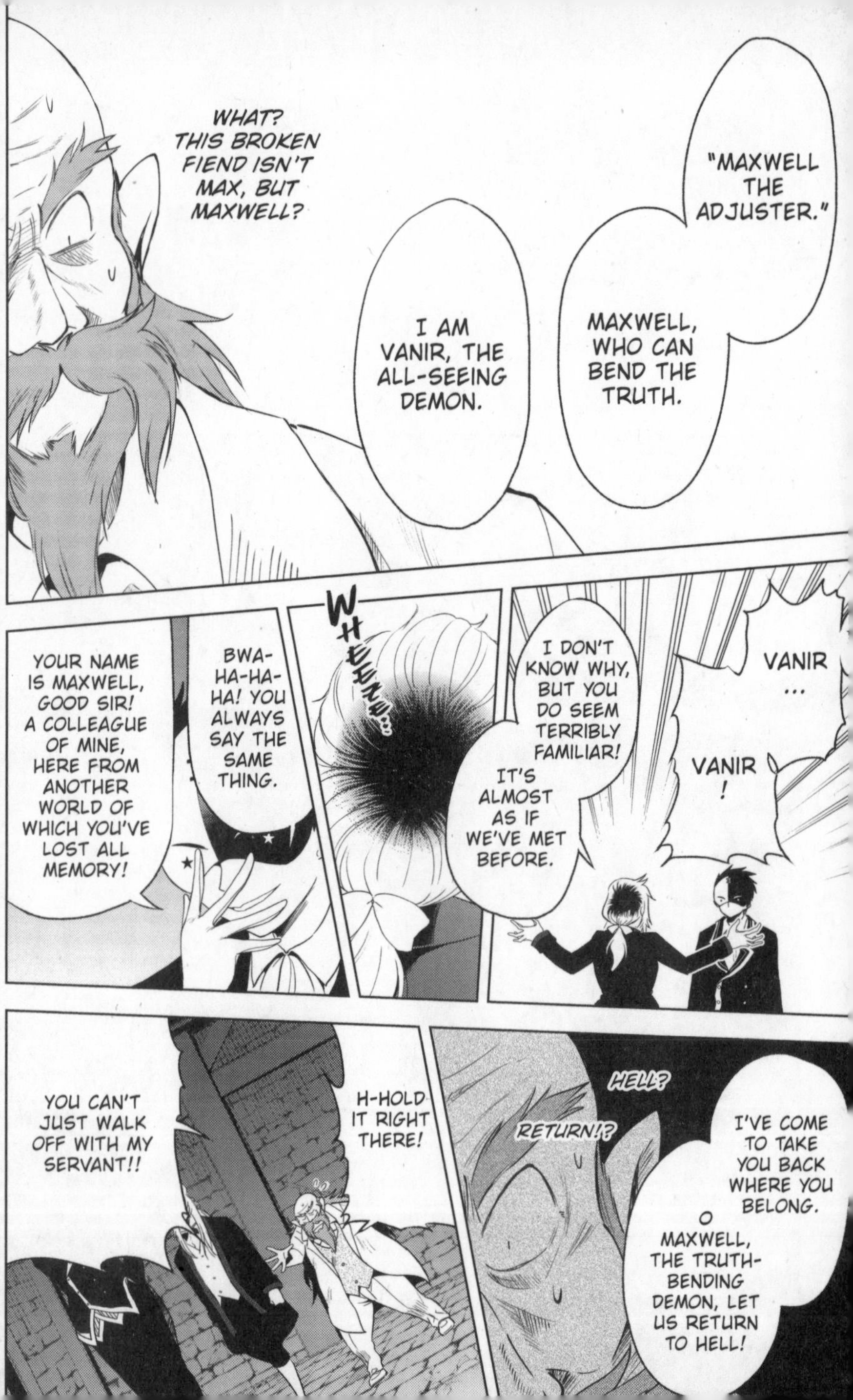
"MAXWELL THE ADJUSTER."
MAXWELL, WHO CAN BEND THE TRUTH.
I AM VANIR, THE ALL-SEEING DEMON.
WHAT? THIS BROKEN FIEND ISN'T MAX, BUT MAXWELL?
VANIR ...
VANIR !
I DON'T KNOW WHY, BUT YOU DO SEEM TERRIBLY FAMILIAR!
IT'S ALMOST AS IF WE'VE MET BEFORE.
WHEEZE...
BWA-HA-HA! YOU ALWAYS SAY THE SAME THING.
YOUR NAME IS MAXWELL, GOOD SIR! A COLLEAGUE OF MINE, HERE FROM ANOTHER WORLD OF WHICH YOU'VE LOST ALL MEMORY!
I'VE COME TO TAKE YOU BACK WHERE YOU BELONG.
O MAXWELL, THE TRUTH-BENDING DEMON, LET US RETURN TO HELL!
HELL?
RETURN!?
H-HOLD IT RIGHT THERE!
YOU CAN'T JUST WALK OFF WITH MY SERVANT!!

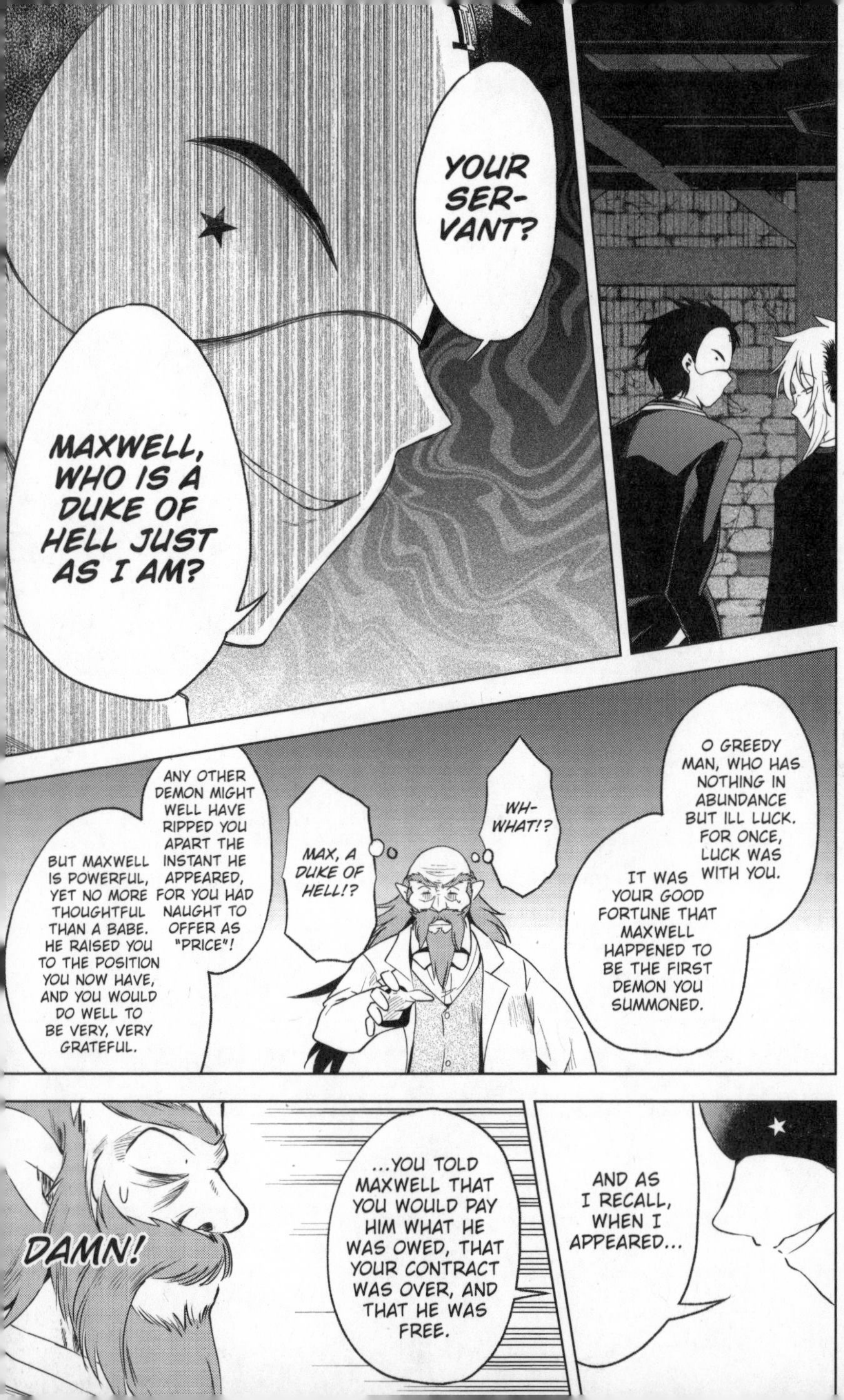
YOUR SERVANT?
MAXWELL, WHO IS A DUKE OF HELL JUST AS I AM?
O GREEDY MAN, WHO HAS NOTHING IN ABUNDANCE BUT ILL LUCK. FOR ONCE, LUCK WAS WITH YOU.
IT WAS YOUR GOOD FORTUNE THAT MAXWELL HAPPENED TO BE THE FIRST DEMON YOU SUMMONED.
WH-WHAT!?
MAX, A DUKE OF HELL!?
ANY OTHER DEMON MIGHT WELL HAVE RIPPED YOU APART THE INSTANT HE APPEARED, FOR YOU HAD NAUGHT TO OFFER AS "PRICE"!
BUT MAXWELL IS POWERFUL, YET NO MORE THOUGHTFUL THAN A BABE. HE RAISED YOU TO THE POSITION YOU NOW HAVE, AND YOU WOULD DO WELL TO BE VERY, VERY GRATEFUL.
AND AS I RECALL, WHEN I APPEARED...
...YOU TOLD MAXWELL THAT YOU WOULD PAY HIM WHAT HE WAS OWED, THAT YOUR CONTRACT WAS OVER, AND THAT HE WAS FREE.
DAMN!

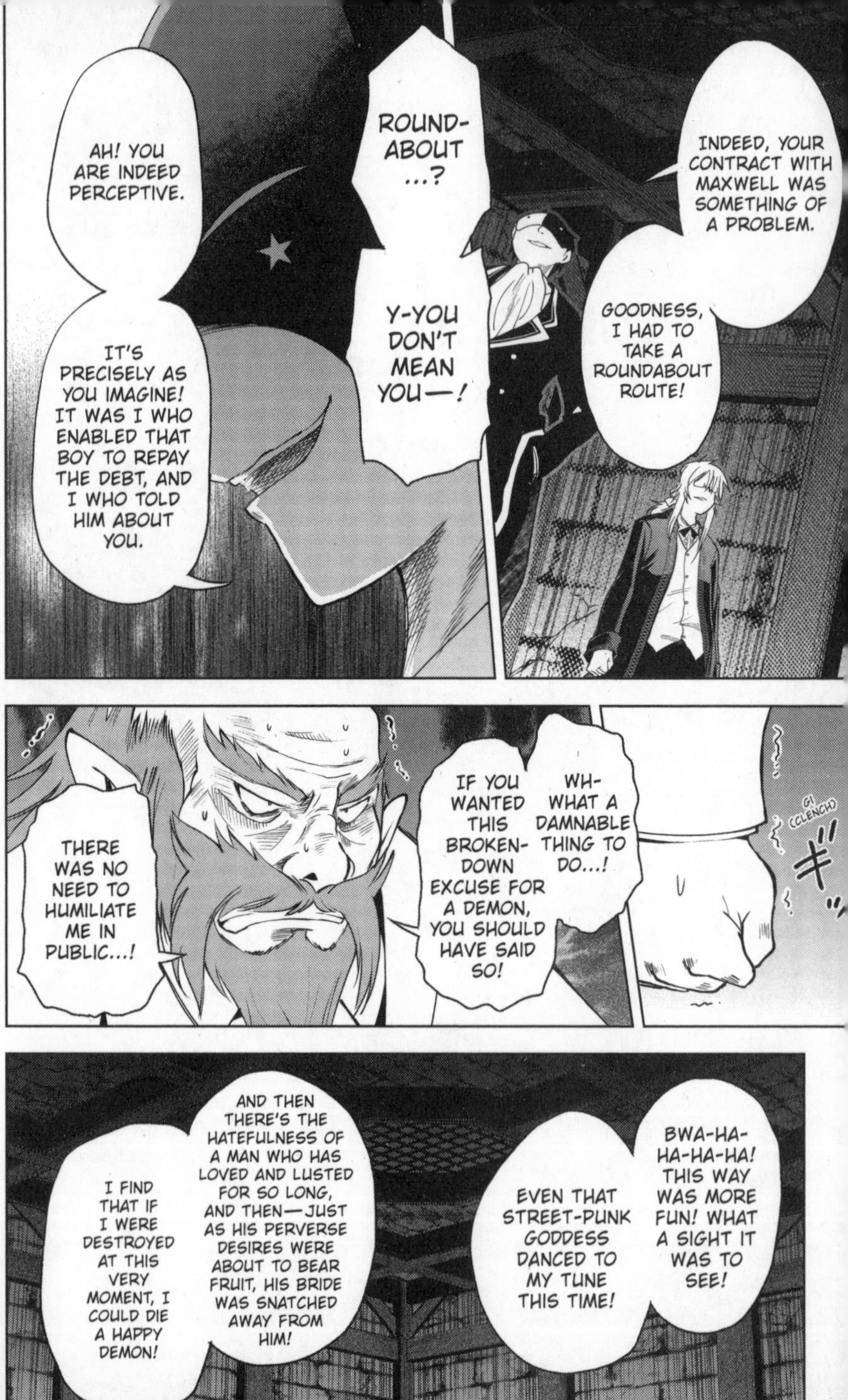
INDEED, YOUR CONTRACT WITH MAXWELL WAS SOMETHING OF A PROBLEM.
GOODNESS, I HAD TO TAKE A ROUNDABOUT ROUTE!
ROUND-ABOUT ...?
Y-YOU DON'T MEAN YOU—!
AH! YOU ARE INDEED PERCEPTIVE.
IT'S PRECISELY AS YOU IMAGINE! IT WAS I WHO ENABLED THAT BOY TO REPAY THE DEBT, AND I WHO TOLD HIM ABOUT YOU.
GI (CLENCH)
WH-WHAT A DAMNABLE THING TO DO...!
IF YOU WANTED THIS BROKEN-DOWN EXCUSE FOR A DEMON, YOU SHOULD HAVE SAID SO!
THERE WAS NO NEED TO HUMILIATE ME IN PUBLIC...!
BWA-HA-HA-HA-HA! THIS WAY WAS MORE FUN! WHAT A SIGHT IT WAS TO SEE!
EVEN THAT STREET-PUNK GODDESS DANCED TO MY TUNE THIS TIME!
AND THEN THERE'S THE HATEFULNESS OF A MAN WHO HAS LOVED AND LUSTED FOR SO LONG, AND THEN—JUST AS HIS PERVERSE DESIRES WERE ABOUT TO BEAR FRUIT, HIS BRIDE WAS SNATCHED AWAY FROM HIM!
I FIND THAT IF I WERE DESTROYED AT THIS VERY MOMENT, I COULD DIE A HAPPY DEMON!

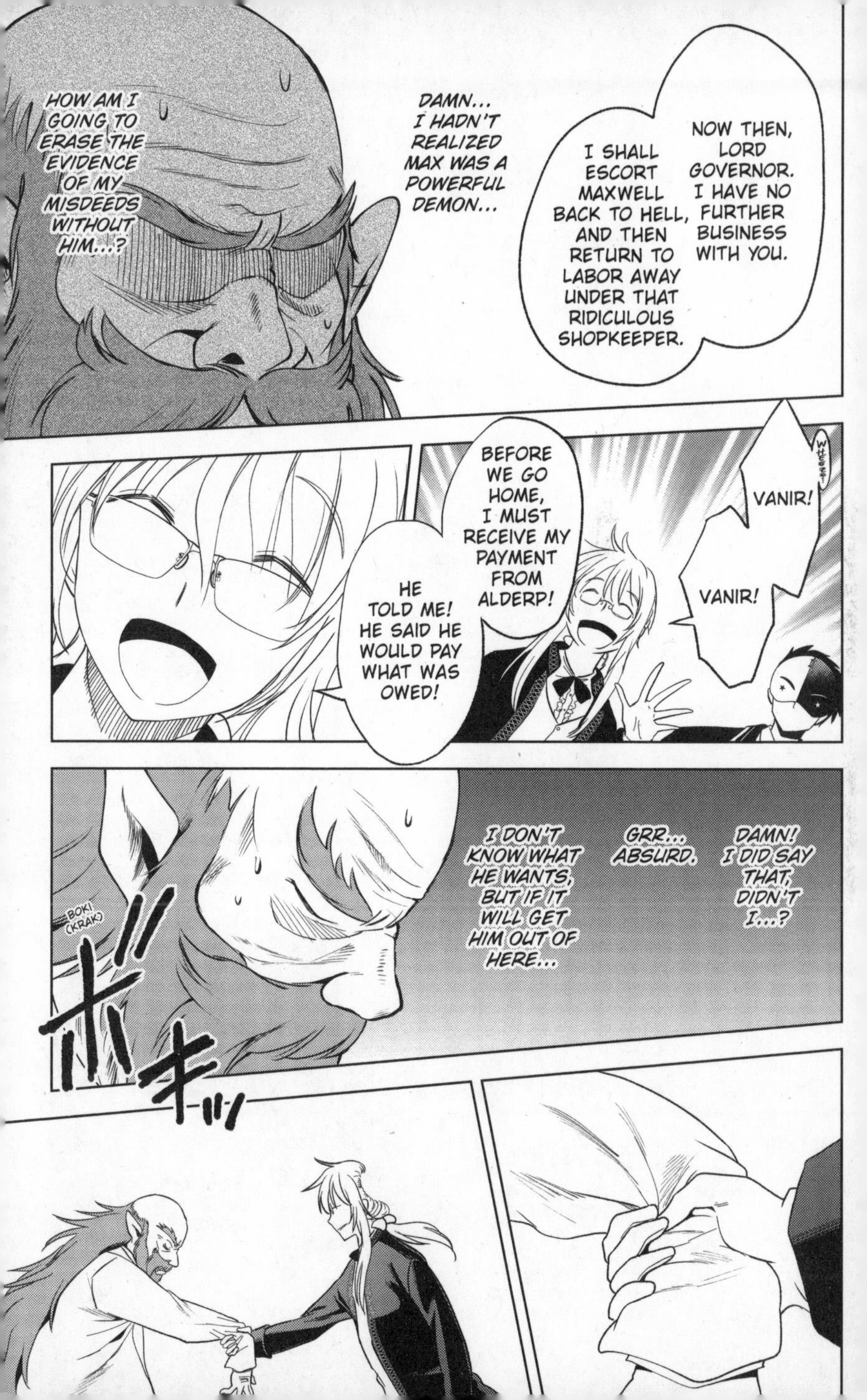
NOW THEN, LORD GOVERNOR. I HAVE NO FURTHER BUSINESS WITH YOU.
I SHALL ESCORT MAXWELL BACK TO HELL, AND THEN RETURN TO LABOR AWAY UNDER THAT RIDICULOUS SHOPKEEPER.
DAMN... I HADN'T REALIZED MAX WAS A POWERFUL DEMON...
HOW AM I GOING TO ERASE THE EVIDENCE OF MY MISDEEDS WITHOUT HIM...?
VANIR!
VANIR!
BEFORE WE GO HOME, I MUST RECEIVE MY PAYMENT FROM ALDERP!
HE TOLD ME! HE SAID HE WOULD PAY WHAT WAS OWED!
DAMN! I DID SAY THAT, DIDN'T I...?
GRR... ABSURD.
I DON'T KNOW WHAT HE WANTS, BUT IF IT WILL GET HIM OUT OF HERE...
BOKI (KRAK)

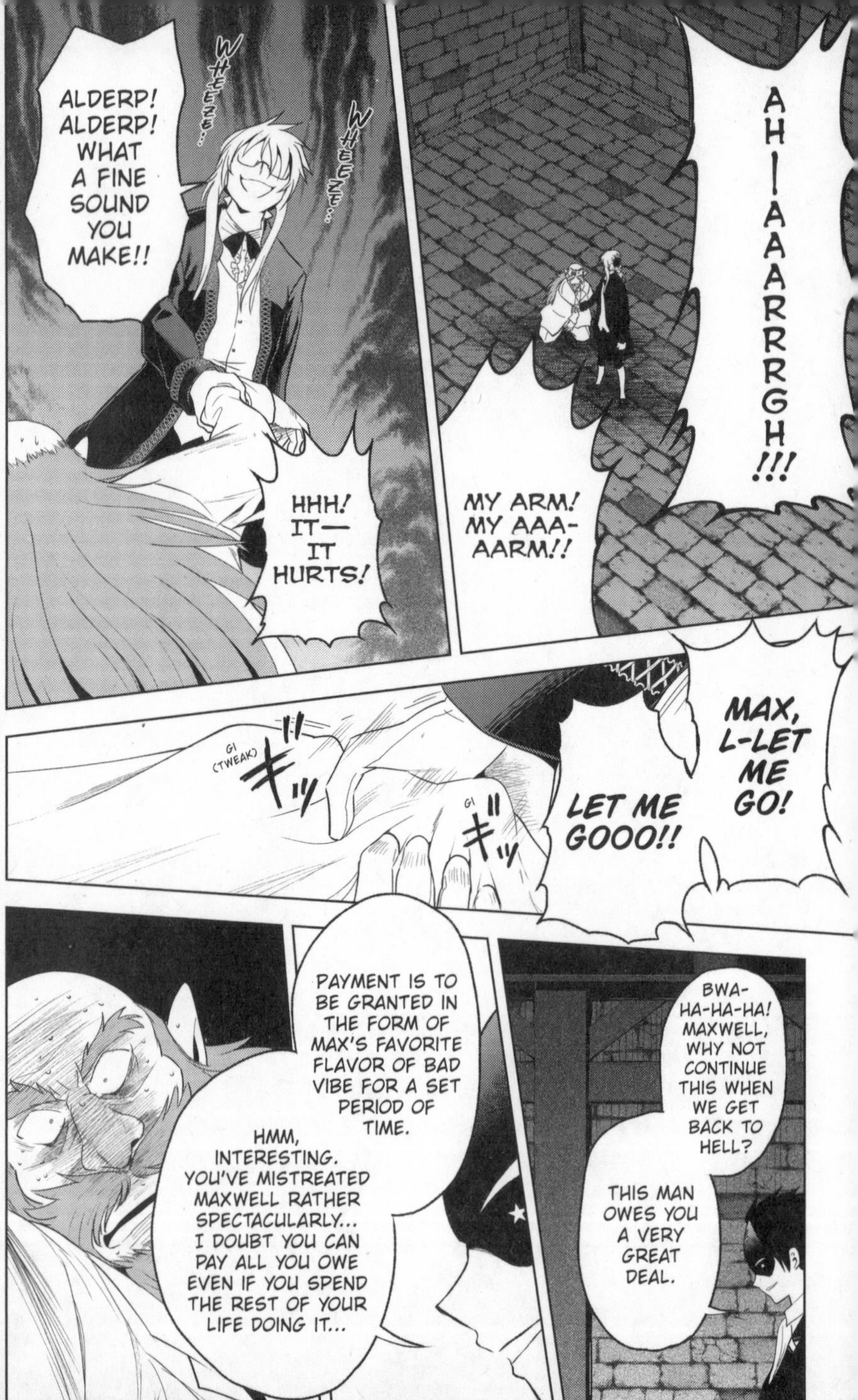
AHIAAAARRRGH!!!
MY ARM! MY AAA-AARM!!
WHEEZE...
WHEEZE...
ALDERP! ALDERP! WHAT A FINE SOUND YOU MAKE!!
HHH! IT— IT HURTS!
MAX, L-LET ME GO!
LET ME GOOO!!
ギッ GI
ギッ GI (TWEAK)
BWA-HA-HA-HA! MAXWELL, WHY NOT CONTINUE THIS WHEN WE GET BACK TO HELL?
THIS MAN OWES YOU A VERY GREAT DEAL.
PAYMENT IS TO BE GRANTED IN THE FORM OF MAX'S FAVORITE FLAVOR OF BAD VIBE FOR A SET PERIOD OF TIME.
HMM, INTERESTING. YOU'VE MISTREATED MAXWELL RATHER SPECTACULARLY... I DOUBT YOU CAN PAY ALL YOU OWE EVEN IF YOU SPEND THE REST OF YOUR LIFE DOING IT...

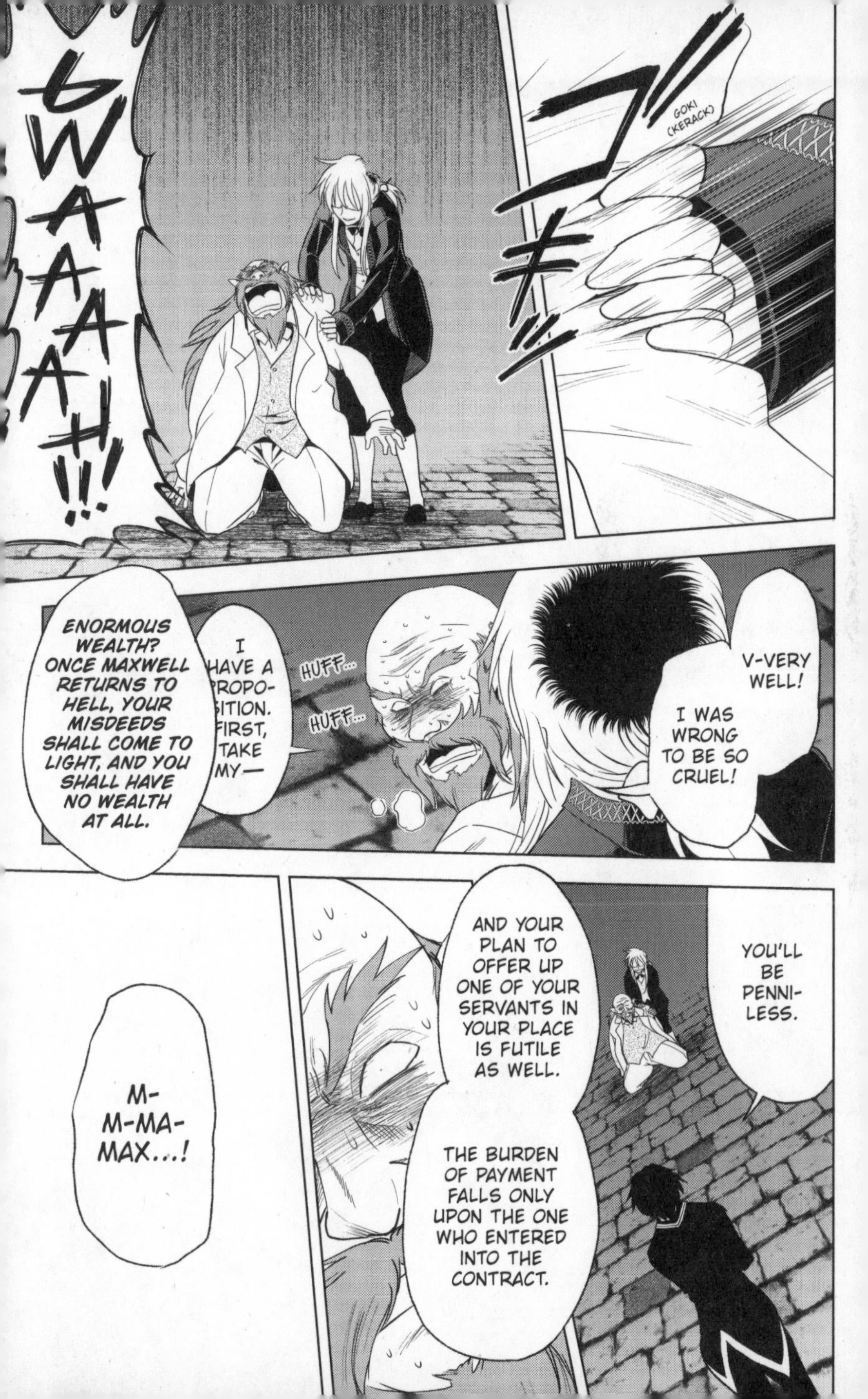
GOKI (KERACK)
GWAAAAH!!!
V-VERY WELL!
I WAS WRONG TO BE SO CRUEL!
HUFF...
HUFF...
I HAVE A PROPOSITION. FIRST, TAKE MY—
ENORMOUS WEALTH? ONCE MAXWELL RETURNS TO HELL, YOUR MISDEEDS SHALL COME TO LIGHT, AND YOU SHALL HAVE NO WEALTH AT ALL.
YOU'LL BE PENNILESS.
AND YOUR PLAN TO OFFER UP ONE OF YOUR SERVANTS IN YOUR PLACE IS FUTILE AS WELL.
THE BURDEN OF PAYMENT FALLS ONLY UPON THE ONE WHO ENTERED INTO THE CONTRACT.
M-M-MA-MAX...!

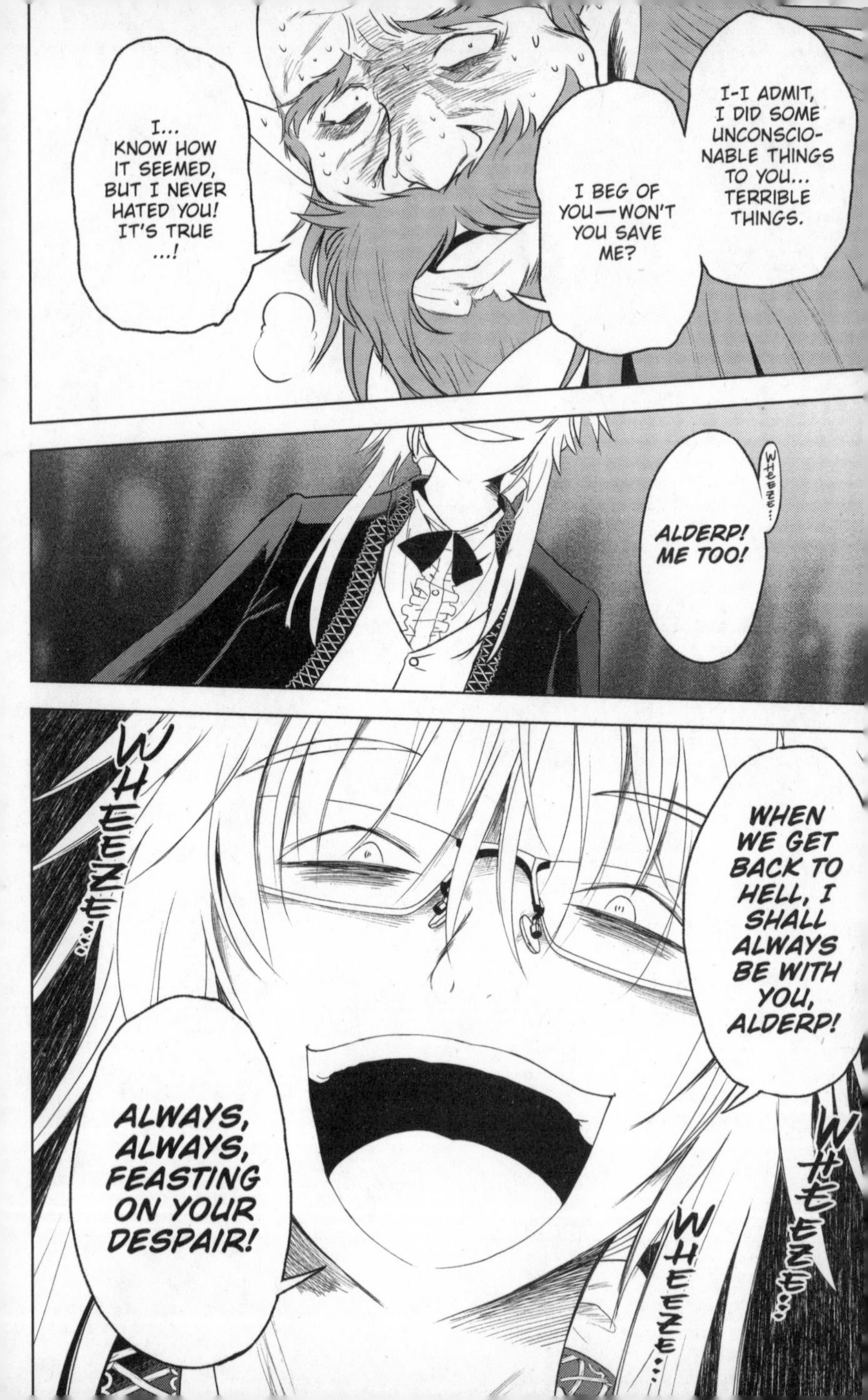
I-I ADMIT, I DID SOME UNCONSCIO-NABLE THINGS TO YOU... TERRIBLE THINGS.
I BEG OF YOU—WON'T YOU SAVE ME?
I... KNOW HOW IT SEEMED, BUT I NEVER HATED YOU! IT'S TRUE ...!
WHEEZE...
ALDERP! ME TOO!
WHEN WE GET BACK TO HELL, I SHALL ALWAYS BE WITH YOU, ALDERP!
WHEEZE...
WHEEZE...
ALWAYS, ALWAYS, FEASTING ON YOUR DESPAIR!
WHEEZE...

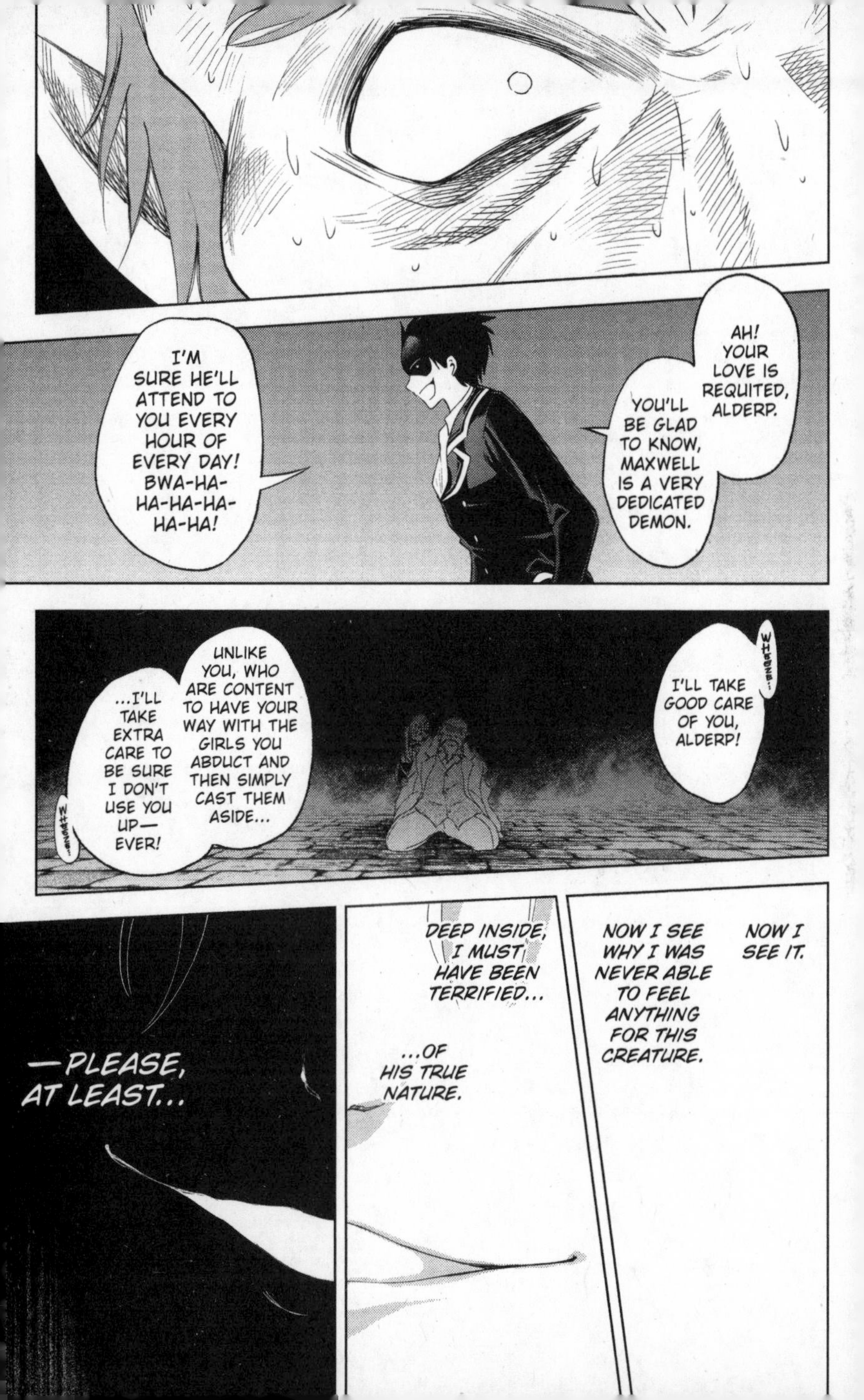
AH! YOUR LOVE IS REQUITED, ALDERP.
YOU'LL BE GLAD TO KNOW, MAXWELL IS A VERY DEDICATED DEMON.
I'M SURE HE'LL ATTEND TO YOU EVERY HOUR OF EVERY DAY! BWA-HA-HA-HA-HA-HA-HA!
WHEEZE...
I'LL TAKE GOOD CARE OF YOU, ALDERP!
UNLIKE YOU, WHO ARE CONTENT TO HAVE YOUR WAY WITH THE GIRLS YOU ABDUCT AND THEN SIMPLY CAST THEM ASIDE...
...I'LL TAKE EXTRA CARE TO BE SURE I DON'T USE YOU UP—EVER!
WHEEZE...
NOW I SEE IT.
NOW I SEE WHY I WAS NEVER ABLE TO FEEL ANYTHING FOR THIS CREATURE.
DEEP INSIDE, I MUST HAVE BEEN TERRIFIED...
...OF HIS TRUE NATURE.
—PLEASE, AT LEAST...

...AT LEAST LET THIS BROKEN DEMON TIRE QUICKLY OF HAVING HIS WAY WITH ME, AND GRANT ME A SWIFT DEATH...

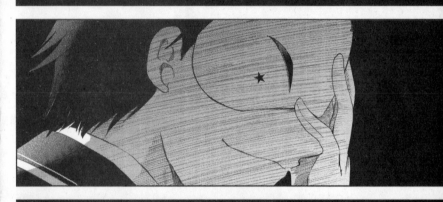

GOD'S
BLESSING
ON THIS
WONDERFUL
WORLD!

13

GOD'S
BLESSING
ON THIS
WONDERFUL
WORLD!

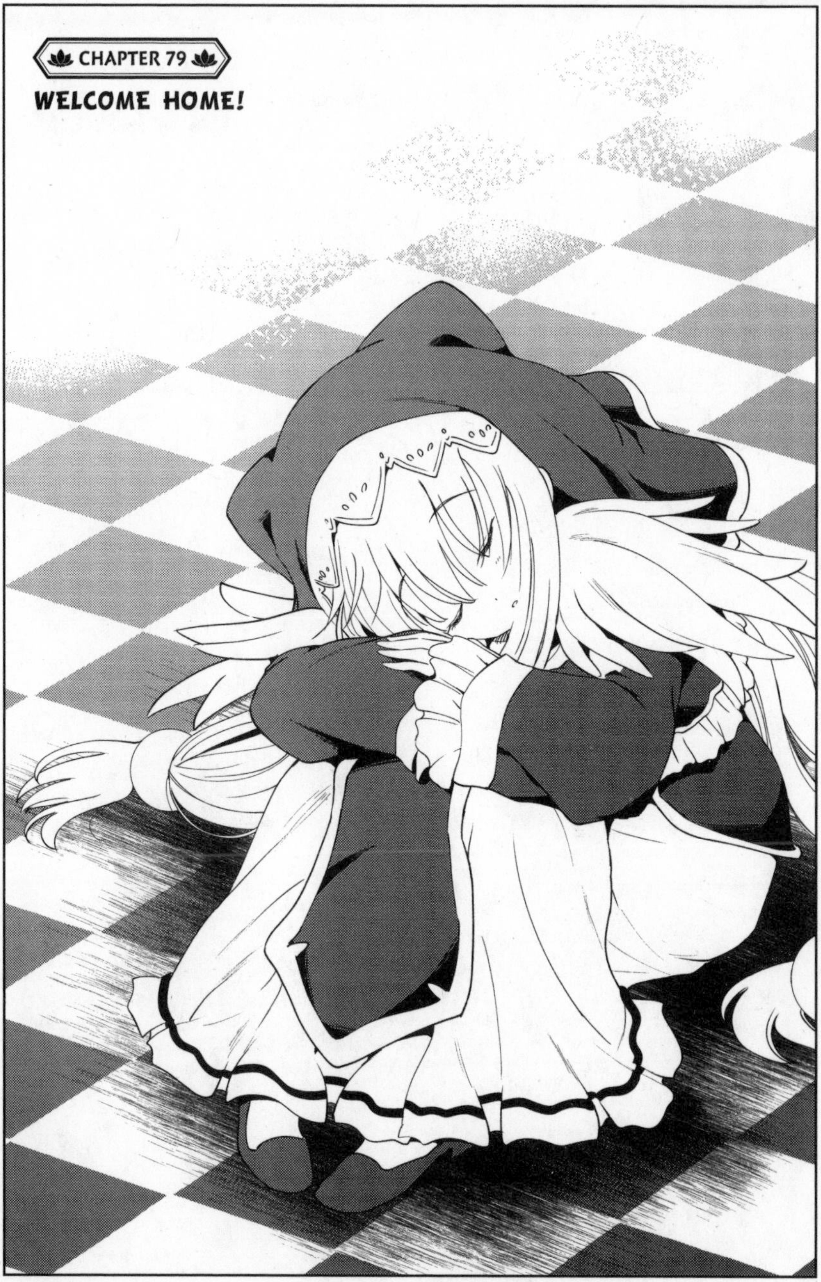
CHAPTER 79
WELCOME HOME!

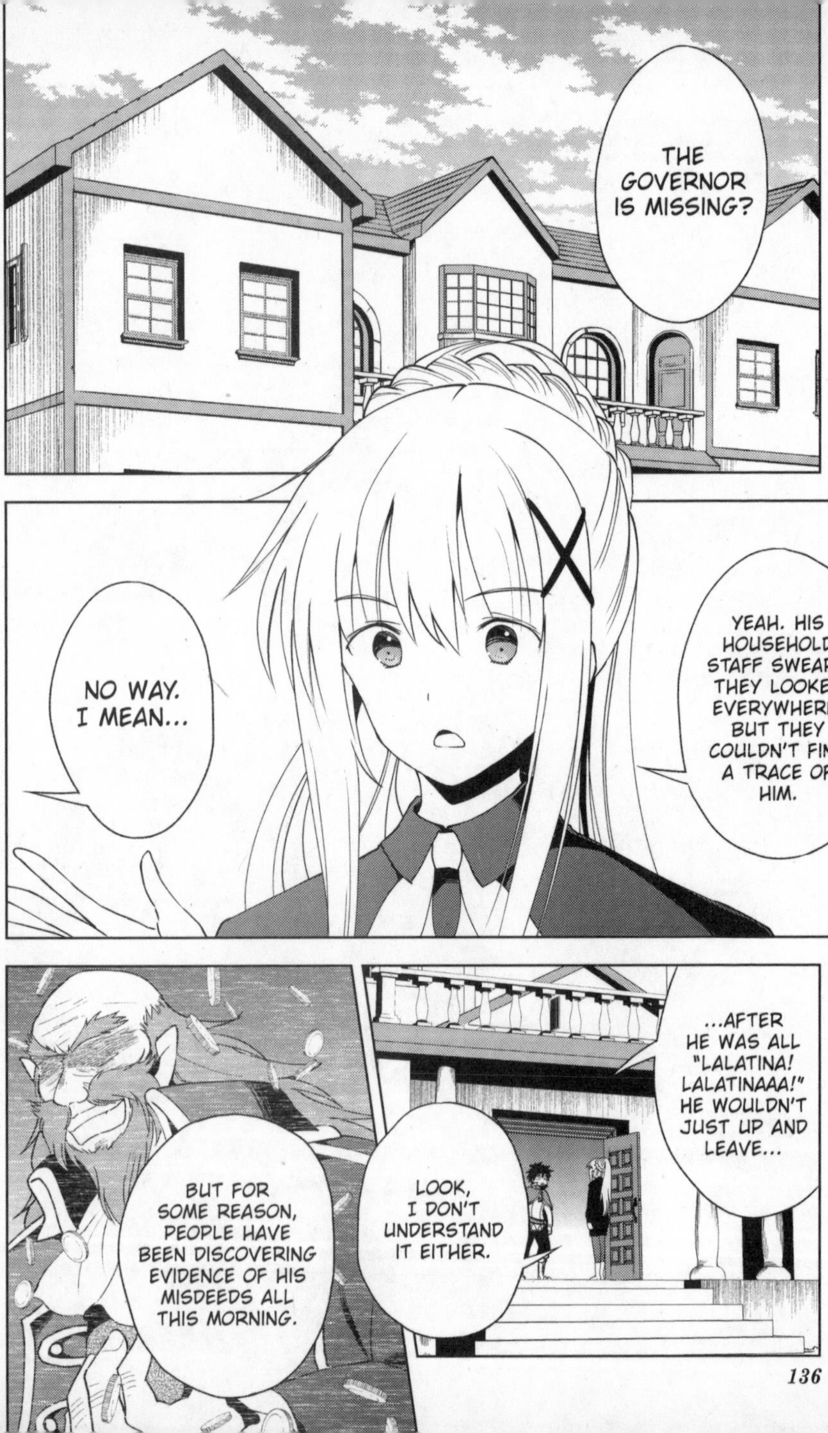
THE GOVERNOR IS MISSING?
YEAH. HIS HOUSEHOLD STAFF SWEARS THEY LOOKED EVERYWHERE, BUT THEY COULDN'T FIND A TRACE OF HIM.
NO WAY. I MEAN...
...AFTER HE WAS ALL "LALATINA! LALATINAAA!" HE WOULDN'T JUST UP AND LEAVE...
LOOK, I DON'T UNDERSTAND IT EITHER.
BUT FOR SOME REASON, PEOPLE HAVE BEEN DISCOVERING EVIDENCE OF HIS MISDEEDS ALL THIS MORNING.

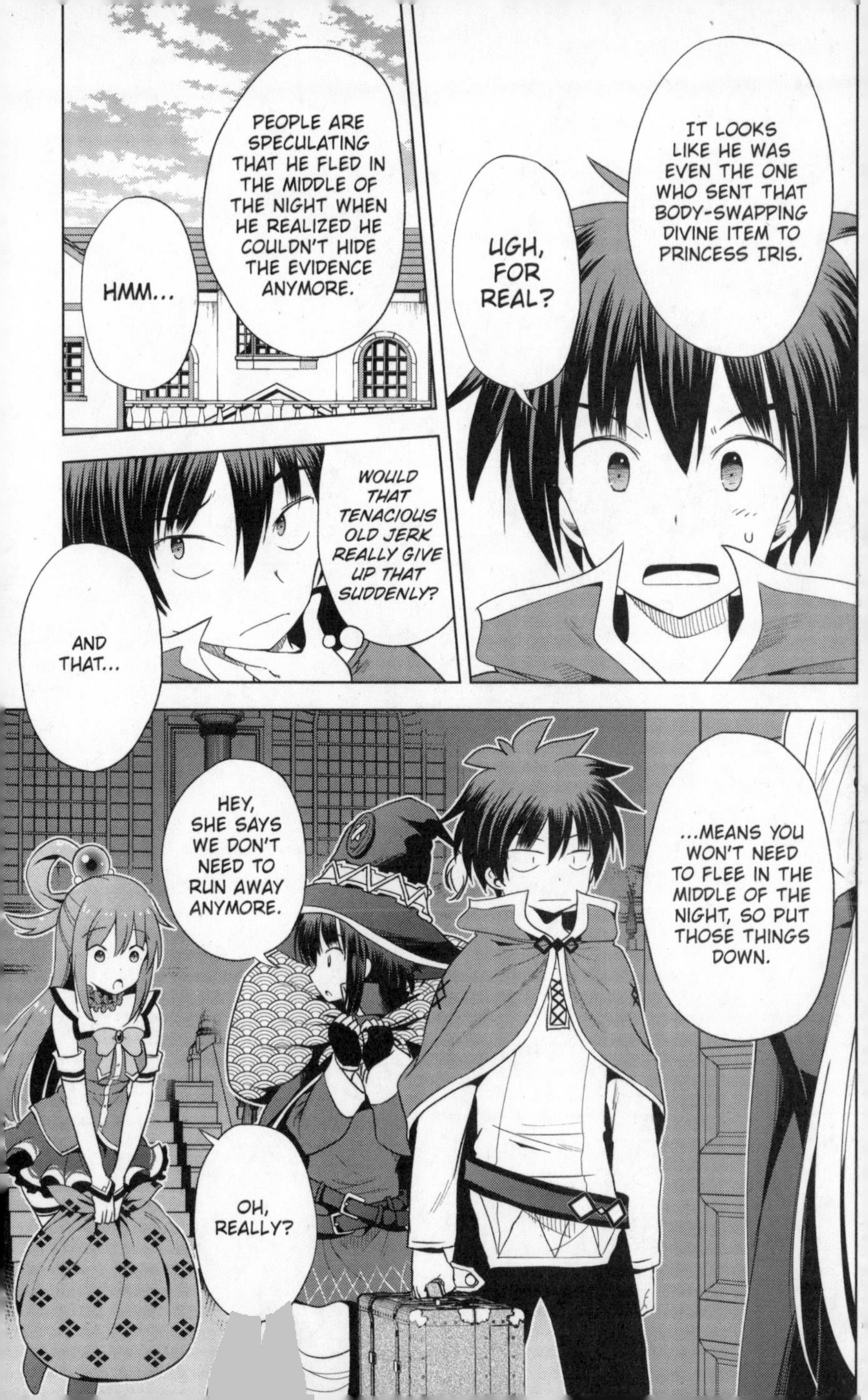
IT LOOKS LIKE HE WAS EVEN THE ONE WHO SENT THAT BODY-SWAPPING DIVINE ITEM TO PRINCESS IRIS.
UGH, FOR REAL?
PEOPLE ARE SPECULATING THAT HE FLED IN THE MIDDLE OF THE NIGHT WHEN HE REALIZED HE COULDN'T HIDE THE EVIDENCE ANYMORE.
HMM...
WOULD THAT TENACIOUS OLD JERK REALLY GIVE UP THAT SUDDENLY?
AND THAT...
...MEANS YOU WON'T NEED TO FLEE IN THE MIDDLE OF THE NIGHT, SO PUT THOSE THINGS DOWN.
HEY, SHE SAYS WE DON'T NEED TO RUN AWAY ANYMORE.
OH, REALLY?

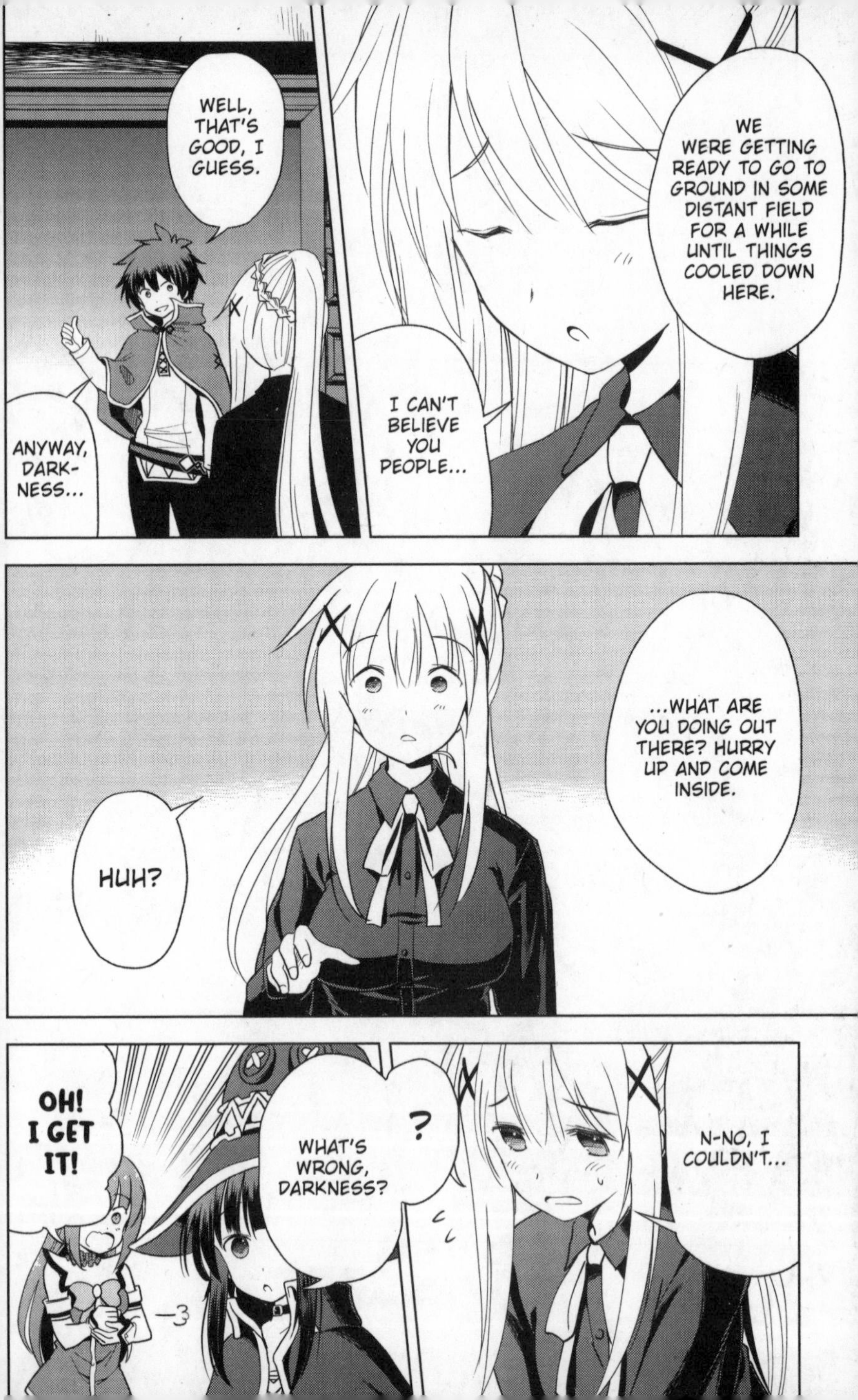
WE WERE GETTING READY TO GO TO GROUND IN SOME DISTANT FIELD FOR A WHILE UNTIL THINGS COOLED DOWN HERE.
I CAN'T BELIEVE YOU PEOPLE...
WELL, THAT'S GOOD, I GUESS.
ANYWAY, DARK-NESS...
...WHAT ARE YOU DOING OUT THERE? HURRY UP AND COME INSIDE.
HUH?
N-NO, I COULDN'T...
WHAT'S WRONG, DARKNESS?
OH! I GET IT!

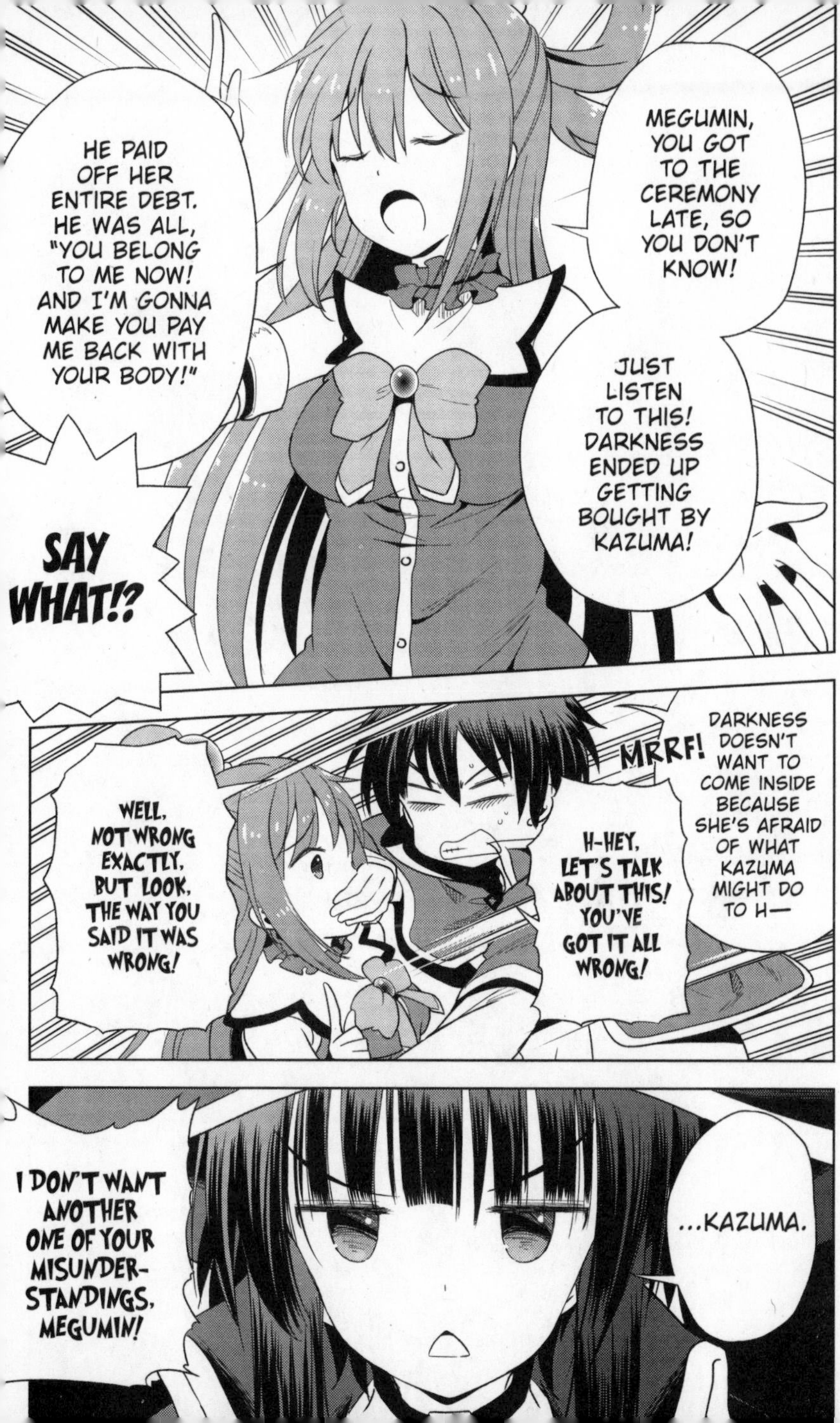
MEGUMIN, YOU GOT TO THE CEREMONY LATE, SO YOU DON'T KNOW!
JUST LISTEN TO THIS! DARKNESS ENDED UP GETTING BOUGHT BY KAZUMA!
HE PAID OFF HER ENTIRE DEBT. HE WAS ALL, "YOU BELONG TO ME NOW! AND I'M GONNA MAKE YOU PAY ME BACK WITH YOUR BODY!"
SAY WHAT!?
DARKNESS DOESN'T WANT TO COME INSIDE BECAUSE SHE'S AFRAID OF WHAT KAZUMA MIGHT DO TO H—
MRRF!
H-HEY, LET'S TALK ABOUT THIS! YOU'VE GOT IT ALL WRONG!
WELL, NOT WRONG EXACTLY, BUT LOOK, THE WAY YOU SAID IT WAS WRONG!
...KAZUMA.
I DON'T WANT ANOTHER ONE OF YOUR MISUNDER-STANDINGS, MEGUMIN!

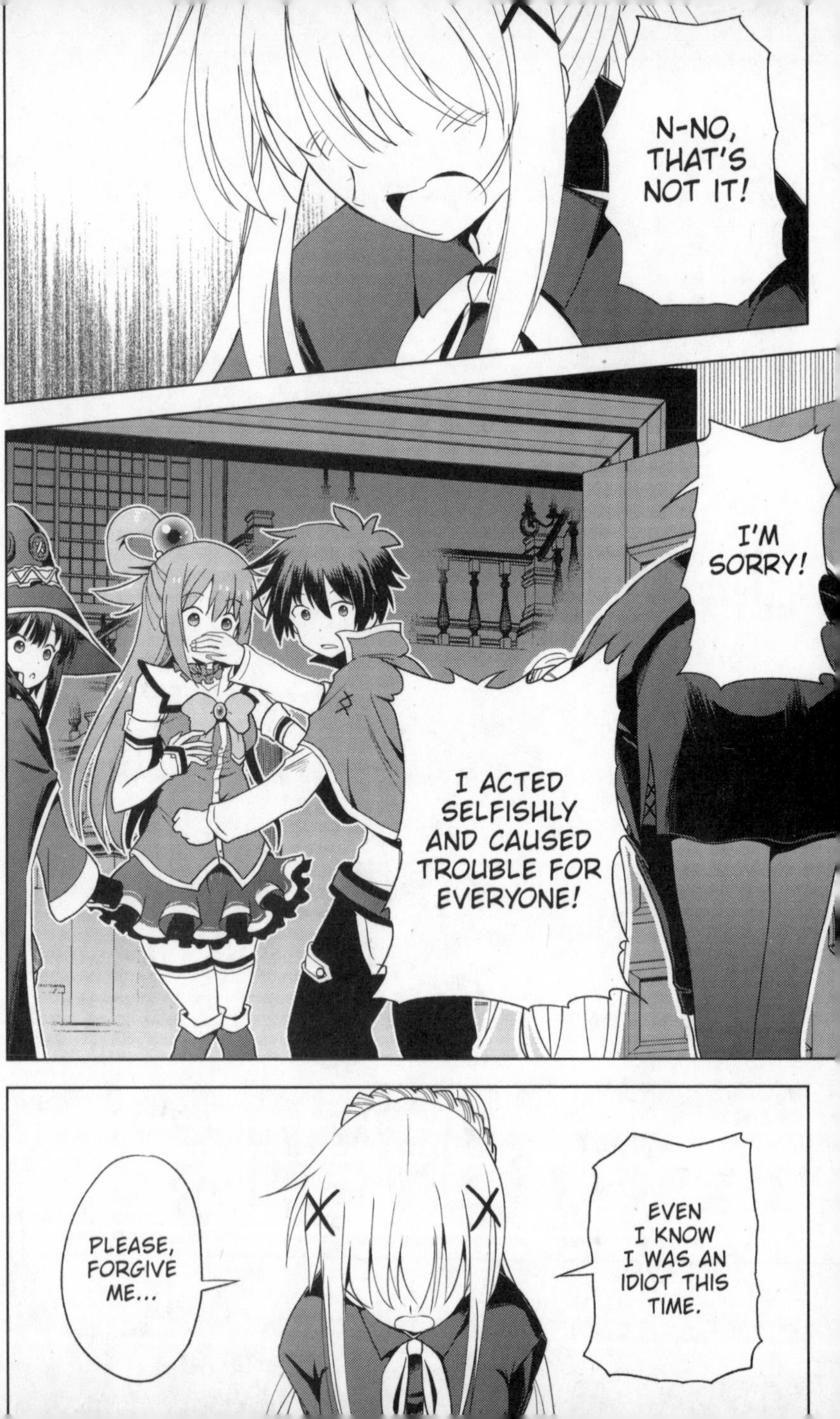
N-NO, THAT'S NOT IT!
I'M SORRY!
I ACTED SELFISHLY AND CAUSED TROUBLE FOR EVERYONE!
EVEN I KNOW I WAS AN IDIOT THIS TIME.
PLEASE, FORGIVE ME...

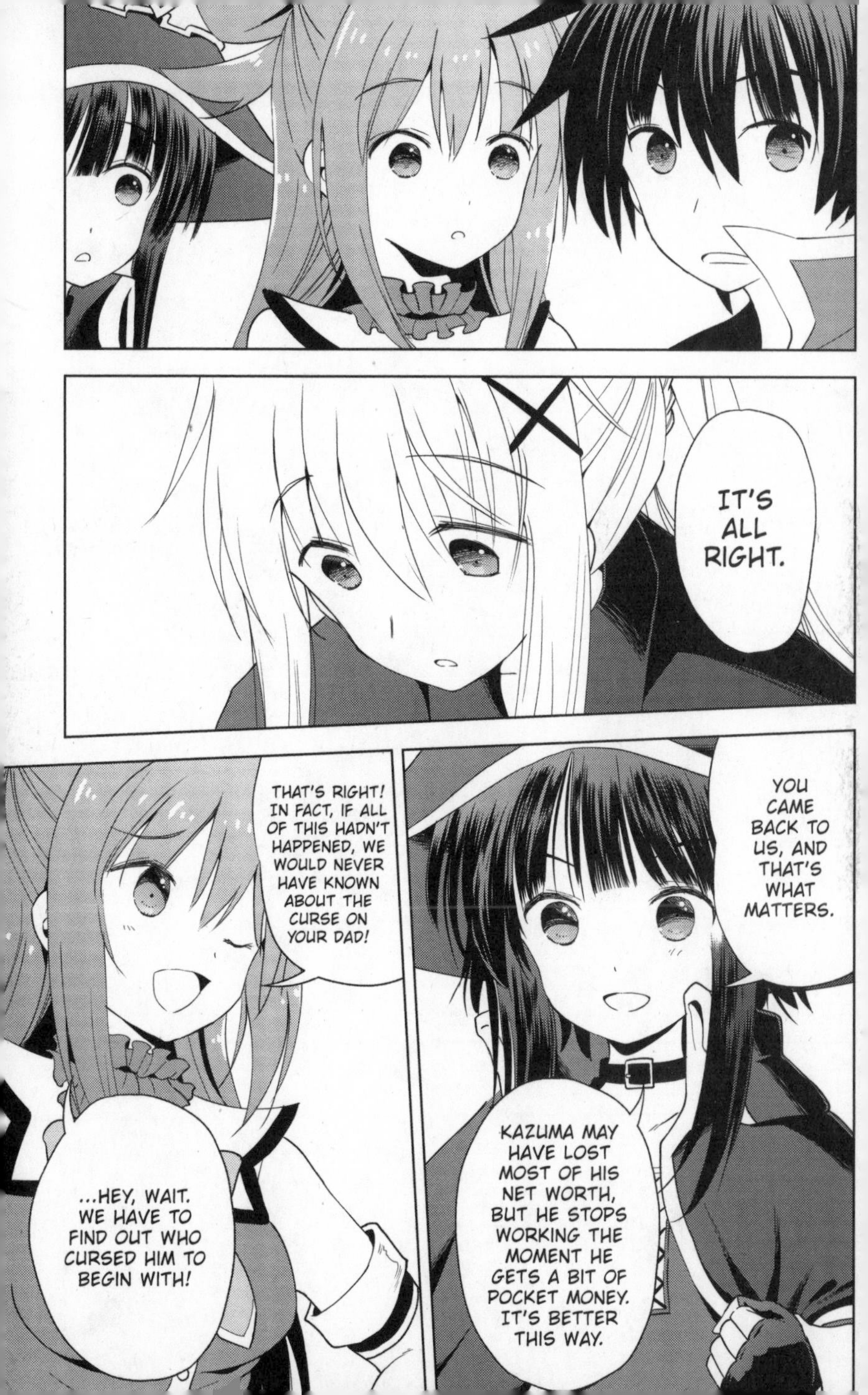
IT'S ALL RIGHT.
YOU CAME BACK TO US, AND THAT'S WHAT MATTERS.
KAZUMA MAY HAVE LOST MOST OF HIS NET WORTH, BUT HE STOPS WORKING THE MOMENT HE GETS A BIT OF POCKET MONEY. IT'S BETTER THIS WAY.
THAT'S RIGHT! IN FACT, IF ALL OF THIS HADN'T HAPPENED, WE WOULD NEVER HAVE KNOWN ABOUT THE CURSE ON YOUR DAD!
...HEY, WAIT. WE HAVE TO FIND OUT WHO CURSED HIM TO BEGIN WITH!

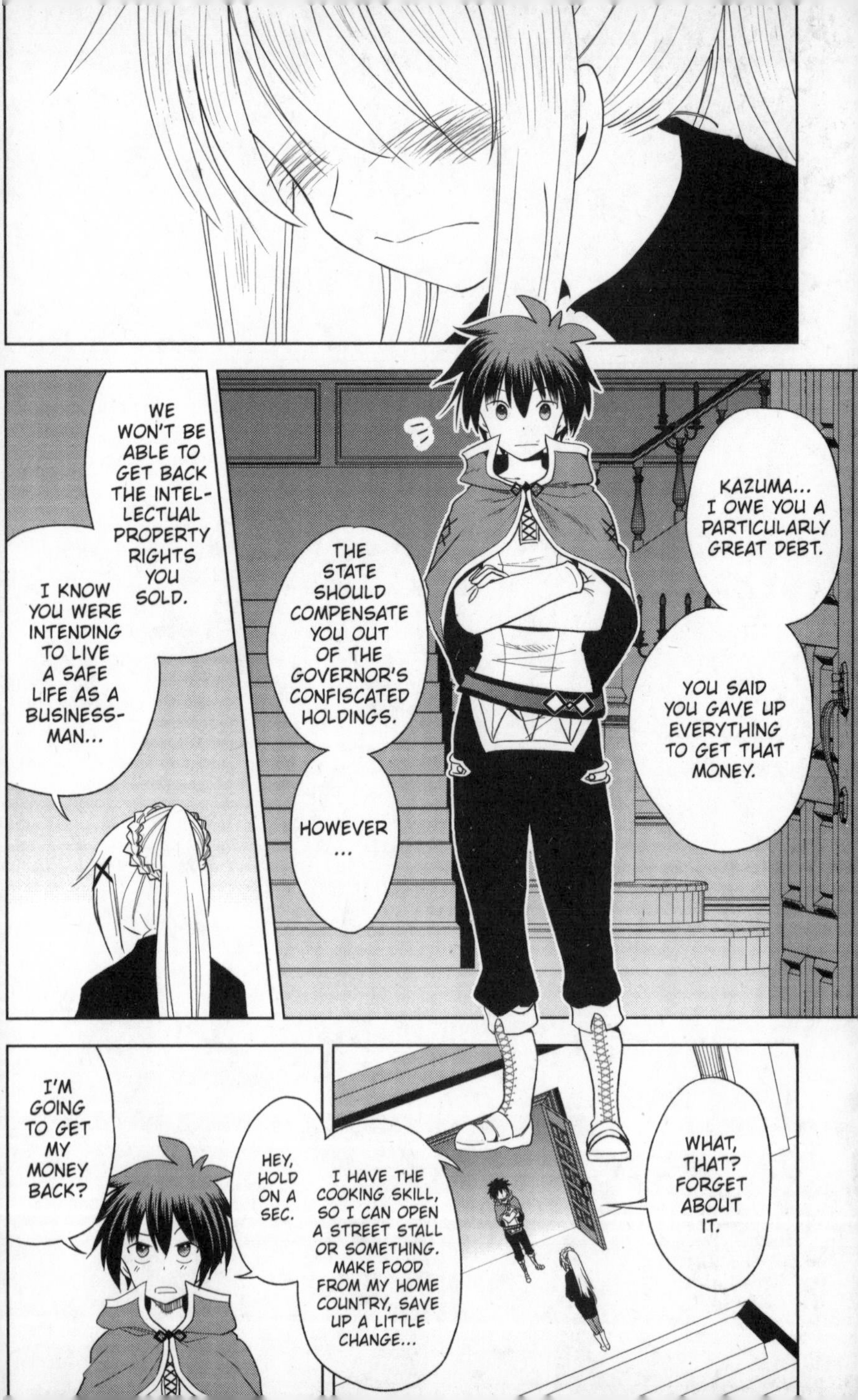
KAZUMA... I OWE YOU A PARTICULARLY GREAT DEBT.
YOU SAID YOU GAVE UP EVERYTHING TO GET THAT MONEY.
THE STATE SHOULD COMPENSATE YOU OUT OF THE GOVERNOR'S CONFISCATED HOLDINGS.
HOWEVER...
WE WON'T BE ABLE TO GET BACK THE INTEL-LECTUAL PROPERTY RIGHTS YOU SOLD.
I KNOW YOU WERE INTENDING TO LIVE A SAFE LIFE AS A BUSINESS-MAN...
WHAT, THAT? FORGET ABOUT IT.
HEY, HOLD ON A SEC.
I HAVE THE COOKING SKILL, SO I CAN OPEN A STREET STALL OR SOMETHING. MAKE FOOD FROM MY HOME COUNTRY, SAVE UP A LITTLE CHANGE...
I'M GOING TO GET MY MONEY BACK?

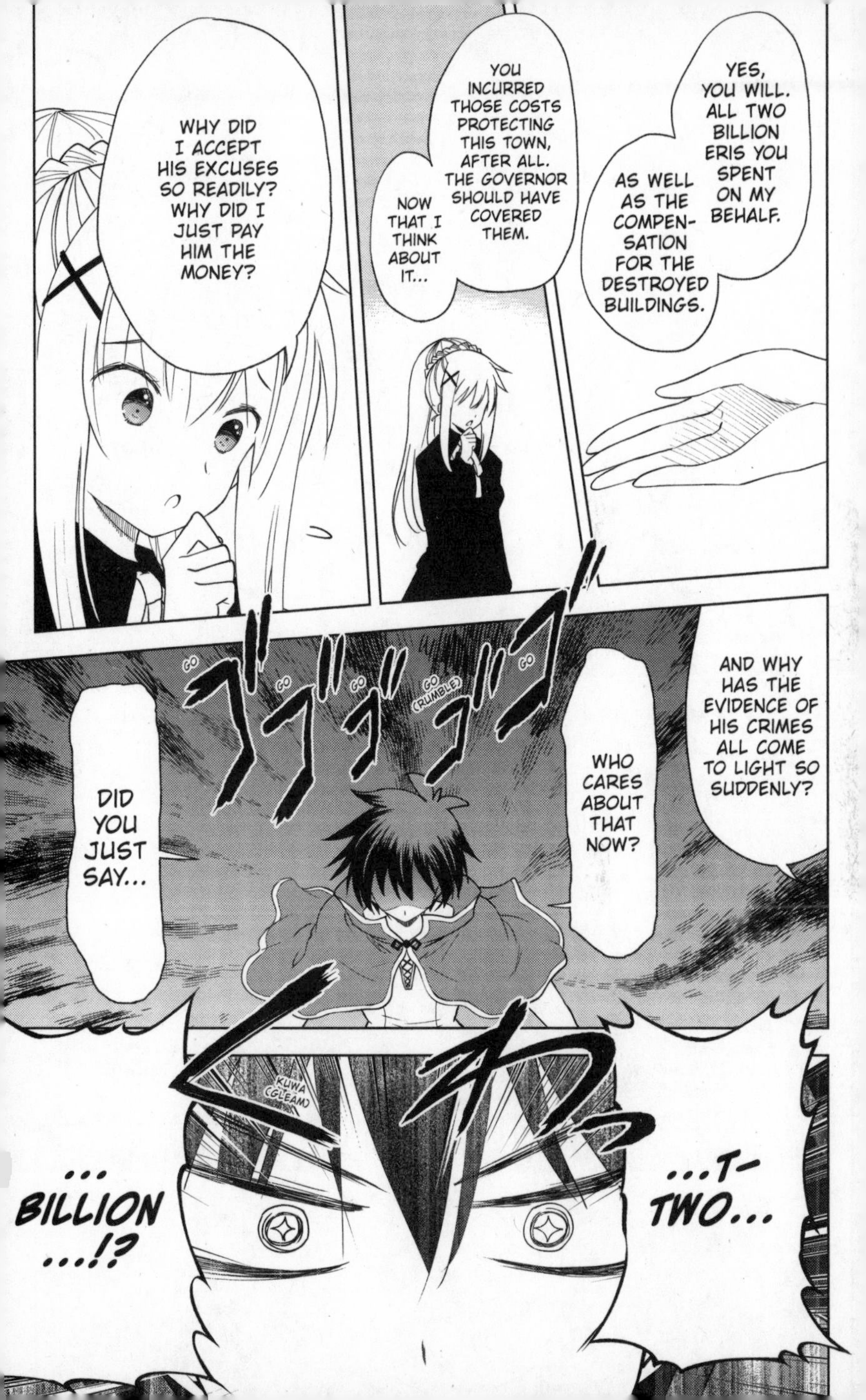
YES, YOU WILL. ALL TWO BILLION ERIS YOU SPENT ON MY BEHALF.
AS WELL AS THE COMPENSATION FOR THE DESTROYED BUILDINGS.
YOU INCURRED THOSE COSTS PROTECTING THIS TOWN, AFTER ALL. THE GOVERNOR SHOULD HAVE COVERED THEM.
NOW THAT I THINK ABOUT IT...
WHY DID I ACCEPT HIS EXCUSES SO READILY? WHY DID I JUST PAY HIM THE MONEY?
AND WHY HAS THE EVIDENCE OF HIS CRIMES ALL COME TO LIGHT SO SUDDENLY?
WHO CARES ABOUT THAT NOW?
GO
GO (RUMBLE)
GO
GO
GO
DID YOU JUST SAY...
...T- TWO...
KUWA (GLEAM)
...BILLION ...!?

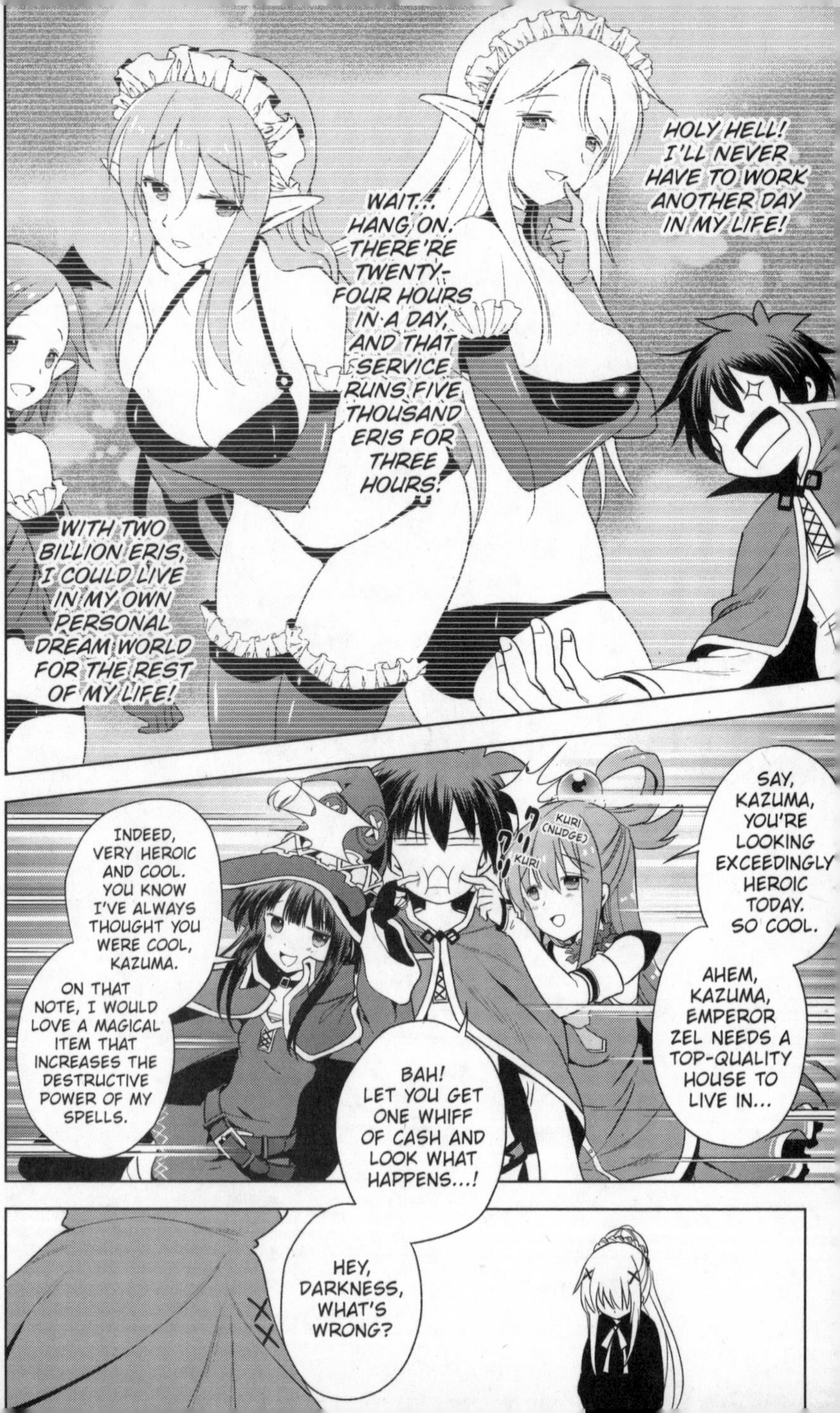
HOLY HELL! I'LL NEVER HAVE TO WORK ANOTHER DAY IN MY LIFE!
WAIT... HANG ON. THERE'RE TWENTY-FOUR HOURS IN A DAY, AND THAT SERVICE RUNS FIVE THOUSAND ERIS FOR THREE HOURS.
WITH TWO BILLION ERIS, I COULD LIVE IN MY OWN PERSONAL DREAM WORLD FOR THE REST OF MY LIFE!
SAY, KAZUMA, YOU'RE LOOKING EXCEEDINGLY HEROIC TODAY. SO COOL.
AHEM, KAZUMA, EMPEROR ZEL NEEDS A TOP-QUALITY HOUSE TO LIVE IN...
KURI (NUDGE)
KURI
INDEED, VERY HEROIC AND COOL. YOU KNOW I'VE ALWAYS THOUGHT YOU WERE COOL, KAZUMA.
ON THAT NOTE, I WOULD LOVE A MAGICAL ITEM THAT INCREASES THE DESTRUCTIVE POWER OF MY SPELLS.
BAH! LET YOU GET ONE WHIFF OF CASH AND LOOK WHAT HAPPENS...!
HEY, DARKNESS, WHAT'S WRONG?

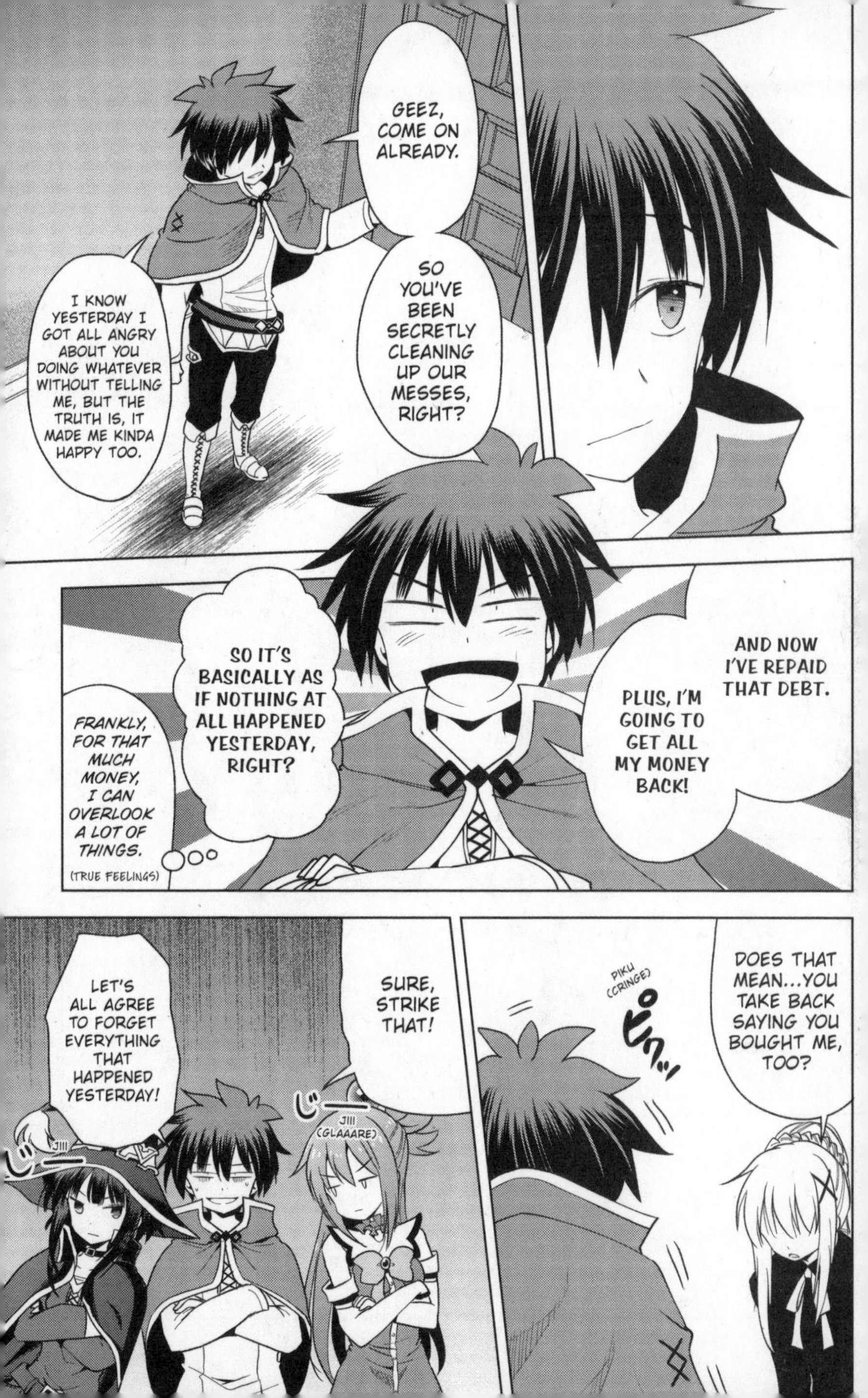

GEEZ, COME ON ALREADY.
SO YOU'VE BEEN SECRETLY CLEANING UP OUR MESSES, RIGHT?
I KNOW YESTERDAY I GOT ALL ANGRY ABOUT YOU DOING WHATEVER WITHOUT TELLING ME, BUT THE TRUTH IS, IT MADE ME KINDA HAPPY TOO.
AND NOW I'VE REPAID THAT DEBT.
PLUS, I'M GOING TO GET ALL MY MONEY BACK!
SO IT'S BASICALLY AS IF NOTHING AT ALL HAPPENED YESTERDAY, RIGHT?
FRANKLY, FOR THAT MUCH MONEY, I CAN OVERLOOK A LOT OF THINGS.
(TRUE FEELINGS)
DOES THAT MEAN...YOU TAKE BACK SAYING YOU BOUGHT ME, TOO?
PIKU (CRINGE)
SURE, STRIKE THAT!
LET'S ALL AGREE TO FORGET EVERYTHING THAT HAPPENED YESTERDAY!
JIII (GLAAARE)
JIII

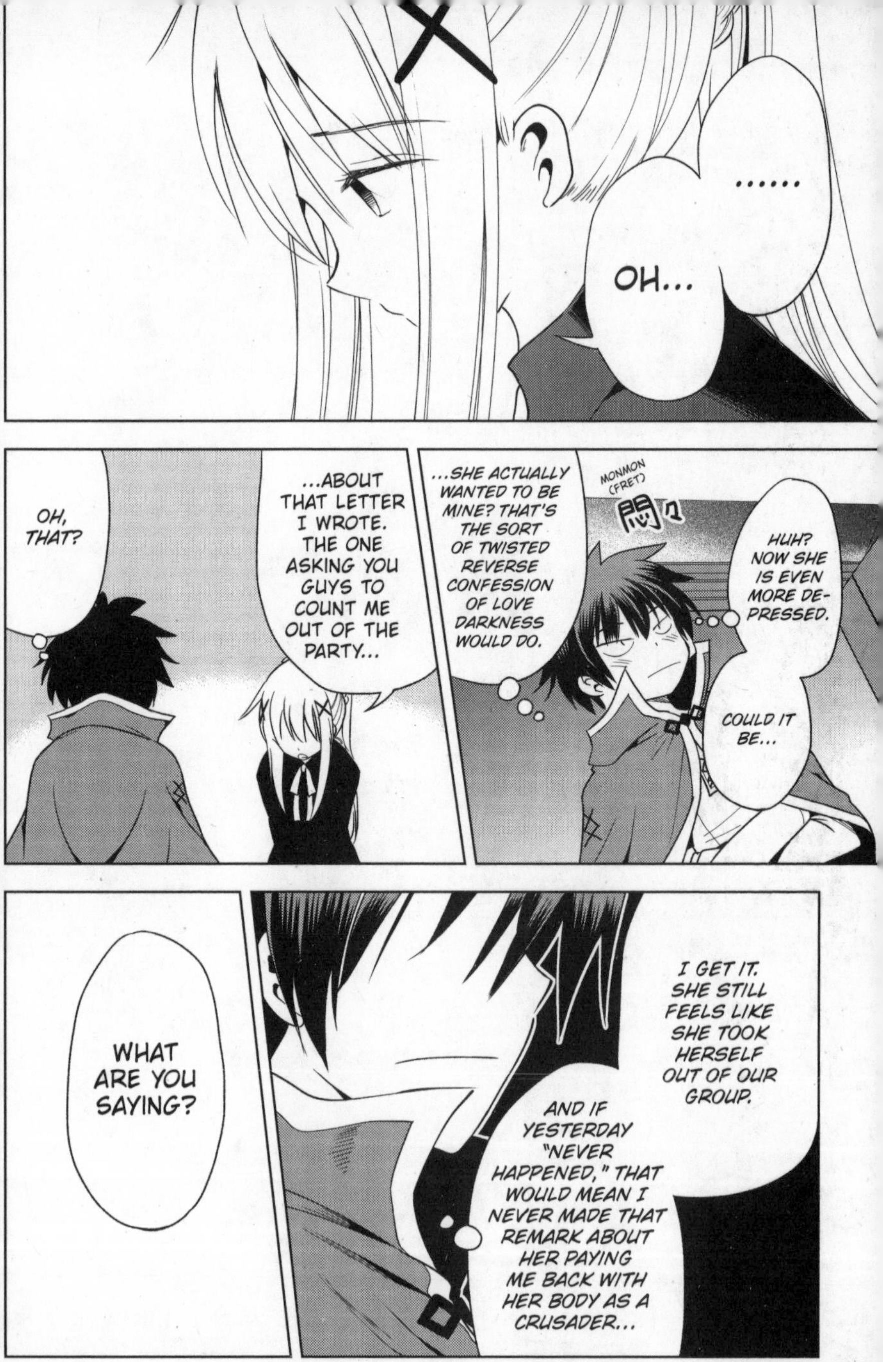
......
OH...
MONMON (FRET)
悶
HUH? NOW SHE IS EVEN MORE DE-PRESSED.
COULD IT BE...
...SHE ACTUALLY WANTED TO BE MINE? THAT'S THE SORT OF TWISTED REVERSE CONFESSION OF LOVE DARKNESS WOULD DO.
...ABOUT THAT LETTER I WROTE. THE ONE ASKING YOU GUYS TO COUNT ME OUT OF THE PARTY...
OH, THAT?
I GET IT. SHE STILL FEELS LIKE SHE TOOK HERSELF OUT OF OUR GROUP.
AND IF YESTERDAY "NEVER HAPPENED," THAT WOULD MEAN I NEVER MADE THAT REMARK ABOUT HER PAYING ME BACK WITH HER BODY AS A CRUSADER...
WHAT ARE YOU SAYING?

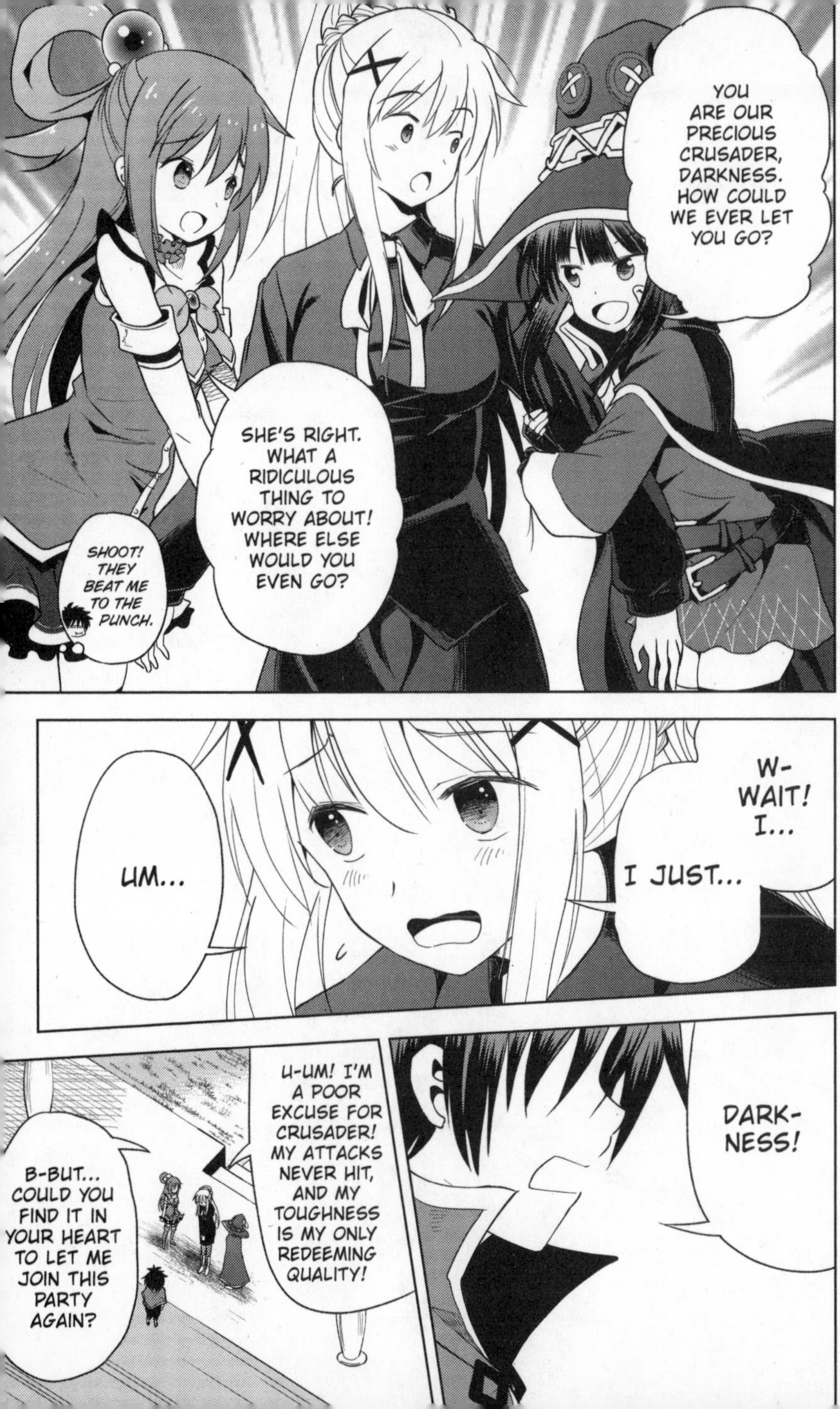
YOU ARE OUR PRECIOUS CRUSADER, DARKNESS. HOW COULD WE EVER LET YOU GO?
SHE'S RIGHT. WHAT A RIDICULOUS THING TO WORRY ABOUT! WHERE ELSE WOULD YOU EVEN GO?
SHOOT! THEY BEAT ME TO THE PUNCH.
W-WAIT! I...
I JUST...
UM...
DARK-NESS!
U-UM! I'M A POOR EXCUSE FOR CRUSADER! MY ATTACKS NEVER HIT, AND MY TOUGHNESS IS MY ONLY REDEEMING QUALITY!
B-BUT... COULD YOU FIND IT IN YOUR HEART TO LET ME JOIN THIS PARTY AGAIN?

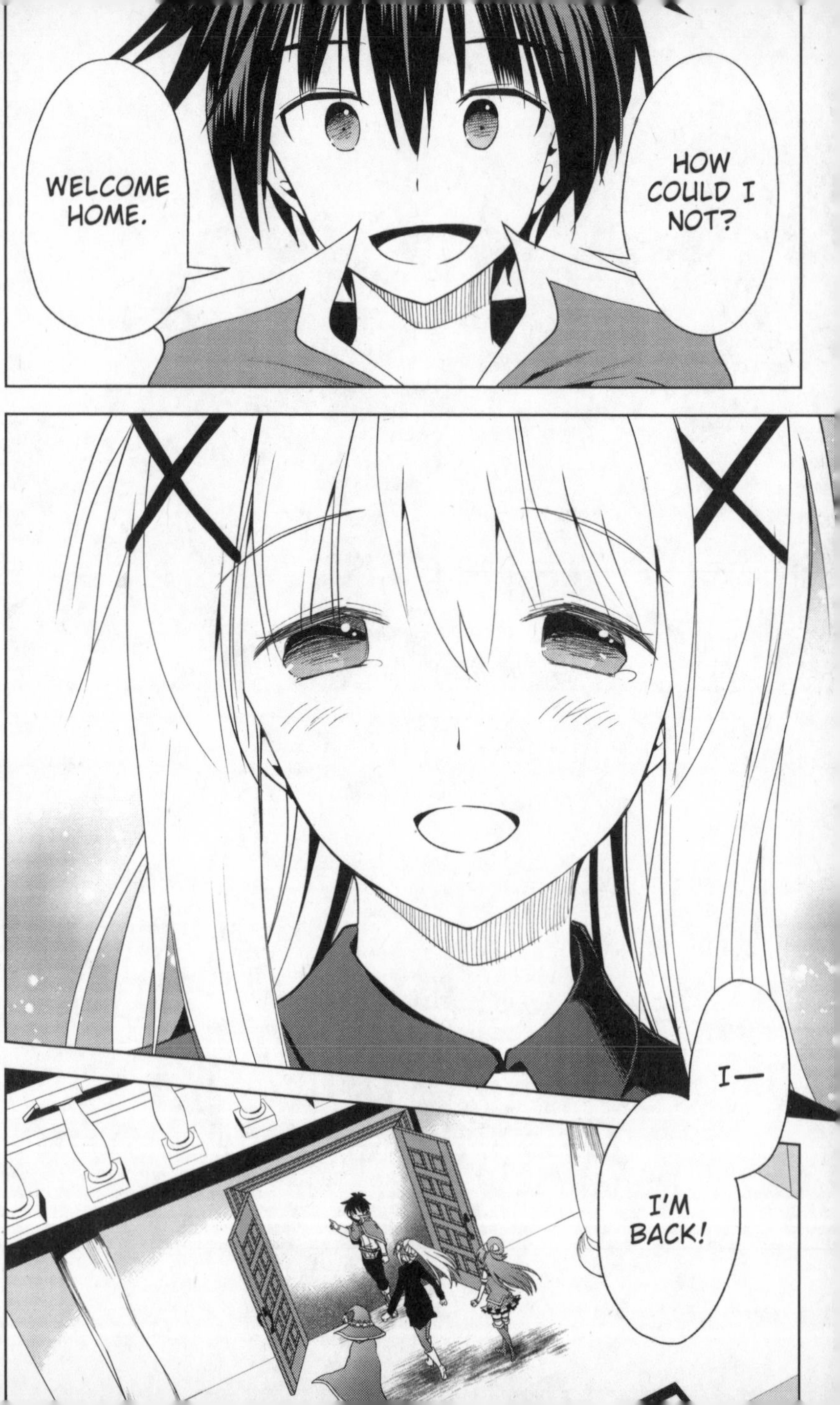
HOW COULD I NOT?
WELCOME HOME.
I—
I'M BACK!

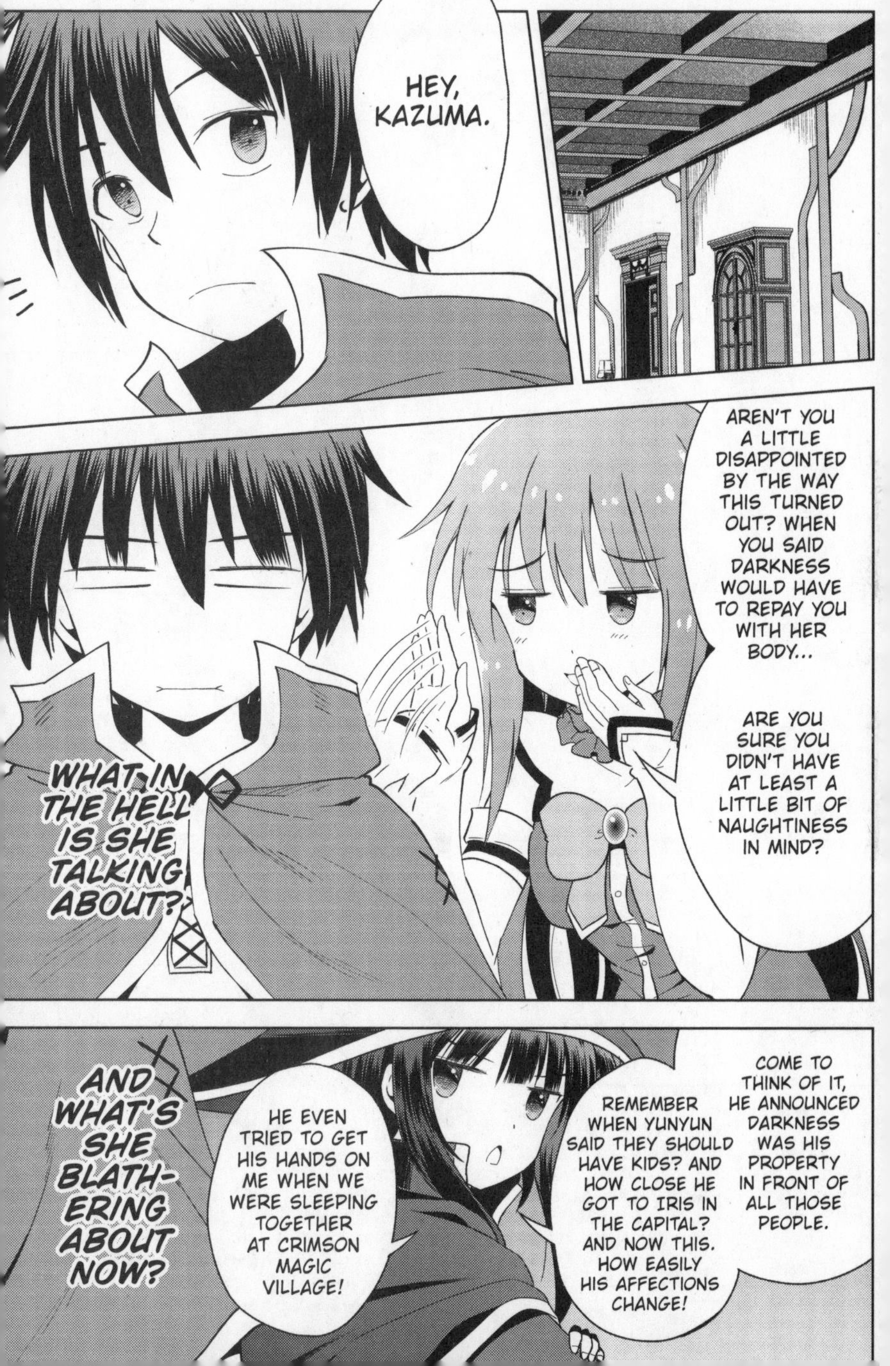
HEY, KAZUMA.
AREN'T YOU A LITTLE DISAPPOINTED BY THE WAY THIS TURNED OUT? WHEN YOU SAID DARKNESS WOULD HAVE TO REPAY YOU WITH HER BODY...
ARE YOU SURE YOU DIDN'T HAVE AT LEAST A LITTLE BIT OF NAUGHTINESS IN MIND?
WHAT IN THE HELL IS SHE TALKING ABOUT?
COME TO THINK OF IT, HE ANNOUNCED DARKNESS WAS HIS PROPERTY IN FRONT OF ALL THOSE PEOPLE.
REMEMBER WHEN YUNYUN SAID THEY SHOULD HAVE KIDS? AND HOW CLOSE HE GOT TO IRIS IN THE CAPITAL? AND NOW THIS. HOW EASILY HIS AFFECTIONS CHANGE!
HE EVEN TRIED TO GET HIS HANDS ON ME WHEN WE WERE SLEEPING TOGETHER AT CRIMSON MAGIC VILLAGE!
AND WHAT'S SHE BLATH-ERING ABOUT NOW?

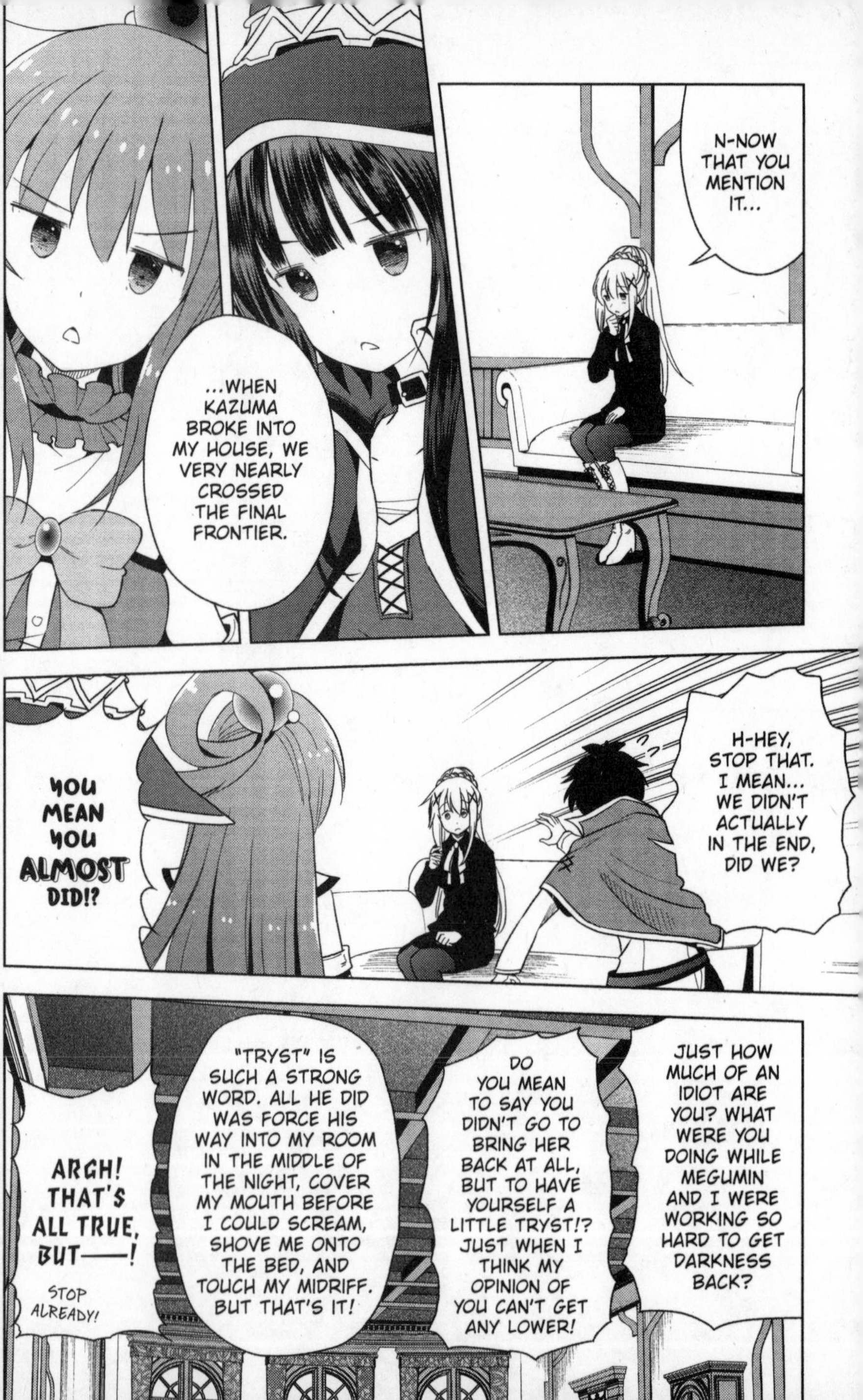
N-NOW THAT YOU MENTION IT...
...WHEN KAZUMA BROKE INTO MY HOUSE, WE VERY NEARLY CROSSED THE FINAL FRONTIER.
H-HEY, STOP THAT. I MEAN... WE DIDN'T ACTUALLY IN THE END, DID WE?
YOU MEAN YOU ALMOST DID!?
JUST HOW MUCH OF AN IDIOT ARE YOU? WHAT WERE YOU DOING WHILE MEGUMIN AND I WERE WORKING SO HARD TO GET DARKNESS BACK?
DO YOU MEAN TO SAY YOU DIDN'T GO TO BRING HER BACK AT ALL, BUT TO HAVE YOURSELF A LITTLE TRYST!? JUST WHEN I THINK MY OPINION OF YOU CAN'T GET ANY LOWER!
"TRYST" IS SUCH A STRONG WORD. ALL HE DID WAS FORCE HIS WAY INTO MY ROOM IN THE MIDDLE OF THE NIGHT, COVER MY MOUTH BEFORE I COULD SCREAM, SHOVE ME ONTO THE BED, AND TOUCH MY MIDRIFF. BUT THAT'S IT!
ARGH! THAT'S ALL TRUE, BUT——!
STOP ALREADY!

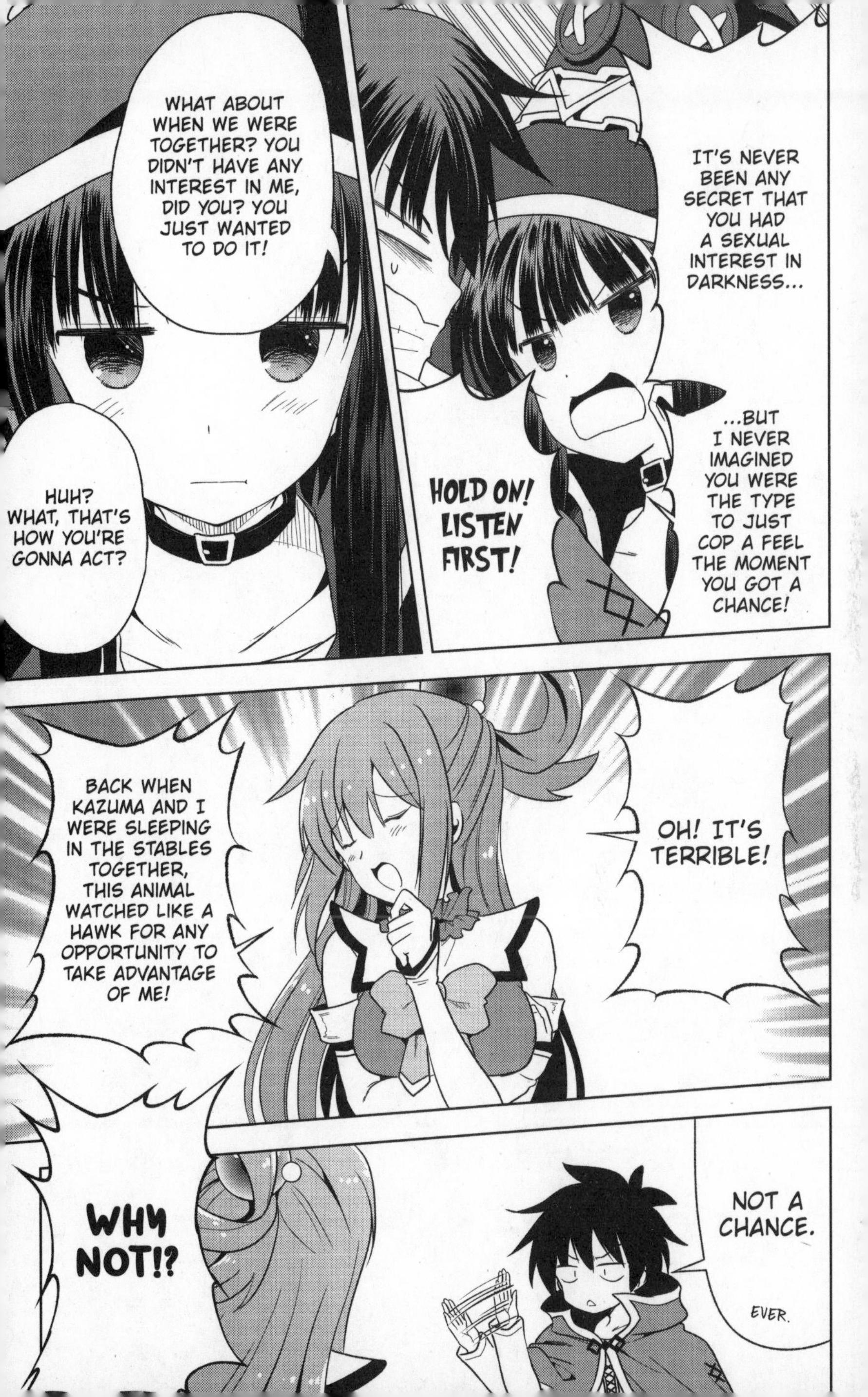
IT'S NEVER BEEN ANY SECRET THAT YOU HAD A SEXUAL INTEREST IN DARKNESS...
...BUT I NEVER IMAGINED YOU WERE THE TYPE TO JUST COP A FEEL THE MOMENT YOU GOT A CHANCE!
HOLD ON! LISTEN FIRST!
WHAT ABOUT WHEN WE WERE TOGETHER? YOU DIDN'T HAVE ANY INTEREST IN ME, DID YOU? YOU JUST WANTED TO DO IT!
HUH? WHAT, THAT'S HOW YOU'RE GONNA ACT?
OH! IT'S TERRIBLE!
BACK WHEN KAZUMA AND I WERE SLEEPING IN THE STABLES TOGETHER, THIS ANIMAL WATCHED LIKE A HAWK FOR ANY OPPORTUNITY TO TAKE ADVANTAGE OF ME!
NOT A CHANCE.
EVER.
WHY NOT!?

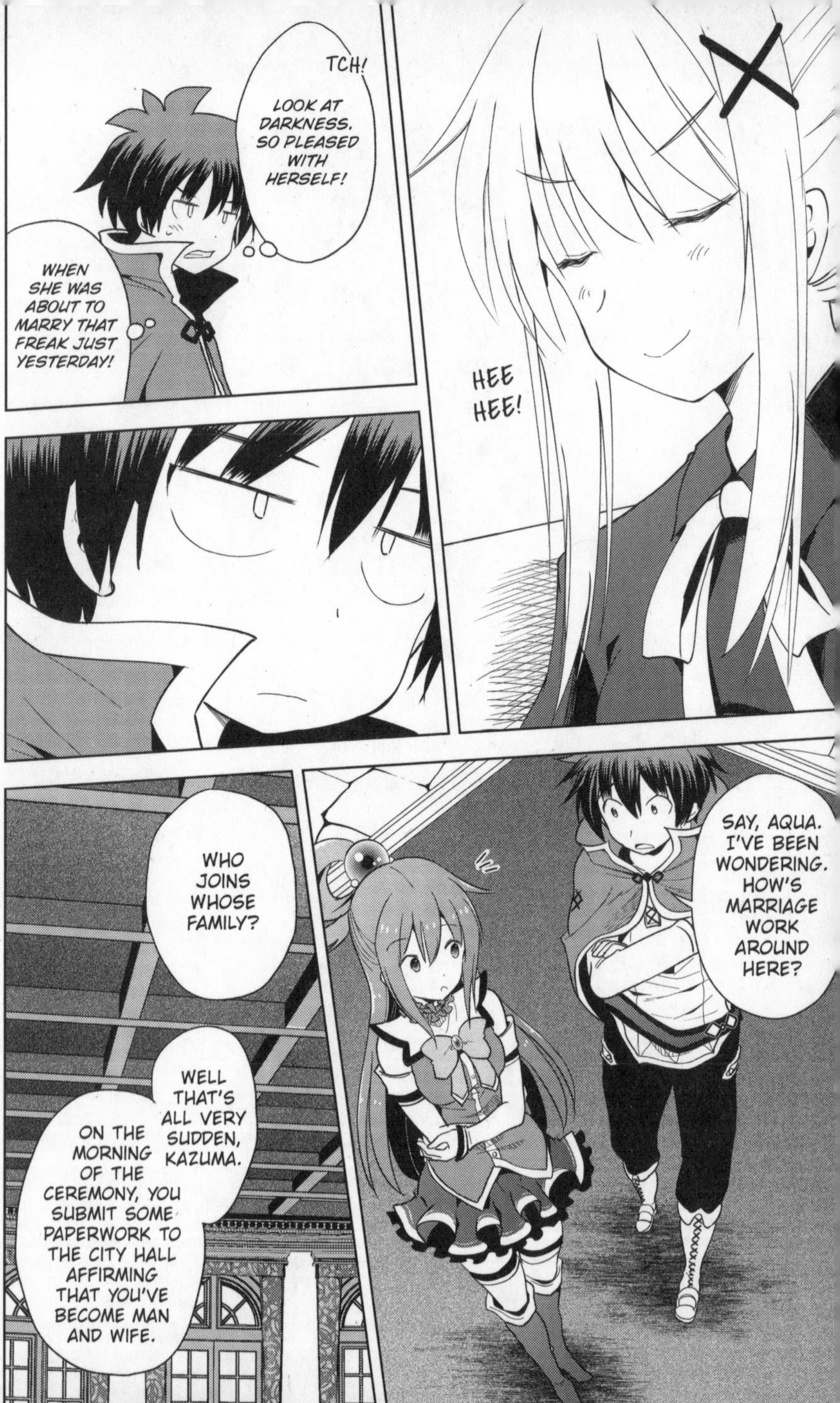
HEE HEE!
TCH!
LOOK AT DARKNESS. SO PLEASED WITH HERSELF!
WHEN SHE WAS ABOUT TO MARRY THAT FREAK JUST YESTERDAY!
SAY, AQUA. I'VE BEEN WONDERING. HOW'S MARRIAGE WORK AROUND HERE?
WHO JOINS WHOSE FAMILY?
WELL THAT'S ALL VERY SUDDEN, KAZUMA.
ON THE MORNING OF THE CEREMONY, YOU SUBMIT SOME PAPERWORK TO THE CITY HALL AFFIRMING THAT YOU'VE BECOME MAN AND WIFE.

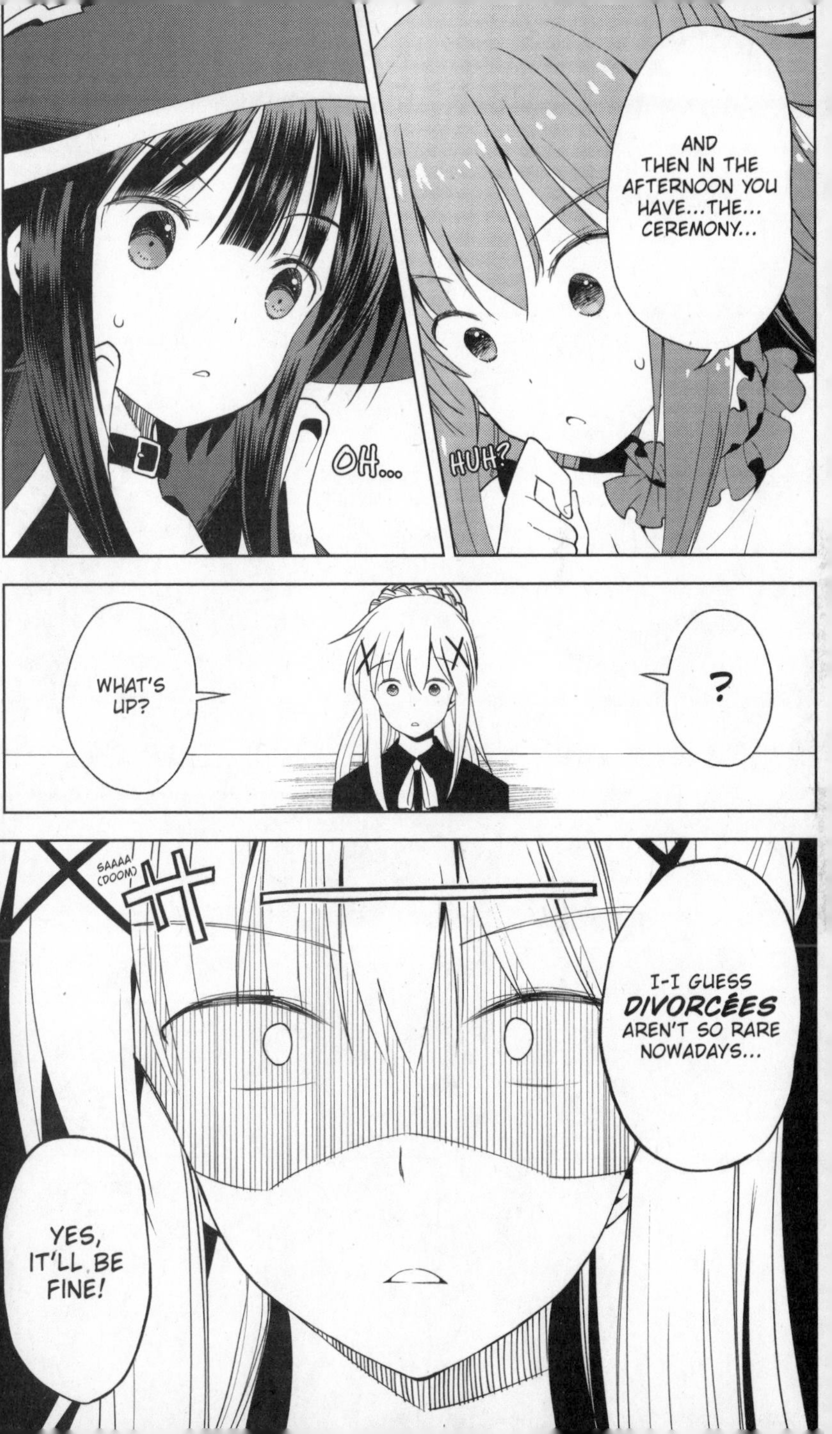
AND THEN IN THE AFTERNOON YOU HAVE...THE... CEREMONY...
HUH?
OH...
?
WHAT'S UP?
I-I GUESS DIVORCÉES AREN'T SO RARE NOWADAYS...
SAAAA (DOOM)
YES, IT'LL BE FINE!

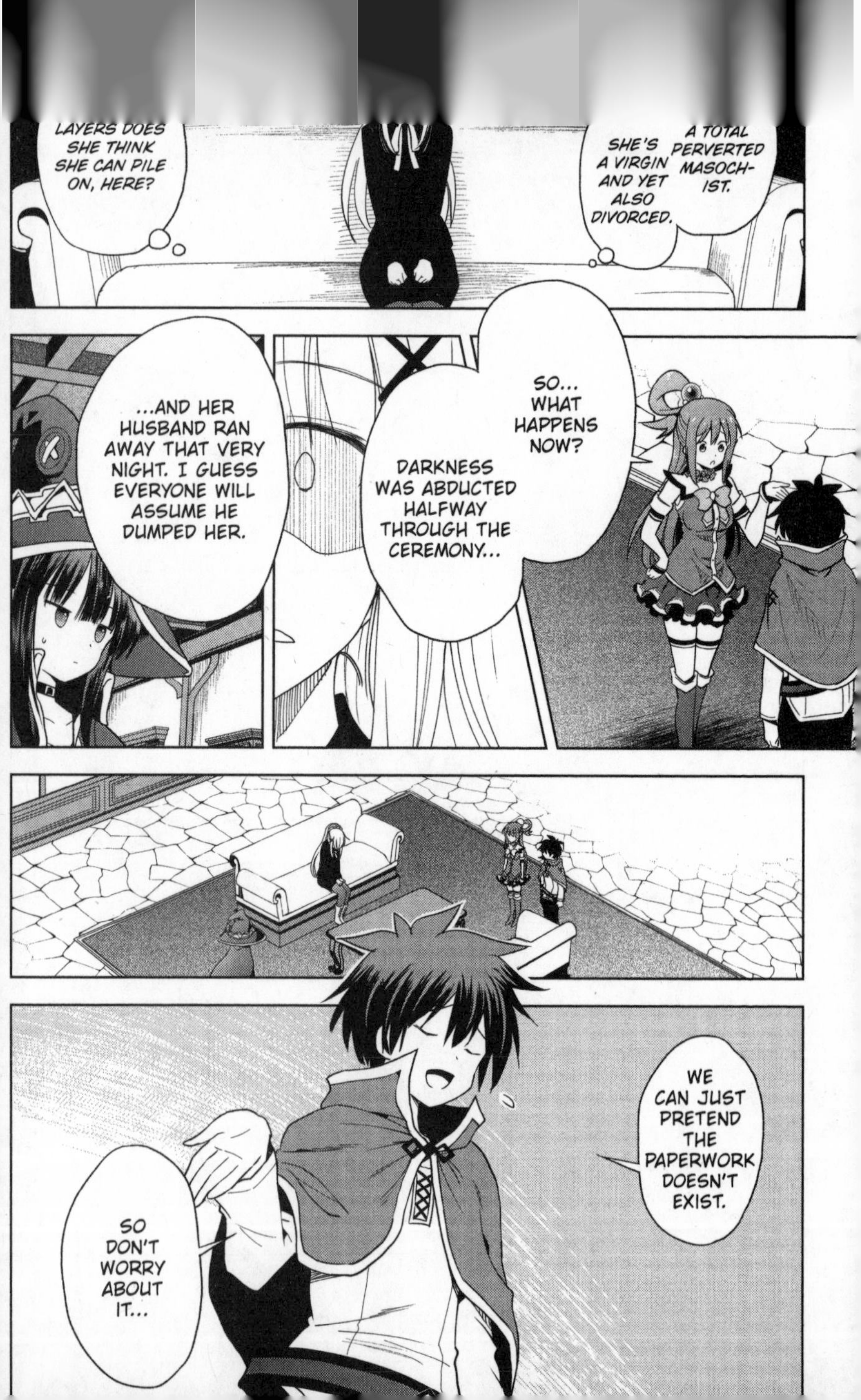
A TOTAL PERVERTED MASOCH-IST.
SHE'S A VIRGIN AND YET ALSO DIVORCED.
LAYERS DOES SHE THINK SHE CAN PILE ON, HERE?
SO... WHAT HAPPENS NOW?
DARKNESS WAS ABDUCTED HALFWAY THROUGH THE CEREMONY...
...AND HER HUSBAND RAN AWAY THAT VERY NIGHT. I GUESS EVERYONE WILL ASSUME HE DUMPED HER.
WE CAN JUST PRETEND THE PAPERWORK DOESN'T EXIST.
SO DON'T WORRY ABOUT IT...

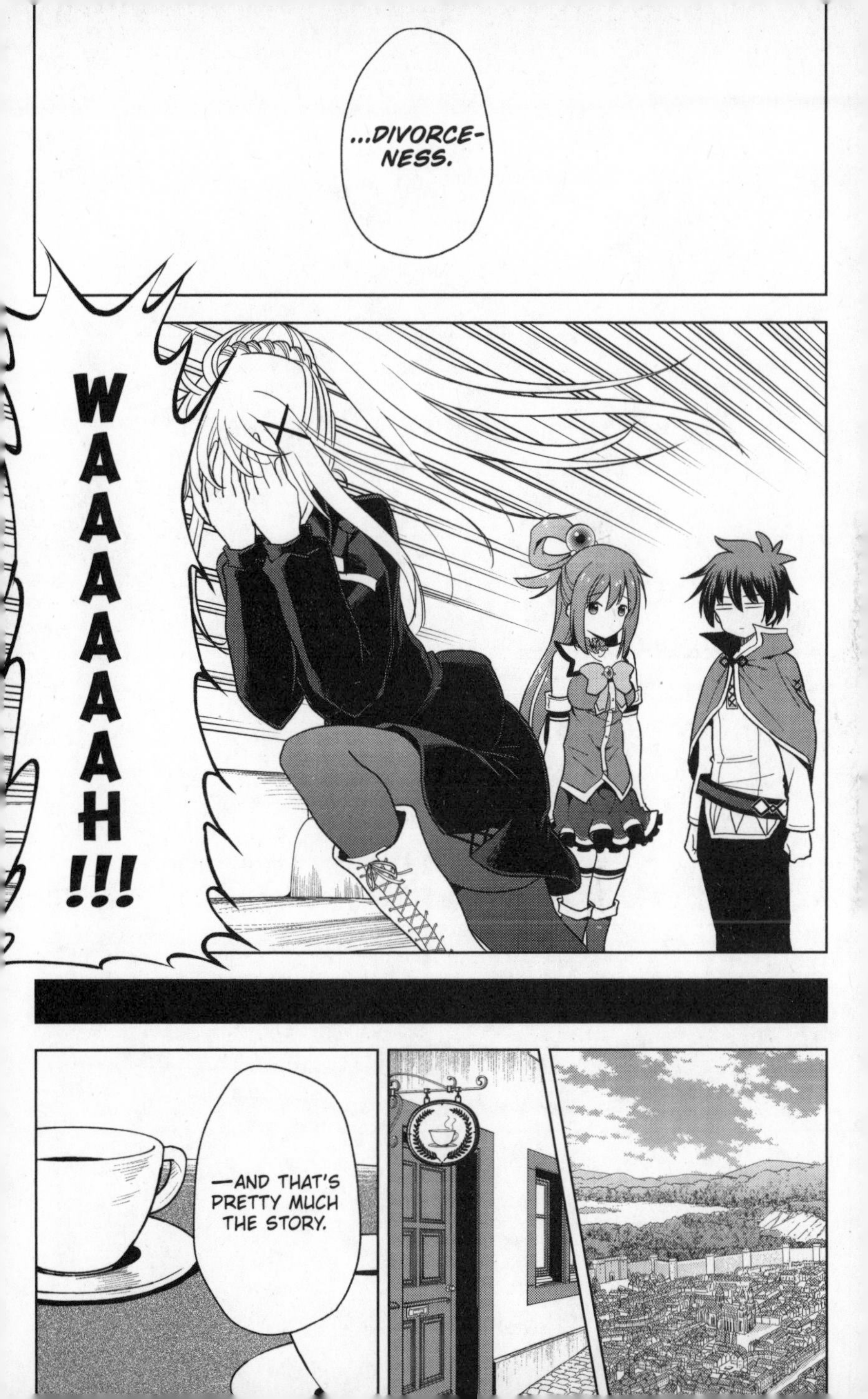
...DIVORCE-NESS.
WAAAAAAAH!!!
—AND THAT'S PRETTY MUCH THE STORY.

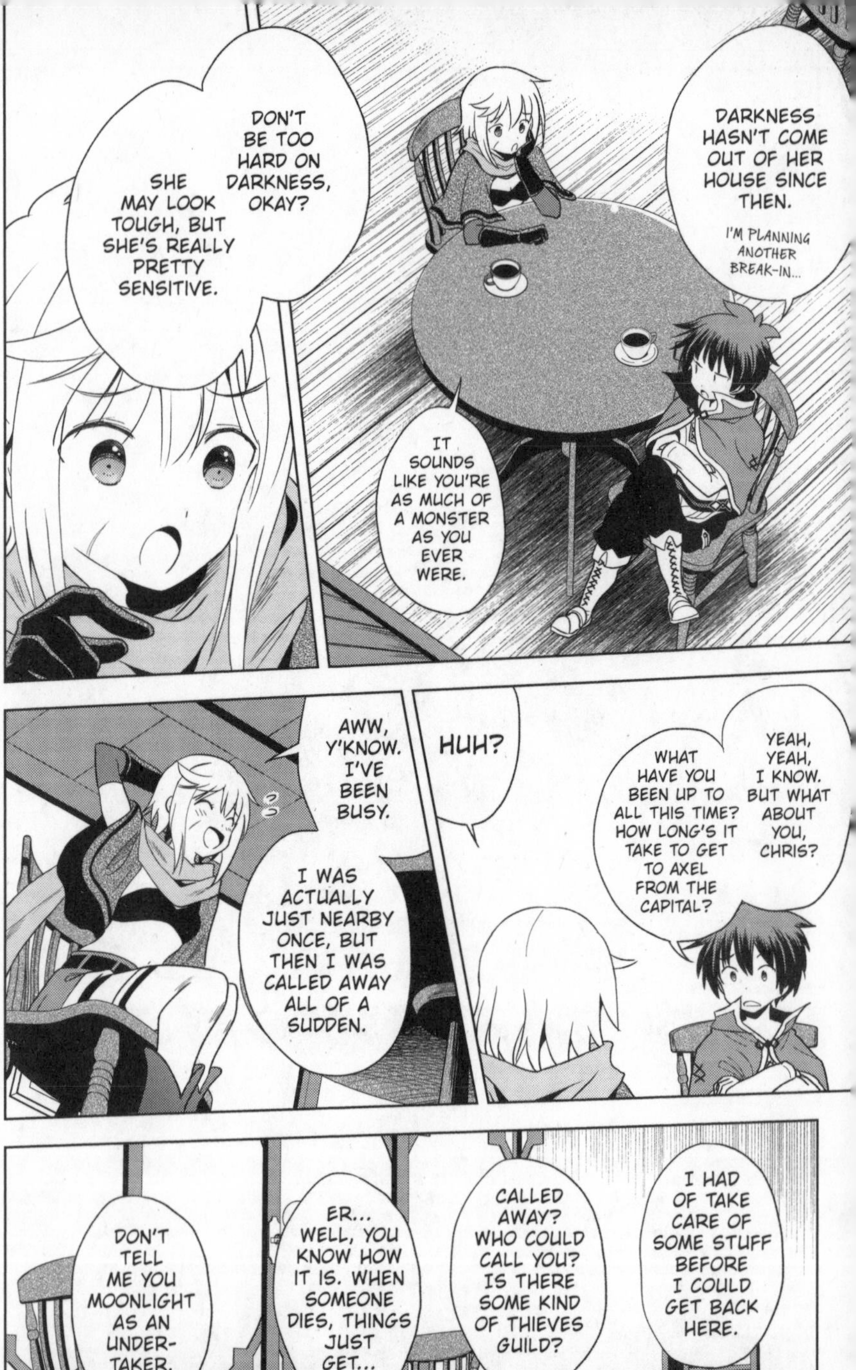
DARKNESS HASN'T COME OUT OF HER HOUSE SINCE THEN.
I'M PLANNING ANOTHER BREAK-IN...
IT SOUNDS LIKE YOU'RE AS MUCH OF A MONSTER AS YOU EVER WERE.
DON'T BE TOO HARD ON DARKNESS, OKAY?
SHE MAY LOOK TOUGH, BUT SHE'S REALLY PRETTY SENSITIVE.
YEAH, YEAH, I KNOW. BUT WHAT ABOUT YOU, CHRIS?
WHAT HAVE YOU BEEN UP TO ALL THIS TIME? HOW LONG'S IT TAKE TO GET TO AXEL FROM THE CAPITAL?
HUH?
AWW, Y'KNOW. I'VE BEEN BUSY.
I WAS ACTUALLY JUST NEARBY ONCE, BUT THEN I WAS CALLED AWAY ALL OF A SUDDEN.
I HAD OF TAKE CARE OF SOME STUFF BEFORE I COULD GET BACK HERE.
CALLED AWAY? WHO COULD CALL YOU? IS THERE SOME KIND OF THIEVES GUILD?
ER... WELL, YOU KNOW HOW IT IS. WHEN SOMEONE DIES, THINGS JUST GET...
DON'T TELL ME YOU MOONLIGHT AS AN UNDER-TAKER.

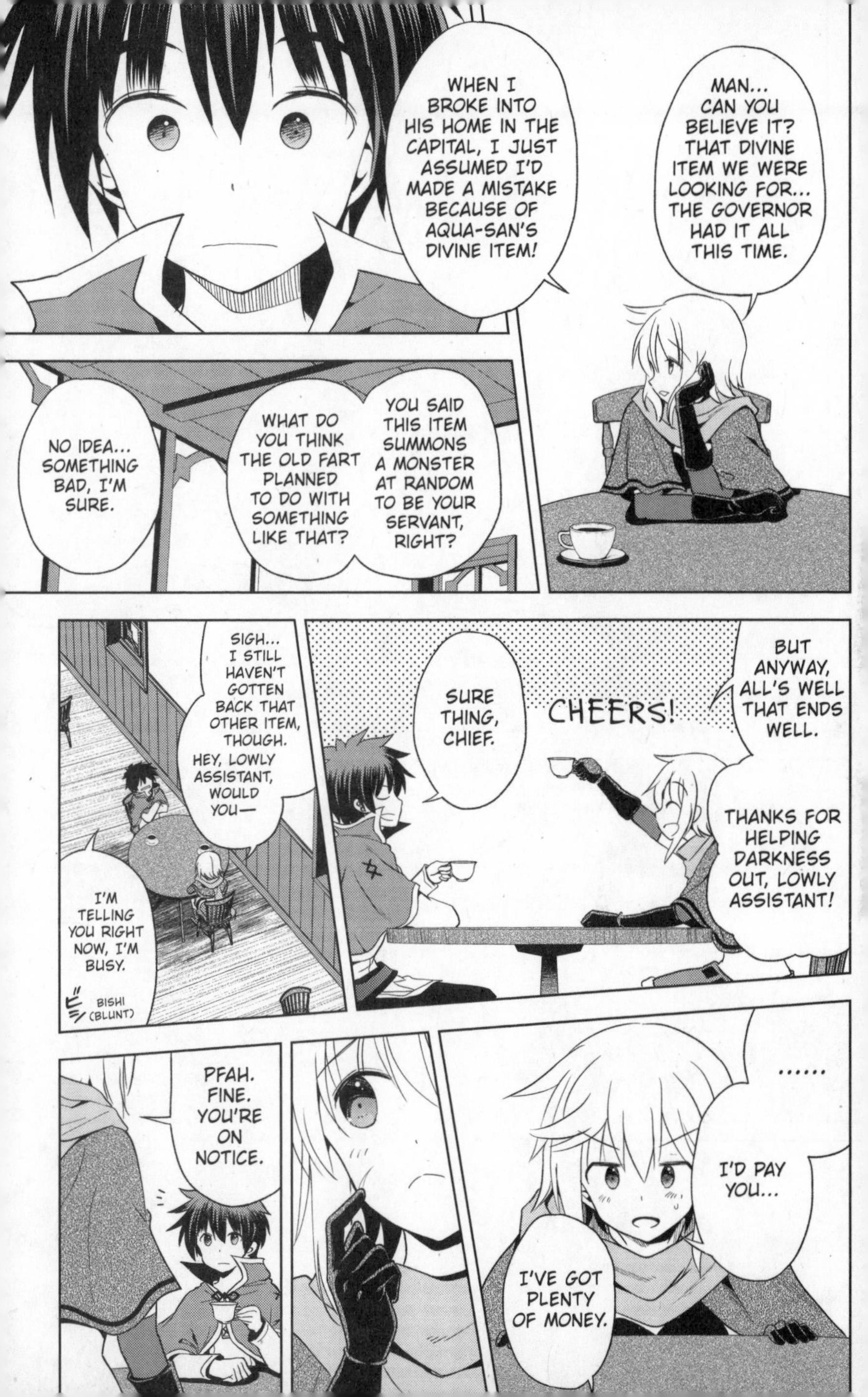
MAN... CAN YOU BELIEVE IT? THAT DIVINE ITEM WE WERE LOOKING FOR... THE GOVERNOR HAD IT ALL THIS TIME.
WHEN I BROKE INTO HIS HOME IN THE CAPITAL, I JUST ASSUMED I'D MADE A MISTAKE BECAUSE OF AQUA-SAN'S DIVINE ITEM!
YOU SAID THIS ITEM SUMMONS A MONSTER AT RANDOM TO BE YOUR SERVANT, RIGHT?
WHAT DO YOU THINK THE OLD FART PLANNED TO DO WITH SOMETHING LIKE THAT?
NO IDEA... SOMETHING BAD, I'M SURE.
BUT ANYWAY, ALL'S WELL THAT ENDS WELL.
CHEERS!
SURE THING, CHIEF.
THANKS FOR HELPING DARKNESS OUT, LOWLY ASSISTANT!
SIGH... I STILL HAVEN'T GOTTEN BACK THAT OTHER ITEM, THOUGH. HEY, LOWLY ASSISTANT, WOULD YOU—
I'M TELLING YOU RIGHT NOW, I'M BUSY.
BISHI (BLUNT)
......
I'D PAY YOU...
I'VE GOT PLENTY OF MONEY.
PFAH. FINE. YOU'RE ON NOTICE.

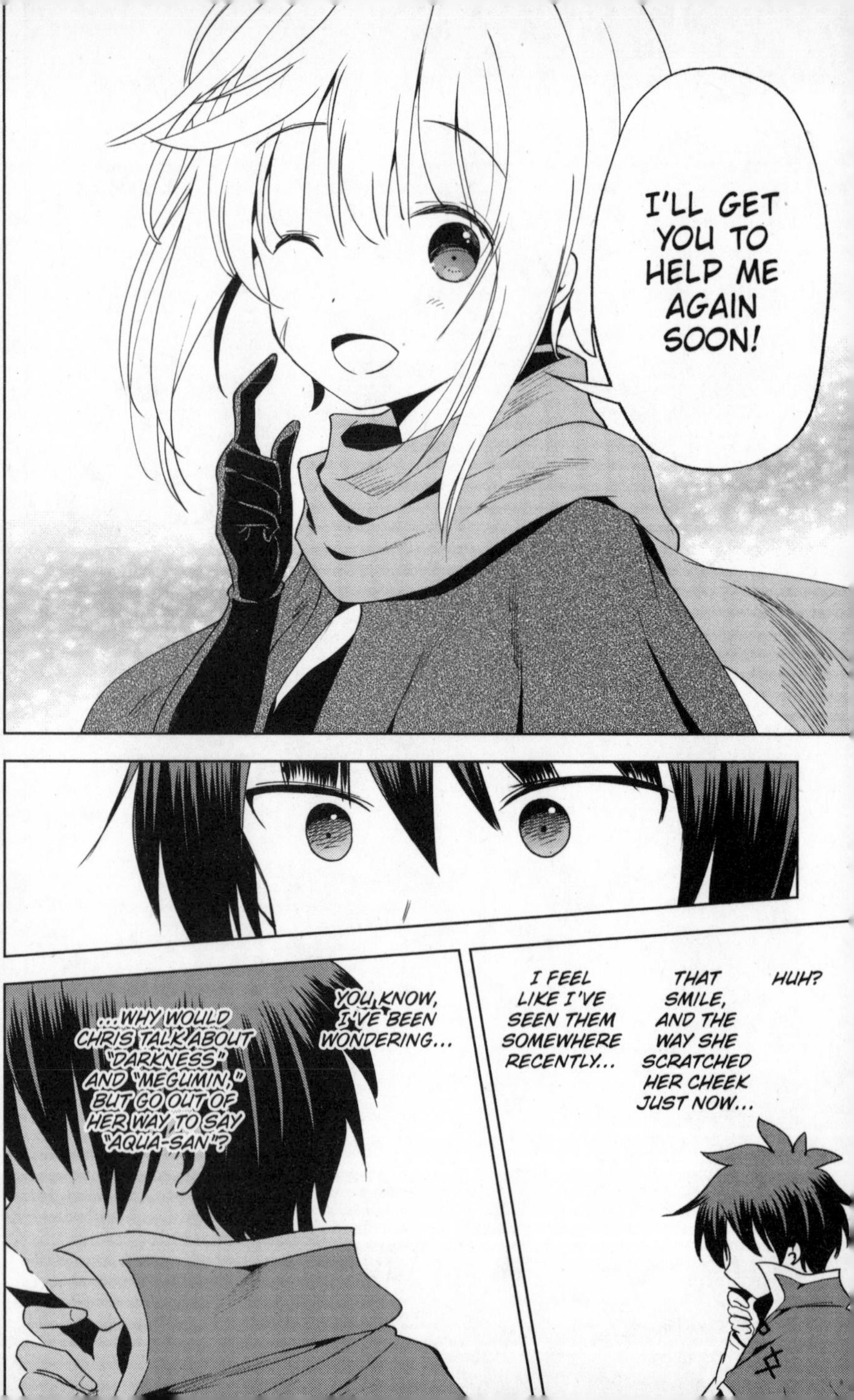
I'LL GET YOU TO HELP ME AGAIN SOON!
HUH?
THAT SMILE, AND THE WAY SHE SCRATCHED HER CHEEK JUST NOW...
I FEEL LIKE I'VE SEEN THEM SOMEWHERE RECENTLY...
YOU KNOW, I'VE BEEN WONDERING...
...WHY WOULD CHRIS TALK ABOUT "DARKNESS" AND "MEGUMIN," BUT GO OUT OF HER WAY TO SAY "AQUA-SAN"?

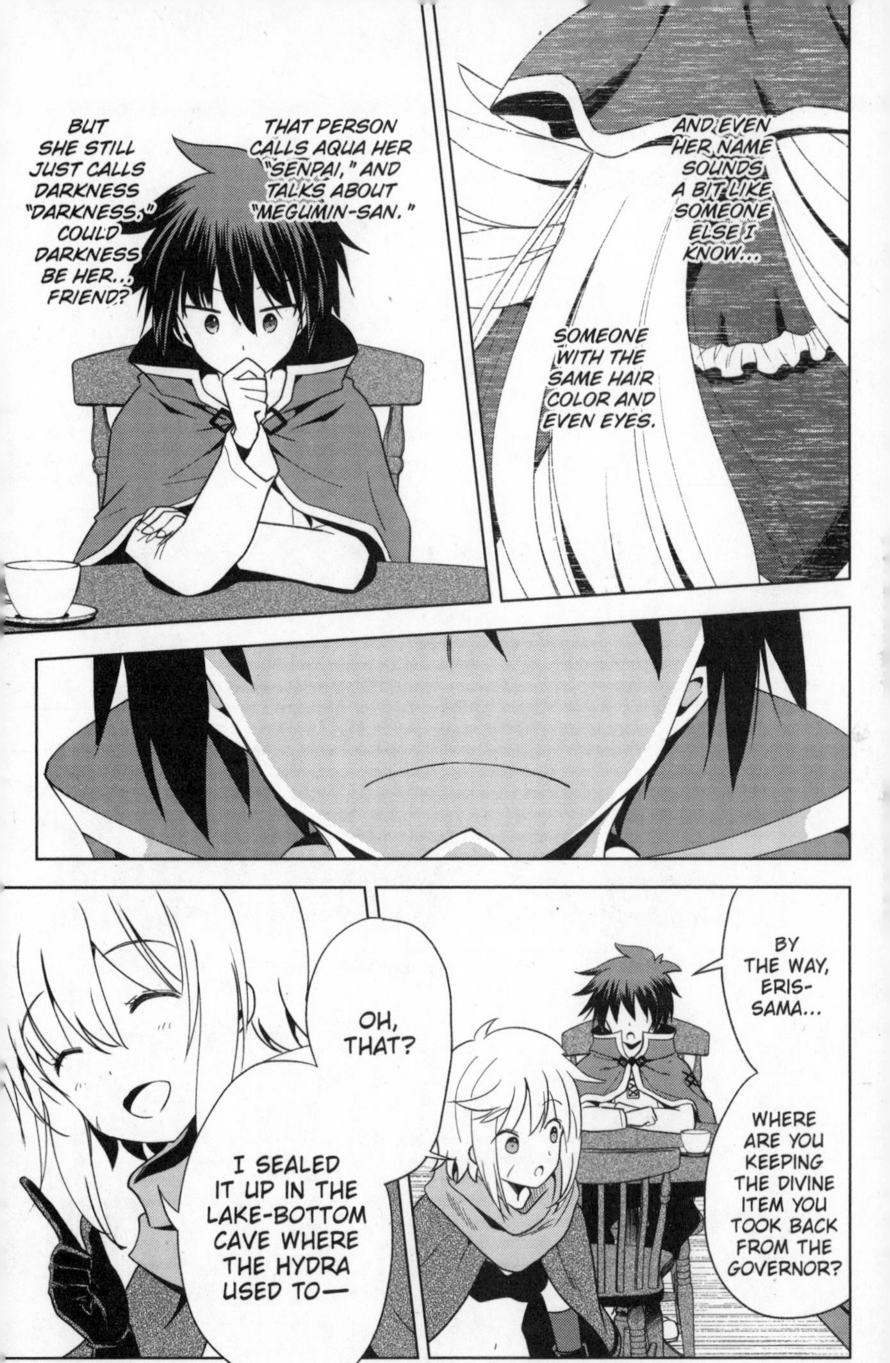
AND EVEN HER NAME SOUNDS A BIT LIKE SOMEONE ELSE I KNOW...
SOMEONE WITH THE SAME HAIR COLOR AND EVEN EYES.
THAT PERSON CALLS AQUA HER "SENPAI," AND TALKS ABOUT "MEGUMIN-SAN."
BUT SHE STILL JUST CALLS DARKNESS "DARKNESS." COULD DARKNESS BE HER... FRIEND?
BY THE WAY, ERIS-SAMA...
WHERE ARE YOU KEEPING THE DIVINE ITEM YOU TOOK BACK FROM THE GOVERNOR?
OH, THAT?
I SEALED IT UP IN THE LAKE-BOTTOM CAVE WHERE THE HYDRA USED TO—

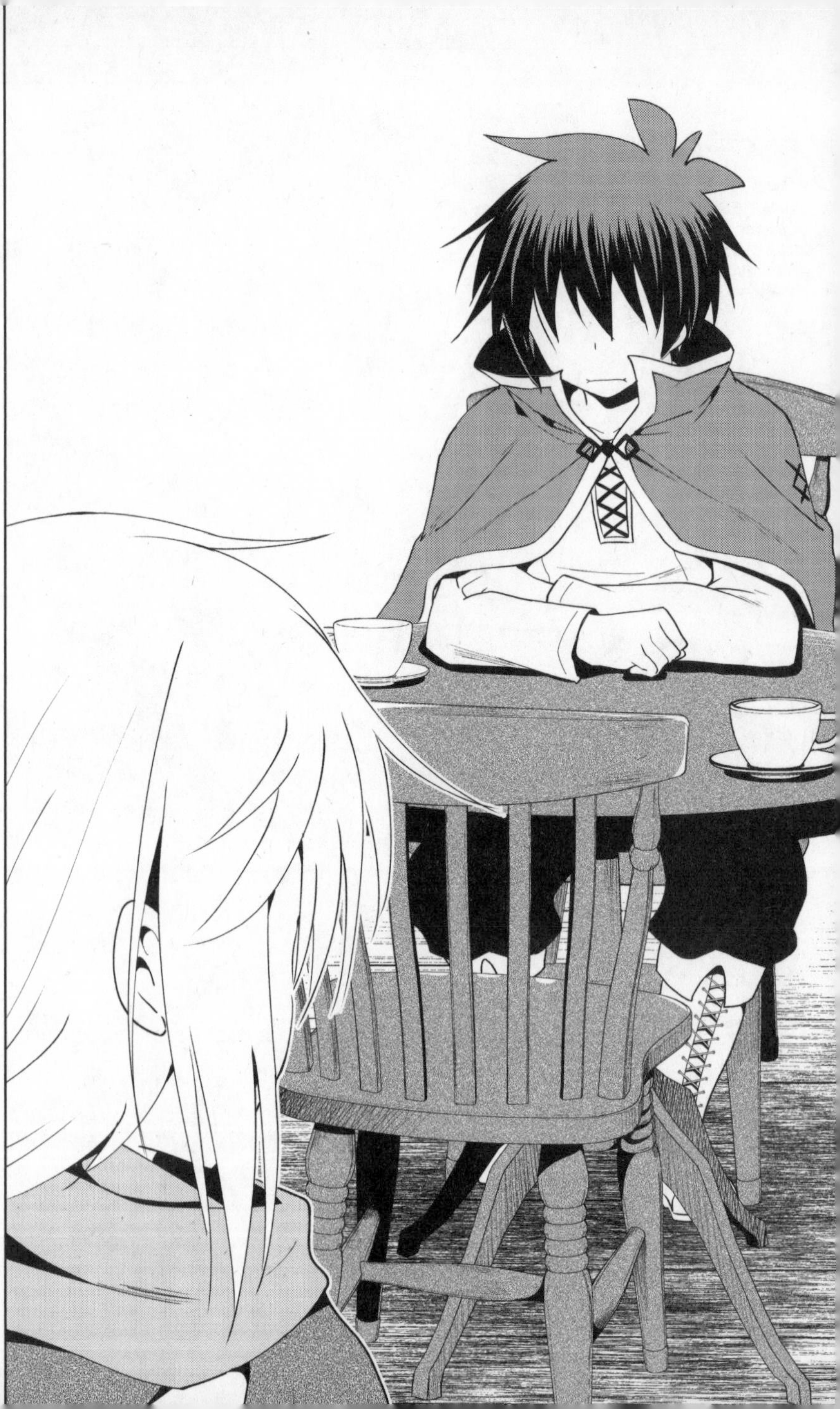